AF540930

KASHMIR
Looking Back in Time

Politics, Culture, History

KHALID BASHIR AHMAD

7/22, Ansari Road, Darya Ganj, New Delhi
Tel.: +91-11-4077 5252, 2327 3880
E-mail: orders@atlanticbooks.com
Web: www.atlanticbooks.com

Reprint 2026

Published by Atlantic Publishers & Distributors (P) Ltd.

Disclaimer

The author and the publisher have made every effort, to the best of their skill, expertise, and knowledge, to provide correct material in the book. However, if any mistakes persist in the content of the book, the publisher does not take responsibility for them. The publisher shall have no liability to any person or entity with respect to any loss or damage caused, or alleged to have been caused, directly or indirectly, by the information contained in this book.

The author has made every effort to follow copyright law. However, if any work is found to be similar, it is unintentional, and the same should not be used as defamatory or to file a legal suit against the author.

All disputes are subject to the jurisdiction of the Delhi courts only.

Printed & bound in India by Atlantic Print Services

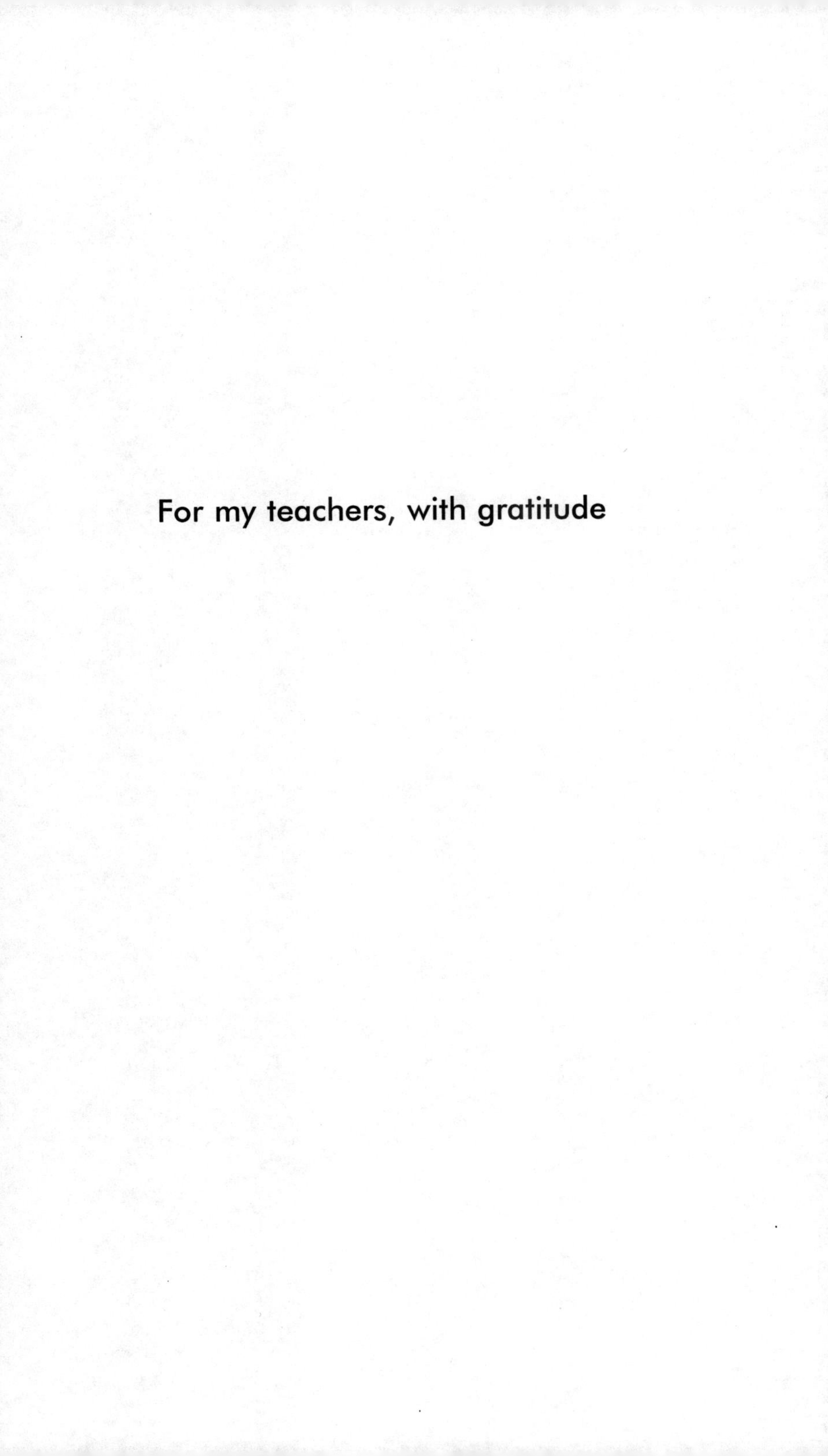

For my teachers, with gratitude

Prologue

This book is set in the twentieth century, mostly, in its first half, when Kashmir witnessed several major developments that stirred up its political and cultural landscape. It is an entrancing peek into the recent past of the Himalayan Valley, offering a closer view of the people who influenced the course of its history. The book also takes a reader through the cultural setting of the land and the huge loss it has suffered in terms of its invaluable inheritance. The material for the book is sourced from archival literature, published works, travelogues, and eyewitness account. Divided into three sections—politics, culture, and history, each thoroughly researched and supported by authentic sources—it captures the mood and scene of the Valley through its tumultuous decades of the last century.

For fifty years beginning 1931, Sheikh Mohammad Abdullah ruled the politics of Jammu and Kashmir, both from within and outside of jail as well as within and outside of power. One of the most enigmatic politicians of his time, he was accused of having conflicting views on issues depending on the time and place he was positioned in. He was loved and hated in equal measure by his admirers and adversaries. His politics was known to be pro-India and anti-India at the same time. A considerable period of his political career, over a decade, was spent in jail which he blamed on New Delhi for misunderstanding him. Architect of the constitutional autonomy of Jammu and Kashmir within the framework of the Indian Constitution—the status diluted over the decades and finally scrapped on 5 August 2019 through a Presidential order—Abdullah was a strong opponent of Muhammad Ali Jinnah's Two Nation Theory and Jammu and

Kashmir joining Pakistan in 1947. Yet, his adversaries within India refused to see in him a pro-India politician. Recently, there have been some overt efforts to, what his supporters feel, dislodge him from the history of Kashmir by withdrawing the annual public holiday on account of his birthday and renaming a police gallantry award named after him.

The first section of the book essays the flip side of politics of Kashmir's mass leader and how this *Lion of Kashmir* reneged from some of his publicly declared cherished ideals, like building and nurturing of the Jammu and Kashmir Muslim Conference and dissolving it when it had attained political muscle against a despotic regime; fighting an all-out battle against an autocratic ruler and ending up in taking oath of allegiance to him and his progeny; and inspiring and patronizing a well-organized 22-years-long struggle for holding of plebiscite in Kashmir and winding it up to take oath as the Chief Minister of the State—a far lower position in power and esteem than what he had held when he was removed and arrested as the Prime Minister in 1953. The material used in this section includes important archival documents not written or spoken about earlier.

The section on culture presents the richness and variety of Kashmir's heritage and its tragic loss over the decades. The Valley's cultural inheritance is manifested in its archaeological finds, artefacts, manuscripts, and old-printed literature. For long, this priceless wealth has been preyed upon by art smugglers and other unscrupulous persons emptying its past. *Tale of a Mammoth Loss* exposes a contemporary crisis by bringing to light the loss of history and intellectual tradition suffered by Kashmir. It brings to the fore complicity of inefficient bureaucracy, complicit curators, wily outsiders, and corrupt political leadership in robbing the Valley of its rich heritage. It also chronicles the loss that natural disasters, like fires and floods, have inflicted on Kashmir's archival wealth.

One of the significant cultural developments taking place in Kashmir during the early 1930s was opening of the first cinema hall in Srinagar. For a long time, Kashmiri society did not accept its youth visiting cinema halls. In fact, as late as up to the 1960s, parents seeking matrimony of their daughter would first convince themselves that the prospective groom was not a cinema or a hotel going guy. A woman visiting a cinema hall was a taboo. Gradually, the number of college going girls and working women visiting cinema halls picked up and during 1970s ladies watching a movie in a theatre was a common sight. With the inception of armed militancy in Kashmir in 1989, the entertainment avenues in the Valley were shut and it was curtains down for cinema halls. There were some efforts by the Government to reopen these but without much success. After some time, the two or three odd cinema halls that had reopened were again closed down. Today, many of the cinema halls have been converted into commercial buildings. *The Celluloid Years* is a story of the beginning and colourful journey of cinema in Kashmir. It recreates old times taking a reader through minute details including of the first film shooting in Kashmir.

The people of Kashmir have deep roots in religion and spirituality despite rapid intrusion of modernity in their lives. As one of the five fundamentals of Muslim Faith, performing *Haj* has always remained close to their hearts and those who return from this pilgrimage are considered Allah's chosen people and revered by all. In the olden times, journey to and from the sacred cities of Makkah and Medinah was arduous and time consuming that, given the poor economic conditions, only few people could afford. It entailed a long and tiresome road and train journey to Bombay or Karachi before sailing to Jeddah or Eden after which a pilgrim would either walk or travel on a camel's back to reach the City of Ka'ba. The scenario has gone a massive change over the decades and reduced the weeks' long journey into few hours' flight. *Kashmir to Ka'ba* is about what it was like setting out on the *Haj* pilgrimage from Kashmir of 1930s-40s.

In recent years, we have seen many cities and places in India being renamed. Allahabad became Prayagraj, Faizabad was changed to Ayodhya, and the Mughal Sarai Railway Station was renamed as Pandit Deen Dayal Upadhyaya Junction. A walk through the history of Kashmir acquaints us with similar developments taking place in the past as well as in the recent years, where names of places were changed. Drawing from archival sources and etymology, *Changing Place Names* tells us stories about how and when these places in Kashmir underwent name changes.

Srinagar, the famed 'capital of Kashmir for five thousand years', is a city with rich culture. Each of its quarters has a distinct identity and a bundle of interesting stories to share. One such area is Sonawar, an uptown neighbourhood and the Green Zone of Kashmir with an ancient existence. *Story of An Uptown Quarter* chronicles its journey from a small village nestled between a hill and a river to the favourite abode of rulers, bureaucrats, and foreign tourists. It takes a reader down the lanes of history to connect with some of its amazing stories including about people and places that had made it a lively place.

Kashmir has always mystified visitors. Old accounts of travellers open up mysteries and magic that defines the place and its inhabitants. People were simple and lived a modest life. Trade and commerce were conducted through barter system. It may sound incredible but as late as up to the last decade of the 19th century, money prices did not exist in Kashmir and salaries to the army and civil officials were paid in grain. The highest revenue official in Kashmir, the Settlement Commissioner, was also asked to take oil-seeds in payment of his salary. *Of Prices and Fares* reconstructs the era when prices of essential commodities were too low to sound true. The chapter takes the reader through a gripping detail on prices and fares prevalent in Kashmir of yesteryears when a sheep cost half a rupee and most of the essential commodities were bought against domestic produce like eggs and grain.

In the olden times, the capital city of Srinagar was a hotbed of political gossip and a fertile nursery of rumours. One would always find eager people gathered around news-fabricators and rumour mongers. *Romance with Rumours* is a story about the fascination of the people of Kashmir for rumour and gossip, and how rumour mongering was successfully used as a political tool in the fight against autocracy.

The section on history is an assortment of interesting, yet important, developments taking place in Kashmir during the Dogra Rule (1846–1947). Otherwise reckoned as one of the most oppressive periods of Kashmir's history, the 101-year long rule also offers some interesting tales related to the affairs of governance and individuals at the helm. The rising of Kashmiris against tyranny in 1931 was met with disproportionate force and oppression, generating a wave of sympathy and solidarity from certain quarters in British India, especially from Punjab. One of the famous Lahore-based vocal exponents of Kashmir was poet Allama Mohammad Iqbal who is considered as the guardian philosopher of political awakening of the Kashmiris during 1930s. He spoke, wrote, and mobilized public opinion about their plight. As a consequence, he became a target of apologists of the autocratic dispensation. *Sir Mohammad Iqbal: The Untold Story* chronicles how the bard was assailed to dissuade him from creating awareness about the affairs in Kashmir. In the light of evidence, it analyses the allegation that Iqbal wanted to become the Prime Minister of Jammu and Kashmir and, after failing to achieve his objective, joined the forces inimical to the Dogra Rule. It also untangles the riddle why a religious community with whom he shared common ancestry and about whom he waxed lyrical, forsake him when people across religious divide celebrate him.

In 1939, Kashmir witnessed a violent agitation launched by its minority Kashmiri Pandit community against the Government takeover of a temple in Srinagar. The agitation was the second outpour of the community in seven years after the *Roti Agitation* launched against the Glancy Commission recommendations on grievances of the Muslims. The showdown continued for several days during which the members of the community took out huge processions through the streets of Srinagar, boycotted work in government offices, pelted stones on the police, and held sit-ins in the temple premises where community leaders made speeches against the government of the last Hindu ruler of Kashmir, Maharaja Hari Singh. *The Temple Agitation* traces the origin of the confrontation and its volume, and presents graphic account of the chaos and confusion in the Valley, especially in the capital city of Srinagar which was pushed into the turmoil for weeks until a settlement was reached between the two warring sides.

Through the Dogra Rule is a narration of stories allowing an insight into the working of the government and the psyche of its administrative elite. It throws up dubious characters associated with the regime including a superstitious ruler, a Rasputin *guru*, an embarrassed *Maharaja*, collaborative *Molvis*, passport seeking beggars, and a snooping Resident, then the highest British official in Kashmir.

A Bowl of History is another extensive and riveting narration on the Dogra period connecting Kashmir's famous hill station, Gulmarg and its European visitors with important historical and cultural developments. It presents interesting details about the events and people leading to formulation of many laws and rules, like the law against cruelty to animals, municipal laws, rules for protection of wild flowers, and restriction on constructions. It also chronicles visits of important persons like Lady Curzon and Viceroy of India, Lord Linlithgow, and his wife, Doreen Maud Milner, besides taking a reader through the years when, apart from golf, polo and cricket matches also were played in the bowl. Further, the chapter traces the launch of the first hotel at Gulmarg, the prevalent modes of transport, and a broke Residency requesting the Kashmir Government to waive off ₹ 213 as it did not have money to clear the outstanding on purchase of furniture for a hut at Gulmarg.

Although the first newspaper in Kashmir was started in 1875, the evolution of journalism is attributed to the rule of Maharaja

Hari Singh (1925–47) during whose reign several newspapers were published from Srinagar. *Dateline Kashmir* traces the birth and growth of print media in the Himalayan Valley and brings to the fore interesting developments including how a reluctant ruler in 1904 when requested to grant permission for starting a newspaper, asked his Prime Minister to issue an order forbidding even receiving such an application in future. It also enlightens a reader about the first press conference held in Kashmir and a government employee used by the Administration as the first embedded journalist in the Valley.

The *Appendixes* carries three important documents including correspondence between Sheikh Mohammad Abdullah and the President of Iranian Parliament on the issue of convening of the Constituent Assembly in Jammu and Kashmir, where the latter unsuccessfully tries to persuade Abdullah to drop the idea of proceeding with the Assembly. The third document, a long letter addressed by Maharaja Hari Singh to the President of India, is an important historical text about developments taking place in Kashmir immediately before and after the Partition of India. It is a straight-from-the horse's-mouth account in which the erstwhile Maharaja of Jammu and Kashmir, besides expressing bitterness on what, he explains, the Government of India and Sheikh Mohammad Abdullah did to him, discloses how right from September 1947 he had acted on the advice of the Government of India, and also allows an insight into how the people of the then princely state were placed with regard to the question of accession.

I am grateful for the help and assistance received from different persons and institutions in completing this work. Peerzada Mohammad Ashraf, former Deputy Director of Archives, Archaeology and Museums, and his team at the Archives Repository, Jammu, deserve special thanks for allowing me access to some important archival material. Peerzada also liberally shared his personal archival collection. The staff at the Archives Repository, Kashmir, were equally helpful and facilitated my research. Mushtaq Ahmad Beigh deserves a special mention.

For valuable inputs, I am also thankful to Manmohan Singh Gauri, Mohammad Yusuf Chapri, Prof. Margoob Banihali, Prof. Shafi Shauq, Lalit Gupta, Imdad Saqi, Javed Azar, Mehmood Ahmad Shah, Tariq Ahmad Rather, Dr. Ayaz Rasool Nazki, Syed Zeeshan Fazil, Dr. Quddus Javed, Showkat Wani, Ali Mohammad Khan, Ghulam Hamzah, Mohiuddin Reshi, Bashir Budgami, Rajinder Singh Raina, Shabir Mujahid, Zareef Ahmad Zareef, Altaf Hussain, Bakhshi Anwar Aftab, Prof. Mohammad Assadullah Wani, Mohammad Amin Wani, Farooq Ahmad Akhoon, Nazir Nazar, Ghulam Mohammad Bhat, Aijaz Kakroo, Riyazul Hassan, Prof. Bashir Ahmad Nehvi, and Dr. Taskeena Fazil.

I express my respectful gratitude to my worthy teachers from first primary to post-graduation, who taught me to read, write, and explore. Head Masters (Late) Ghulam Hassan Shah and Ghulam Ali Shaheed Salmani deserve a very warm mention. There are several others like them whose individual mention here may not be possible but who, nonetheless, deserve my respectful thanks.

Last, but not the least, my thanks go to the Atlantic Publishers and Distributors (P) Ltd. for bringing out of this book.

Contents

Politics

1

Muslim Conference to National Conference: Anatomy of a Conversion

Following the killing of two dozen unarmed civilians by Maharaja Hari Singh's army in Srinagar on 13 July 1931, Sheikh Mohammad Abdullah (1905-82) emerged as the symbol of resistance and ruled—both from inside and outside of jail—the political scene of Kashmir for the next half a century. A teacher by profession, who had recently returned from the Aligarh Muslim University with Masters in Chemistry, he plunged into politics to fight for the basic political, economic, and religious rights of his people denied to them for long. His foray into active politics was stirred by an incident of blasphemy of the Holy *Qura'n* at Jammu, 300 kms south of Srinagar, in June 1931 against which he led a massive protest demonstration at the Jama Masjid, Srinagar on 9 June. He made a fiery speech before a 30,000-strong gathering which made him an instant hero of the masses. Besides, strongly condemning the blasphemous act, he "reminded the Muslims [of Kashmir] of their slavery and called upon them to fight for their birth rights."[1] Thousands of people followed him in a procession as he left the mosque for his home.[2] Soon, he became an undisputed leader of the people. Notwithstanding his wavering politics and changing goalposts, his leadership literally remained unchallenged for five decades. For his people, he was the *Sher-i-Kashmir* (Lion of Kashmir) who fought for restoration of their usurped rights and valiantly took on an oppressive rule of Hari Singh, the fourth-generation Dogra Maharaja from a Rajput Hindu family of Jammu that ruled Kashmir for a century (1846-1947).

Gulab Singh, founder of the Dogra rule, had obtained Kashmir in the foulest of transactions ever made in the history of mankind wherein the British East India Company, after defeating the Sikhs—who also ruled the Valley from 1819 to 1846—in the First Anglo-Sikh War, sold Kashmir along with its inhabitants and resources to him for ₹ 75 lakh. For the next 101 years, the regime used every conceivable brutality against its subjects, 97 percent of whom comprised the Muslims. Economically crippled, socially humiliated and politically disempowered, they were discriminated against in comparison to their fellow citizens from the minority community. Any peaceful resentment (like the *Shawlbaf Agitation* of 1865 and the *Silk Factory Agitation* of 1924) against this discrimination was militarily crushed. The formation of political associations was banned due to which an organized resistance against oppression was impossible. However, it was during early 1920s that some freshly educated young Muslim men organized themselves as a group known as the Reading Room Party, and began to voice their grievances. They wrote articles in newspapers published from the Punjab and submitted memoranda to the British Viceroy as well as the local government inviting their attention to the plight of their community. Abdullah became one of the active members of this group.

As soon as the ban on freedom of association was eased following the recommendations of the Glancy Commission[3] constituted in 1931 to look into the grievances of the majority community, the Muslims decided to organize themselves as a political party to launch a movement for their basic rights. The choice for leadership fell on Abdullah, an eloquent speaker who charmed his audience with melodious recitation of verses from the *Qura'n* and couplets of Allama Mohammad Iqbal, famous Urdu and Persian poet with Kashmiri lineage. In anticipation of building a cohesive political platform, Abdullah visited Jammu and important towns of Kashmir including Sopore, Baramulla, Islamabad (Anantnag), Pulwama, Kulgam, and Tral where enthusiastic masses, looking up to him as their leader, warmly received him. During these massive public contacts, people were told that now was the time to work under a formal organization to achieve the objects of their movement.[4] The minority Kashmiri Pandit community was also approached to join but they showed no inclination. One of their frontline leaders, Kashyap Bandhu found the concept of a joint political party commendable but did not agree to the suggestion as his community was "not yet mentally ready for an alliance with the Muslims."[5]

The organisation thus born in 1932 was named as the Jammu & Kashmir Muslim Conference (here onwards referred to as the Muslim Conference only) to serve as "an advance guard of the national interest".[6] Abdullah later wrote that he discussed the founding of the new party with his colleagues and other prominent people in Kashmir and Jammu. "Everybody was in favour of a State-wide organization."[7] Although Abdullah was chosen as the founder President of the new party, it remains somewhat unclear whether he was the brain behind its formation. Chaudhri Ghulam Abbas, Abdullah's colleague and later President, Muslim Conference writes [translation]:

> [I]t was decided that in order to unite the Muslims of Jammu and Kashmir at one platform, a meeting of the representatives from across the State should be held to form the Jammu & Kashmir Muslim Conference. Sheikh Mohammad Abdullah was also consulted who welcomed the idea.[8]

Abbas' take on the subject presents a different view according to which the idea of forming a political party of the Muslims of Jammu & Kashmir was born in Jammu, although there were some Muslim leaders there like Chaudhri Gauhar Rehman, who opposed the idea of a single party for both Kashmir and Jammu, the two provinces of the then State of Jammu & Kashmir. Abdullah was invited to Jammu to thrash out the issue[9] where he was engaged in discussions with leaders including Abbas, Mistri Yaqoob Ali, Sheikh Ghulam Qadir, and Allah

Rakha Sagar. "It was unanimously decided to float a single organization embracing Muslims from all parts of the State."[10] There are others who consider the Lahore-based All India Kashmir Committee (AIKC) as being "largely responsible"[11] for the formation of the Muslim Conference. The AIKC was set up by prominent Muslims of British India including poet Allama Mohammad Iqbal, within a fortnight of the 13 July Massacre to extend support to the Kashmiris.

On 14, 15 and 16 October 1932, a convention of the Muslim representatives was held at the Pathar Masjid in Srinagar where the Muslim Conference was formally launched with Abdullah as its President. The AIKC had also sent its representative delegation. The Mirwaiz of Kashmir, Molvi Mohammad Yusuf Shah, also attended the session along with his followers irrespective of differences between him and Abdullah that had broken out in public recently. The birth of the organization became the centre of aspirations of the Muslim majority of Jammu & Kashmir and its launch generated hope among them. As Abbas puts it, the party was the "sole outcome of the struggle, oppression and incarceration of the Muslims".[12] Recalling the launch of the party, Abdullah's associate and an eyewitness, Pir Mohammad Afzal Makhdoomi writes [translation]:

> Besides delegates, several prominent personalities from the Frontier Province were seated on the podium. At the outset, a green flag spotting crescent and star in white was unfurled and all the participants rose in reverence to salute it. It was an electrifying scene of enthusiasm which still envelops one with the warmth of faith. The sincerity, tolerance, brotherhood, selflessness and humility that were on display are now a thing of the past. Soon after unfurling of the flag, Hakim Mohammad Aminuddin Qureshi recited verses of the *Qura'n* which left the audience ecstatic. Chaudhri Lahori recited a poem of Iqbal. After this, Chaudhri Ghulam Abbas Khan proposed the name [of Abdullah] for the Chair. The Presidential Chair [on the podium] was vacant till then. The delegates from Mirpur, Poonch, Akhnoor, Muzaffarabad, Islamabad, Sopore and all other areas, one

> after another, endorsed Chaudhri Sahib's proposal. Of all the endorsements, the one by Maulana Saifuddin Shah Lolabi, brother of Sheikh-ul-Hadith Maulana Anwar Shah Kashmiri Deobandi, was unique and beautiful. He said in matters of religion, politics, morality or trade, two witnesses are enough as per Islam. But here, dozens of personalities have seconded the proposal on Sheikh Sahib's President-ship. So, I endorse the chain of these endorsements. Sheikh Sahib was requested to take the Chair. Clad in a cream-colour suit, he took the charge of the proceedings. The hall reverberated with slogans and for 15 minutes voices of jubilation ruled supreme. From the roof of the Pathar Masjid, umpteen firecrackers were exploded. From the Fateh Kadal and the Zaina Kadal[13] also, there was display of fireworks. After a melodious rendering of a revolutionary poem by Maulana Baihaqi, the Chairman delivered the Presidential speech.[14]

In his address, Abdullah spelt out demands of the Muslims which included immediate revocation of the law dispossessing a Hindu subject of his property if he converted to Islam; freedom of press and platform and forming of association; due representation of Muslims in recruitment to the army and withdrawal of all obsolete rules laid down in this connection; expansion of municipal committees and district boards and holding of elections to these bodies; representation to Muslims in the Praja Sabha [Assembly] in accordance with their population; and implementation of the Glancy Commission Report in respect of *jagirdars* and *chakdars* holding large tracts of agricultural lands. Giving an idea of the new organization's pan-Jammu & Kashmir representative character, he also demanded representation to the people of Poonch in the State Assembly and appointment of an independent commission to look into their grievances; extension of the laws prevalent in Jammu & Kashmir to Poonch and Chenahni and withdrawing of powers of Sessions Judge from the Raja of Chenahni; abolition of grazing tax and immediate redress of grievances of the nomadic communities of the Gujjars and Bakerwals. Abdullah rejected the claim of the government that Muslims with Matriculation qualification were not available for recruitment as clerks and pointed out that 132 Matriculate Muslims who had applied for jobs were ignored. He spoke about the use of force by the Dogra rule to subjugate the masses and muzzle their voice, and thanked the Muslims of India, especially those of Punjab, and the Muslim Press for having effectively represented their case. Importantly, he assured the minorities that the movement was not directed against them and that their grievances would be redressed. At the same time, he asked them to "respect our just rights."[15] Earlier, Waliullah Zainul Aabideen, representative of the AIKC who unfurled the party's flag, also affirmed that the party would be the harbinger of love, peace, and guarantor of brotherhood among different communities. He said:

> Today, the hoisting of green flag with crescent opens a new chapter in the history of Kashmir. As such, it is the duty of the Kashmiris to see that it remains hoisted always. This flag of the Conference is the harbinger of love, peace and brotherhood among all the communities living in the State and it is the guarantor of peace, progress and happiness for all subjects of the Maharaja.[16]

The Muslim Conference soon plunged into an intense political activity, threatening civil disobedience against non-implementation of the Glancy Commission recommendations on restoration of mosques and shrines, grant of proprietary rights to the tenants, freedom of press and platform, setting up of a legislative assembly and facilities for extension of education. The party again tried to reach out to the Kashmiri Pandit community for a joint front against the government but, again, without any positive outcome. A committee was constituted to engage with them and seek their cooperation which failed in its effort in view of their refusal to cooperate.[17] The Kashmiri Pandits viewed the Muslim Conference as a threat to their interests which lay with the continuity and strength of the Dogra rule. The community enjoyed monopoly over government services which position, its leaders thought, was in danger in case the majority community pursued education and sought its share in government jobs.

As the Muslim Conference grew into a strong voice of people, it soon became an eyesore for the government and its supporters. However, more than external forces, the party was dented by a serious rift within the Muslim community itself. The factional politics pursued by Sheikh Mohammad Abdullah and Mirwaiz Mohammad Yusuf Shah struck a serious blow to the unity of the Muslims in general and the Muslim Conference, as their unified voice, in particular. Their feud had preceded the birth of the party and attempts by some well-meaning prominent persons had bought truce between the two sides which, however, did not last long. On 2 September 1932, the Mirwaiz told a gathering at the Jama Masjid in Srinagar that many respectable persons had approached him for reconciliation but he did not agree. "However, now a Turkish prince has come who wants accord [between him and Abdullah] and I have accepted peace on the condition that the Mirzayis—whom the Muslims do not consider among the faithful—will be ousted [from the Muslim Conference] or they will seek atonement."[18]

The Mirwaiz was accused of soft pedaling with the government and, in return, being a recipient of an annual royal grant of ₹ 600 and a *khillat*.[19] The Chief Cleric was believed to have been tricked by a canny Prime Minister Hari Kishan Kaul into accepting government favours in order to drive him into a permanent animosity with Abdullah and thereby break the Muslim unity. He walked into the trap but in the face of severe public criticism, soon realized his mistake and at a congregation at the Jama Masjid returned the royal favour as "unacceptable".[20] His detractors accused him of bashing Abdullah for feeling threatened by his rising popularity. "The Mirwaiz strongly felt that it was he who had brought Abdullah on the forefront and introduced him to the people but now he himself was getting sidelined."[21] On the other hand, Abdullah considered the Mirwaiz as an obstacle to his becoming the sole leader of Kashmir. Chaudhri Ghulam Abbas who as a colleague closely watched the feud between these two leaders, observes that "the Mirwaiz had felt that [popularity of] Abdullah would now destroy the position his family held and the old respect and grandeur of the Mirwaizs would be gone. On his part, Sheikh Abdullah knew that as long as the Mirwaiz household enjoyed strong political, religious and social influence he would be unable to become the sole leader of Kashmir."[22]

The Mirwaiz, however, refuted the allegation and stated that his only objection was to Abdullah's proximity with the Mirzayi leaders and the latter's influence on the Muslim Conference. It was actually the Ahrar-Mirzayi feud in the All India Kashmir Committee, Lahore that had its trickling effect in Kashmir. Both Ahrars and Mirzayis—also known as Qadianis or Ahmadis—wanted to exert their influence on the Kashmir Movement. While the former were close to the Mirwaiz, the latter had propinquity with Abdullah for which the Mirwaiz dubbed him as a Mirzayi and criticised him for, what he alleged, "shaving clean his beard, embezzling nation's money and promoting obscenity at women's meetings."[23] Abdullah also used public meetings to level all kinds of accusations on the Mirwaiz, including embezzlement of public money and dubbing his party as the King's Party.[24] At one point in time, when under the pressure from the Ahrars, Mirza Bashiruddin Mehmood, leader of the Mirzayi community, was ousted as President of the All India Kashmir Committee, the Mirwaiz announced cessation of hostility to Abdullah and showed readiness to work with him. On 12 May 1933, he told a congregation that there was agreement [between him and Abdullah] on their demands and the only point of disagreement was Mirzaiyat.[25] The lull, however, proved temporary.

The Abdullah-Mirwaiz bickering snowballed into group clashes, often violent, between the followers of the two leaders and ruined the chances of a united front against autocracy. Poet and Kashmir watcher, Allama Mohammad Iqbal appealed the warring factions to close their ranks. On 12 October 1933, he wrote to Abdullah, "I was sorry to learn that many an organisation has recently sprung up [in Kashmir] because I have no doubt that your mutual differences will greatly obstruct your march. Unity is the only way through which you can achieve your political and social ends."[26] But thanks to mutual intolerance of the two leaders, the Muslims of Kashmir were rendered a divided house at the most crucial and painful period of their history. The Mirwaiz quit the Muslim Conference and formed his own Azad Muslim Conference (also known as Azad Party)[27] which Abdullah alleged "ruined the garden that we had laid out in the shape of the Muslim Conference."[28] It was alleged that the Azad Party had "joined hands with the Hindus to dismantle the Muslim Conference."[29] For years, the two leaders held separate public meetings where they tore apart each other while their supporters engaged themselves in vicious clashes to pin each other down. Amid this strife, on 6 November 1933, foundation stone of the official headquarters of the Muslim Conference was laid adjacent to the Pathar Masjid on the left bank of the Jhelum River. The building was named Mujahid Manzil (The House of Warriors).

As unity between the two feuding factions of the Muslims seemed a far cry, Abdullah again looked upto the Kashmiri Pandit leaders for a joint fight against the government. It was not long ago when he had publicly expressed his anguish over their alleged attempts to 'break the Muslim resistance' against the government. On 28 July 1934, during a public meeting at Rainawari, he warned them that "both the communities have to live in this country; they should not take advantage of our present weakness and must remember that we have taken on the Government far stronger than them."[30] It may be recalled that Kashmiri Pandits had launched the Roti Agitation in 1932 against the Glancy Commission conceding some demands of the majority community to remove discrimination against it in matters of employment and education. This time, Abdullah was successful in enlisting the support of Pandit leaders and held joint public meetings with Jia Lal Kilam, Kashyap Bandhu, Prem Nath Bazaz and Sardar Budh Singh, a Sikh leader.

Abdullah's extension of hand of cooperation to the Kashmiri Pandit leaders was followed by a visit to Kashmir in July 1935 by Saifuddin Kitchlew, Indian National Congress leader with Kashmiri ancestry and a close associate of Jawaharlal Nehru. On 30 July, Ahmadullah Shahdad, a prominent local Abdullah supporter, hosted Kitchlew at his house where Abdullah was also invited. The meeting proved ominous for the Muslim Conference. Next day, a public meeting was held at the Hazuri Bagh (Iqbal Park) where, for the first time in Kashmir's history, the slogan of *Gandhiji Zindabad* was raised.[31] It was the first public statement on change in Abdullah's political outlook and a clear hint at the future of Muslim Conference. On 3 August, Kitchlew made another speech in Srinagar where he was more open and emphatic. He said that Kashmir was a part of India and asked the Kashmiris not to forget it.[32] He followed it with another speech on 4 August. Kitchlew also released the first issue of the weekly *Hamdard* published jointly by Abdullah and Prem Nath Bazaz who "was already in touch with the Congress leaders".[33] The idea was to base the policy of the newspaper on secular outlook of the Indian National Congress and it published articles of the same tenor.[34]

Abdullah's warming up to the Indian National Congress had begun in early 1930s soon after the launch of the Muslim Conference. In 1934, he toured Punjab and met Congress leaders there. These meetings influenced his thoughts and within a year, he was mulling over winding up of the Muslim Conference. On 28 May 1935, a joint public meeting of Muslims and Kashmiri Pandits was held at Sheetal Nath, a Hindu stronghold, where besides Abdullah, Jia Lal Kilam and Kashyap Bandhu made speeches. In his long address lasting quarter to three hours, Abdullah said that they were busy molding a united nationhood.[35] Ideologically, Abdullah's mind had already taken a tectonic shift but he was not yet ready to spell it out. On 24 October 1935, in the company of Abbas, he participated in a river procession comprising about 1500 boats, taken out by the Muslim Conference from Abi Guzar downstream to Pathar Masjid.[36] The entire city had poured on the banks of the Jhelum to greet the procession. Less than two months later, Jia Lal Kilam resigned from the Sanatan Dharam Yuvak Sabha (Youngmen's Association) and it was public knowledge that Abdullah will soon follow suit and leave the Muslim Conference to pursue 'nationalist politics'. Breaking the news of Kilam's resignation, the *Kashmir Times* foretold Abdullah disassociating himself from the Muslim Conference so that both of them will "live up to their new ideal of national outlook."[37] The Indian National Congress—Jawaharlal Nehru in particular—seized the opportunity with both hands and its leaders started trickling into

Kashmir and meet Abdullah. In 1936, Nehru sent Purushottam Das Tandon and some others to Kashmir to specifically meet Abdullah and strengthen his new found love for nationalism. Next year, Abdul Gaffar Khan and R.K.M. Ashraf also arrived in Srinagar in an effort to bring the Kashmir movement closer to the Indian National Congress.

The seeds of dismantling the Muslim Conference and building over its debris a 'nationalist and secular' party had been sown and the turning point came in 1937 when Abdullah had his first meeting with Jawaharlal Nehru at the Lahore Railway Station and, on the latter's request, accompanied him on his visit to the Frontier Province. The meeting culminated in Abdullah's formal baptism in nationalism and his discarding the apparel of the leader of Muslims of Jammu & Kashmir. His one-time colleague and later adversary, Chaudhri Ghulam Abbas, sarcastically recalls that Abdullah "returned from this meeting heavily intoxicated with the wine of nationalism whose hangover did not leave him thereafter."[38] He had fallen in love with Nehru's persona and later admitted that "the magic of his personality had brought us closer to the [Indian National] Congress."[39] He was determined to answer the wishes of Nehru to open his party for non-Muslims, although they had refused to cooperate with him despite much of his efforts. Abbas recalls [translation]:

> Immediately after his return, he had a closed door discussion with me on nationalism. First, there was a cool exchange of opinion on its justification and absence of it but I was saddened to feel that the matter had crossed the boundaries of national gain and loss. Sheikh Abdullah was adamant that this issue should be decided during the ongoing three-day annual session of the Muslim Conference.... He had returned after drinking the wine of nationalism at the hands of his nationalist friends. Unfortunately, this friendship created a visible wall between our principles and the means [to achieve these].[40]

During his stay in Punjab, Abdullah addressed a press conference at the residence of Saifuddin Kitchlew where he said, "My future programme would be to act according to the principles of the Congress. After returning to Kashmir I would lay foundation of an organisation which would serve the national interests."[41]

Back in Kashmir, Abdullah did not have a smooth sail in selling his nationalist politics to colleagues and people. There was opposition to the idea of dissolution of the Muslim Conference. It would be incorrect to believe, as some suggest, that Kashmir overwhelmingly supported Abdullah's line on the conversion of the Muslim Conference. The educated Muslims, in particular, were against it. Even his close aides like Mirza Mohammad Afzal Beg and Bakshi Ghulam Mohammad too expressed themselves against the conversion.[42] The bulk of population, uneducated and oppressed under a ruthless autocratic rule as it were, had no idea of the import of the decision and, accordingly, could not fathom its implications. They blindly trusted the leader who had stood up for their rights and believed that wherever he led them it would be in their interest. Jammu was altogether a different case. There, Abdullah did not command much following and had to beat a hasty retreat in the face of a stiff resistance when he tried to test the waters for the dissolution of the Muslim Conference. The Muslims of Jammu province, constituting a majority of roughly 61% of the total population of the region [Census of 1941], barring a few like Raja Mohammad Akbar Khan of Poonch, were vehemently against the conversion. Apart from the challenge that he saw to his leadership in the person of the Mirwaiz, Abdullah also felt insecure of the educated and eloquent youth among his own supporters. "There was this talk in the Valley that he was, one by one, pushing them into taking Government jobs to ensure that he remained [in the field as] the sole leader."[43] Although Abdullah complained that they had their own compulsions like family responsibilities to take up government jobs and could not dedicate themselves to the national service, "the fact is that if he had wanted, many of his colleagues like Molvi Abdur Rahim would not have joined the government service."[44]

Abdullah now found himself in a tight spot. On the one hand, his nationalist outlook did not have many takers among the Muslims and, on the other, his financial position was very weak. At one point in time, he told his colleagues that he had run in debt. Under the circumstances, he even thought of migrating from Kashmir to earn a livelihood. His colleagues were making appeals for donations to ensure financial support for him.[45] On 8 July 1934, Mohammad Yahya Rafiqi asked for some relief money to be provided to Abdullah every month "since he had dedicated his life [to the cause of the people]".[46] On 17 September, Ahmadullah Shahdad hosted a tea party for 200 people and informed them that Abdullah was financially in a tight spot and might go out of Kashmir to seek employment in some Muslim State. He told them that "if you want he should stay here then you must arrange ₹ 10,000 which will be invested in some business whose profit will be passed on to Sheikh Sahib".[47] On 6 November 1934, Habibullah Zargar hosted a party where Abdullah informed the invitees that he would find a way out to make both ends meet and hinted at going to England for studying law. "I am running a debt of ₹ 3,000 which I will settle up before I leave"[48], he told them. In response, he was told that he need not repay the amount as the money was given to him for the 'national cause' and he had not embezzled the amount. Molvi Abdullah told him that for the last two months his financial crisis had occupied their thoughts and when they discussed this with educated [government] employees they refused to help, arguing that "Sheikh Sahib had done nothing for them and whatever they had achieved was on their own merit."[49] On 5 December 1934, Abdullah told a group of youth that "if [the] Aligarh [Muslim University] helps me out I will go to England and pursue a career in law, otherwise I will start a newspaper and a school [for a living]."[50] On 12 October 1935, several prominent Kashmiri Muslims including Ghulam Ahmad Ashai, Habibullah Mir, Abdul Aziz Fazili, Ghulam Rasool and Ghulam Nabi Gilkar assembled at the residence of Ghulam Ahmad Jeweler where Abdullah's monetary hardship was discussed. Jeweler informed the select gathering:

> Sheikh Mohammad Abdullah is now in a precarious financial situation. Some arrangement has to be made to help him out. Some people will have to monthly contribute money and initially make six month's advance

contribution to be deposited in a bank and drawn every month.[51]

Again, on 29 July 1936, at a similar gathering where Abdullah was also present, financial assistance to the poor was discussed. Abdullah said that "if some society were to come to my aid I would like to go to England for three years to pursue a degree in law."[52] Later, Munshi Mohammad Ishaq came to Abdullah's rescue. He earmarked a certain part of his income from his transport company for his financial assistance and also gifted him a private motor car purchased from an Englishman.[53]

In the meanwhile, a Jammu-based Muslim newspaper, *Pasban* in 1936 lambasted Abdullah for, what it wrote, reneging from the Muslim cause and advocating a national movement. Abdullah was so annoyed with the newspaper that he had an 'important meeting' of the General Council of the party held in Srinagar in August that year. The meeting condemned the *Pasban* "for writing against Mr. S.M. Abdullah and the national movement which he advocates."[54] A resolution was passed to express full faith in Abdullah who was unanimously elected President for the next session. Importantly, the meeting formed a committee which, besides Abdullah, Chaudhri Ghulam Abbas, Mian Ahmad Yar Khan and Mohammad Afzal Beg, included non-Muslim leaders like Prem Nath Bazaz, Sardar Budh Singh and Pandit Prem Nath Dogra, to "draw a scheme for Responsible Government in the State."[55]

At the sixth session of the Muslim Conference at Jammu held in June 1938, Abdullah publicly put forth the idea of "broad-basing the Muslim Conference and converting it to a nationalist party". He summoned a special session of the Working Committee of the party on 24 June during which a resolution was piloted by Raja Mohammad Akbar Khan recommending that "in the next session of the Muslim Conference suitable changes should be made in the constitution of this party so that all the people who want to take part in this struggle irrespective of their color, race, caste, creed or religion should have an opportunity to become members of this party."[56] The resolution was opposed by Chaudhri Ghulam Abbas, Chaudhri Hamidullah, Allah Rakha Sagar and Abdul Majid Qarshi who had earlier also expressed themselves against this in a meeting of the General Council of the party.[57] Others who opposed the resolution included some close aides of Raja Mohammad Akbar Khan. The resolution fell flat. The Working Committee, however, recommended that a resolution for amending the constitution of the Muslim Conference to broad-base it be placed before the General Council. The Muslims of Jammu planned an "unprecedented procession" to oppose Abdullah's "nationalism and style of function."[58] Given his huge popularity in Kashmir, he was confident that he could overrule any opposition and persisted with his plan to dissolve the Muslim Conference and raise a new party named the Jammu & Kashmir National Conference (here onwards the National Conference only). Meanwhile, in a significant development, Abdullah's candidate for the Leader of the Party in the Assembly was massively defeated. He could muster only two votes out of 19 while his rival supported by the Abbas-group was elected with a thumping majority.[59] The development, if anything, served as a hastener in the process of dissolution of the Muslim Conference, as "the defeat left Abdullah fretting and fuming".[60]

Besides opposition from within his party, Abdullah also encountered resistance from his wife against the dissolution of the Muslim Conference. Begum Akbar Jahan tried to persuade her husband against taking such a step but he was adamant. The issue resulted in bitter arguments taking place between the couple threatening their marital life. Convinced that he was determined to go ahead with his idea, Akbar Jahan left her husband's home and moved into her parental house. The Begum was under the influence of her mother who, as a family friend recalls, was averse to the idea. Mohammad Sidiq Parray, a close friend of Harry Nedou, father of Akbar Jahan, recalls that there appeared ideological differences between Abdullah and his wife who was "a strong supporter of the Muslim Conference."[61] Bitter arguments would take place between the two over this issue and one day Akbar Jahan left her husband's house and shifted to her parental residence. Parray recollects:

> I was with the Nedous and came to know that Akbar Jahan was upstairs and had quarreled with her husband

> over the issue of dissolution of the Muslim Conference. She stayed put there for 15 days and after persuasion by her brother, Akram, who pleaded with her that as a devout wife she had to follow her husband, she returned to him [Abdullah]. Akram told her that if she did not go back her husband might divorce her and take another wife. Subsequently, she relented and Akram and I accompanied her to her husband's house. While Akram went inside the house with her I remained in the outer room. After this incident, she fell in line and followed her husband's political course.[62]

On 5 July 1938, some Muslim youth held a public meeting at Bulbul Lankar in the interior city of Srinagar and, in opposition to Abdullah's pursuit of national politics, formed a new political party named the Muslim League.[63] During the proceedings, Abdullah was severely criticized. Abdul Salam Dalal, in particular, made a strong speech against him. The Muslim League, led by Ashiq Hussain, was established by a group of youth who were very critical of Abdullah's nationalist outlook and, at a public meeting held on 29 June at the Pathar Masjid, vowed to defeat it. The meeting was also attended by a student leader from Lahore, Inayatullah.[64] In the meanwhile, unruffled by opposition, Abdullah focused on espousing his nationalist outlook through various ways. On 23 June 1938 at a public meeting at Arampora, Nawa Kadal, he laid "too much of stress on nationalism without which, he said, the country could not be served."[65] Three weeks later on 13 July, he led the Martyr's Day procession wearing *Khaddar ka kurta pyjama*,[66] the trademark attire of the Indian National Congress leaders. On 19 July, he made a speech at Dab Tal in old Srinagar city and spoke about nationalism and tried to convince his audience that "the struggle for their rights was not a fight between Hindus and Muslims but between the oppressor and the oppressed; between the poor and the rich."[67] He continued with holding joint public meetings with Kashmiri Pandit leaders and sent his close associate, Bakshi Ghulam Mohammad and R.N. Dhar to Delhi to meet Mahatma Gandhi. They appraised Gandhi and the President All India Congress Committee about the current situation in Kashmir.[68]

The bond between Abdullah and the Congress leaders was getting stronger by the day and on 12 March 1939 he was invited to the Tripura Session of the Indian National Congress where Nehru introduced him to the leaders of the party. He was also asked to preside over one of the sittings of the Session. The Tripura Session played a very important role in "cementing ties"[69] between Abdullah and the leaders of the Indian National Congress. Returning from Tripura, he visited Bombay (now Mumbai) where in an interview with the *Bombay Chronicle* he stated: "The Working Committee of the Muslim Conference has resolved to run the party on Nationalist lines and open its doors for the non-Muslims."[70] Prime Minister of Jammu & Kashmir, Gopalaswami Ayyangar, accused of working overtime to break the Muslim Conference, had promised Abdullah that if even a nominal nationalist structure was erected in the State at least two popular ministers would be inducted in the Government. Abdullah argued that since some non-Muslim political workers had desired to work with him for national cause he cannot ignore them.[71] Those 'some non-Muslim political workers', alleges Abbas, were "Ayyangar's special agents and both the Government and the Hindus, alarmed by the results of the Assembly elections, wanted to split into pieces the national unity of Muslims by breaking the Muslim Conference."[72] The alleged plot against the party also found expression in the poetry of a contemporary versifier, Niaz Kamraji, who wrote verses on political developments. In an Urdu poem laced with English words, '*Muslim Conference par Hareefun ki Yurish*' (Rivals' Attack on the Muslim Conference), he accused Finance Members of the government, Messrs Mehta and Kartar, of engineering dissention in the Muslim Conference and employing insiders like Messrs Mirak and Zirak to achieve their 'evil objective'. The poem goes like this:

Jab se hai is mulk mai qayam huee
Jammu wa Kashmir Muslim Conference
Meharba'n is par hamesha se rahay
Mehta-o-Kartar Member Finance

Is ko malyamait karnay ke liye
Imtihaa'n mai la chukay hain loose guns
Jab rahay nakaam to phir phoot par
Kar diye tayyar chand aik non-sense
Halwa-o-gushtaba ke dildaadgaa'n
Paas jin ke phoot ka hai license
Mirak-o-Zirak bhi in mai mil gaye
Kar chukay zaaya hain apna conscience
Parcham-i-baatil ko lehraatay huey
Jab badhay aagay gaye daldal mai phans
Sarbulandi mai surraya tak badha
Parcham-i-iqbal-i-Muslim Conference
Itehad-i-quam ka hissan haseen
Dekh ye zillat diya duniya ne hans
Tha yahan tak hi abhi puhancha Niaz
Kaan mai awaaz aaayi silence.[73]

[Ever since the Muslim Conference was established, it has been constant target of [un] kind treatment of Messrs Mehta and Kartar, the Finance Members [of the Government]. To destroy the party, they have employed loose guns. As they failed [in achieving their designs] they used some non-sense persons—the lovers of *halwa* (sweet pudding) and *gushtaba* (ball of minced mutton cooked in yogurt) who possess license to engineer dissentions. Mirak and Zirak who have lost their conscience, also joined them. Bearing the flag of the falsehood, when they marched ahead they were stuck in a swamp. The fortune of the Muslim Conference's flag rose to the heights of the Plied. The abased state of the fort of nation's unity caused the world to cast a sarcastic smile. Niaz had reached only this far when a voice whispered in his ear: 'Silence'.]

The hour of reckoning had arrived. On 11 June 1939, at a specially convened session of the party, the Muslim Conference was dissolved and replaced with the National Conference, opening its doors for other communities. The conversion resolution was piloted by Abdullah loyalist Mohammad Sayeed Masoodi and passed with a majority vote. The flag of the party was changed from the 'green with a white crescent' to the 'red with a white plough'. The conversion was great news for some and a sad one for few others. For Prem Nath Bazaz, it was "the happy news";[74] for Sheikh Mohammad Abdullah, it represented "a dream-come-true" moment,[75] and when Raja Mohammad Akbar Khan who was in jail, came to know about it, "[h]is joy knew no bounds over this development."[76] On the other hand, Munshi Mohammad Ishaq considered the conversion of the party as tantamount to breaking the oath taken in the historical meeting on 21 June 1931 with the *Qura'n* as the witness. He lamented that "the Muslim Conference was buried by one of its prominent founders with his own hands."[77] Chaudhri Ghulam Abbas, a frontline Muslim Conference leader who had earlier opposed its conversion, spoke in support, as did Chaudhri Hamid Ullah. Abdullah read out congratulatory telegrams sent to him by Jawaharlal Nehru and Mahatma Gandhi on the formation of the National Conference.[78] Abbas later wrote that there were certain conditions laid down for the conversion like including in the aims and objectives of the National Conference fight for religious, economic, political and administrative grievances of the Muslims; continuing with their separate electorate for the Assembly and other public institutions; Sheikh Abdullah not to embrace politics of the Indian National Congress nor support the party; the Muslim League as the sole representative party of the Muslims of India not to be opposed in any form; and all communities living in the State to join the freedom struggle against Maharaja Hari Singh.[79] Recalling the event, Abbas writes [translation]:

> These conditions were placed by me before an open session and agreed to by the other side [Abdullah and his nationalist group]. We made an announcement that we were ready to join the National Conference under a contract and will observe for some time the political conduct of the proponents of the united nationality before taking a final decision.[80]

Decades later, Abdullah admitted that besides Abbas, Bakhshi Ghulam Mohammad, Mirza Afzal Beg, Molvi Abdullah Vakil and Ahmad Din Banihali, also opposed the conversion of the Muslim Conference at one stage[81] but maintains silence on any conditions agreed to before dissolution of the Muslim Conference. Abbas believed that Abdullah had slipped out of their hands and had started considering Nehru as his guru and, possibly, his spiritual leader.[82] Justifying his falling in line, he writes, "In view of the obtaining political situation and a particular policy adopted by the Hari Singh Government towards the Muslims, any discord among them was akin to mass suicide by the community."[83] All prominent workers were in agreement that the State cannot afford two parties of the Muslims. Considering the 80% Muslim majority population of the State, they believed that inclusion of non-Muslims was unlikely to affect the separate status of the Muslims and that the Hindus were co-opted only as a political agreement between the two communities. Abbas counts the advice of Muhammad Ali Jinnah also as the reason for his change of heart on the conversion of the Muslim Conference to the National Conference.

During his visit to Kashmir in 1936, Jinnah had advised the Muslim Conference leadership to strive for the cooperation of the minorities and give them an assurance that equality and justice shall be secured to them in the State. "I will also say this that without winning the confidence of minorities and without assuring them of equal treatment with the majority, the obstacles in your political path will not be removed,"[84] he had cautioned them. At no point in time, however, had Jinnah advised them to disband the Muslim Conference and form a new party. Interestingly, Abdullah also claimed to have been guided by the advice of Jinnah. That, however, is an overstatement. Jinnah's advice to him on the minorities came in 1936 while, as we have observed in the preceding, Abdullah had as early as in 1935 decided to discard the Muslim Conference and live up to his new ideal of nationalist politics. Jinnah, it may be recalled, was against Abdullah's proximity with the Indian National Congress that he believed was "a Hindu-ridden organisation and enemy of Muslim interests."[85] On 1 April 1939, two months before the dissolution of the Muslim Conference, he told Kashmiri students at the Aligarh Muslim University:

> I can say with certainty that he [Sheikh Mohammad Abdullah] is in the wrong. Having got himself ensnared by the Congress, which is thoroughly a Hindu organization,

> he has put the ship of his community in a whirlpool. I understand that he is doing this out of ignorance and some misunderstanding. But I am fully satisfied that he will soon realize his mistake and will return to the right path, and will come to know that those whom he is considering his friends and at whose beck and call he is acting, are not his true friends but his enemies.[86]

The National Conference was launched with Abdullah as its President but the preconditions for its formation Abbas refers to were ignored. The latter accused Abdullah of reneging from the pledge he had made to the members of the Muslim Conference who were opposed to the conversion of the party. "Had Sheikh Abdullah and his colleagues stuck to the mutual contract then possibly nationalism alone would have been the remedy for people's pain. But that did not happen,"[87] Abbas wrote in his biography, *Kashmakash*, first published 10 years after the formation of the National Conference. He referred to Abdullah as "the Incorrigible Kashmiri Gandhi who very quickly came before the Muslims in his true colours."[88]

After the dissolution of the Muslim Conference, there was a feeling of dissatisfaction among the Muslims especially the educated youth affecting somewhat Abdullah's popularity. His proximity with the Indian National Congress and opposition to the Two Nation Theory did not go well with a sizeable section of the population. This fact was also reflected in the Administration Report of the government for 1940-41 which reads:

> A section of the Muslims could not tolerate Sheikh Mohammad Abdullah's opposition to Pakistan scheme of the All India Muslim League. Some of them revived the Muslim Conference and openly declared their support of Pakistan claiming to be better Muslims than the Muslims in the National Conference party. They repudiated the claim of the National Conference to represent the Muslim population of the State.[89]

Five days after the National Conference was formed, there was an attempt by the rival side to take possession of the *Mujahid Manzil*, erstwhile headquarter of the Muslim Conference now under the control of the National Conference. On 16 June 1939, some youth from the Muslim League hoisted Islamic flag at the Hazratbal shrine and then proceeded to the *Mujahid Manzil* with the aim to wrest the building from the National Conference and hoist their flag on it. Abdullah was present there with his supporters and resisted the attempt of the youth to occupy the building by throwing stones at them. It was an interesting development when Kashmir's frontline political leader was seen pelting stones at a rival group of the youth. Recording the event in his daily diary, Molvi Mohammad Shah Sa'dat writes, "Yesterday, when the Muslim League people entered the *Mujahid Manzil*, Sheikh Mohammad Abdullah and his colleagues hurled stones at them and injured them."[90] Next day, the police arrived at the venue and arrested some workers of the National Conference. Another attempt was made in 1940 when, on 26 March, a group of educated youth held a meeting at Badam Wari, an almond garden in old Srinagar, raised pro-Muslim Conference slogans and made speeches. Later, they marched to the *Mujahid Manzil* and hoisted a flag atop the building. Mohammad Sayeed Masoodi, who was present there, had the flag removed and the youth thrashed.[91] Another development took place that year on 10 October when several political leaders including Sardar Gouhar Rehman, Sardar Fateh Mohammad Khan, Mirza Attaullah Khan, Qazi Abdul Gani, Pir Zia-ud-Din, Babu Abdullah, Chowdhary Abdul Kareem, Chowdhary Hamidullah, Munshi Mohammad Din Fouq, Syed Hussain Shah Jalali, Mohammad Yousuf Qureshi, M.I. Sagar, Ghulam Haider Gori and Syed Meerak Shah met at Badam Wari and resolved to revive and galvanise the Muslim Conference.[92]

To his dismay, Abdullah soon found that the Kashmiri Pandits were not attracted to the National Conference barring a few youth leaders who, in his own words expressed decades later, joined the party only to "mould its policies according to their wishes but having failed in their objective opted for an exit from the party."[93] He alleged that they had "struck a dagger into the heart of the people's movement of Kashmir and began to dance to somebody else's tune."[94] They left the party shortly on one or the other pretext after raising objections to public meetings starting with the recitation of verses from the Holy *Qura'n* or shouting of slogans like *Allahu Akbar*. Abdullah's predicament was obvious:

> [H]e was confronted by enraged Pandit leaders including Jia Lal Kilam, Kashyap Bandhu and Prem Nath Bazaz who made a big fuss over his description of Prophet Muhammad (pubh) as the Final Messenger and the *Qura'n* as the Last Revelation from God. He was addressing a *Miladun Nabi* function and had spoken only what as a Muslim the divine scripture taught him and what he believed in as an article of faith. The Pandit trio made such an issue of it that Kilam and Bandhu resigned from the National Conference and Bazaz followed suit soon. They had objected to raising of the slogan, *Naar-e-Takbeer,* and recitation of verses of the *Qura'n* in public meetings. Owing to the Pandit hostility towards him, an upset Abdullah, on 28 July 1941, wondered: "What is the use of preaching nationalism to Pandits who cannot even tolerate the washing of hands and face by us on the banks of [the] Jhelum?"[95]

Abdullah was caught in an unenviable situation on the issue of conversion of the Muslim Conference. On the one hand, his own colleagues were resenting the conversion and considered the move against the interests of the Muslim majority of the State and, on the other, Kashmiri Pandits were not enthusiastic on joining his National Conference. There was yet another front where Abdullah was facing hostility and extreme opposition. The Hindu leaders and opinion makers outside Jammu & Kashmir advised the Kashmiri Pandits against joining Abdullah's National Conference. They viewed 'change of re-orientation of his policy' with suspicion. One such person was Lala Khushal Chand, owner of the daily *Milap* published from Lahore, who rejected as "a new hoax" the conversion of the Muslim Conference and lamented the "orthodoxy" of Hindus coming in the way of reconversion of Kashmiri Muslims to Hinduism during the rule of Maharaja Ranbir Singh, thereby stopping Kashmir from becoming a Hindu majority land. When Abdullah was working for a Hindu-Muslim unity, Lala was accusing him of spreading communalism. Writing in the special *Satyagraha Number* of the *Desh Sewak*, Jammu, he wrote:

> It was the orthodoxy of the Hindus of Maharaja Ranbir Singh's time which stood in the way of the reconversion of the Hindus proselytized by the Muslim rulers; otherwise Kashmir should have been a Hindu majority... Mr. Abdullah has been spreading communalism in the State for the last several years. Now, he had created a new hoax regarding the conversion of the Muslim Conference. How can Hindus rely on him! He should first throw the Glancy Commission Report in the river Jhelum. What is required is that the Hindus and Sikhs should sink their differences and strengthen the hands of His Highness [Maharaja Hari Singh].[96]

As later developments suggest, burial of the Muslim Conference was the single most crucial development leading to political uncertainty that plagues Kashmir ever since. The decision proved to be as momentous as it was controversial. For, in 1947, it turned the flow of events in a direction that subsequently left even Abdullah a bitter man. Decades after undergoing long incarceration following dismissal and arrest as Prime Minister in 1953, he regretfully recalled Jinnah warning him that people he counted as his friends [read Jawaharlal Nehru and other leaders of the Indian National Congress] and at whose beck and call he was acting were not his true friends but his enemies, and cautioning him against ignoring his advice.[97]

Soon after the formation of the National Conference, there was unease, especially among its Muslim leaders who had earlier agreed to the conversion of the Muslim Conference on certain assurances, over the manner the party was being run and the increasing influence of the Indian National Congress over it. They were also uncomfortable with the behaviour of their non-Muslim colleagues in the party for their vehement opposition to certain matters sacred and emotional to the majority community like raising the slogan of *Allahu Akbar* at public meetings to instill fervor among the audience. These public meetings comprised of Muslim audience with literally no or miniscule participation of Kashmiri Pandits, apart from a few of their leaders sharing the dais. These Muslim leaders felt that the community for whose inclusion a strong and on-the-rise political party of the Muslims was dismantled to raise a new political party at a crucial juncture of their fight against tyranny were now searching for excuses to pin it down.

Following the dissolution of the Muslim Conference, Nehru remained in constant touch with Abdullah and even made several visits to Srinagar, despite his preoccupations back home. On 30 May 1940, accompanied by Khan Abdul Gaffar Khan, he arrived in Srinagar where he stayed till 12 June during which time he attended public meetings, visited schools and also attended a meeting at the *Mujahid Manzil*.[98] He asked the Kashmiri Pandits to join the National Conference. There were several demonstrations against Nehru's visit and an annoyed Sheikh Mohammad Abdullah warned Mirwaiz Mohammad Yusuf Shah to stop these protests or face consequences. The important fallout of the Nehru visit was the exit of Chaudhri Ghulam Abbas from the National Conference. Next year, Nehru again visited Kashmir and addressed a public meeting in Srinagar on 2 October 1941.[99] These visits had a clear political motive—to hold Abdullah firmly on to the side of the Indian National Congress. "Nehru appears to have honed in early on Sheikh Abdullah as his man in Kashmir, a role that the Sheikh played with admirable aplomb up to a point."[100] His proximity with the leaders of the Indian National Congress and identifying the National Conference with its policies had caused concern among many of his colleagues in the party. The coldness shown by the Kashmiri Pandit leaders was adding to their unease. A feeling was gaining ground in the party that the dissolution of the Muslim Conference was a grave mistake that should be undone.

On 10 October 1940, a special meeting of several political workers including Sardar Gauhar Rehman, Chaudhri Hamidullah Khan, Syed Hussain Shah Jalali, Khawaja Mohammad Yusuf Qureshi *et al.* was held in Srinagar.[101] Chaired by poet and author Munshi Mohammad Din Fauq, the meeting resolved to revive the party and constituted a committee which unanimously rejected the National Conference.[102] In a statement issued on the occasion, the meeting observed that at present it did not want to enter into the debate about how the formation of the National Conference had damaged the larger interests of the Muslims but concluded that "the purpose for which the so-called nationalist elements among the Hindus desired the formation of the National Conference was to kill two birds with one stone; they were not able to do so by themselves and, therefore, resorted to the help and co-operation of Muslim leaders."[103] Earlier, in June 1940, Mohammad Yusuf Qureshi through his weekly *Paigham* had started a campaign for the revival of the Muslim Conference. Another newspaper, weekly *Al-Islah* chipped in to condemn the formation of the National Conference and demand the revival of the Muslim Conference.[104]

Finally, on 13 June 1941, the Muslim Conference was resurrected. Abbas, who had distanced himself from the National Conference and returned to Jammu, was informed about the decision. After remaining politically inactive for two years, he finally joined the revived Muslim Conference in 1942. He had developed serious differences with Abdullah on the latter's all out embrace with the Indian National Congress. The flashpoint came in 1940 when the Prime Minister of Jammu & Kashmir, Gopalaswami Ayyangar[105] took two major decisions which the Muslims considered seriously detrimental to their interests. These included imposition of Devnagri script in schools and allowing the Hindus to possess arms at the exclusion of the Muslims. Abdullah took a very controversial stand on these important matters. On the script issue, after initial opposition, he took a sudden U-turn and declared that "if the Indian National Congress opted for the Sanskrit script he would readily go with it."[106] On both these issues significant for the Muslims of Jammu & Kashmir, the National Conference chose to sit on the fence in the State Assembly.[107] Following this development, Abbas' relations with Abdullah "were broken forever."[108] Ayyangar was seen as being supportive of the National Conference and Abdullah, almost confirming the perception, later claimed that he had "influenced Nehru's decision to pick Ayyangar as a minister in his cabinet."[109] Within the National Conference also, many leaders were not happy with the state of affairs and at one point in time, there was a serious move to dissolve the National Conference and return to the Muslim Conference. In the meanwhile, Abdullah was consolidating his relations with the Indian National Congress. On 7 September 1942, a procession was taken out in Srinagar in solidarity with the Indian National Congress, which passed through different parts of the city and terminated at the Goal Bagh where Abdullah and Kashmiri Pandit leaders, including Shiv Naraian Fotedar and Jia Lal Kilam, addressed the gathering.[110]

During his last visit to Kashmir in 1944, Mohammad Ali Jinnah tried to wean Abdullah away from the Indian National Congress but did not succeed. Jinnah asked him to lead the Muslim Conference instead of the National Conference, reminding him that he had started his movement for the protection of rights of the Muslims and his support base also comprised only Muslims.[111] He made an offer to him by assuring that he would ask Chaudhri Ghulam Abbas to return to his legal profession and the Mirwaiz Mohammad Yusuf Shah to religious preaching, leaving the political field vacant for him.[112] He knew that among the Kashmiri leadership, Abdullah alone had the ability to unite the Muslims on one platform and, in fact, told the leadership of the Muslim Conference, "You donot have a leader like Sheikh Abdullah who without fear knows how to play with fire. If you have to stay in politics then produce a Kashmiri speaking leader."[113] About the Mirwaiz and Abbas, he did not have such an opinion. He was aware of the Mirwaiz as a naïve politician and of Abbas' language handicap as a non-Kashmiri. Recalling his personal experiences with the Congress, Jinnah told Abdullah that he had quit that party after seeing 'double face' of its leaders. The Indian National Congress, he cautioned him, will deceive you after its interests were met and you would repent one day. The advice of Jinnah did not make any impact on Abdullah other than making him bitter with the former. Years after he was dismissed as the Prime Minister of Jammu & Kashmir and had spent a long time in jail, he said at a reception held at a New Delhi hotel in 1968 [translation]:

> The *Quaid-e-Azam* had told me that I am like your father. Look at my gray hair. It has not grayed under the sunshine. I have spent my entire life in politics. Initially, I had joined these very Hindu leaders and dreamt of a united India but was forced to part ways. Remember! If you do not listen to my advice you will repent one day.[114]

In his memoirs, Abdullah quotes Jinnah as further saying to him that his experience was that Hindus cannot be trusted and that they can never be your friends. "Time will come when you will recall my words and feel sorry", he told Abdullah and asked him, "How can you trust a people who consider it a sin to accept water from your hands?"[115] He narrated an incident to him when Madan Mohan Malviya, citing religious reasons, had refused to have food with him on the same table when he called on Jinnah at the latter's residence.[116] Abdullah was not impressed.

Meanwhile, frustrated with disinterest of non-Muslims towards the National Conference, the Kashmiri leadership within the party mulled its reconversion to the Muslim Conference in 1944, and almost reached a consensus on the issue. The General Secretary of the party, Mohammad Sayeed Masoodi, being away in his hometown, Muzaffarabad, the Acting General Secretary, Ghulam Mohiuddin Qarra, sent registered letters to other members of the Working Committee and sought their views on the subject of reconversion of the party. Senior political leader and author, Krishan Dev Sethi, who chanced upon such a letter addressed to Raja Mohammad Akbar Khan, the lone Muslim leader from Jammu who had earlier opposed the suggestion, recalls the development thus [translation]:

> In 1944, due to disinterest shown by non-Muslims towards the National Conference and in view of Sheikh Mohammad Abdullah's other consideration, the reconversion of the National Conference to the Muslim Conference was under consideration and the Kashmiri leaders had almost arrived at a consensus on the issue. The General Secretary of the National Conference, Maulana Mohammad Sayeed Masoodi had gone to his native village, Lorat, in Muzaffarabad district. Ghulam

> Mohiuddin Qarra was the Acting General Secretary. He sent registered letters to other Muslim members of the Working Committee on the subject [informing them] that members from Kashmir had reached a consensus on this change and [now] you may give your opinion.[117]

Abdullah's Muslim colleagues kept on impressing upon him that the experiment of nationalism had failed. Although disillusioned with non-cooperating Kashmiri Pandit leaders, he was not ready to undo the National Conference. He held meetings with them and complained that they were not extending their hand of cooperation to him due to which he was facing pressure to revive the Muslim Conference. He told them that only if they strengthened his hands could he foil such a move. Simultaneously, he addressed series of public meetings in the Pandit-dominated areas and was accused by opponents of adopting their religious symbols to appease them but without any success. "At the first such meeting held at Rainawari, he appeared on the stage wearing vermillion on his forehead and, against his earlier routine, read out [albeit] with wrong pronunciation, verses from the *Bhagavad Gita*, Hindu religious scripture, instead of the *Qura'n*, as he would normally do, and, in the end, raised the [Hindu religious] slogan *Har Har Mahadev*."[118] The Kashmiri Pandits were not impressed, forcing him to discontinue with such public meetings. The leaders of the Muslim Conference again tried to win a disillusioned Abdullah over to their side but instead of agreeing to the merger of the National Conference with the Muslim Conference, he proposed a united front of the two parties. Abbas accepted the proposal on the condition that Abdullah would have to part ways with the Kashmiri Pandits. "For Sheikh Abdullah", writes Shabnam Qayoom, "leaving the Kashmiri Pandits was akin to leaving Pandit Nehru whom he would just not annoy. Hence, the talks broke down."[119]

The dissolution of the Muslim Conference and creation of the National Conference brought about a seemingly perennial enmity between the followers of Abdullah and the Mirwaiz. The ideologically divergent groups were involved in many a bitter and violent battle, dividing the Muslims of Kashmir into two feuding sides. For years, this bitterness and group fight adversely affected people to people relations and destroyed many families, leading to divorces where spouses came from rival backgrounds. Frequent and violent *Sher-Bakra* (nick names given to supporters of Abdullah and the *Mirwaiz*, respectively) clashes took place with warring groups fighting out their differences on the streets of Srinagar city and giving each other bloody noses and broken bones. Such was their animosity against each other that separate rounds of Eid prayers were held at the same place and at the same time. On 7 January and 16 March 1935, the Mirwaiz and his followers offered *Eid* prayers inside the Srinagar's Aali Masjid while Abdullah and his supporters did so in the open outside the mosque.[120]

The fracases that had broken out between the two sides in 1930s turned violent and frequent during 1940s. Residential houses of opponents were attacked, properties vandalized and unsuspecting individuals ambushed, beaten and left severely injured. For their numerical strength and an organized 'attack-force', the National Conference had an upper hand in such clashes and in most of the cases the supporters of the Mirwaiz bore the brunt. Abdullah's colleague and later *bête noir*, Bakhshi Ghulam Mohammad had raised a volunteer corps mostly comprising of ruffians and nicknamed as the 'Maisuma Regiment', which frequently attacked the followers of the Mirwaiz and allegedly enjoyed Abdullah's patronage. "Sheikh Mohammad Abdullah gave them full support and encouragement and was sometimes found moving with these groups with a hockey stick in his hand."[121] In 1942, on the day of Muslim festival of *Eid*, when clashes erupted in Srinagar between the supporters of Abdullah and the Mirwaiz, the former "beat with his hockey stick many innocent people at Amira Kadal in broad daylight."[122]

The *Sher-Bakra* feuds were not restricted to political beliefs. Religious affiliations and institutions were also targeted. On 12 October 1942, Abdullah allegedly let loose his men to "finish the Yusuf Shahi Muslims"[123] at the Eidgah in Srinagar where the Mirwaiz had gone to lead the congregational *Eid* prayers. A large number of Mirwaiz supporters were injured. The offices of the Muslim Conference were attacked and vandalized throughout the city limits. The vengeance was writ large on the faces of the attackers who would not mind indulging even in blasphemous acts to teach the adversary a lesson. At Khawaja Bazar, a green flag with the inscription of *kalima shahadah* was pulled down from the roof of a Muslim Conference worker's house, tore into pieces and thrown into a gutter.[124] The City Office of the Muslim Conference at Zaindar Mohalla was broken open and many articles including "Islamic flag hoisted at the top of the office, sign board bearing the name of the party, one Remington type-writer, ₹ 165 in cash and many important documents"[125] were stolen.

In another incident of alleged high-handedness, the *Anjuman Darsul Islam*, a religious institution running a night school at Reshi Mohalla, was locked by the workers of the National Conference on 26 March 1943. A prominent worker of the Muslim Conference, Mohammad Yusuf Khan, was beaten up by the attackers.[126] The institution remained locked for a long time with the police taking no action to unlock it or proceeding against the culprits, forcing the *Anjuman* to urge the Governor of Kashmir to "spare no pains to see that law and order is maintained in the Allaqa [area] and issue orders to see our office transferred honourably."[127] The National Conference workers were incensed on seeing green flags flutter on offices of the Muslim Conference. In Ward No. 6, the office of the party was vandalized and broken down for the green flag fluttering on its top.[128] The building of the office was the property of one Mohammad Sheikh who had rented it out to the Muslim Conference. He had been threatened with demolition of the house if he did not bring down the flag. The Muslim Conference alleged that the police was taking the side of the attackers and Prime Minister Ayyangar was befriending Abdullah at the expense of the Muslim Conference.

The months of March and April 1943 especially turned out to be very hot for the workers of the Muslim Conference in Srinagar. Their person and property were subjected to, what the party alleged "Nazi type of aggression". On 16 April, the General Secretary of the party wrote to the Governor of Kashmir:

> For about last three weeks, daily we get harassing news from different corners of the city telling therein sad occurrences and Nazi type of aggression played freely by the National Conference workers. It is highly sad and I am bold enough to say that there exist worst type of fifth columnists in the Police Department. We have till now often and on brought these facts in to the notice of concerned authorities, but that served no purpose. On the contrary, it enhanced Nazi tactics of the Gundas.[129]

Another incident of intimidation was reported from Maharaj Bazar, Srinagar where an 'Islamic flag' had been hoisted atop the office of the Muslim Conference which the activists of the National Conference demanded to be immediately removed. On 16 April, the 'final ultimatum' with threat of severe reprisal was served, and within hours, despite prior information to the police, the Muslim Conference supporters in Maharaj Bazar were assaulted, resulting in injuries to many. The assault party was led by Qadir Khan alias *Nata*,[130] President National Conference Halqa Committee Goni Khann who, in later years, attained infamy as a frontline muscleman used by his party to silence dissent.[131] Amidst these violent incidents, an interesting situation developed when M. Sultan, a prominent leather and handicraft merchant and a Mirwaiz loyalist who ran a shop at The Bund, alleged that his residential house at Shamaswari in downtown Srinagar was being stoned "every now and then". Sultan, who had recently shifted residence to this locality dominated by the National Conference loyalists, had been called along with his workmen, to Jammu by Maharaja Hari Singh for making his shoes. Owing to insufficiency of tools he had to return to Srinagar to make the shoes right. During his absence from Srinagar, stones were thrown at his house several times, breaking window panes and causing fear among the inmates. On 8 May 1943, he complained to the District Magistrate that "last night there was again a heavy shower of stones on my house", and expressed his inability to leave for Jammu to have the shoes tried by Hari Singh "as my family is badly frightened by this incident, and they do not allow me to leave this place even in the day time, not to speak of the night."[132] He also sent a telegram to the Maharaja. Since the complainant had access to the ruler, police investigation was quickly ordered and uniformed and plain clothed policemen were deployed to keep a watch. "There has been no stone throwing for the last two days now and it is expected that nuisance will ease", Lt. Col. Rao Baldev Singh, Senior Superintendent of Police, Srinagar wrote to the District Magistrate on 12 May 1943.[133]

During Muhammad Ali Jinnah's last visit to Kashmir in 1944 also, the workers of the Muslim Conference and the National Conference engaged themselves in clashes and thrashing each other at various places, especially on May 10 when he was driving through south Kashmir on his way to Srinagar. At Khanabal Dak Bungalow, where the Muslim Conference had arranged tea for the visiting leader, workers of the National Conference gate-crashed into the premises, scuffled with the host party and snatched and tore its flags. At Bijbihara, similar clashes took place between the supporters of the two parties, abusing and assaulting each other. A school teacher and a supporter of the Muslim Conference, Mohammad Ismail, filed a police report alleging that he was assaulted, his clothes torn into pieces and ₹ 45 removed from his pocket.[134]

There were also incidents where the Mirwaiz supporters laid ambush on the National Conference supporters and thrashed them whenever an unsuspecting victim among them passed through their area. In one such case, one Ghulam Qadir Wani was waylaid near the Jama Masjid and beaten to the pulp. The injured Wani was taken in a procession to the Pathar Masjid and 'a platoon of National Conference workers' raided the alleged prime assailant, Ali Mohammad Darail, at Dab Tal where he was thrashed and whisked away, besides his house ransacked.[135]

During these internecine feuds among the Muslims, Abdullah was successful in dislodging the Mirwaiz Mohammad Yusuf Shah from the podium of Hazratbal shrine and capture it for his own benefit as a political platform that he used to the fullest till his demise. Likewise, he also took over the shrine of Dastgeer Sahib at Khanyar. For the Mirwaiz, both shrines were source of support and powerful centers for dissemination of political and religious messages and losing these was a great setback for him. On 5 January 1943, the Mirwaiz was supposed to address a large congregation at Hazratbal in connection with an auspicious occasion connected with one of the four close Companions of Prophet Muhammad (pubh). Since on such occasions the Holy Relic at the shrine is displayed for public viewing a huge gathering of devotees was expected but the National Conference had a different plan. The party sent large number of its supporters to the shrine through both surface and water routes to stop the Mirwaiz from taking the podium. The caretaker of the shrine, Abdur Rahim Banday, sensing serious trouble, forbade the Mirwaiz from entering the shrine premises. After taking control of the Hazratbal shrine, Abdullah led his supporters to Khanyar to seize the Dastgeer Sahib shrine. "Ahead of the procession, pipers and drummers played music to rouse the onlookers and different groups in the procession acted like jumping monkeys."[136] To further weaken the Mirwaiz politically, the National Conference targeted its main support-base, the *wazas*, a community of chefs specializing in the famous multi-course Kashmiri cuisine, *wazwan*, served on marriages and special occasions. They were beaten up and their copper utensils looted to force them against supporting the Mirwaiz. People were asked to boycott them unless they displayed certificates of loyalty issued from the National Conference Headquarters.[137]

Within days of Jinnah's departure from Kashmir in 1944, the two factions of Muslims settling scores with each other on the streets of Srinagar, found time and urge to accord a rousing reception to Maharaja Hari Singh, the 'fountainhead of oppression' they were fighting against. Singh's Minister-in-Waiting, Ram Chandra Kak, was successful in bringing around Abdullah to publicly show his loyalty to the Maharaja in return of a promise of some public welfare schemes. On the other side, Kak advised Hari Singh to visit the interiors of the city where he assured him a warm reception awaited him. Not to be left out, the Mirwaiz also jumped on the bandwagon. In July 1944, on his return from the Middle East where he had gone to cheer up his troops fighting on the side of the British Forces in the World War II, Hari Singh was accorded a grand reception in Srinagar. Both the National Conference and the Muslim Conference vied with each other in the display of loyalty to the throne. The city was decorated with colourful arches. As he drove through the streets, the Maharaja was showered with flower petals. "On the roadside at *Mujahid Manzil*, Sheikh Sahib with his head bowed, garlanded the autocrat and showered flowers on him."[138] Whether or not the Maharaja announced any public welfare scheme, Kak was successful in securing for himself the post of Prime Minister.

On 16 March 1945, a grand *Miladun Nabi* procession was taken out in the Srinagar city under the aegis of the Muslim Conference which passed through different areas. The procession, for the first time in Kashmir, raised slogans of *Muslim League Zindabad* and *Pakistan Zindabad*, infuriating the National Conference workers. The Congress leaders in Delhi were alarmed and Nehru rushed Diwan Chaman Lal to Srinagar to check with Abdullah what was happening there.[139] On 6 July that year, the Muslim Conference held a large public meeting in Poonch where the Mirwaiz and Abbas were accorded "royal reception".[140] Nehru viewed these developments with concern. On 28 July, he arrived in Srinagar and was followed immediately by Khan Abdul Gaffer Khan, Maulana Abul Kalam Azad and Mian Iftikhar-ud-Din Ahmad. The National Conference organized a river procession in their honour. However, at several places from Nawa Kadal upstream to Zaina Kadal the Muslim Conference supporters held black flag demonstrations, raised pro-Jinnah and anti-Nehru slogans and pelted stones at the procession injuring, among others, Khan Abdul Gaffar Khan.[141] The National Conference retaliated by attacking workers of the Muslim Conference, the Muslim League and the Muslim Students League and vandalizing their offices and schools. Shabnam Qayoom recreates the scene thus [translation]:

> Through the National Army comprising drivers of the Lorry Adda, butchers, Tonga drivers and vendors, the supporters of the Muslim Conference, the Muslim League and the Muslim Students League were apprehended and beaten, injuring many and rendering several incapacitated. Wherever a flag, signboard or office of the Muslim Conference, Muslim League or the Muslim

> Students League was spotted it was razed to the ground. At Nawab Bazar, Krala Khud, Chinkral Mohalla, Sona Masjid, Maisuma, Batamaloo and Chhatabal, offices of the Muslim Conference were vandalized. Later, Muslim schools were targeted. The Islamia Schools at Drugjan and Amira Kadal were threatened with closure.[142]

Inspired by the Quit India Movement launched by Gandhi against the British rule in 1942, Abdullah announced the Quit Kashmir Movement against Maharaja Hari Singh in 1946. Before the launch of the Movement, there was again some effort to bring peace between the Muslim Conference and the National Conference and form a joint front. Leaders from both sides toned down their opposition against each other and talked about the need to jointly take on the 'oppression and tyranny' of the government. Abdullah declared that he was not out to fight the Muslim Conference and would 'shed his blood' for a worker of that party. In response, Abbas addressing a gathering at the Jama Masjid on 8 May 1946, described Abdullah a "Great Leader" and assured him that he was prepared to "make any sacrifice for the revolution the latter was out to cause in the State."[143] A meeting of the General Council of the National Conference was scheduled for its reconversion to the Muslim Conference but the move was sabotaged by the government through "arrest of its leaders and hundreds of workers"[144] including Abdullah who was arrested at Garhi on 20 May 1946. The Muslim Conference developed cold feet towards the Quit Kashmir Movement after it was assured by the government that it would support Pakistan and oppose the Congress.[145] The National Conference alleged that the Muslim Conference was in league with the government and resignation of its members from the Praja Sabha earlier and declaration of the "Direct Action" programme were only a hoax.

In the meanwhile, situation was fast changing in the subcontinent. India and Pakistan had emerged out of the Partition as independent sovereign states in mid-August 1947 and Maharaja Hari Singh was still withholding his decision on accession to any of the two Dominions. He was under tremendous pressure to quickly decide on the future of Jammu

& Kashmir even as he was toying with the idea of independence from both countries. The Muslim Conference too was persuading him to opt for a semi-independent status for Jammu & Kashmir with himself as a constitutional head. The party had passed a resolution on 19 July 1947 asking the Maharaja to declare internal autonomy of the State, set up a constituent assembly and accede to Pakistan in matters of defence, communication and foreign affairs.[146] For Hari Singh, time was fast running out of his hands. Leader after leader had arrived from Delhi to persuade him to accede to India. Acharya Kriplani, President Indian National Congress, Sikh rulers of Kapurthala, Faridkote and Patiala and the RSS Chief, Guru Golwalkar, visited Srinagar one after another to persuade him to decide for India.[147] A request by Jinnah to visit Kashmir around this time was turned down by him. Building the pressure further on Hari Singh, Mahatma Gandhi announced his visit to Kashmir, even as the Mirwaiz cautioned the Maharaja against joining 'Hindu India' under his influence and warned him of serious breach of peace in case he did so.[148]

On 1 August 1947, Gandhi reached Lahore on way to Kashmir. Different sets of National Conference leaders received him at the Lahore Railway Station, Kohala and Baramulla, where he faced protest and hostile slogans from the Muslim Conference workers.[149] Abdullah was in jail and his wife, Begum Akbar Jahan proceeded to Shalateng in the outskirts of Srinagar to welcome Gandhi. In Srinagar also, Gandhi was surrounded by some protesters who attacked his vehicle and raised loud slogans of "Go back Gandhi". Journalist and historian Rashid Taseer recalls that at Lal Chowk, the city center, Gandhi was asked by a protesting crowd to shout pro-Pakistan and pro-Jinnah slogans and he obliged them.[150] However, no unpleasant incident took place. Later, Akbar Jahan along with some Muslim workers of the National Conference joined Gandhi at his prayer meeting at the Abhinanda Home and with him and other Hindu devotees clapped and chanted *Raghupati Raghav Raja Ram*, a hymn that Hindus sing in praise of their god, Ram Chanderji.[151] Gandhi also visited the *Mujahid Manzil* to meet the National Conference workers where he was requested to speak for

Kashmiris' right to self-determination but he excused himself by invoking his "promise to not interfere with the politics of Kashmir".[152] During his stay in Srinagar, he met Maharaja Hari Singh, his wife Tara Devi, Prime Minister R.C. Kak and the palace priest, Swami Sant Dev. The immediate fallout of Gandhi's Kashmir visit was the sacking of pro-independence Prime Minister, Ram Chandra Kak, on 10 August 1947. For little over a month, Thakur Janak Singh functioned as the stop-gap Prime Minister until 15 October when Mehar Chand Mahajan, a Government of India recommended person was appointed on the post.[153] Before taking up his Kashmir assignment, Mahajan had a meeting with Prime Minister Jawaharlal Nehru in New Delhi.[154] As he wrote to his Home Minister, Vallabhbhai Patel, on 8 October 1947, Nehru was "sure things [for India in Kashmir] would improve when Justice Mahajan takes over the Prime Ministership."[155] The National Conference celebrated the ouster of Kak who, after Abdullah assumed power, was humiliated and dragged on the streets of Srinagar handcuffed where party workers even spat on his face.[156] By the third week of October, situation in Kashmir became highly volatile with large number of armed Tribal groups racing into Kashmir to dethrone Maharaja Hari Singh. The Maharaja fled to Jammu and sought military intervention from India to clear Kashmir of intruders. The Indian Army troops were air dropped in Srinagar. Abdullah was sworn in as the Emergency Administrator.

As Abdullah took over the reins of administration—first, as the Emergency Administrator and, later, as the Prime Minister—he cracked down on the Muslim Conference cadre, a large number of whom were arrested or exiled to Pakistan for supporting Jammu & Kashmir's accession to that country. A *Giriftaar Committee* was formed which supervised arrests of pro-Muslim Conference workers who were dubbed as the "Fifth Columnists of Pakistan". "The *Giriftaar Committee* also sent innocent people to jail."[157] False cases were slapped on them. Houses were raided and searches conducted, leaving the inmates in horror and shock. An atmosphere of terror was created to suppress dissenting voices. In early 1948, the Enemy Agents Ordinance was promulgated and used to stifle people with opposing ideology. On 6 September 1947, Mirwaiz Mohammad Yusuf Shah had secretly escaped to Pakistan in disguise, though being under constant watch. Till he crossed the State boundary at Kohala and sent a telegram of his safe arrival there, Khawaja Ahmad Ullah Makai, a lookalike and friend of the Mirwaiz, was put up at the *Mirwaiz Manzil* to mislead the intelligence sleuths in believing that the Mirwaiz was at home.[158] The Maharaja banned re-entry of the Mirwaiz in Kashmir and when Abdullah came to power he did not revoke this ban. The Mirwaiz lived the rest of his life in exile in Muzaffarabad where he rose to the position of the President of Pakistan Administered Jammu & Kashmir, the post he held twice between December 1951 and September 1958. Other prominent leaders of the Muslim Conference including Chaudhri Ghulam Abbas, Allah Rakha Sagar, Molvi Nooruddin, Molvi Abdur Rahim, Aga Showkat Ali and Ghulam Nabi Gilkar were also sent across the border. Hundreds of other Muslim Conference workers and their kin were pushed across the border even as thousands more voluntarily migrated for the fear of reprisal by Abdullah administration back home. Majority of them thought they were moving out temporarily and would return with the resolution of Kashmir dispute between India and Pakistan which they believed was happening soon.

2

A Loyal Rebel

On 31 October 1947, when Sheikh Mohammad Abdullah took oath of office as the Administrator of an Emergency Government in Jammu & Kashmir under Maharaja Hari Singh, the Dogra ruler had lost control over one-third of his territory while another one-half from where he had fled to safety, was at the verge of fall. Of the total 2,22,236 sq kms that Jammu & Kashmir comprised of, 83,294 sq kms (37.47%) in the form of Gilgit, Baltistan, Mirpur, Muzaffarabad and Kotli had fallen in the hands of the rebels. Another 15,948 sq kms, comprising Kashmir Valley including the capital city of Srinagar, and 86,904 sq kms comprising the region of Ladakh were facing similar danger. These areas accounted for 1,02,852 sq kms (over 46%) of the total territory. The Tribal Raiders had penetrated deep into the Valley and were less than 15 kms from the royal palace while large number of troops of the State Army were withdrawing from the battlefield. In simple words, when in the face of a serious threat Maharaja Hari Singh fled to Jammu, his native land, he had fully or partially lost control over a substantial part of the Princely State.

Abdullah's oath-taking took place in a state of acute crisis amid landing of Indian troops in Srinagar to "clear Jammu & Kashmir of raiders from Pakistan." On Jawaharlal Nehru's intervention, he was taken out from the prison where he had been lodged for fighting for the rights of his people to pave way for his coronation. Nehru had prevailed upon a weighed down Maharaja Hari Sing to hand over administration to Abdullah in order to save the situation for both the Maharaja and India. The

Maharaja had acted all through from September 1947 under the advice of the Government of India. Earlier, the appointment of Mehar Chand Mahajan as Prime Minister too, as Hari Singh later pointed out in a letter to President Rajendra Prasad, had been made on the suggestions from the Government of India as early as in September 1947. Singh wrote:

> In September 1947, it was suggested to me that it would be a wise move on my part to appoint Shri Meher Chand Mahajan as my Prime Minister as he would be able to handle the affairs of the State in the then critical period firmly and in a statesmanlike manner. Before Shri Meher Chand Mahajan took up his appointment he discussed with Sardar Patel about immediate requirements of the State and Sardar Patel promised him full support and cooperation on behalf of the Government of India.[159]

For Nehru, Abdullah was the only hope to bring Kashmir into the Indian fold. It was important for him to see Abdullah in a position where a 'grateful' Kashmiri leader could deliver for India in the hour of need. Pressure was built on Hari Singh to assign the administration of Jammu & Kashmir to its rebel leader "without whom solution to any issue in Kashmir is impossible."[160] Burdened by the pressure, Hari Singh issued an order on 30 October 1947 assigning Abdullah with "the function of the administration with powers to deal with the emergency." The short order signed by the Maharaja reads:

> We are hereby pleased to command that pending the formation of the Interim Government as agreed upon and in view of the exigency that has arisen I charge Sheikh Abdullah to function as the Head of the Administration with power to deal with the emergency. Sheikh Mohamed Abdullah be sworn in by the Chief Judge or any other Judge of the High Court at Srinagar.[161]

Next day, Chief Judge of Jammu & Kashmir High Court, S.K. Ghose, administered the oath of office to Abdullah. As Ghose initiated him into taking the oath, Abdullah, swearing allegiance and loyalty to Hari Singh and his heirs and successors, repeated the text of the oath after him:

> I, Sheikh Mohammad Abdullah having been appointed Head of the Administration of the Jammu & Kashmir State do solemnly swear that I will be faithful and be truly loyal to His Highness Maharaja Hari Singhji Bahadur of Jammu & Kashmir, his heirs, successors, my country, and nation and that I will faithfully discharge the duty upon which I am about to enter.
>
> I further do solemnly swear that I will not directly or indirectly communicate or reveal to any person or persons any matter which shall be brought under my consideration, or shall become known to me as Head of the Administration, except as may be required for the due discharge of my duties as Head of the Administration or as may be specially permitted by His Highness.[162]

Abdullah's oath of allegiance to Hari Singh came close on the heels of his letter to the Maharaja on 26 September 1947, written after the latter's announcement of 'amnesty', in which he affirmed:

> In spite of what has happened in the past I assure Your Highness that myself and my Party have never harboured any sentiment of disloyalty towards Your Highness's person, throne or dynasty. The development of this beautiful country and the betterment of its people is our common aim and interest and I assure Your Highness the fullest and loyal support of myself and my organization.... Before I close this letter, I beg to assure Your Highness once again of my steadfast loyalty and pray that God may grant me opportunity enough to make this country attain under Your Highness' aegis such an era of peace, prosperity and good Government that it may be second to none and be an ideal for others to copy.[163]

In his memoirs, *Aatash-i-Chinar* (Flames of the Chinar) published four years after his death in 1982, Abdullah recalls his assumption of office on 31 October with a sense of pride for being the "first Kashmiri Muslim to be appointed to the post after 28 Prime Ministers since [the inception of the Dogra rule in] 1846."[164] Evidently, he was either mistaking himself as the

Prime Minister when a Prime Minister in the person of Meher Chand Mahajan was very much in office and had been sworn in only a fortnight ago for a period of five years, or his amanuensis had failed to notice Mahajan in the chair.

The text of the oath makes it clear that Sheikh Mohammad Abdullah, revered by his people as the Lion of Kashmir for taking on a despotic regime, joined the Administration as a subordinate to Hari Singh with first and foremost allegiance and loyalty to him and his heirs and successors. This was a strange coincidence, for here was a rebel swearing allegiance and loyalty to an autocrat against whom he had led from the front a popular agitation and served him the ultimatum of "Quit Kashmir" only a year back. As Head of the Administration now, he took an oath to serve the interests of not just the same Maharaja but even his progeny. On 19 November 1947, Hari Singh abolished the post of Deputy Prime Minister, relieving Ram Lal Batra of the office and appointing him Hazoor Secretary, in-charge of Private and State Departments, thereby giving enough indication that Abdullah's status was no more than an officer subordinate to the Prime Minister. Legally, Abdullah's appointment was in no manner different from that of the advisors, ministers and prime ministers the Dogra ruler had earlier picked for assistance in running the affairs of his State, and who served only till his pleasure. Meanwhile, the fast deteriorating situation in Kashmir led to open armed hostilities between India and Pakistan with the dispute over its title reaching the United Nations. The Jammu Province was engulfed by flames of communalism where the Maharaja's administration was accused of actively abetting the killing of Muslim subjects.

The Government of India now being actively involved in the affairs of Jammu & Kashmir, Hari Singh watched helplessly his authority slipping out of his hands. Nehru exerted pressure on the Maharaja to appoint Administrator Sheikh Mohammad Abdullah as the Prime Minister of Jammu & Kashmir. In fact, the declaration of his appointment by Maharaj Hari Singh was drafted in and sent from New Delhi. On 1 March 1948, Gopalaswami Ayyangar, a Minister in Nehru's cabinet, wrote in unequivocal terms to Hari Singh to fall in line:

> Messrs V.P. Menon and Mahajan are going to Jammu this afternoon to discuss and finalize with you the draft of the Proclamation which Your Highness has to issue for appointing Abdullah as Prime Minister and others on his advice. The draft has been very carefully considered by myself, Pandit Ji [Jawaharlal Nehru] and Sardar Ji [Vallabhbhai Patel] and we are of the opinion that the whole of it should be accepted by you. Anything less would not satisfy the requirements of the present situation.[165]

Ayyangar, a former Prime Minister of Maharaja Hari Singh for six years between 1937 and 1943, did not mince words in seeking Abdullah's appointment on the terms set by the Government of India to use it as strength to its cause on Kashmir issue at the Lake Success[166] where he was going to fight India's case. In fact, he had foretold the Security Council that the Maharaja of Kashmir was appointing Abdullah as the Prime Minister. He spelt out this plan in his letter to Hari Singh thus:

> As a friend of yours, I consider it most important that Your Highness must make a very big gesture in order to rally the maximum percentage of the population of the State behind you with the help of Abdullah. Things are moving very fast and we have yet to fight a great battle at Lake Success. I have already stated during the discussion at Lake Success that Your Highness had only been waiting for Sheikh Abdullah to return from America to convert the Emergency Administration into an Interim Council of Ministers with Abdullah as Prime Minister. I am leaving Delhi for Lake Success the day after tomorrow, and it would be a great strength to the cause I have to plead there on behalf of Kashmir if this Proclamation is issued before I leave. I have not the slightest doubt that the issue of this Proclamation at this juncture is, in the circumstances that confront us at present, in the best interests of yourself and your people.[167]

Ayyangar's letter is a testimony to how strong Nehru and his government felt about Abdullah as their asset maintaining Kashmir's accession to India. Ayyangar counseled the Maharaja:

> It is further very important that everything that has happened in the past should be forgotten and forgiven and that Your Highness should take Sheikh Abdullah into your fullest confidence. In fact, I was almost going to suggest that you should give up your usual reserve, come out in the open and put yourself at the head of your people, both Muslims and non-Muslims, for the purpose of consolidating and strengthening the large volume of support for preserving the integrity of the State and maintaining its accession to India, which thanks to Sheikh Abdullah and the Indian Army, you have already behind you.[168]

A beleaguered Hari Singh had no option but to implement directions from New Delhi. So, on 5 March 1948, he ordered swearing-in of Abdullah as the Prime Minister of Jammu & Kashmir. The oath of office was administered to the new Prime Minister by the Chief Justice of Jammu & Kashmir High Court, Janki Nath Wazir, at Darbargarh Jammu. Besides Abdullah, seven ministers, including Ghulam Mohammad Bakshi, Mirza Mohammad Afzal Beg, Sardar Budh Singh, G.M. Sadiq, Shyam Lal Saraf, Girdhari Lal Dogra and Colonel Pir Mohammad Khan, were also administered the oath of office.

The Royal Command appointing Abdullah as the Prime Minister reads:

> Whereas We being graciously pleased to give and grant during Our pleasure unto Sheikh Mohammad Abdullah, the office of Prime Minister constituted and appointed under and by virtue of the Jammu & Kashmir Constitution Act of 1996 [Samvat] passed in the fourteenth year of Our Reign. We do by these Our presents hereby constitute and appoint him the said Sheikh Mohammad Abdullah, to be Prime Minister during our pleasure with all the interest, powers, titles, authorities, privileges and duties appertaining unto and vested in the said office.[169]

After the oath ceremony, Abdullah made a brief speech during which he used an Urdu allegory that, for decades following his ouster from power in 1953, served as his favourite expression to describe the prevailing situation in Kashmir. "Our ship is in a whirlpool", he said and sought support of "my colleagues and my people" to weather this storm.[170] Students of Kashmir history would recall that after 1953 till his return to power in 1975, during public meetings he would without fail use the expression: "*Hamari kishti manjdhaar mai phansi hai.*"

Once Abdullah was saddled in power with the full support of Nehru and his government, the relation between Hari Singh and his Prime Minister soured rapidly. Abdullah, Singh complained, soon backed out of the promises and assurances that he had given before the assumption of office. He was obviously referring to Abdullah's letter of steadfast allegiance and oath of loyalty to him and his family. With Nehru nursing a grudge against him, things became hot for Hari Singh. The relation between Hari Singh and Jawaharlal Nehru was less than cordial and both nursed a sentiment of dislike for each other. In 1946, Nehru set out for Kashmir to provide legal assistance to his jailed friend, Sheikh Mohammad Abdullah, but was denied entry into the territory of Jammu & Kashmir and arrested at Kohala. Nehru did not take this kindly. The Government of India asked Hari Singh to leave Jammu & Kashmir which he did in 1949 after appointing his son and heir, Karan Singh, as his Regent and himself remaining the titular Maharaja. Singh felt that Nehru and Abdullah schemed and got rid of him. In an agitated mood, he asked of the President of India, "Are myself and my dynasty to be pawns in the game which Sheikh Abdullah is playing with the Government of India on the representation that he is actively helping India in the case before the UN Security Council?"[171] He felt that Sheikh Abdullah was not "a synonymous term with the people of Kashmir" and threw a challenge: "Let the people of Jammu and Kashmir freely decide between me and Sheikh Abdullah without interference from the Government of India."[172]

Although he asserted himself against Hari Singh and succeeded in having him eased out of Jammu & Kashmir,

Abdullah as the Prime Minister continued to represent the Maharaja and worked under the shade of the Royal Seal that so pompously represented the 100 years of the Dogra rule over Kashmir. As Prime Minister, he communicated with Indian and foreign leaders using the Seal of the *Suryavanshi* Dogra monarchy. The Dogra rulers, it may be pointed out, considered themselves members of the *Suryavanshi* family, a mythical dynasty of ancient India whose 67th king is said to be Rama, a Hindu God. The *Surya devta* or the Sun God being the *kul devta* of the dynasty commanded a special significance in personal and State affairs of a *Suryavanshi* ruler. This significance was amply reflected in the State Flag and the Seal of Dogra rulers with *Surya devta* occupying the central place. The detail of the Dogra Seal includes two soldiers standing on the either side of an image of *Surya devta* with a sword each in one hand and the royal flag with an image of the Sun in the other. The legend inscribed under the feet of the two soldiers reads: "*Raj Dharmo Raghu Kula Adarsho*" meaning "A just rule is the ideal or motto of the family of *Raghu*". The legend would vary from office to office using the Seal. The British suzerainty was represented in the Seal by an image of the Crown.

That Sheikh Mohammad Abdullah used this Seal as the Prime Minister of Jammu & Kashmir is established by official correspondence carried out by him and the Prime Minister's Office. To quote only two instances, his letter of 15 August 1951 to the Chairman of the Parliament of Iran, Abul Qasim Kashani, and his Private Secretary's letter of 19 January 1952 to D.P. Dhar, Abdullah's junior colleague then camping in Paris, prominently carry the Royal Dogra Seal. The legend in the Seal of Abdullah's Private Secretary reads: "*Prashasht Ranveerta*" which means "Valour in war is praiseworthy".

In 1951, through an election in Jammu & Kashmir that returned all but two out of the total 75 National Conference candidates elected unopposed, the State Constituent Assembly was set up. This was followed by abolishment of the monarchy and appointment of Maharaja Hari Singh's son, Karan Singh as the *Sadr-e-Riyasat* of Jammu & Kashmir. Till August 9, 1953 when he was dismissed and arrested, Abdullah was his *bête noir*, Hari Singh's appointed Prime Minister. His popularity as a mass leader being undisputed, the fact remains that when in 1953 he was dismissed and sent to jail, he was not an elected Prime Minister. Ironically, his appointment and dismissal both came on the directions of his bosom friend, Jawaharlal Nehru.

3

The Plebiscite Ruse

Following the outbreak of armed hostility between India and Pakistan, the United Nations brokered a ceasefire in 1949 to end their first war over Jammu & Kashmir, the erstwhile princely state now divided between the two estranged south-Asian neighbours. On 5 January 1949, the Security Council passed a resolution calling for a plebiscite to decide the State's future, and spelled out the mode of holding the proposed referendum. Pertinently, in December 1948, both India and Pakistan had communicated to the world body their acceptance of the principles of the Resolution which stated that "the question of the accession of the State of Jammu and Kashmir to India or Pakistan will be decided through the democratic method of a free and impartial plebiscite."[173]

The UN-monitored referendum, however, was never held and both countries hold each other responsible for non-implementation of the Plebiscite Resolution. Pakistan accuses India of backing out on its promise to the world community for the fear of losing the vote on future of the Muslim majority Jammu & Kashmir. India, on the other hand, blames its western neighbour of failing to fulfill the precondition of vacating its troops, as envisaged in the Resolution, from the disputed territory before a referendum was held. India claims that there was no Kashmir dispute except with regard to the occupation of a portion of the erstwhile Princely State by Pakistan and that Maharaja Hari Singh's accession to India was an irrevocable decision making Jammu & Kashmir its integral part. Pakistan counters the Indian stand by referring to the UN Resolutions as being evidence of the erstwhile State's 'disputed status'.

At the time of Partition, Jammu & Kashmir existed as a geographical entity, outside British India, with an area of 2,22,236 sq kms. There was already discontent and public upsurge in Kashmir against the autocracy even as Maharaja Hari Singh faced armed rebellion in different parts of Jammu & Kashmir. In the wake of reverses suffered by his army after uprising in Poonch and Gilgit, and armed assault on Kashmir by Tribal groups in late October 1947, the Maharaja fled to Jammu. There, Nehru's emissary, Krishna Menon, obtained his signatures on the Instrument of Accession and Hari Singh appointed Sheikh Mohammad Abdullah as the Administrator of an Emergency Government.

Following the dispute over the status of Jammu & Kashmir, the United Nations debated for years its future while India and Pakistan strengthened their control over the respective parts of the erstwhile princely state; steadily converting the territory into the world's highest militarized zone. Maharaja Hari Singh, who had submitted to the sovereignty of India in matters of defence, communication and external affairs, was eased out in 1949 and sent on forced exile to Bombay (Mumbai) where eventually he died a bitter man, complaining about broken assurances and ill treatment meted out to him by the Nehru-led Government of India and Sheikh Mohammad Abdullah. In his long Memorandum written on 16/17 August 1952 to the President of India, Dr. Rajendra Prasad, he gave an account of how his subjects were positioned on the future of Jammu & Kashmir. Singh candidly stated that only "Hindus of Jammu and all the people of Ladakh were for affiliation with or Accession to India."[174] About the Border Feudatory Territories such as Hunza, Nagar and Chitral and the District of Gilgit, he conceded that these were "definitely for accession to Pakistan and were pressing me to accede to Pakistan without delay and threatening me with dire consequences if I did not act according to their suggestion."[175] Likewise, "Muslims from parts of Jammu such as, Mirpur, Poonch, Muzaffarabad, were for accession to Pakistan."[176] About Kashmir, he wrote, that a portion of its population "was also for accession to Pakistan" while Muslims of Kashmir and some Muslims of Jammu wanted to decide the question [of accession] "independent of me" and "obstructed me in deciding the question of accession instead of helping me to accede to India."[177]

After the Security Council passed the Plebiscite Resolution in 1948, there were some developments that appeared like the World Body was seriously considering holding a referendum in Jammu & Kashmir. At one stage, it seemed so close to be happening that the Press Officer of the United Nations Commission for India and Pakistan (UNCIP), M.D. Capite, in a letter dated 25 April 1949 to M.L. Bhardwaj, Deputy Principal Information Officer, Government of India, asked if facilities like radio stations, community receiving sets, sounds trucks, printing of pamphlets and posters, and 16 mm and 35 mm film projectors were available for publicising the plebiscite in Kashmir. "The reason I am asking these questions is that I am trying to get an idea of what equipment—radio, films, printing—we must import from Lake Success to compliment the equipment and facilities that are already here,"[178] Capite explained. In the subsequent years, however, refusal by both India and Pakistan to withdraw their armed forces from Jammu & Kashmir prior to holding of a referendum blocked the implementation of the UN resolution on plebiscite.

When in late 1940s and early 1950s the United Nations was deliberating on holding of a "free and fair plebiscite" in Jammu & Kashmir, Sheikh Mohammad Abdullah was in power and representing Indian standpoint at the Security Council as part of the delegation arguing the Indian case. He demanded vacation of Pakistani forces from the territory of the State held by that country and disbanding of the "Azad Jammu & Kashmir Government", and rejected the UN proposal of a plebiscite mooted by some of its members without achieving this end. He declared: "No plebiscite is possible without the sovereignty of the legally constituted Government of Jammu & Kashmir being effectively extended over the entire territory of the State, disbanding of the so-called Azad Kashmir Government and its forces and the withdrawal of Pakistani troops and nationals."[179] Again, in another statement, he said, "But there can be no plebiscite in Kashmir unless and until the Pakistan and the so-called Azad Kashmir forces are withdrawn from the State territory, refugees are rehabilitated and the sovereignty of the legal head of the State over the entire territory of Jammu & Kashmir is recognized."[180] He also issued a press statement in Srinagar in which he reiterated his demand of restoration of the State to the "lawful Government" and liquidation of "Azad Kashmir Government and disbandment of its forces."[181]

The situation, however, changed in 1953 when, on 9 August, Abdullah was sacked as Prime Minister and sent to jail. Two years later, his supporters started a movement for holding of plebiscite under the banner of *Mahaz-i-Rai Shumari* or the Plebiscite Front. His lieutenant, Mirza Mohammad Afzal Beg, assumed the leadership of the movement. The Front was launched on 9 August 1955 on the second anniversary of Abdullah's dismissal, but effectively came into being in 1958. In the process of mass movement, many people were killed, thousands arrested and families ruined. To the people's credit, they stood firm behind their leadership despite trials and tribulations. Slogans like *Rai shumari foran karao* (Hold plebiscite at once), *Jis Kashmir ko khoon se seencha woh Kashmir hamara hai* (Kashmir that we irrigated with our blood belongs to us) and *Yeh mulk hamara hai iska faisla hum karaingay* (This country is ours and we alone will decide its future) rent the Valley's air during those years. The Plebiscite Front leadership successfully turned a massive public outburst over the theft of Holy Relic from the Hazratbal Shrine in December 1963 into a mass agitation for release of Abdullah from jail.

Officially, Sheikh Mohammad Abdullah never associated himself with the demand for plebiscite. He neither assumed leadership of the Plebiscite Front nor registered himself as its basic member. At 59, he excused himself from leading the Front, saying that he was too old to lead the organisation. This he told at a wayside public meeting at Bijbihara on 18 April 1964 while returning from Jammu after being released from jail.[182] However, in 1975 when he returned to power at the age of 70 he did not think twice in assuming the President-ship of his revived National Conference. In fact, the first thing he did after disbanding of the Plebiscite Front was to obtain membership of the revived National Conference and taking over as its President. Earlier, through 1930s-40s also, he had headed the Muslim Conference, the National Conference and the State People's Convention. Although the Plebiscite Front was launched under his patronage while he was in jail, he strategically maintained an arm's length distance from the Front when he was out of power while fully using it for furtherance of his political agenda. In power, he was averse to holding of plebiscite in Jammu & Kashmir. His government came down heavily on those who pursued this goal during his rule, and even used against such people the draconian Public Safety Act, originally enacted by him to tackle timber smuggling.

One of the oft-repeated arguments to justify Abdullah changing course in 1975 when he returned to power following an agreement with Prime Minister Indira Gandhi, is that the dismemberment of Pakistan in the Indo-Pak War of 1971 had convinced him about futility of pursuing estrangement with India. That, however, is an oversimplified view of the facts. In pursuit of his politics, he had never countenanced Islamabad as a factor beyond having reconciled to her control over a part of the territory of Jammu & Kashmir. As Prime Minister, his official correspondence with the Government of India [for instance, letter dated 14 April 1950 addressed to Vishnu Sahay, Secretary for Kashmir Affairs, Ministry of States] is an indication of this, where he refers to the territory as "Azad Kashmir" [Free Kashmir] and "Azad territory"[183] like Pakistan would call it. Other than the years of plebiscite movement when Pakistan *qalmay, dirmay, sukhany* [through written and spoken word, and money] helped him in Kashmir, the country did not factor much in his politics. Her dismemberment in 1971 only offered him an excuse and an expressway for an outreach with India, the desire and process for which, however, had started years earlier.

Before the fall of Dacca (now Dhaka) when East Pakistan had revolted against Islamabad and India was supporting insurgents there, Abdullah had told Balraj Puri that he thought he should start the process of dialogue with India even if it took "its own time." Puri, as a first step, suggested him to issue a statement in support of India's Bangladesh policy. "India was at that time prepared to pay," what Puri observes, "the maximum price for support to Bangladesh. Since Sheikh Sahib was the tallest Muslim leader of the subcontinent, his support was most valuable", Puri wrote in the weekly *Mainstream*.[184] Abdullah asked Puri to draft a statement for him on these lines which he did. However, on his advisor's suggestion, he held back from issuing such a statement at the last minute.

Abdullah's supporters cite the Simla Agreement of 1972 between India and Pakistan as a reason for his looking towards New Delhi. They argue that the Agreement shut the doors on the demand for a plebiscite in Jammu & Kashmir. However, what is missed here is that the Simla Agreement kept the Kashmir issue open for resolution through bilateral dialogue between the two south-Asian neighbours while in the Indira-Abdullah Accord, as Indira Gandhi informed the Parliament, Abdullah had accepted the finality of accession of Kashmir with India, and thus stamped the option of plebiscite out for all the times to come. Another important fact, as readers will observe in the succeeding paragraphs, that nullifies the argument on Pakistan's defeat in the Indo-Pak War of 1971 or the Simla Agreement being the reason behind Abdullah's change of heart and looking towards New Delhi, is his and the Plebiscite Front's drifting away from the demand of plebiscite and accepting electoral politics under the framework of the Indian Constitution as early as in 1969.

The 'seriousness' with which Abdullah dealt with the demand for a referendum in Jammu & Kashmir can be gauged from his voluminous memoir of 73 chapters, *Aatash-i-Chinar*, where he talks about everything under the sun related to Kashmir and its turbulent history but steers himself clear of discussing plebiscite or how he patronized a 22-year long people's movement for it while he was out of power. A study of archival papers related to the years from 1949 to 1953 throws up some interesting details with regard to lack of his commitment with the demand for plebiscite right from the beginning. When the Security Council passed resolutions on Jammu & Kashmir, Abdullah had already moved into the corridors of power under the still existing shadow of Maharaja Hari Singh. A plebiscite in the Princely State would have undermined his authority as a vast majority of people outside the Valley of Kashmir—both Muslims and Hindus—did not accept him as their leader nor subscribed to his politics. Within the Valley, a section of people did not like him for his pro-India stand. He was aware of the result of an impartial vote under the aegis of the United Nations. Further, Pakistan had raised objection to his being in power while a vote on the future of Jammu & Kashmir was taken, alleging that he was partial towards India. Abdullah apprehended that the Plebiscite Administrator might turn out to be a parallel or over-riding authority while he himself administered Kashmir. He thought if he was removed from the government, it would be construed as "a victory of Pakistan"[185] before the plebiscite was actually held.

Interestingly, post-Accession and as early as on 10 November 1947, Abdullah had said that "there may not be a referrandum [in Kashmir] at all."[186] He was speaking to pressmen in Srinagar during a visit of Jawaharlal Nehru to Kashmir. At one stage in 1952, Abdullah's close associate and representative in the Indian Parliament, Mohammad Sayeed Masoodi, had sold to Jawaharlal Nehru the idea of holding a plebiscite limited to the Kashmir Valley so that "all the evils associated with a plebiscite limited to the Valley could be satisfactorily avoided".[187] Abdullah was always confident of his wide support base in Kashmir while a referendum in the whole of Jammu & Kashmir would be altogether a different story. Masoodi made this suggestion in a meeting Prime Minister Jawaharlal Nehru had convened in New Delhi on August 18, 1952 where, besides the members of the Foreign Affairs Committee and others, Abdullah's ministerial colleague, D.P. Dhar, was also present. Before the start of the meeting, Nehru called in Dhar to have a brief discussion on the proposed talks with the UN Representative on Kashmir, Dr. Frank P. Graham. Dhar suggested that "the provision of a plebiscite limited to the Kashmir Valley should be dropped completely for very well-known reasons and substituted by arrangements other than a plebiscite."[188]

While the United Nations was deliberating on the future of Kashmir through an 'impartial plebiscite', Abdullah announced convening of the Constituent Assembly to throw a spanner and decide the issue of accession of Jammu & Kashmir. Holding of plebiscite, which at the moment looked like a happening thing, would have jeopardized the applecart of both Nehru and Abdullah in Kashmir. To pre-empt such a possibility, Abdullah put pressure on New Delhi to declare accession of Jammu & Kashmir to India as final.[189] The Kashmir issue being under debate in the United Nations, India was reluctant to take such a step but advised Abdullah to convene the Constituent Assembly and have the matter decided by it.[190] The convening of the Constituent Assembly, however, was opposed by the Anglo-American Bloc in the United Nations. Nearer home, Iran also objected to it as an impediment in reaching to a peaceful settlement on Kashmir dispute. Cautioning India of imperialistic aims of foreign powers "to reduce Asia to a position of serfdom,"[191] Iran was watching developments in Kashmir. The Chairman of the Parliament of Iran and a prominent Shia cleric, Abul Qasim Kashani, sent various telegrams to Jawaharlal Nehru and Sheikh Mohammad Abdullah, urging them to resolve Kashmir dispute. In one of his long telegrams, Kashani appealed Abdullah to "make a bold and determined contribution by voluntarily withdrawing your proposal to proceed with the Constituent Assembly".[192] "This step", he argued, "I am sure will help considerably in creation of congenial atmosphere so necessary for initiating negotiations for a peaceful and a satisfactory solution of this most important problem."[193] In his response dated 15 August 1951, Abdullah justified his decision to convene the Constituent Assembly to "take the initiative into their [people's] own hands"...[as] a fair and just solution was not likely to be affected soon through the Security Council." The Constituent Assembly "is the only way out of the present impasse",[194] he wrote back to Kashani. Pertinently, at one stage, Maharaja Hari Singh also objected to the convening of the Constituent Assembly and stopped his son and the Regent, Karan Singh, from signing and issuing the Proclamation. One of his objections was that the Proclamation should be signed by him as the ruler of Jammu & Kashmir and not by his Regent. However, Abdullah managed to have Hari Singh pressurized by the Government of India which unequivocally impressed upon him that no purpose would be served by any of his act that held up "the signing and issue of the Proclamation by Shri Yuvraj [Karan Singh]" (see Appendix III). Singh fell in line.

In October 1951, ahead of a meeting of the Security Council on Kashmir in Paris, where Abdullah was also to participate as a non-official member of the Indian delegation, he forwarded a draft of his proposed speech to the Government of India for approval wherefrom it returned with some changes. One of the changes made by New Delhi was to keep the provision of a plebiscite open. While Abdullah readily accepted other changes, he resented the commitment of the Indian Government to a plebiscite. In a communication addressed to G.S. Bajpai, Secretary General, Ministry of External Affairs, on 30 October 1951, he objected to keeping the offer of a plebiscite open, arguing that "the pronouncement by the Constituent Assembly on the question of accession would lose its effect if an element of uncertainty is introduced in sharp terms again in regard to its finality."[195] Referring to, what he claimed, a majority opinion of "My colleagues", he impressed upon Bajpai that "a specific mention of the plebiscite offer would not be desirable as that is bound to have psychological reaction among the people here.... I regret this part has been dropped in the final draft. The rest of the changes have been duly incorporated."[196] Abdullah wrote:

> On reaching Srinagar yesterday, I had immediately a meeting with my colleagues to discuss the changes in my speech. I explained the background of the suggestions and I am glad to say that they have agreed to almost all the changes except one. This relates to the provision of keeping the offer of a plebiscite open if in future requisite conditions for it are restored in the State. It was pointed out that the pronouncement by the Constituent Assembly on the question of accession would lose its effect if an element of uncertainty is introduced in sharp terms again in regard to its finality. My colleagues argued that a specific mention of the plebiscite offer would not

> be desirable as that is bound to have psychological reaction among the people here.... I tried to persuade my colleagues to accept the change, but as all of them were of the opinion that it was not necessary to bring it in, I regret this part has been dropped from the final draft. The rest of the changes have been fully incorporated.[197]

Abdullah also did not take kindly the Indian representative Brajeshwar Dayal's assurance to the Security Council that so far as the Government of India was concerned, the convening of the Constituent Assembly in Jammu & Kashmir was not to sabotage efforts of the Security Council to resolve the Kashmir issue or impede in any manner the Council's way. Dayal's assurance to the Security Council annoyed him to the extent that "I thought it useless to discuss the issue of accession in the Constituent Assembly because the country with which we wanted to ratify our decision to accede had on international level expressed her inability to accept the decision."[198] Quoting a Persian couplet, Abdullah lamented over India behaving like "my beloved who fulfills everybody's wishes; drinks wine with me and offers prayers with the pious."[199]

If there was any doubt about Abdullah's stand on the plebiscite, it was soon removed by a communication of his government. On 19 January 1952, R.C. Raina, Prime Minister Abdullah's Private Secretary, in a letter to D.P. Dhar, then in Paris, spilled the beans. Raina wrote:

> The Consembly [J&K Constituent Assembly] has appropriately come into the picture now and there is no doubt that it will come in for a good deal of drubbing [at the Security Council]. This is all the more reason to stress its importance *in order to play down the plebiscite*.[200] [Emphasis added]

That explains the stand of Abdullah on plebiscite till his ouster from power and arrest in 1953. However, by 1955, when it appeared that neither the government in Kashmir nor Prime Minister Nehru were inclined to set him free, much less reinstate him to the position of power, his colleagues and supporters embarked on a new political strategy. On 9 August 1955, they launched with Abdullah's patronage, the *Mahaz-i-Rai Shumari* or the Plebiscite Front to fight for a popular plebiscite to decide if the Jammu & Kashmir should remain part of India or join Pakistan. The Front, questioning the accession of Jammu & Kashmir to India, declared holding of plebiscite as the core of its political struggle.

For the next two decades, the *Mahaz-i-Rai Shumari* spearheaded a movement for plebiscite with mass public support. In between, Abdullah was released from jail in 1958, then re-arrested and freed again in 1964, again arrested and then released in 1968. As a caged bird, he observed through these years a smooth transition of power taking place in Jammu & Kashmir among his once junior colleagues—Bakshi Ghulam Mohammad, Khawaja Shamsuddin, Ghulam Mohammad Sadiq and Syed Mir Qasim. The years in jail were not easy for him and long separation from his family 'in trouble' back home was one difficult aspect of it. However, he kept himself busy with different activities including gardening, playing badminton and raring poultry and sheep of which "some I brought with me on my release".[201] As a prisoner at the Kud Sub-Jail in Jammu province, he once had a dream during which he entered a splendid palace, met a person, took him around and showed him the bathroom of the castle. "Pointing to the mirror, I told him that it has been brought from Switzerland. Passing through the corridor, I went inside several rooms. In one of the rooms, I saw golden chairs and thought it to be the Crown Chamber. As I was coming out of the room, my mother-in-law put a fine soft shawl on my shoulders"[202], Abdullah later wrote in his memoirs. Did the dream prove seeding of the event that ultimately unfolded itself on 24 February 1975?

Years before he returned to power in 1975, Abdullah had made up his mind to shun separatist politics and mend fences with India. On 5 August 1965, his close aide, Mirza Mohammad Afzal Beg, was shifted from Otacamund to Srinagar where Union Home Secretary met him and started negotiations under the ambit of Indian Constitution.[203] On 25 April 1967, Beg was flown from Srinagar to Delhi on the pretext of treatment. Soon, Abdullah too was shifted, again, on the pretext of treatment, from Kodaikanal, where he was in detention, to Delhi to facilitate talks on his return to the Indian mainstream politics. It may be recalled that Abdullah and Beg were arrested at the Palam Airport in New Delhi in May 1965 after their return from Haj pilgrimage and tour of Egypt and Algeria where, among others, they had met Egyptian President, Gamal Abdel Nasser and Chinese Prime Minister, Chou en-Lai. They were interned in Otacamund and, later, Kodaikanal, the two south-Indian hill stations. On his return from Delhi in June 1967, Beg told Munshi Mohammad Ishaq, senior leader and three-time ad-hoc President of the Plebiscite Front, in Srinagar that he would soon be released while Abdullah would be kept in house arrest in Delhi where, according to Ishaq, secret negotiations were soon started with him.[204] The engagements of Abdullah and Beg in Delhi were seen in Kashmir with suspicion.[205]

Abdullah's externment was revoked and he returned to Srinagar on 4 March 1968 where he convened a meeting of the State People's Convention to which he invited prominent socialist leader of India, Jayaprakash Narayan. Besides Narayan, leaders of other political parties of India including the Indian National Congress, the Jan Sangh and the Communist Party of India also participated in the Convention that Abdullah described as "a beginning of a new era of accord with India and gave enough hint of a send-off to the fifteen years of struggle [the Plebiscite Movement]."[206] He wanted the participating divergent political groups to "deliberate on the solution of the existing situation in Kashmir."[207] This was a clear signal of his having no faith in the plebiscite as an instrument to resolve the Kashmir issue. The pro-Pakistan members within the Plebiscite Front led by Munshi Mohammad Ishaq were unhappy over Abdullah's move and came down heavily on him. Ishaq writes [translation]:

> To find a solution to the Kashmir issue, Sheikh Mohammad Abdullah organized in October 1968 a meeting of the State People's Convention at the Mujahid Manzil and committed the third mistake by repeating the history of 1939.[208] Sheikh Sahib himself became the President of the Organizing Committee of the Convention with Prem Nath Bazaz as its Convener. Bazaz Sahib was the

> chief advisor of Sheikh Sahib in the burial of the Muslim Conference and the birth of the National Conference. After achieving his mission, he resigned from the National Conference, became its critic and sang songs of praise of the Ram Chandra Kak Government.... Now when plans were afoot to bury the Plebiscite Front, Sheikh Sahib thought of Bazaz Sahib.[209]

What followed the Convention was a public meeting held at the Hazuri Bagh in Srinagar where Narayan unraveled the plot. He dismissed the demand for a plebiscite as "redundant".[210] There were hostile slogans from a section of the audience. Next day, Narayan addressed a press conference where he openly termed plebiscite and return to the pre-1953 position as "impossible".[211] Significantly, he offered his services for a rapprochement between the leaders of Kashmir [read Abdullah] and the Government of India to reach a solution "within the constitutional framework of India."[212] In this connection, he underscored the role of the People's Convention as "crucial."[213] This, according to Munshi Mohammad Ishaq was "the voice of Abdullah's heart".[214] Following the Convention, the Plebiscite Front, on 22 March 1969, decided to contest the Panchayat elections which it would boycott earlier.[215] Abdullah had wanted the Front to participate in elections and even tried very hard for it by sending from Delhi, where he was detained, messengers and emissaries to convince sympathizers of the party to contest elections.

Recalling the development, Ishaq writes [translation]:

> In Kashmir, our leaders, Sheikh Mohammad Abdullah and Mirza Mohammad Afzal Beg, who were in the white list of the people, were dithering. On 22 March 1969, in a meeting of the Executive Council of the Plebiscite Front, a resolution proposing participation in the elections, which were so far being boycotted, was passed. I openly opposed the resolution. People and a particular group of workers are with me. If resources are available I am ready to stand in opposition, whatever the consequences. In this connection, Molvi Mohammad

> Farooq and Molvi Abbas Ansari came to me and, in a hushed voice, promised their support.[216]

The resolution was adopted by a joint meeting of the Executive Council and the General Council of the Plebiscite Front on 24-25 June 1969, notwithstanding the fact that the General Council did not exist that time and it was constituted by unconstitutionally nominating members.[217] Addressing the joint meeting, Abdullah declared the resolution as 'historic' and pressed for its adoption. The only thing historic about the resolution, wrote Ishaq's son and compiler of his memoirs, Munshi Ghulam Hassan, was burial of the Plebiscite Front and gaining power through the support of the Government of India.[218] The Plebiscite Front fought the Panchayati elections. On 7 August 1969, Ishaq, who opposed the Front entering into the electoral fray, held a press conference declaring that elections were not a substitute to the plebiscite. He said that if some members of the Plebiscite Front and their 'lackeys' were unconstitutionally fighting the elections it did not mean that the Front was participating in the electoral process. Angered by Ishaq's statement, the pro-election leaders in the Plebiscite Front labeled him as a traitor and insincere person.

The participation in the Panchayat elections was followed by the Front's announcement to take part in the Parliamentary elections in 1971. Prime Minister Indira Gandhi had declared mid-term polls for the Lok Sabha (Lower House of the Indian Parliament) on 28 December 1970 and, on 4 January 1971, President of the Plebiscite Front, Mirza Afzal Beg, called a meeting of the Working Committee, Parliamentary Board and important workers for 9 January to finalize the list of candidates. On 8 January, he announced that the Front would fight these elections "under the framework of Indian Constitution."[219] However, before that could happen, the Government of India externed Abdullah, Beg and G.M. Shah from the State and banned the Plebiscite Front on 12 January 1971. It is important to recall here that while unsuccessfully fighting the ban before the Unlawful Activities (Prevention) Tribunal, Beg argued that they had publicly said that "our attitude on plebiscite is not rigid, and through Sheikh Mohammad Abdullah the Central Government could explore other alternatives for finalizing the

[Kashmir] dispute."[220] That was about a year before the fall of Dhaka and a year and half before the Simla Agreement.

In 1972, Abdullah sent his wife, Begum Akbar Jahan, to Srinagar for actively campaigning for an independent candidate, Shamim Ahmad Shamim, to ensure the defeat of his *bête noir*, Bakshi Ghulam Mohammad, in an election to the Lok Sabha. In the meanwhile, he had reached out to the Government of India and convinced it about his willingness to renounce separatist politics and join the electoral politics. Talks between Abdullah and Prime Minister Indira Gandhi were conducted by their respective emissaries, G. Parthasarthi and Afzal Beg. The negotiations culminating on 13 November 1974, returned Abdullah to power. Beg, who till then had led on his behalf a mass movement for a plebiscite under the banner of the Plebiscite Front, justified his leader's 'homecoming' by dismissing the people's two decade long struggle as 'wandering in the wilderness'. Abdullah justified his political U-turn as a 'change in the strategy while the goal remained the same'. However, on 24 February 1975, while he was taking oath as the Chief Minister of Jammu & Kashmir, the words of his oath, for his adversaries, sounded like the last post at the funeral of plebiscite in Kashmir.

The Indira-Abdullah Accord was 'a milestone event' from the Indian point of view, the talks for which were held behind the back of the people of Kashmir including veteran leaders of the Plebiscite Front like its senior Vice-President, Sofi Mohammad Akbar. In between signing of the Accord and oath taking, Beg convened a meeting of leaders of the Plebiscite Front at the *Mujahid Manzil* where a pamphlet justifying the Accord was distributed. Akbar, a long-time associate of Abdullah and his staunch follower, was taken aback. There were some murmurs and within 15 minutes or so, Malik Mohiuddin, an aide of Beg, took the pamphlets back from the participants but Akbar refused to part with the leaflet. Terming the Accord as "a sellout and a fraud on the people", he got up in anger, hastily collected his bedding from an adjacent room allotted to him as the party's senior Vice-President, and left for his native place, Sopore, never to look back.

Sheikh Mohammad Abdullah, it may be recalled, had assured people that he would take them into confidence before reaching an agreement with New Delhi and proceed further only if they approved of it. However, what they were informed about was that he had entered into an accord with Mrs. Gandhi and was taking over as the next Chief Minister of Jammu & Kashmir. The development was received in Kashmir with a feeling of shock and bewilderment. To show their rejection of the Accord, a complete and unprecedented shutdown was observed by people in the Valley on 28 February, the call for which was given by the then President of Pakistan, Zulfikar Ali Bhutto. Ironically, however, a week after assuming power, Abdullah entered the Valley to a grand public reception. Days later, when a group of students led by Ghulam Mohiuddin Sofi called on him at his private office to know reasons for his quitting the resistance movement, he lost his cool and had them chased away by his staff.

Five months after Abdullah's taking over as the Chief Minister of Jammu & Kashmir, the Plebiscite Front was dissolved on 5 July 1975 in a meeting of the Front's General Council that Vice-President, Sofi Mohammad Akbar, boycotted. In a protest letter, he wrote to the founder President of the Plebiscite Front, Mohammad Afzal Beg, that the dissolution was an "open betrayal with the martyrs of 9 August 1953 [when Abdullah was dismissed and arrested] and asked him how he would face them on the Day of Judgment."[221] A former interim President of the Front, Ghulam Nabi Hagroo, wondered if "our whole struggle was only for a chair."[222] Beg's reply was that "it is the edict of Sheikh Sahib and you have to accept it. One who does not fall in line has no place in the organization."[223]

Known for drawing prickly caricatures of leaders and coining pungent slogans, Kashmiris reacted to the 'burial of plebiscite' with a peppery catchphrase: *Raishumaeri beren dabas¸Aelve Babas Mubarak* [Congratulations to Potato Patron for locking plebiscite in a box]. Pertinently, Abdullah had at one point in time asked people of a rice-deficient Kashmir to eat potatoes to pursue their dream of self-reliance. His detractors gave him the nickname of *Aelve bab*. A powerful caricature by ace cartoonist Bashir Ahmad Bashir was published in the *Srinagar Times* in which a bowing Abdullah with his *Qarraqul* cap donning head in his hands was shown offering it to Indira Gandhi for coronation.

During his last years, Sheikh Mohammad Abdullah was believed to be remorseful. Within two years, the ruling Congress Party, with whose support he had become the Chief Minister in 1975 despite describing a few years ago its leadership and workers as "worms of a gutter" and calling for their social boycott, pulled the rug under his feet leaving no option for him but to quit the office. He felt betrayed as none of the promises made to him during the talks on the Accord or after its signing were met by the Government of India. He had to be contended with the designation of a Chief Minister, like any other of his counterparts in about two dozen states of India, compared to that of the Prime Minister he held before his ouster from power in 1953.

The accord with Indira Gandhi did bring Abdullah back to power after 22 years albeit with reduced position and authority than he enjoyed earlier. Soon, he was in for a rude shock and humiliation. In spite of assurances contained in the Accord, New Delhi did not review any of the Central Laws extended to Jammu & Kashmir after 1953. Indira Gandhi tersely told him that the hands of the clock cannot be turned back. Gandhi's Congress Party showed him down on many occasions. He was even denied the prerogative of inducting into his cabinet a lady educationist, Tahira Shahmiri, and was made to include the Congress nominee, Zainab Begum, in her place. On another occasion, he had to cut a sorry figure when on the instructions of Indira Gandhi, the swearing-in ceremony to induct three ministers who had changed sides from the Congress Party to the National Conference, was cancelled by the Governor. Frustrated, he later told journalist Kuldip Nayyar that the Government of India was treating him "like a peon."[224] Ultimately, the Congress Party pulled the rug under his feet and he had to resign as the Chief Minister.

Before his demise, a hurt Abdullah is said to have dictated to his amanuensis some 'revealing' things for his memoirs, *Aatash-*

i-Chinar, which, however, did not find space in the book that was released four years after his death on 8 September 1982. His supporters later sought to float the perception that he wanted to have the struggle for a plebiscite revived. A former leader of the Plebiscite Front, Hakim Mohammad Yusuf, claims that soon after the Accord, Abdullah had confided in Sofi Mohammad Akbar that New Delhi had betrayed him once again and that he (Akbar) must continue with his movement for plebiscite. Akbar's close associate, Advocate Mohiuddin Mandloo rejects this as a "travesty of facts" and recalls that the senior separatist leader never forgave Abdullah for "betraying the people's trust".[225]

4

A Letter to New York

In 1950, Sheikh Mohammad Abdullah had just returned to Delhi after, what he himself described, 'a comfortable journey' from New York where he had gone as a member of the Indian Delegation to present its case on Kashmir in the Security Council. En-route, he spent a night at the Claridges in London and met G.S. Bajpai, India's Secretary General, External Affairs, who had freshly called on the British Prime Minister, Clement Attlee, in an effort to win him over to the Indian side on Kashmir. Soon after his arrival in Delhi, Abdullah met the topmost leadership of the country including President Rajendra Prasad, Prime Minister Jawaharlal Nehru and Home Minister Vallabhbhai Patel. He also discussed his visit with Minister for Railways and Transport, Gopalaswami Ayyangar, his former team-head in the Security Council and a former Prime Minister of Kashmir during Maharaja Hari Singh's reign.

Earlier, in 1948, Abdullah as Head of the Administration in Jammu & Kashmir, had been to New York as a member of the Indian delegation where on 5 February 1948 during his speech in the Security Council at Lake Success, he put the whole blame of creating the Kashmir problem on Pakistan and, countering the Pakistani Delegation's accusation of his partiality in the Kashmir dispute for being Nehru's friend, shot back with those now-famous lines:

> Yes I admit that [I am a friend of Pandit Jawaharlal Nehru]. I feel honoured that such a great man claims me as his friend. And, he happens to belong to my own country; he is also a Kashmiri. Blood is thicker than

> water. If Jawaharlal gives me the honour, I cannot help it. He is my friend.[226]

Eight months later when Nehru was in Kashmir, Abdullah reiterated his sentiments about him thus: "I assure Pandit Nehru on behalf of Kashmiri people that Kashmir belongs to him and he belongs to Kashmir. Now no power of the world can separate you or us from each other."[227]

In January 1950, when Abdullah was again in New York, India was all but feeling comfortable in the Security Council where on the issue of Kashmir the Anglo-American Bloc seemed more inclined towards Pakistan's point of view, or, at least, India felt so. Home Minister Vallabhbhai Patel observed that India should resist American pressure tactics even if it meant foregoing any loans from the US.

Abdullah returned from New York on January 30. Next day, he shot a letter to his Deputy Home Minister, Durga Prasad Dhar, who had been asked to stay put in New York to advise the Indian delegation on the ensuing voting on Kashmir in the Security Council. Dhar, as Abdullah would later allege, "played the vile role in the wicked drama of my arrest [in 1953] and [consequent] atrocities on Kashmiris" and who worked as "an agent of the Indian intelligence creating misunderstanding"[228] between Abdullah and New Delhi. In 1950, however, the two enjoyed cordial relations. Dhar was a close aid of Abdullah who, in turn, was to him "yours affectionately".[229]

In the letter, Abdullah informs Dhar about his meeting with Indian leaders and how nobody in Srinagar or Delhi was "in a mood to yield to the persuasions of our friends"[230] [read Anglo-American bloc at the UN]. "It is the common opinion here that firmness on our part is the greatest need at the present moment and it is now for Sir B.N. [Rau] and yourself to take advantage of this mood so as to press for the proposals envisaged by us,"[231] he advised Dhar. He was confident that "our case was safe in the hands of Sir B.N."[232] In the meanwhile, when President of India wanted to recall Rau from New York to take over as the Election Commissioner of India, Abdullah urged the former to "let him continue as that would suit the interests of India best."[233] Rau, like Ayyangar, it may be recalled, had served as the Prime Minister of Jammu & Kashmir under Maharaja Hari Singh during 1940s.

From his letter, Abdullah appears at pains to emphasize on how important it was for India to retain Rau at the Security Council which had "not yet taken a decision with regard to the Kashmir question."[234] He asks from Dhar if he had met any member of the Security Council after his [Abdullah's] departure and advised him to call on the Norwegian member and "explain our position in detail", besides giving "my Salams to the Egyptians."[235]

The letter also talks about belated heavy snowfall in Kashmir, continuous rains in Jammu for a couple of weeks, 'satisfactory' supply position in the Valley and measures against black-marketing. It also talks about Bakshi Ghulam Mohammad with his family being in Jammu and informs Dhar that "your people are all well and you need have no worry about them. I met your mother this morning and she gives you her blessings."[236]

The author of the letter writing about issues related to the future of Jammu & Kashmir takes a sudden turn to switch over to a mundane subject. Overtaken by parental love, the 'tallest leader of Kashmir' draws up a long list of gifts for Dhar to send for his sons and daughters, and, to be fair to him, for his colleagues too. The list includes air-guns for the three sons, Farooq, Mustafa and Tariq and, additionally, a watch for the latter. For daughters Khalida, Suraiya and [Khalida's] baby the choice of gifts was left to Dhar. Interestingly, Abdullah had only a day earlier arrived from New York when "everyone expected a present from me",[237] and yet he chose to himself return empty handed. Within 24 hours of his arrival, he asked his junior colleague to arrange for the gifts. The concluding portion of the letter makes an interesting read. Here it goes:

> Khalida and Shah Sahib have come down to Jammu and the baby is alright. Everyone expected a present from me and I postponed their disappointment with the assurance that all the presents had been stocked with you. I might warn you that in my next letter you will have a fairly

> long list of presents to be brought here with details. Meanwhile, here are some requisitions. Bakhshi Sahib wants a watch. Beg, Sadiq, Raina, Shamlal and R.C. need necklaces. Farooq, Tariq and Mustafa would be proud to have good air-guns and Tariq wants a watch besides. I leave the choice to you for presents to Khalida, Suraiya and baby. Khwaja Ahsan Ullah wants to have a Rolliflex camera.[238]

As a post-script, there is this important instruction for Dhar: "Please send your letters direct to me and not through diplomatic bag." That, perhaps because letters sent through the Diplomatic Bag would first land, and possibly be read, in the Foreign Office in New Delhi.

In the meanwhile, Dhar, through a cablegram received in Jammu on February 27, 1950, sought permission to "return immediately to explain the Security Council Resolution personally or", it added, "should I continue my fruitless stay for another ten days during which time the matter is expected to be over."[239]

In his memoirs, *Aatash-i-Chinar*, published in 1986, Sheikh Mohammad Abdullah devotes a full chapter to his engagements in New York. From his narration, it appears that he had spent quite a busy time—meeting diplomats, making speeches, receiving accolades (for once, from the Russian representative) and taking on a hostile British representative, Philip Noel Baker, who after "my reply was lost for words and felt embarrassed."[240] However, an official communication originating from the Prime Minister Abdullah's office in Jammu on 19 January 1952 belies this claim.

As the next meeting of the Security Council on Kashmir was scheduled at Paris to discuss the Report of Dr. Frank P. Graham, United Nations Representative for India and Pakistan, India was feeling the heat since Russia had drastically intervened in the Kashmir dispute amid speculation about posting of UN troops in the State. The Government of India was "making a frantic search for a man to go to Paris."[241] Prime Minister Nehru asked Abdullah to accompany the Indian Delegation. Abdullah was reluctant to go to avoid, what his Private Secretary's letter to Dhar in Paris, suggests, the "utterly discomfortable experiences of his last two visits and he is anxious that similar moments of boredom should not await him in Paris too."[242] On January 24, 1952, however, the Government of India announced the composition of its Delegation to Paris which, besides the Attorney General M.C. Setelvad and G.S. Bajpai, included Sheikh Mohammad Abdullah as a non-official member. A Ministry of External Affairs' order mentioned "hotel accommodation (sitting room and bed room with bath) in Paris and London and £150 (lump sum) for expenses", as entitlement of Abdullah for his visit to Paris.[243]

Culture

5

Tale of a Mammoth Loss

During a study tour on 31 August 2000, when some teachers and students of the Degree College Sopore stumbled over a fossil of a mammoth at Pampore, 15 kms south of Srinagar, geologists in Kashmir were exhilarated. The find, comprising a skull with complete lower and upper jaws, a broken tusk and a vertebra, was highlighted as "the largest ever unearthed in the subcontinent". A little distance from the site a huge tusk measuring eight feet and three inches was also unearthed. Further excavation threw up '58 Paleolithic (stone) and three bone tools' in the same fossil bearing strata, a claim yet to be scientifically ascertained. As news about the discovery spread, the site turned into a huge attraction with enthusiastic people jostling each other to have a glimpse of the find.

On the basis of carbon dating of the upper strata of Pampore karewa, the initial reports described the fossil to be at least 50,000 years old. The fact that it was discovered from lower stratum its life further going back in time—a million years or more—remained a possibility. Experts believed it had catapulted Kashmir into the great mammoth era. The significance of the find lay in the strong prospect of its redefining natural and climatic history of Kashmir. Given the discovery of stone and bone implements, the find could alter the widely held belief about the oldest evidence of human presence in the subcontinent, especially Kashmir. In short, the unearthing of the fossil was supposed to be one of the most significant archaeological developments regarding Kashmir's past.

The euphoria was still high when in 2007 news broke that the precious find was missing from its makeshift tin shed at the excavation site. On 3 April 2007, Dr. Abdul Majid Dar, one of the two geology teachers who had chanced upon the find, visited the site and, to his shock and disbelief, found both the skull and the tusk missing. He feared that these had been smuggled out of Kashmir for sale in the international market. The incident left people in general and lovers of Kashmir heritage in particular appalled. Incidentally, five years before the theft, fears had been expressed in the State Legislature about the safety of the find whereupon the government had assured of proper watch and ward arrangements at the site, besides promising to declare the area as a protected site once the authenticity of the findings was established. However, the assurance proved false.

As days passed, the fossil was found parked in the Jammu University's Geology Department. It turned out that a teacher of the Kashmir University, Dr. G.M. Bhat, who was earlier co-opted for excavation of the fossil, on his return to the Jammu University—his parent institution—had illegally taken away the prized collection and, shockingly, also bragged about the theft. "Yes, I have shifted it. I didn't need permission from anybody. I have done whatever I had to do. They can go to court", he was quoted as saying in the *Himalayan Mail*, a subsidiary publication of the *Indian Express*, issued from Jammu.[244] When voices for getting back the stolen fossil began to rise in Kashmir, an artificial opposition by students of the Jammu University was engineered to thwart its return. A four-member recovery team sent to Jammu met with hostile situation there and returned empty handed.

In 2011, news came from Jammu that "the rare fossil is gathering dust in the corridor of the Jammu University's Geology department" and that "exposure to changing climatic conditions and the elements in the air for over eight years has started taking its toll on the fossil, with officials helplessly watching its destruction."[245] Fourteen years after its removal from Kashmir and assurances on its return held out by the then Vice Chancellor, Jammu University, the fossil is still illegally held by the Jammu University. In fact, it is now permanently installed at the newly set up Wadia Museum of Natural History giving enough indication that the University has no plans to return it to Kashmir. Not to talk of return, it even refuses to share information on the status of the fossil terming it 'out of the realms of public interest'. In response to an RTI application seeking information about the status of the fossil and why it was not returned to Kashmir, the university asked the applicant to "justify the public interest involved in the disclosure of the information sought".[246] When confronted with a counter argument that if seeking information on the theft of a priceless object holding information on natural and climatic history of the land of seven million people was not of public interest what else would be, the Public Information Officer (PIO) of the university wrote back that the information "will be supplied in due course". The Kashmir University that financed the excavation of the fossil, took the cover of a ruling by the Apex Court in a certain case to deny information. Obviously, both universities were helping each other out in keeping facts from the public domain. Incredibly, nobody was held responsible for the theft, nor for illegally holding the fossil. The height of insensitivity of the government could be measured by the fact that it failed to perform even the basic responsibility of filing a case against the daylight robbery. An inquiry committee announced by the Kashmir University in 2007 never took off. The Chief Minister's instructions to get back the fossil from Jammu remained proverbial *Hukm-i-Nawab ta dar-i-Nawab* (the ruler's orders are obeyed not beyond his door).

No less scandalous than the conduct of the two universities was the response of the Government of Jammu & Kashmir which not only failed to act and recover the stolen fossil but literally handed it over to the alleged thief. It constituted a committee to not investigate the brazen heist and recommend action against the culprits, but suggest measures for the safety of the fossil and identify its age—a clear indication that it did not intend to attend to the basic issue of return of the fossil and punishment to the culprits.[247] Intriguingly, none of the members of the committee was a paleontologist to ascertain the age of the fossil. The composition of the committee is beyond belief; it is, in fact, an offence to both public sentiment and demands of legal morality, for it includes the alleged mastermind of the fossil heist. Rather than punishing him the government bizarrely honored him with the membership of the committee.[248]

The discovery and purloin of a mammoth fossil from Kashmir was not the first incident of its kind. An elephant tusk and bones were excavated from the same area in 1931 by Dr. de Terra, then Research Associate at the Carnegie Institution of Washington who was twice sent on expedition to India by Yale. On his return from the first expedition, Terra took the mammoth with him and installed it in New Haven. When Maharaja Hari Singh came to know about it, he wrote to the university asking for the return of the mammoth. Although Terra claimed that he had a written authorization from the Kashmir Government to take the fossil out "but as I wanted to go back to Kashmir, I decided to return it."[249] Hari Singh had the mammoth installed in his palace for, lo and behold, "using its tusk as coat-hangers"[250]. When in 1935 he left Kashmir where he had extracted so much inspiring information in his search for traces of pre-historic man, Dr. de Terra felt "as though we had laid a foundation on which pre-historic research on early man in India can be built in the years to come."[251] The 1931 fossil is now in the Sri Pratap Singh (SPS) Museum Srinagar. The Museum was established in 1898 at the Maharaja's Summer Guesthouse. Among its initial collection were shawls and armoury obtained from the State *toshkhana*. Subsequently, it developed into one of the best museums in the subcontinent, displaying artefacts and objects, which it has now about 80,000, covering subjects like archaeology, numismatics, decorative art, arms and armoury, paintings and textiles.

Nineteen years after its establishment, a major theft took place in the SPS Museum. As many as 68 objects including precious *jamawars*, silk brocades, Shah Pasand Kani Tosa Shawls, Pashmina robes, Agate and Turquoise stones, were stolen.[252] The thieves broke open six almirahs and three glass cases to make good with the loot. On 16 December 1917, the *tehvildar* of the Museum informed the Home Minister about the theft of the objects with a book value of over ₹ 16,500 (₹ 16,518 *annas* two and *paise* six to be precise). The stolen articles related to the Afghan, Sikh and Dora rule over Kashmir.[253] The burglary happened in spite of the fact that the Museum was guarded by two policemen, one posted on its southeast and the other on western side. One guard, as police report revealed, was posted at a point where he "could see nor observe the commission of burglary"[254] while the other was in a position to observe the burglars inside the museum or hear "cracking of opening of doors and almirahs" but was "unable to give any information."[255] The electric lamp in the museum was found broken and its switch removed. The two *chowkidars* on watch and ward duty of the museum and the nearby observatory also expressed ignorance about the incident.

The fact that burglary was committed in spite of the police guard at the Museum annoyed Maharaja Pratap Singh, after whom the museum is named. He passed mocking remarks about the police. "This theft has been committed in a state building, and if the theft remains untraced it will be very disgraceful on the part of the Kashmir police. The very fact of a theft having been committed in *ajaib ghar* shows that the thieves are not afraid of the Kashmir police",[256] he observed. A reward of ₹ 1,000 was announced by the government for information leading to the recovery of the stolen objects as police failed to make any headway in the case. Soon thereafter, on 26 March 1918, the Police claimed recovery of a part of the stolen property, including 23 shawls and some stones valued at ₹ 2832 *annas* three and *paise* six, from a canal near the Maharaja's Palace at Shergarhi. Major part of the looted property, however, remained untraced.

In 1973, another major theft occurred at the Museum. On 10 August, Curator J.L. Bhan reported theft of six (five bronze and one wooden) antiques. The stolen objects included Standing Buddha (Bronze), Jain Figure, Buddha (Wooden), Tara (Bronze), Seated Buddha (Bronze) and Ardha Nari Shawara (Bronze). In the First Information Report (FIR), Bhan stated that at 11 A.M.

when the Museum was opened a showcase in the Archaeology Section was found broken open with six antiques missing. Within hours of filing an FIR about the theft, however, he informed the police that one object, Ardha Nari Shawara, was found in the Textiles Section near the window. On the previous day, he claimed, the Museum was closed in the presence of the in-charge guard. The police investigated the case without success. In 1975, the Deputy Inspector General of Police reported that the "theft of articles has been closed as untraced".[257]

Thirty years later, the Museum was again struck by thieves, this time an invaluable 17th century Arabic manuscript of the Holy *Qura'n* was stolen. On 12 July 2003, the Curator of the Museum reported to his Director that "one manuscript titled holy Quran bearing seal of [Emperor] Aurangzeb" was found missing from the showcase "at 3.30 P.M. yesterday (11 July 2003)". The manuscript, believed to have been written in the hand of the Mughal ruler, besides its antique value was an object of religious reverence for the people in Kashmir the theft of which caused great anguish. The burglary was reported to the police for investigation and recovery of the stolen object. On 6 July 2004, the Station House Officer (SHO), Police Station Raj Bagh wrote to the Curator, SPS Museum, "During the course of investigation many persons were questioned regarding the occurrence but unfortunately no clue has been found." The letter added that "there is no hope to find out any clue regarding the occurrence and the case has been closed as untraced". In 2013, however, the Chief Secretary, referring to a report by SHO, Police Station Raj Bagh, informed the J&K High Court that the case was "under investigation with the Crime Branch, Srinagar". The High Court was not satisfied with the probe and on 22 September 2016, ordered its transfer to the Central Bureau of Investigation (CBI) which is now investigating the theft.

There were also reports of many rare coins going missing from the Museum collection. On 24 March 2008, the *Greater Kashmir* published a news report claiming that 84 gold and silver coins were missing from the SPS Museum. The newspaper quoted a report allegedly prepared by officials of the Department of Archives, Archaeology & Museums in 2003 after "verification of Gold and Silver coins displayed in the museum". The gold coins, the report alleged, were "lying with the then Curator for purpose of identification but the [accession] register doesn't say what happened to the coins later". Likewise, the news report referred to a list of 2000 coins prepared in 1900 by G.B. Bleazely, the then Accountant General of Jammu & Kashmir, which "hardly coincides with the stock of silver coins housed in the museum". In 2007, the Valley Citizens' Council, a Non-Governmental Organization (NGO), through a Public Interest Litigation (PIL) informed the Jammu & Kashmir High Court that "8 gold and 76 silver coins were also reported to be missing". The Museum officials reject this notion. However, an in-house survey conducted in 2012 by a team of officers of the Department of Archaeology, Archives and Museums on the directions of the court, among other things, recommended verification of the gold collection of the Museum for authenticity of metal and their genuineness.

Another incident of theft happened in 1989 when nine terracotta tiles of immense archaeological value, were stolen from Harwan, 'the earliest surviving Buddhist site'. The tiles with figural and symbolic forms, dating back to 3rd-4th century AD, represented an independent local artistic tradition and depicted a high degree of sophistication. Thirty-two years after the theft, the priceless artefacts are yet to be recovered. The Archaeological Survey of India sits pretty over the incident after "necessary formalities", which it would not specify and which in all probability mean filing of an FIR, were "carried out for its recovery."[258]

In 1995, paramilitary forces during a raid on a suspected militant hideout at Chandpora, Shalimar in the outskirts of Srinagar, claimed recovery of 35 (some newspapers mentioned 32) antique objects related to the 8th-10th century AD which made big news. At a press conference, the recovered antiquities were displayed. An official of the SPS Museum was called to ascertain the antiquity of the objects. "We had gone to seek custody of the recovered objects but the security forces refused to give those to us. Overnight, the antiquities were shifted to New Delhi and handed over to the National Museum",[259] recalls Jamshed Ahmad, the then Curator SPS Museum. The images were of Hindu deities and mostly in stone. According to a former officer of the Department of Archives, Archaeology and Museums, the objects are now on display at the National Museum in Delhi.

Incidents of theft of artefacts from the SPS Museum did not come in the way of Jammu & Kashmir Government liberally gifting prized heritage objects to various museums and institutions. The first documented beneficiary of the government munificence was Moti Lal Nehru Children Centre (MLNCC), Lucknow. In 1958, the MLNCC was gifted at least 30 objects (25 from Numismatics Gallery, three from Natural History Gallery and two from Decorative Art Gallery). However, in 2013, when in pursuance of a court order the Government of Jammu & Kashmir was asked to get back all the gifted artefacts, the MLNCC expressed inability to locate the objects.

Barely two months after a major theft in the Museum in 1973, as heritage lovers in Kashmir were still under shock the State Government announced an open-handed gift of 35 precious artefacts, including 31 antique coins, to the Government of Himachal Pradesh for setting up a museum at Shimla (previously Simla). On 26 September 1973, an order was issued, pursuant to a decision of the State Cabinet headed by Chief Minister Syed Mir Qasim and subsequent instructions by Education Minister Abdul Gani Lone, under which the artefacts were taken out of the SPS Museum and the Research Section of the Department of Libraries and transferred to Shimla. The objects included coins, manuscripts, armoury and paintings related to ancient and medieval Kashmir. The 31 copper and silver coins dating from the earliest Hindu period (225 AD) to the Dogra rule (1846-1947) represented the reigns of Spalapati Deva (225 AD), Tormana (500 AD), Samanta Deva (900 AD), Ananta (1028 AD), Kalasa (1081 AD), Dida (1085 AD), Harsha (1089), Zainul Aabideen (1479 AD), Fateh Shah (1483 AD), Akbar (1556 AD), Jahangir (1627 AD), Shah Jahan (1658 AD), Aurangzeb (1707 AD), Shah Alam (1712 AD) and Farrukh Siyar (1719 AD). Other artefacts included a Persian manuscript,

Magaz-un-Nabi (Wars of the Prophet) by famous 16th-century Kashmiri poet, scholar and spiritual personality, Shaikh Yaqoob Sarfi, one gun of the Dogra period, a Sharda manuscript and a Kashmiri painting depicting Swchanda Bhairva. The objects reached Shimla on 11 October 1973.

The largest 'gift pack' of 209 antiquities, however, went to the newly set up Central Asian Museum of Kashmir University in 1980. Three days after a missive from the Chief Minister's Office, Director Archives, Libraries and Museums, ordered on 25 August 1980 that "all Central Asian Antiquities be transferred to Prof. S. Maqbool Ahmad, Director, Centre of Central Asian Studies, University of Kashmir on the day he reports in the SPS Museum, Srinagar, under proper receipt." The direction was issued in pursuance of the orders of the Chief Minister to the undersigned."[260] The artefacts were taken out from textile, decorative art, archaeology and numismatics galleries. When in 2012, the SPS Museum asked for their return in the light of a court directive, the Centre of Central Asian Studies refused to oblige, arguing that these were properly transferred, handed over-taken over and registered with the Government of India under the Antiquities and Art Treasure Act of 1972 in the name of the Central Asian Museum. Subsequently, however, it relented.

Besides gifting away artefacts from its collection, the government also exhibited casual approach towards preserving and protecting Kashmir's heritage wealth, a glaring instance of which is sending outside the Valley 'Stone Age' objects for carbon dating and then caring less to bring them back. In 1963, these artefacts including stone axes and tools made of animal bones, unearthed from the Neolithic Burzahom in 1930s, were sent to a laboratory in Calcutta (now Kolkata) to scientifically determine their age. The objects were never brought back. More than half a century later, nobody even knows where the treasure is located now. Further excavation at Burzahom by Dr. de Terra and his team was stopped due to sinking of land there.[261] However, the work was resumed many years later when Superintending Archaeologist Triloki Nath Khazanchi was able to unearth more Stone Age tools.

Old hands in Kashmir archaeology recall, at least, two incidents when precious artefacts were stolen from official premises. In the first case, Khazanchi had discovered a Buddha image at Harwan which was still under his study when it disappeared from his table. In another case, a 7th-8th century stone *Shivlingam* discovered from Parihaspora and weighing 5-6 quintals went missing from the Darbar Garh premises before it could be accessioned and transferred to the SPS Museum. About four decades back, poet and filmmaker, Faiyaz Dilbar was doing a write up for a radio talk on heritage which led him to visit the Museum a couple of times where his attention was drawn by a small but elegant bronze statue. "It was a beautiful sculpture with Shiva in the middle and different incarnations of Vishnu around its oval-shaped frame. After a fortnight, when I again visited the Museum I was shocked to see the head of Shiva's image missing", he recalls.[262] Around this time, antique traffickers in the Valley were known to be active, with a Srinagar art dealer nicknamed *Cherry Budha* after a rank in one of the four suits of playing cards he resembled with, allegedly being in the forefront.

On 17 October 1979, stone images and stone fragments related to the 10th-11th century AD were discovered from Khurhama in Kupwara district of north Kashmir. Soon thereafter, there were allegations that some of these objects were pilfered during shifting from the excavation site to the Museum. A case of corruption was filed against an officer of the Department of Archives, Archaeology and Museums. The missing objects were believed to be of high antique value. As part of the investigation, the Anti-Corruption Department seized 22 objects from the Museum[263] which remained in its custody for 24 years until released on 29 January 2013 through intervention of the court. The case is still undecided and the accused official has since passed away. Earlier, in 1965, as many as 461 copper coins and one fragment of copper ring were unearthed by one Ghulam Rasool Kumar from his private land at Kulgam in South Kashmir. He refused to part with the treasure when the Department of Archives, Archaeology and Museums asked him to handover the find. The matter went to the Court of Munsif (Magistrate)

Kulgam which seized the coins in connection with the case titled State *vs* Ghulam Rasool Kumar and Others. The artefacts were still in the custody of the court when the government informed the High Court about their status in 2013.[264]

Kashmir artefacts adorn museums around the world and all of these are not legally transferred. Illegal trafficking of priceless objects has slowly depleted heritage reserves of Kashmir. The long turmoil and the resultant law and order failure beginning 1989 is especially believed to be a period when art smugglers robbed Kashmir of its priceless articles "which now adorn homes of private collectors and museums in western countries."[265] In 2012, a 10th-century Durga statue in greenstone, stolen from a temple in Tengpora village of Pulwama, was spotted at Linden Museum, Stuttgart (Germany). The role of an Indian art dealer, who was arrested in Germany in 2011, was suspected in smuggling the idol out of Kashmir.[266] During her visit to New Delhi in October 2015, German Chancellor, Angela Merkel, returned the 18-armed Durga sculpture which is now installed at the SPS Museum. Archaeologist and former Director Centre of Central Asian Studies, Dr. Ajaz Ahmad Banday, was "surprised to see Harwan Tiles at a museum in France". A 6th century AD Gajalakshmi (Stone) was discovered in village Brah of Anantnag district during early 20th century. The photograph of the image was first published in 1913-14. Ever since, a host of archaeologists, including Banday, have used the picture in their publications but nobody knew where the image was actually located until recently when it was discovered at a museum in Japan.[267]

With regard to the structural and archaeological heritage of Kashmir, most of the important sites and monuments—precisely 31—like Burzahom, Martand and Awantipora are under the supervision of the Archaeological Survey of India (ASI) which is accused of leaving these literally uncared for since 1990, although the organization wants us to believe that "all the Sites/ Monuments are well preserved, maintained and in presentable condition."[268] Further, no fresh excavation was undertaken after Kanishpora, Baramulla in 1998-99. The working of the

ASI in Kashmir also came in for criticism by the Jammu & Kashmir High Court when in an interim order pronounced on 11 December 2012, a Division Bench comprising Chief Justice M.M. Kumar and Justice Muzaffar Hussain Attar observed: "[A] survey report of archaeological excavation conducted by the Archaeological Survey of India, J&K, 2012 has also been filed. We have been taken through the photographs which show that efforts are being made to discover and identify these excavated sites but no steps have been taken which may lead us to record our satisfaction". Against the well-established norms, the ASI has not set up any site museum at its archaeological sites in Kashmir to showcase the excavated objects. Instead, it is accused of shifting the artefacts outside Kashmir. Quoting an instance, senior journalist, Ghulam Nabi Khayal refers to "[t]he Terracotta tiles of 2nd and 3rd [century] BC excavated here were shifted to Ramgad, Udhampur in the name of security and thus Kashmiris were deprived of their rich history."[269] The ASI, Srinagar Circle admits that "a portion [of the excavated material in Kashmir] has been shifted", for, what it describes, "its reporting part."[270] It attributes its failure to build a site museum in Kashmir to "land dispute", as if every ASI protected site is in dispute.

In a situation where the government and institutions have literally abdicated their responsibility to stand guard against loot and rot of Kashmir's rich heritage, journalist and social activist, Imdad Saqi woke people up to the perilous state of affairs. In 2007, he filed a PIL in the J&K High Court through his NGO, the Valley Citizen's Council, seeking appropriate directions for the protection and conservation of Kashmir's artefacts, monuments and excavation sites, and return of artefacts gifted by the State to different museums and institutions. The PIL revealed a sad tale of government negligence and insensitivity. Taking cognizance, the court ordered return of the treasure gifted away by the government. Thanks to the PIL, the SPS Museums received back 35 artefacts it had gifted to a museum in Shimla in 1973. Another 209 Central Asian antiquities were also returned by Kashmir University. The 22 artefacts seized by the Anti Corruption Department in 1979 too were released and received in the Museum. More significantly, the PIL renewed hopes of recovery of one of the most precious artefacts of the Museum—the 17th-century manuscript of Holy *Qura'n* bearing the seal of Aurangzeb—after the High Court ordered the CBI to investigate its theft. The court was not satisfied with the investigation by the Crime Branch.

The condition of the protected monuments and sites being what it is, the status of unprotected heritage, like private residences and institutional buildings, is vulnerable to vandalism, inappropriate additions and alteration or even demolition, risking their long term survival. The worst instance of this vandalism was the demolition of the famous 17th-century Persian poet Gani Kashmiri's house at Razay Kadal in Srinagar city in 2001 in the name of its preservation, and rebuilding it in brick and mortar. According to Altaf Hussain, Convener Indian National Trust for Art and Cultural Heritage (INTACH), Kashmir Chapter, "Most buildings under private ownership are suffering from several issues of conservation due to lack of knowledge and resources. The floods of 2014 have amplified these problems as many heritage houses in some prominent neighbourhoods were demolished and reconstructed as the owners deemed them unfit for rehabilitation."[271]

One of the least talked about yet serious case of heritage plunder happening under the nose of, if not in connivance with, the government is the pillage of Valley's geological and heritage treasure—its karewas. World over, the karewas are valued and explored for global climate record of the recent past—so vital for predicting future climate. The most significant evidence of Kashmir's earliest human life like at Burzahom and Gufkral were discovered from the karewas. Sadly, the government appears working hand in glove with land mafia in vandalizing these scientific and anthropogenic sources. Massive construction activities, especially filling of flood plains and marshes for building new housing colonies and laying of railway track and new roads in Kashmir, has resulted in destruction of its karewas.

Another instance of government insensitivity towards heritage is reflected in the construction of the *Tehzeeb Mahal.* After several foundation-laying ceremonies at different places since early 1980s and identifying some existing buildings for the purpose, the government finally appeared making a serious effort when on 22 January 2013 it laid the first stone of the ₹ 72 crore project near the Tourist Reception Centre in uptown Srinagar. Five years and an expenditure of ₹ 4.82 crore later, the then incumbent government stopped funding the construction, citing unsuitability of the location as the reason. The aesthetically designed building would have added beauty to the skyline, besides being a centre of attraction for people and tourists for its multiple facilities like a heritage museum, art gallery, seminar hall, book shop, auditorium for literary and cultural activities, and a coffee shop. The work on the project has stopped since 2014 and reappearance of the State Road Transport Corporation buses on the abandoned site gives enough clues about encroachment of the land.

In the olden times, art traffickers and traders travelling on the Silk Road are believed to have taken out huge heritage wealth of Kashmir. In many cases, travellers and scholars collected material of immense cultural value and returned to their native places with the amassed wealth. The 7th-century Chinese Buddhist monk, scholar and traveller, Heun Tsang, arrived in Kashmir in 631 AD after travelling through Turkistan, Tashkent, Gandhara and Hazara. He stayed in Kashmir for two years and was accorded imperial reception and lodged in the royal palace where the king provided him, besides five servants, 20 copyists for copying religious texts and manuscripts. He left Kashmir through the Pir Panjal and visited many north and south Indian cities. When after his extensive travel he returned to China, he had 20 horse-loads of manuscripts, books and Buddhist relics with him.[272] The 19th-century Hungarian-British explorer and the celebrated translator of Kalhana's *Rajatarangini*, Sir Aurel Stein, is known for his enormous contribution to the promotion and development of Sanskrit literature of Kashmir. His pioneering works remain a must read on Kashmir history, culture and literature. However, what is little known about Stein in this part of the world is that for removing priceless manuscripts, paintings and sculptures during his several expeditions to Central Asia, he was reviled as an "imperialist thief". *Reinterpreting Exploration:*

The West in the World edited by Dane Kennedy, talks about archaeologists from seven nations (including Britain, France, Germany, Russia and the United States) removing "literally by the ton, huge wall paintings, sculptures, priceless manuscripts and other works of art and shipped them home. The sites were ransacked for objects that now stock the great museums of Europe and North America. Aurel Stein comes top of the list of offenders."[273] During his fourth Central Asian visit he was forbidden by Chinese authorities from digging.

Stein visited Kashmir many times between 1888 and 1905 and collected a huge wealth of Sanskrit manuscripts, most of which he took with him to the United Kingdom. Later in 1911, he deposited 350 manuscripts with a library, now part of the New Bodleian Library, Oxford where these remained hidden from public eye for a century. Some of these manuscripts he gifted to other people, one among them being Georg Buhler who in 1875 himself collected from Kashmir "more than 300 manuscripts, many of them in Sharda script written on birch bark leaves".[274] The Hoernle collection at the British Museum also consists of manuscripts collected by Captain Stuart Hill Godfrey who was Joint Commissioner of Ladakh in 1896 and Assistant to the Resident in Kashmir between 1897 and 1899, and Sir Adelbert Cecil Talbot, Resident in Kashmir from 1896 to 1900. Europeans such as these have been accused of taking away Kashmir's intellectual wealth and making its cultural landscape poorer.[275]

One glaring instance of taking away Kashmir's heritage is the transfer, on the pretext of safety, of the Gilgit Manuscripts from Srinagar to Delhi in 1948. As armed conflict was going on between India and Pakistan over the status of Kashmir, the Prime Minister of India, Jawaharlal Nehru, convinced the Emergency Administrator, Sheikh Mohammad Abdullah, that these manuscripts were in danger of being lost to arson and must be shifted to Delhi till the situation in Kashmir normalized. He sent a special plane to take the manuscripts out of Kashmir, never to be returned.[276] With a keen eye on history and culture, Nehru knew the importance of the treasure as much as he knew the cavity in his promise to return it. Abdullah naively waited for his friend to fulfill his promise. After returning to power in 1975, he asked for these manuscripts from Delhi but beyond Prime Minister Indira Gandhi writing to him that she has asked details from the Ministry of Culture,[277] the Government of India did not pay any heed. In fact, it feigned ignorance whenever the matter was raised. An RTI application seeking information from the National Archives of India on whether it would return the Gilgit Manuscripts is awaiting answer since 20 November 2017. Notwithstanding the silence maintained by the Government of India, a former Director Conservation at the National Museum, S.P. Singh, admitted that the manuscripts were in the Museum. "They [National Museum] have exhibited Gilgit Manuscripts in exhibitions as their prized possession. I have seen these manuscripts in original form and they are still kept in the National Museum", Author Mohammad Yousuf Taing quotes Singh as saying in a seminar at Srinagar in 2005.[278]

The Gilgit Manuscripts, dating back to 5th-6th century AD, hold "the key to the exact evolution of Sanskrit, Buddhist, Chinese, Korean, Japanese and Tibetan literatures"[279] and deal with the teachings of Buddhism, philosophy and social customs. The texts throw light on the social life of Kashmir's earliest people and Buddhism, and establishment of *vihars* in Kashmir.[280] Some manuscripts provide information on flora of Kashmir, especially the *chinar* establishing its indigenous status. Kashmir having been an important centre of Buddhist faith and literature for over a millennium underscores the importance of the Gilgit Manuscripts for the land. During the 2nd century AD ruler, Kanishka, a World Buddhist Conference was held in Kashmir marking the birth of a new and progressive Buddhism known as the Mahayana. The Gilgit Manuscripts written on birch bark were discovered per chance in 1931 by a shepherd at Naupur, a village in Gilgit. He was grazing his sheep when he stumbled over the treasure which lay in several half-buried wooden boxes. He informed his fellow shepherds who distributed the booty among themselves. When the Governor of Gilgit, a part of the erstwhile Princely State of Jammu & Kashmir, came to know about it he sent his men to recover the find. The officials seized many manuscripts, some were destroyed by people for the fear of reprisal by the government and some they sold for peanuts. The seized manuscripts were brought to Srinagar where Maharaja Hari Singh ordered their preservation. A team of experts including Dr. Nilinakasha Dutt, Dr. Surinder Nath, Prof. D.M. Bhattacharya and a local scholar, Vishinath Shastri. Studied the manuscripts and attested to their immense cultural value.[281] The first news about the Gilgit Manuscripts was broken to the world by the *Statesman* on 24 July 1931.[282]

Not only the Gilgit Manuscripts, hundreds of other manuscripts sent to Delhi for repair or other purposes have not been returned. The record of the Research Library Srinagar reveals that in 1948, as many as 212 Sanskrit manuscripts were sent to the National Archives, New Delhi which it has held back since. The manuscripts form the first 212 indexed items of the Library established in 1904 as Research and Reference Department. Some of these manuscripts are titled *Bodha Taddhati, Hari Tattva Muktawali, Chanderaleka* with commentary, *Rasamanjan* with commentary, *Alankarodaharma, Upadesa Ratna Panchaka, Upanishads* (1) *Mundika,* (2) *Prasana,* (3) *Chchandogya,* (4) *Kathavali,* (5) *Aitareya,* (6) *Isavasya,* (7) *Mandukya,* and (8) *Kena, Samptika Parvan of the Mahabharta* with *Bhavadipa, Ramaswamidha* of the *Padma Purana, Sisupala Vadha* with commentary, *Anarghareghava Nataka, Alankara Sarvasva, Alankara Vimarshini* and *Bhagvadgita* with commentary.

Kashmir has witnessed pillage of its intellectual heritage also in the shape of valuable books that people have borrowed from public libraries but never returned. In 2013, the Department of Libraries and Research ran a media campaign requesting borrowers to return the books they were withholding for many years, after a stock audit in 2011 threw up shocking statistics. From public libraries across Jammu & Kashmir, 36,696 books were 'outstanding with borrowers' while another 33,200 were recorded as 'missing'. Kashmir accounted for 24,819 and 9044 books in the two categories, respectively. A substantial number of these books included rare and reference titles. Srinagar's SPS Library alone accounted for 2616 outstanding and 5365 missing titles. The Research Library records showed 153 outstanding and 867 missing books. The defaulters with various public libraries include, besides common borrowers and middle rung officials, former heads of departments, advisors, administrative secretaries, and heads of the Department of Libraries and Research itself. On 6 December 1994, one former Advisor to the Head of the State borrowed from a public library *Travels in the Mughal Empire, Kalhana's Rajatarangini* (Vols. I and II) and *The Gardens of Mughals in India* which are still outstanding against him. A former boss of the state bureaucracy failed to return books like *Alberuni's India, Account of an Embassy to the Court of Tashoo Lama in Tibet* and *History of Hindustan* (Vols. I and II) which he had borrowed in 1988 and 1996. One of his successors has *The Warning of Kashmir, Things Seen in Kashmir, Zulfi Bhuttoo of Pakistan: His Life and Times* and *Prepare or Perish* outstanding against him since 1993. Another is withholding *History of Jammu & Kashmir* and *Kashmir Saivism* since 1997. A former head of the Department of Libraries and Research has not returned *Valley of Kashmir, Kashmir: Past* and *Present, Civil Service Examinations and Complete Guide to PSC* since 1998. Another senior officer of the department, who later rose to become a legislator, has eight books outstanding against him since 1991 and 1993 which include *Kashmir Crisis, Iqbal: An International Missionary of Islam, Prepare or Perish, Kashmir: Pakistan's Proxy War, Kashmir Under the Sultans* and *With Pen and Rifle in Kashmir.* The 'worthy' defaulters include quite a few who have since travelled to the other world.

The Reference & Research Section of the J&K Information & Public Relations Department is a similar story. At one point in time, it was one of the best reference libraries on Kashmir which is now in a bad shape due to inadequate space, lack of professional management, ravages of fire and flood, and questionable behaviour of its borrowers. Over the decades, the greens of the library were grazed by everybody—scholars, officials of the department, journalists and bureaucrats—and not all have returned the borrowed books. To quote a few instances, a former head of the department who later held a constitutional position in the state is yet to return books like *Buddhist Kashmir, The Western Frontiers of Kashmir, Kalhana's*

Rajatarangini, Freedom at Midnight, Ghalib Shinasi and *Best Quotations.* Books shown outstanding against one of his successors include *Islam in Modern History, Development of Islamic State and Society, Handbook of Muslim Jurisprudence* and *Introduction to Kashmir and its Geography.* Yet another did not return *Keys to Kashmir* and *Qura'n-i-Sharief.* A lower rung official has seven books outstanding against him which include *Last Years of British India, Decline & Fall of Roman Empire, The Kashmiri Pandits, The Indian Press: Profession to Industry, Punjab Today* and *A History of Europe.* Among the defaulters are men from the fourth estate also. Seven such gentlemen have not returned at least 18 reference books to the library. The titles include *Gilgit: The Northern Gate of India, The Islamic Bomb, Heir Apparent, Kashmir Problem, Essential Documents and Notes on Kashmir, The Arabs, News Reporting, Journalists' Handbook, Ladakh Crossroads, History of Freedom Struggle in J&K, Terrorism and Security, Kashmir in Sunlight & Shade, From Jinnah to Zia, Pictures of the Kashmiri Autumn, Newsweek Bound File, The Constitution of J&K, Cultural Heritage of Kashmir* and *Aatash-i-Chinar.*

A case of theft of valuable books, earlier privately talked about by some people privy to the information, recently came in the public domain through an article published in a periodical of the J&K Academy of Art, Culture & Languages. As is well known, in the wake of Partition and resultant conflagration in Kashmir in 1947, many people from the Valley migrated, or were forced to go, to Pakistan leaving behind their properties including private libraries. After the J&K Academy of Art, Culture & Languages was set up in 1958 these collections were handed over to the institution by the Custodian Evacuee Property. Few years back, a former officer of the Academy, writing for *Sheeraza,* a journal of the institution, alleged that some valuable and quality books were swindled before landing in the Academy's library.[283] One of his former colleagues recalls that these books came from private collections of people like Abdur Rehman Afandi. Afandi was among many people like Mirwaiz Mohammad Yusuf Shah, Brigadier Rehmat Ullah, Sana Ullah Wani of Sopore, Ghulam-ud-Din Wani of Baramulla, Ashiq

Hussain of Srinagar and the Rajas of Kohli, Chikar, Dopatta and Kathai whose properties were confiscated on 2 March 1948 under the Enemy Agents Confiscation of Property Ordinance (1948).[284] An un-edited portion of an article, copy of which came to the fore during an inquiry into some controversial portions of an Academy publication, alleges mysterious disappearance of a valuable painting which, the author of the article alleges, still adorns a wall of one of his former boss' house. Allegations of pilferage of the institution's intellectual wealth often come up in private discussions while those who have knowledge about it avoid speaking on record. There was this manuscript of significance titled *Majmuai-e-Bayaz* by Jaffer Malik that was allegedly shown outstanding against a noted researcher, son of a legendary poet of Kashmir, a year after his death. Through an order issued on 29 June 1981, the manuscript referred to as "now beyond the scope of recovery" was written off from record but allegedly appropriated by an officer of the institution.

The Archives Repository Srinagar has about 6,00,000 files but, unlike the Archives Repository Jammu which has a larger collection, no index register. Over a period of time, some say, the repository has suffered substantial pilferage which in the absence of an index register is difficult to locate. Added to it, the government has not since decades transferred any record to the repository, save a few hundred files from the Chief Secretary's office in recent years. The Randhawa Committee Report on the Reorganization of Libraries, Research & Museums (1976) had recommended that various government departments should "not weed out their old records without scrutiny of the Research Department, and the archives should be transferred to the Directorate."[285] The recommendation was observed only in breach leading to the most crucial post-1947 period of Kashmir history including the Holy Relic Movement (1963-64), the Plebiscite Movement (1955-75) and the armed insurgency since 1989, not forming part of the record. Established in 1954, the Repository houses some post-1947 record of the civil secretariat and other government departments, and 'thousands of files' of the Governor of Kashmir's office under the Dogra rule. Fortunately, the great flood of 2014 did not reach the stone building of the repository but, God forbid, a short circuit can blow up the paper treasure. The building is an old structure with anything but congenial ambiance for housing such a huge and important collection on Kashmir history. Few years back, the government had started digitization of the record. Strangely, however, after completing 25,80,000 pages the process was stopped. Former Director Doordarshan, Leh and a frequent visitor to the repository, Rajinder Singh Raina, finds the record "at risk due to lack of space and absence of scientific environment for preservation and protection". During long turmoil in Kashmir, he observes, "the archival record has suffered for want of proper care and management."[286]

Besides individuals and institutions eating into the intellectual wealth of Kashmir, calamities, both natural and manmade, have also depleted its sources of scholarship. Massive damage was inflicted by burning down of the *Jamia Madinat ul Uloom*, Hazratbal on 21 February 1992 turning into ashes a collection of 16,000 books and manuscripts including a 400-year-old copy of Holy *Qura'n*, titles on history, politics and religion and works by noted scholars on the life of Prophet of Islam (peace be upon him), Islamic jurisprudence and interpretation of *Qura'n*. Most of the collection was in Arabic and Persian languages with some translations also in English and Urdu. Tragically, the institution was again ravaged by fire on 30 April 2015 that perished a collection of 2700 books serving as important sources of Islamic studies bought from countries like Egypt and Lebanon. Likewise, the library of the Islamia College Srinagar went up in flames in an act of arson in which the college was burnt on 15 October 1990. About 65,000 books were lost to the blaze including titles like *Al-Khilafat: Its Rise & Fall, Literary History of Arabs, Tawaseen of Mansur Al-hilaj,* acclaimed commentaries on *Al-Qura'n,* earliest books on the life of Prophet Muhammad (peace be upon him) and a collection on Islamic art and science. More shocking was the fact that not a single student or faculty returned any book out of the hundreds, if not thousands, that were outstanding against them at the time of the disaster. Another educational institution that went up in flames on 25 July 1989 was the S.P. Higher Secondary School

(Boys), Srinagar established in 1874 AD. The biggest loss to the school was razing of its rich library comprising over 12,000 books painstakingly built over a century. During the intervening night of 9 and 10 June 1999, the Head Office of the J&K Academy of Art, Culture & Languages caught fire resulting in the loss of several important paintings including one of Zaina Dab, the famous palace of King Zainul Aabideen, adorning the walls of the building, manuscripts, books and artefacts. Further damage was caused by water used by fire tenders to douse the flames. The Academy at a specially held presser, refuted media reports about any loss other than office record suffered by the institution in the incident but knowledgeable sources point out that the employees of the institution were directed not to speak a word about the fire incident. As advised, they reportedly remained off-duty on the day press conference was held in the premises of the institution.

Kashmir has a long tradition of scholarship and private libraries. The 12th-century versifier, Bilhana refers to the scholarly discussions held during his time in the high rising buildings situated on the banks of the Jhelum.[287] His more famous contemporary, Kalhana, consulted at least 11 earlier manuscripts while composing the *Rajatarangini.* Zainul Aabideen, the 15th-century ruler of Kashmir, had many old Sanskrit works including the Kalhana's tome, translated into Persian. The 16th-century Islamic scholar, author and spiritual personality, Shaikh Yaqoob Sarfi, had a magnificent library in Srinagar with a collection of 15,000 books.[288] In 1875 when Georg Buhler visited Kashmir, he found "All the Sanskrit-speaking Pandits, as well as some of the traders and officials, possess larger or smaller libraries."[289] He mentions by name 22 Pandits in Srinagar city alone who possessed "the most considerable collection".[290] He felt that the lists furnished to him were not complete and spoke of libraries at Sopore, Islamabad [Anantnag] and Baramulla also. Over the centuries, the tradition of families inheriting large collections of books and manuscripts lost roots among new generations who sold as scrap many rare and priceless collections. Peerzada Muahammad Ashraf who surveyed manuscript collections in Kashmir under the National

Mission Manuscripts, a Government of India project, and National Register of Records to create a country-wide database on manuscripts, found that of the surveyed collections about 35,000 manuscripts in Kashmir were with private individuals and institutions. There are many more manuscripts whose owners were reluctant to share information. In several cases, the manuscripts were unsafely stashed or moth infested. The largest collection of 5824 manuscripts in a government institution in Kashmir is with the Research Library. These are in languages including Persian, Sanskrit, Arabic, Kashmiri, Urdu, Punjabi, Bakha, Brej Basha, Hindi, Dogri, Turkish, Pashtu, Balti, Dogri, Tibetan and English. The entire collection is digitized.

Peerzada believes that due to "our negligence and indifference a large portion of our old manuscripts have landed in foreign libraries and museums. We have sold our heritage for peanuts." Many Kashmiri Pandit families migrating from the Valley in 1990 left behind private libraries that, they alleged, were burgled or torched. Among such persons, Dr. V.N. Drabu, Trilok Koul, P.N. Kachru and Dr. K.L. Chowdhary claimed that their rich collections of books and paintings were looted.[291] Rajinder Singh Raina recalls having seen in 1993 truckloads of books and Persian and Sanskrit manuscripts being sold at Baba Demb, Srinagar. These included inherited collections of families whose new generation sold these as scrap. Manzoor Ahamd Daik who runs Kashmir Research Institute at Brein, Nishat with an impressive collection of books and manuscripts blames governments in New Delhi and Srinagar for "not [being] interested in our rich history in the form of manuscripts and old books and, in fact, [they] would like all of it was destroyed". Daik, who possesses rare manuscripts like Persian translation of the *Rajatarangini* of Kalhana, 23 volumes of Bhagwad Gita in Sharda script and English translation of Lal Ded's poetry by Grierson, claims to have approached every who-is-who in Srinagar and New Delhi including Chief Ministers and Prime Ministers asking for measures and financial assistance to preserve and protect treasures of manuscript wealth of Kashmir but, sadly, with no result. The only 'noteworthy' step the State Government took few years back was the creation of an independent ministry of culture whose only contribution was undesirable bureaucratic and ministerial interference in the affairs of an autonomous institution—the Jammu & Kashmir Academy of Art, Culture & Languages.

As if other adversities were not enough, the flood of 2014, one of the worst that ever hit Kashmir, played havoc with libraries in Srinagar city. In a radius of about two kilometers from the Radio Kashmir to the J&K High Court on the one side and the Amar Singh College to the Government Girls Higher Secondary School, Kothi Bagh on the other, over 2,50,000 books were lost in government institutions alone. According to the statistics made available by these institutions, in the SPS Library, Kashmir's largest public library, 15,501 titles, about 5% of which were reference books, were destroyed. Another 300 to 400 books were partially damaged. Some of the rare titles lost in the deluge included *Mathnavi Molvi Roum* (1873) with commentary by Abul Ali Mohammad Behrul Aloom, *Hayat-i-Afghani* on history of Afghanistan (1867) by Mohammad Hayat Khan, *Tazkira-e-Rausa-i-Punjab*, *Saheef-e-Zareen* (1902) on Indian rulers by Parag Narain Bhargav, Himalayan Journals (1854) and Survey of International Affairs (1925). The flood took a heavy toll of books at the Amar Singh College, Government College for Women, M.A. Road, Sri Pratap College and the College of Education. Housed in the ground floor, the Amar Singh College library lost 44,000 books out of a collection of 60,000. Fortunately, the reference section of the library comprising 16,500 reference and 3500 rare books was saved for its location in the first floor and timely rescue efforts of the library staff. The Sri Pratap College library lost around 55,000 books including about 3,000 reference titles. The flood consumed another 43,000 books at the Government College for Women and about 50,000 titles including rare books and old manuscripts of the nearby College of Education. The library of the J&K High Court with a collection of about 15,000 books also perished. The libraries of Radio Kashmir, Srinagar and Doordarshan Srinagar were fully consumed by the flood. The two institutions had about 8,500 and 6,000 books respectively, which included subjects like history and literature.

The Government Girls Higher Secondary School, Kothi Bagh lost its entire collection of 22,071 books (about 1000 partially and the rest fully) including reference titles and encyclopedias.

The great deluge also severely hit the J&K Academy of Art Culture & Languages where 3000 books, including 137 rare titles, were damaged. Further, from a collection of 5000 stock copies of books and journals, including a large number of out-of-print titles, published by the Academy over the past 60 years, 1050 were "severely damaged". Most of the retrieved books "have undergone changes in their respective physical shape and form; pages stuck together. Majority of them have been affected by fungal growth too."[292] Out of the total 626 manuscripts of the Academy, 142 were damaged, 79 totally. Some rare manuscripts, however, were saved for being located higher than the flood level. Experts from National Research Laboratory for Conservation of Cultural Property, Lucknow, found "sporadic and fluffy fungal growth and enormous presence of blackish spores" on the affected manuscripts which had "aesthetically spoiled such valuable unbound paper manuscripts."[293] A serious conservation problem, they observed, was the "transfer of bleeding color from the supporting packing material to the original documents".[294] The Report further added: "Deposition of mud had obscured the script and in addition had caused physical deformation.... Most of the manuscripts in bounded volumes were seen affected by water percolation which caused sticking of paper folios together and also stained."[295] The painting collection including the works of giants like M.F. Hussain, Subramaniyam, Laxman Pai, Gaitondai and G.R. Santosh was also affected. On most of the paintings, experts found "adherence of thick muddy deposition on either side".[296] The only reassuring thing in this gloomy scenario was that the entire collection of Academy's manuscripts, paintings and sculptures was digitized in 2013, making soft copies of the treasure available.

The flood irrevocably damaged the Information & Public Relations Department's 1800 international and Indian newspapers clipping files on Kashmir, representing the period from 1940s to 2000. Newspaper files from 2000 to 2014 were also lost. Immediately after flood water receded, an official of the department who had painstakingly built on and properly maintained this valuable treasure asked for two computers, a few accessories and two hard-coke stoves costing in all about ₹ 2 lakh to dry and scan the files for digital preservation. The response was a snub by the Head of the Department: "This is a tall order. Forget about it". The wreckage of the fungus inflicted files mourned this apathy which only matches with the naked ignorance of an officer who, as head of the department, inspected an archives repository and on observing piles of files of old record admonished his staff for wasting office space for '*raddi ke dher*' (heaps of scrap) and even suggested its auction.

Yet another major casualty of the flood was the SPS Museum. A team of experts from the National Museum, New Delhi comprising R.C. Jain and R.P. Savita assessed the damage suffered by the Museum. The team observed that "[t]he most affected artifacts are of organic nature which includes: Miniature Paintings, valuable Manuscripts, Textiles, Papier Machie, Wooden carvings, Stuffed animals, etc. Also a sizable no. [number] of inorganic material objects are affected due to flood which includes Stone sculptures, Terracotta, valuable mask (made of terracotta), metal artifacts, etc."[297] The report praises the Museum staff for "rescuing a sizable number of museum collection." The damaged objects include 124 paintings, 38 manuscripts, four photo albums, 92 textile items mainly shawls, 24 papier mache [completely damaged], six musical instruments, 14 earthen glass ware, four astronomical instruments, 26 straw ware and 490 objects of natural history. The Gilgit and Sharda manuscripts, currency notes, Sarkari Notes, Certificates, British Stamps, telegraph stamps and other service stamps, Sufi paintings, copper ware and metal seals, minerals specimens, Copper Coins, Silver Coins and Gold Coins were not affected by the flood. However, the condition of Gilgit manuscripts was 'bad' requiring "immediate attention".[298] The National Museum team had submitted a conservation and treatment proposal for the flood affected artefacts that, sadly, hit bureaucratic hurdle.

The tape library of the *Doordarshan Kendra* in Srinagar was completely washed away by the flood. Former Director,

Shabir Mujahid, says that many old recordings had been already lost due to failure in shifting these from obsolete to new technology, and inundation few years earlier when rain water gushed into a wooden barrack housing the library. The huge loss includes footage on shifting of the *Moi-e-Muqaddas* (Holy Relic) from the old to new building at Hazratbal, the first tele-films of Indian television in any language—*Rasul Mir* and *Habba Khatoon*—Sheikh Mohammad Abdullah's public speech at Lal Chowk after his return to power in 1975, his funeral procession in 1982, a rare discussion on Iqbal and Kashmir among Sheikh Mohammad Abdullah, Ali Sardar Jafri and Jagan Nath Azad, and interviews with and performances by legendary Dilip Kumar, Begum Akhtar, Malika Pukhraj, Ustad Bismillah Khan and Runa Laila. Bashir Budgami, filmmaker and former Doordarshan producer who directed *Rasul Mir* and *Habba Khatoon,* describes the loss as "of huge proportion and irreparable".[299] Fortunately, he has a copy each of the two films which he had offered to the Doordarshan for transfer but the reply was a cold shoulder. The tape library of the Radio Kashmir was saved in the flood for being located in the first floor while its book library was washed away.

The loss to private libraries in the city where houses remained submerged for over a week under 10 to 15 feet high water is equally large. Although it is difficult to accurately quantify the loss, Editor *Kashmir Uzma*, Javed Azar, gives a rough estimate of at least 1,00,000 books that the flood consumed in private houses in the city. Peerzada Mohammad Muzaffar, for instance, he adds, lost his lifetime collection of about 3000 books on select topics. The loss to publishers and book sellers was enormous. Sheikh Ajaz of Gulshan Books, a leading publishing house in Kashmir, "lost over 2,00,000 books from hundreds of titles, mainly on Kashmir and Islamic literature." His stocks at five godowns at Maisuma and Bemina were consumed by the flood. The worst hit areas of Lal Chowk, Maisuma and Bemina had about 30 booksellers whose collective loss is estimated to be anywhere between 5,00,000 to 6,00,000 books. The affected area also houses most of the newspaper offices, some of whom lost their entire archives.

6
The Celluloid Years

The beginning and the end of cinema halls in Kashmir is linked with the turmoil it has witnessed for about nine decades now. During the early 1930s, when Kashmir was passing through an uncertain situation following the killing of two dozen people in Srinagar on 13 July 1931, a Punjabi speaking Sikh businessman built the Valley's first cinema hall, the *Palladium Talkies,* at the city centre, later, named as the Lal Chowk. In 1989, when armed insurgency started in Kashmir and a militant outfit, the *Allah Tigers*, ordered closure of cinema houses and liquor shops in the Valley and grenades were hurled at some movie theatres, all of them were shut on 1 January 1990. The State Government's efforts to reopen cinema halls, linking it with the return of normalcy in Kashmir, did not materialize albeit a short lived success when three movie theatres in Srinagar reopened in 1999 but quickly shut down in the face of grenade attacks resulting in the death of at least one person and injuries to many. Today, most of the cinema halls are either converted into commercial centers, including one into a hospital, or serve as camps of paramilitary forces.

The story of cinema in Kashmir is essentially the story of the *Palladium Talkies* started in 1932 by Bhai Anant Singh Gauri, who—unknown to most as a philanthropist—donated over 50 kanals (6.19 acres) of land to the Sher-i-Kashmir Institute of Medical Sciences (SKIMS), Srinagar in 1978. An acknowledgement to this huge gesture is the Institute's Ward No. 4 named after him and dedicated to the treatment of urology patients. A letter of gratitude signed by Sheikh Mohammad Abdullah, the then Chief Minister and the man behind the construction of the SKIMS, on 14 January 1978 welcomed the donation as coming from "a great family of our State which is known for their numerous acts of philanthropy." Bhai Anant Singh's grandson, Manmohan Singh Gauri, claims that the *Palladium Cinema* was the oldest movie hall in north India and would screen Hollywood movies before these were released in Delhi which did not have a good market for English films then.[300] "We had the privilege of hosting a meeting of a leading Hollywood film producing company, the 20th Century Fox", he reminisces. The cinema also held variety shows. In 1940, for instance, it held Mumtaz Shanti Variety Show whose first day's proceeds it gave to the War Fund.[301] Shanti was a famous film actress of 1940s. Before the *Palladium Cinema* was established, one Lala Shiv Nath Nanda had applied for grant of land for construction of a cinema hall in Srinagar. However, the matter did not move further as the then Revenue Minister informed the Governor of Kashmir that the land applied for by Nanda "is the same as has been indented for construction of Motor Garages."[302]

The *Palladium Cinema* was Kashmir's big leap in the entertainment arena. It was run by the *Kashmir Talkies Ltd.* One of the first movies, if not the very first, screened at the cinema was the India's maiden sound picture, *Alam Ara,* released in 1931. Directed by Ardeshir Irani, the film had Master Vithal and Zubaida in lead roles with Prithviraj Kapoor as a supporting actor. In October 1947, when Kashmir was pushed into a tumult, the *Palladium Cinema* was screening *Kismet*, the first blockbuster in Indian cinema, featuring Ashok Kumar and Mumtaz Shanti. The screening of the film had begun on 10 October 1947.[303] After Maharaja Hari Singh fled to Jammu for safety on 26 October in the wake of Tribal Attack on Kashmir, the *Palladium Cinema* became the hub of the Emergency Administration headed by Sheikh Mohammad Abdullah, and his *Peace Brigade*. Many adjacent hotels and other buildings were also used as offices of different wings of the Administration. In front of the cinema hall, the red flag of the National Conference with an image of a plough fluttered on an iron pillar about 30 feet high. The flag was removed later during G.M. Sadiq's Government (1964-71). However, during the Plebiscite Movement, Holy Relic Movement and other political agitations, a protestor would climb the pole to unfurl a black flag. It was in front of the cinema in 1948 that Pandit Jawaharlal Nehru, Prime Minister of India, made a solemn pledge to Kashmiris of holding a plebiscite to determine the future of Kashmir once the situation was normalized. Whether the screening of films was temporary halted in the *Palladium Cinema* is not known. However, the cinema screened *Kasam*, featuring Prem Adib, a Kashmiri origin actor, and Najma, from 16 November 1947. The screening of the film was extended to 30 November, after which films *Taj Mahal* and *Man ki Jeet* were screened.[304] The earliest and the longest serving gatekeeper of the *Palladium Cinema* was Mohammad Abdullah of Dalgate. The *Palladium* was burnt in a major incident of fire in 1993 which consumed many adjacent buildings also. It could not be rebuilt due to a dispute over land lease and the gutted building was taken over and used by paramilitary forces as a security camp. Within the collapsed four walls of the cinema hall different species of plants, especially Himalayan Horse Chestnut, grown over the years have turned into huge trees. The government in 2017 announced that the site would be developed as a heritage museum.[305]

The inauguration of the *Palladium Cinema* was soon followed by the opening of the *Regal Cinema* in Srinagar by Bals, another Punjabi speaking family whose progeny, Rohit Bal, is a leading fashion designer of India. The Bal siblings—Amresh, Prakash and Mahinder—owned two more cinema houses of the same name at Gulmarg and Lahore under the banner of the Universal Pictures Ltd. The *Regal Cinema* at Srinagar was the only theatre which had a bar also. The Annual Administration Report for the year 1940-41 talks about two cinema halls in Srinagar as "one caters chiefly for Europeans and educated Indians and the other provides amusement chiefly to Indian audiences".[306] The *Regal Gulmarg* was a seasonal facility for the European visitors only. The *Palladium* and the *Regal* cinemas were connected with landlines with phone numbers 252 and 138, respectively.

In 1935, one S.D. Puri applied for grant of land for construction of a cinema hall, third in Srinagar. The Revenue Minister recommended to the Prime Minister allotment of two kanals of land to the applicant near the Police Station Kothibagh on the assurance that educational films for school going boys and girls would be screened in the proposed cinema hall twice a week. However, the proposal faced opposition, both within and outside the government. Within the government, it was feared that with crowds of people of all sorts passing the adjacent Zanana Palace (abode of widows in the then ruling family, now Government College for Women) on way to the cinema hall every evening and returning in batches late at night, "the road may not maintain its desired respectable appearance."[307] There was public outcry also against setting up of a third cinema hall in the city. On 11 March 1936, a telegram sent to the Prime Minister by both Muslim and Hindu subjects informed him that due to the current trade depression and unemployment the existing two cinema halls were proving harmful for the people, and urged him to reject permission to "outsider exploiter" for construction of a third cinema hall in Srinagar and "save His Highness' loyal subjects from ruination".[308] The issue was agitated through the press also. The daily *Martand*, owned by the *Yuvak Sabha* of Kashmiri Pandits wrote against starting a third movie hall in Srinagar. In its publication of 30 November 1935, the newspaper cautioned that "a third cinema hall will reduce to extremity a people already depleted of their resources by the existing cinema halls". Ultimately, the State Council decided to reserve the land for government purposes and the question of construction of a cinema hall was "automatically quashed."[309]

There were others who saw 'a great educative and moral value' in the cinema and focused on the need for good selection of movies. That year, a body named Cinema Reform Association was formed to ensure, among other things, reduction in rates and fair selection of movies for exhibition. The association comprised Ramsaran Das Malhotra as President, Fazal Ahmad as Vice-President, Mr. Nishat as Secretary and Yahya Rafiqi as Joint Secretary. The association was "of the opinion that

Cinema Industry has a great educative and moral value & that open competition alone can provide good treatment, reduction in rates and fair selection of pictures."[310]

By the end of 1930s, there were only two cinema houses in Kashmir. However, in early 1940s, the Bals were permitted to construct another movie hall, *Amresh*, named after one of the three owner siblings, behind the then existing *Regal Cinema*.[311] The family used the upper floor of the *Amresh Cinema* as their residence. In 1950, the ownership of the *Regal* and the *Amresh* cinemas changed hands from the Bals to Bakhshi Abdul Majid, brother of the then Deputy Prime Minister of Jammu & Kashmir, Bakhshi Ghulam Mohammad, who later became the Prime Minister of the State in 1953. The two cinema halls were purchased for a sum of ₹ 1,50,000.[312] By 1956, three more cinema halls had come up in Kashmir including the *Samad Talkies*, Sopore, the *Regina Cinema*, Baramulla and the *Nishat Talkies*, Anantnag. Those days, cinema halls were required to send to the government a quarterly statement of gate collections.[313] During the second quarter of 1956, the *Palladium Cinema* made a collection of ₹ 64,367, the *Regal Cinema* ₹ 47,347 and annas six, the *Amresh Talkies* ₹ 48,529 and annas 14, the *Regina Cinema* ₹ 12,688 and annas two, the *Samad Talkies* ₹ 1836 and annas four, and the *Nishat Talkies* ₹ 5231 and annas ten.[314]

On 28 December 1963, a day after the mysterious theft of the Holy Relic at the Hazratbal Shrine, an infuriated mob set ablaze the *Regal* and the *Amresh* cinemas for alleged involvement of the Bakhshis in the sacrilegious act. When the situation normalized, the owners sought permission of the government for reconstruction of the two gutted cinema halls. However, the permission for reconstruction was granted only for one cinema hall following which a new *Regal Cinema* was constructed at the site of the *Amresh Cinema*. It was then the largest cinema hall of Kashmir with a capacity of 1340 seats, almost equal number the *Regal* and the *Amresh* had together. The cinema was inaugurated in 1967 with the Raj Kapoor movie, *Around the World in 8 Dollors*. On the first day, the roof of the entry to the ticket counter collapsed under the weight of the people who had climbed over it to obtain tickets for the late night show. Many of them sustained injuries. It happened to be the auspicious *Shab-i-Baraat* and many people believed that the accident was caused due to 'disrespect' shown by cinema-goers to the sacred occasion.

For two decades after the commencement of the *Amresh Cinema*, Srinagar had no more movie halls until 1964 when the *Shiraz Cinema* was inaugurated in the heart of the old city at Khanyar. The first three cinema halls were located in the uptown area of Lal Chowk. The *Shriraz* opened with *Sangam*, a Raj Kapoor-Vijayanti Mala-Rajindra Kumar starrer, that drew huge rush of people. The residents of Khanyar resented the opening of a cinema in the locality. The permission for construction had been granted to the proprietors of the cinema house, Abdur Rahim and Krishan Gopal, on the recommendations of the Administrator, Srinagar Municipality and Deputy Inspector General of Police. The *Intizamia Committee* of the nearby shrine of *Dastgeer Sahib* claimed that the land on which the cinema house was constructed was the shrine property which had been gifted away to Rahim and Gopal by one of the trustees of the shrine, Ghulam Hassan Gilani for "some unknown consideration".[315]

The decade of 1960s saw rapid expansion of cinemas in Kashmir. After the *Shiraz Cinema*, the *Broadway Theatre* was opened at Sonawar in May 1965 with Shammi Kapoor's *Jaanwar*, and the *Neelam Cinema* at Suthra Shahi near the Civil Secretariat in 1966 with *Dil Diya Dard Liya* featuring Dilip Kumar and Waheeda Rehman. The *Neelam Cinema* was originally built by Gauris as the *Jai Hind Talkies* but the building was acquired by the government to use it as coal storage. After sometime, it was auctioned and its new owner opened it as a movie hall. Bhai Anant Singh Gauri had another cinema house, the *Regina,* built on the present Maulana Azad Road which was also taken over by the government for the Transport Department. The *Regina* was built in 1945-46 and the *Jai Hind Talkies* in 1946-47.[316] Soon, Kashmir was engulfed by turmoil in October 1947 and opening of the two new cinema halls was put on hold. However, when the situation somewhat stabilized, the government refused cinema license to Gauris in either case, allegedly to save Bakhshi Abdul Majid, owner of the *Regal* and the *Amresh* from any competition. The building of the *Regina Cinema* was acquired by the government on 7 January 1953 for ₹ 1,10,000.[317] On 22 November 1949, Majid applied for license claiming that he had taken the *Jai Hind Talkies* on lease and intended to run it as the *Shalimar Pictures*.[318] Later, he stepped back arguing that "it was not the policy of the Government to grant any more licenses for cinemas."[319] In the meanwhile, Gauri approached Bakhshi Ghulam Mohammad, who was now the Prime Minister of Jammu & Kashmir, for issuance of license but without success. The matter lingered on till 1961 when the government acquired the building. Between 1946 and 1948, residents of the locality objected to the proposed cinema in the building, arguing that a mosque, a girls' school and a Muslim graveyard were located nearby. The then District Magistrate, M.A. Shahmiri, had pointed out the undesirability of a cinema hall there.[320] The denial of cinema licenses to Gauri for safeguarding business interests of his brother formed part of the charges of misconduct against the former Prime Minister, Bakhshi Ghulam Mohammad, investigated by a Commission of Inquiry appointed by the government on 30 January 1965.

Following the opening of the *Neelam Cinema*, the next movie hall inaugurated in Srinagar was the *Khayam Cinema,* at Muniwar, on 2 December 1968 with the screening of a Hollywood war movie, *The Dirty Dozen*. It was the first cinema hall in Kashmir with a 70 mm screen. Next in the line were the *Naz Cinema* opposite the Huzoori Bagh and the *Firdous Cinema* at Hawal, which were inaugurated in 1969. The *Firdous Cinema* opened with *Tumse Achha Kaun Hai*, a Shammi Kapoor and Babita starrer. The cinema was thrown open on 13 April on the Baisakhi festival. For the next 14 years, the *Firdous* was the last cinema hall to come up in Srinagar till the inauguration of the *Shah Cinema* at Qamarwari in October 1983.

Besides these nine regular cinema halls in Srinagar, there were few run by the army where civilians also were allowed entry. One such cinema, *Badam Kutir*, was located at the Sadar Bazar in the Badami Bagh Cantonment. Another was an open air projector-and-a-screen facility in the Militia premises near the Huzoori Bagh. Jalaluddin Shah, a geologist by profession who has a remarkable memory of developments taking place in Kashmir since 1960s, recalls that on 9 August 1965 when the Tattoo Ground was attacked by the infiltrators from Pakistan, the cinema was showing the movie *April Fool* with actors Biswajeet and Saira Banu in pivotal roles. Next day, Batamaloo, an adjacent congested locality, went up in flames.

Outside the city of Srinagar, there were cinema halls in Anantnag, Baramulla and Sopore towns and in 1980's a cinema hall at Kupwara also was started. A 1946 archival document mentions existence of a cinema hall each at Pahalgam and Anantnag without mentioning their names.[321] In all probability, the Anantnag cinema was the *Nisaht Talkies* which was an old structure when it got burnt in 1982 at a time when Hindi movie *Surakhsha,* feauring Mithun Chakarvarti, was being screened there. In 1985, a new theatre named *Heevan Cinema* was inaugurated in the town. Other cinema halls included the R*egina* and the *Thimaya Hall* (an Army cinema hall, also known as *Dagger Cinema*) at Baramulla, the *Samad Talkies* and the *Kapara Theatre* at Sopore, the *Zorawar Theatre* (another army cinema hall) at Pattan, and the *Marazi Theatre* at Kupwara. In 1989, when cinema was banned in Kashmir, there were at least 15 functional cinemas in the Valley, nine in Srinagar city alone.

For a long time, Kashmiri society did not accept its youth visiting cinema halls. In fact, up to the 1960s, parents seeking matrimony of their daughter would first convince themselves that the prospective groom was not a cinema or a hotel going guy. A woman visiting a cinema hall was a taboo. During 1940s, only a few of them could go for a movie. Gradually, the number of college going girls and working women visiting cinema halls picked up and during 1970s ladies at a cinema hall was a common sight. The 87-year-old Krishna Misri, a former college principal, would watch films from her childhood and "went to the *Palladium* a lot". "This place", she told BBC Radio 4, "was so dear to me and so familiar to me. I can still picture it clearly in front of my eyes".[322] Author and former professor of English, Neerja Mattoo, too has fond memories of the cinema.

"This cinema had the unique feature of a Lady's Gallery where even unescorted young girls would feel safe to watch a movie", Mattoo recalls.[323] The first film she watched, in the company of her father and grandmother, in the cinema was a mythological movie, *Ram Rajya*. During 1940s, a cinema going daughter of a Muslim civil servant married the Sikh Manager of a cinema hall and created a flutter in a conservative society.

Before 1947, film prints would arrive in Srinagar via the Jhelum Valley Road. However, in the wake of the Indo-Pak hostility over Kashmir the road was closed and film prints, as other commodities, started coming via the Banihal Cart Road, later named as the Srinagar-Jammu National Highway and NH1A. The management of a cinema hall was required to intimate the government in advance about the films it intended to show in the coming weeks. At times, which frequently happened during winters, when the snow caused roadblock and film print could not reach Srinagar the screening of the ongoing film was extended till the arrival of a new movie. Failure in electric supply would also disturb cinema schedules. In 1942, breakdown at the then only power house at Mohura near Uri resulted in the closure of cinema halls in Srinagar for two days.[324] Diesel generators, as alternate electric supply, were not then available to the cinema owners. In early 1930s and 40s, the films screened in Kashmir were generally based on mythological and historical characters, social and moral subjects, and romance and fantasy. Some of the films screened in the *Palladium*, the *Regal* and the *Amresh* between 1942 and 1945 include *Dil ka Daku, Charnu ki Daasi, Daku ki Ladki, Hunter Wali ki Beti, Return of Toofan Mail, Hanso Hanso Duniya Walo, Pistol Wali, School Master, Rustum Sohrab, Hatim Tai ki Beti, Nausherwan-i-Aadil, Bhagat Surdas, Pagli Duniya, Mahatma Vidur, Din-o-Duniya, Circus Queen, Achut Kaniya, Nal Damyanti, Bhagat Kabir, Alibaba Chalees Chor, Krishna Sudama, Vish Kaniya, Shakuntala, Tansen, Ramraj, Laila Majnu, Sangal Deep ki Sundari, Shakuntala,* and *Kadambari*.

Around the same time, the English movies screened at Srinagar and Gulmarg included *Gold Rush, House of Seven Gables, History is Made at Night, The Earl of Chicago, One*

Night in Tropics, Magnificent Obsession, Blossoms in the Dust, How Green was My Valley, The Little Foxes, To Be or Not To Be, Pied Piper, Jungle Book, They All Kissed the Bride, Sailor's Wife, Black Panther, Strange Death of Adolf Hitler, Tarzan Triumphs, Arabian Nights, Sky's The Limit, Bogie Man Will Get You and Wuthering Heights. During later decades, films like *The Godfather, Doctor Zhivago, Lawrence of Arabia, Mackenna's Gold;* World War movies like *Where Eagles Dare, The Great Escape, The Dirty Dozen* and *Patton.* James Bond and Charlie Chaplin movies remained in great demand. Actors Sean Connery, Clint Eastwood, Gregory Peck, Al Pacino and Omar Sharief (more for his Muslim sounding name and Egyptian origin) were among the Hollywood actors watched with interest in Kashmir. A sizeable section of the Hollywood movie watchers would comprise people with little or no knowledge of English language and, amazingly, they understood and enjoyed the movies and appropriately reacted to dialogues with claps or howls.

New films would open on Fridays. It was after Sheikh Mohammad Abdullah's return to power in 1975 that the 1 P.M. show on Fridays was scrapped for it weaned people, especially youth, off the Friday prayers. The decision came after Abdullah, while on way to the Hazratbal Shrine for attending the Friday prayers there, saw a large number of people struggling to enter the *Shiraz* cinema and asked the Kashmir Cinema Owners Association to stop the midday show on Fridays. During 1970s, the *Palladium Cinema* held regular shows of South-Indian and Bengali movies which were screened daily at 10 A.M. The audiences for these films were army and para-military personnel posted in Kashmir. Around that time, *Chan Mahi*, a Punjabi movie from Pakistan, was screened in the *Shriraz Cinema* and drew large number of people, majority of whom did not speak or understand the language of the film.

In 1954, a feature film titled *Pamposh*, set in the backdrop of Kashmir, was screened in the *Amresh Cinema.* The film had many dialogues in Kashmiri language. Significantly, it was the first Indian movie in Geva colour. The film written and directed by Ezra Mir, had Mogli, Savi Multani and Rusi Patel in main roles. Young and handsome G.M. Parray of Sonawar, then Demonstrator (Geography) at the Amar Singh College, also did a supporting role in the film. It so happened that in 1952, Ambalal Jhaverbhai Patel established India's first colour laboratory at Bombay. However, film producers were skeptical of handing over colour processing work to his lab. To demonstrate that the processing by his lab was of high quality, Patel produced *Pamposh* shot on Geva colour film negative which was highly appreciated for its beautiful visual quality.[325] The film, however, did not do well in Kashmir and was removed after few shows.

When *Khana-e-Khuda*, a film based on the annual Islamic pilgrimage of Haj, was screened in the *Shiraz* in 1968 the entire cinema hall was first cleaned and washed to give it a holy ambiance. Many people who came to watch the movie removed their footwear in reverence before entering the cinema hall. Many others showered candies on the screen. The cinema drew heavy rush of people—men and women of all ages. Likewise, many Sikh cine-goers removed their footwear before entering the *Palladium Cinema* where devotional film *Nanak Naam Jahaz Hai* was screened in 1969. Another well-attended 'Islamic' film was the 1970 release, *Ziaratgah-i-Hind—Zeenat.* The film captured all major Muslim shrines of India. Kashmir's two important shrines, Hazratbal and Charar-i-Sharief also figured in the movie. The film's credits were given in Urdu. A versified tribute to the shrines sung by Mohammad Rafi was the main attraction of the film. About the Hazratbal Shrine, the eulogy went like this: *Srinagar mai hai Hazrat e Bal Khuda ke fazl o karam ka saaya Yahin Medinay ka paak tofta naseeb Moi-i-Mubarak aaya* (Hazratbal in Srinagar is the silhouette of Allah's blessings where the sacred gift of Medinah, the Holy Relic has arrived). Films with religious appeal were screened to cater to the interest of a particular community. Jalaluddin Shah recalls that the *Palladium* in particular would screen Hindu mythological movies like *Har Har Mahadev, Sant Tuka Ram and Sampuran Ramayana* on festive occasions like *Shivratri.* A movie with Muslim characters was usually publicized as an '*Islami shahkaar*' (Islamic masterpiece) even if it had nothing to do with Islam, the religion. Ironically, a cinema hoarding on the eve of Muslim festival of *Eid* once read, "*Sex aur maar katai se bharpur Islami tohfa. Eid Mubarak ki khushi par chaar show*" [On the auspicious Eid, an Islamic gift full of sex and fight. Daily four shows.]

The first cinematograph film produced in Kashmir was made somewhere between 1929 and 1931 when G.E.C. Wakefield was the Prime Minister. It was a film with a social message based on the theme of hygiene and unfavourable condition of women. The project was taken up on the directions of Maharaja Hari Singh. The script of the film was written by Wakefield's Political Secretary, Ram Chandra Kak who later rose to the position of Prime Minister of Jammu & Kashmir. The film ran in trouble as Kashmiri Pandits protested against it and opposed its public screening. The government succumbed to the pressure and withdrew the film.

The film was an effective medium of propaganda for social reform but Pandits reacted unfavourably and opposed its public exhibition. When an attempt was made to screen it in Srinagar, some young men resorted to picketting. Wakefield was blamed for interference in the domestic affairs of the community. Base political motives were ascribed to him. Ram Chandra Kak too came in for severe criticism. Telegrams were dispatched to the Maharaja imploring him to intervene. Finally, Wakefield yielded to the pressure and the film was withdrawn and never shown anywhere again.[326]

The Kashmiri Pandits did not forgive Kak for, what they alleged, presenting the community in a bad frame. The matter was also raised as part of charges against Wakefield by the Pandit community before the Riots Enquiry Committee constituted to go into the carnage of 13 July 1931 and the resultant violence. A witness, Pandit Prem Nath, who by his own admission was working for the secret police under the codename of 'Bashir Ahmad' levelled serious charges against Wakefield including being anti-Hindu and inviting applications from Muslims only against three vacancies in the Srinagar Municipality. The third charge that he made against the Prime Minister was appointing "R.C. Kak as his Private Secretary who wrote story of a cinema film depicting the life of a Kashmiri Pandit. All Kashmiri Pandits disliked it. The college students boycotted classes as the film directly insulted their mothers and sisters. But still, the film was not stopped. The Kashmiri Pandits were portrayed in the film as fallen and uncivilized."[327] Kak told his erstwhile neighbour, Jalaluddin Shah, in 1964 that in view of the pressure built by Kashmiri Pandits, the film print was consigned to flames.[328]

In 1968, the *Shriaz* screened the first Kashmiri feature film, *Maenz Raat* (The Night of Henna), which was shot completely on location with Omakar Aima and Mukta in lead roles. The story of the film was written by playwright Ali Mohammad Lone. Other actors included Som Nath Sadhu, Pran Kishore, Shaheen Afroz, Nabla Begum and Pushkar Bhan. In 1970, *Shair-i-KashmirMehjoor*, a biopic on Kashmir's popular poet, Ghulam Ahmad Mehjoor, was released in the *Regal Cinema*. The movie, produced in Urdu, also dubbed in Kashmiri language, had veteran actor Balraj Sahni and his son Parikshat Sahni as the main actors besides several Kashmiri performers. Abdul Gani Wani, an elderly shopkeeper at Sonawar was very upset after watching the film and used uncharitable words against Mehjoor for exhibiting, what he felt, 'shamelessness' by running after girls. It turned out that when he had arrived at the cinema hall he enquired if the film on Mehjoor was being screened there. A person selling tickets in black answered him in affirmative and sold him a ticket at a higher price. Throughout the movie, a naive Wani wearing a yellow turban could not make out that he was watching the Sunil Dutt-Asha Parekh starrer, *Bhai Bhai*, and not *Shair-i-Kashmir Mehjoor* that had been taken off a day earlier.

In 1985, a Hollywood movie inspired youth uprising, later turned into armed militancy, in Kashmir. That summer, producer Moustapha Akkad's *Lion of the Desert,* a film on Libya's resistance led by an uncompromising aged teacher and freedom fighter, Omar al-Mokhtar, against the occupying army of Mussolini's Italy, was screened at the *Regal Cinema*. Portrayed by actor Anthony Quinn, Mokhtar's great courage and wisdom in fighting a mighty enemy and turning down offers of materialistic rewards to end the resistance won the hearts of the audience. They compared Mokhtar with Sheikh Mohammad Abdullah, a mass leader who also had started his career as a teacher, whom they accused of selling out the "sacrifices of Kashmiris for his lust for power". Abdullah had died three years ago after abandoning resistance against Indian rule over Kashmir and embracing power. As the first wave of enraged young viewers came out of the theatre, they raised slogans against Abdullah and pulled down hoardings and banners in Lal Chowk depicting his name and image. Each show of the film brought out more enraged youth and the authorities quickly took off the movie but not before it had inspired a new resistance in Kashmir which erupted in 1989 as a full grown armed insurgency. One of the youth inspired by the movie was militant commander, Mohammad Yasin Malik, currently in prison on charges of terrorism.

Movies on Indo-Pak hostility were not exhibited in Kashmir for the fear of cinema halls being targeted by agitated audience. It was only after the Indo-Pak War of 1971 in which Pakistan lost its eastern flank that the *Broadway* cinema, located in a Cantonment area, broke this tradition and screened a newsreel on the fall of Dacca [Dhaka] and surrender of Pakistan army. The newsreel was shown before each show of the Hindi movie, *Maryada*. Later, a feature film, *Hindustan Ki Kasam*, based on Indo-Pak war was also screened in the cinema.

Dilip Kumar's films would run packed houses in Kashmir. As elsewhere, he had a huge fan following in the Valley. Even the re-runs of his movies would go houseful. Films like *Devdas, Mughal-e-Azam, Naya Daur, Deedar, Aan, Leader, Dil Diya Dard Liya* and *Aadmi* would keep on returning year after year to a huge response. In 1970, when *Gopi* was released at the *Palladium* for an All India premier, Lal Chowk wore a festive look with buntings and colour posters of the film fluttering everywhere, and a huge gathering of Kumar fans jostling each other to reach the ticket window. Dilip Kumar and his wife, Saira Banu, who was his co-star in the movie, also came to the *Palladium* to watch the film. They had a tough time to wade through the river of fans including men with long grey beards, dying to have a glimpse of their favourite actor or shake hands with him. "A beaming Kumar shook hands and exchanged pleasantries with some of them", recalls Javed Azar, a former resident of Amira Kadal. Large crowds of fans were also seen when actors Rajindra Kumar, Shammi Kapoor, Sunil Dutt, Waheeda Rehman, Mehmood and Om Prakash visited the cinema hall on different occasions. Actor Ajit was on several occasions seen sipping local salt tea at the shop of Sultan Joo, a dealer in Kashmir Art. Dev Anand was another popular actor in the Valley. His *Mahal* in 1969 caused a traffic jam in the Regal Chowk and police had to can-charge people to clear the traffic. Raj Kapoor, Raj Kumar, Rajendra Kumar, Dharmendra, Rajesh Khanna and, later, Amitabh Bachchan too were popular actors who had a large fan following in the Valley. So were actresses Madhubala, Nargis, Meena Kumari, Vyjantimala, Sadhna and Asha Parekh. Some ardent fans would go to any length to watch a movie of their favourite actors. When Raj Kapoor's much talked about *Bobby* was released in 1973 many Kashmiri film buffs travelled to Jammu, a 300 km road journey, to watch it there before it was screened in Srinagar.

Films had a deep impact on people. Young boys and girls would dress up like their favourite actors or imitate their mannerism. You had a Dilip Kumar or a Dev Anand or a Rajesh Khanna in every neighbourhood. During 1960s, the Sadhna haircut was very popular among girls. In some cases, the impact was of a different kind. Young Ghulam Nabi Hajam of Drugjan was so consumed by the tragedy afflicting Dilip Kumar in *Devdas* that he turned crazy, grew beard, stopped eating food and wandered on the Bund along the Jhelum for weeks. Ghulam Mohammad Bhat, a 1931 born from uptown Sonawar, was a film buff from a very young age. There was hardly any movie during those times that he missed to watch. So charmed was he by movies that despite being an illiterate, he fancied the idea of writing stories for films and, in fact, dictated one to his cousin. One day, in the midst of narration of a standoff between the hero and the villain he was at a loss for words to carry forward the wordy duel and took a long pause. Waiting for the next lines to jot down, his cousin observed that the silence was getting longer and asked Bhat what he should write now. Using his imaginative skills, Bhat quickly offered a sound filler: "*Zradga'un*!" The script was titled *Mohabbat ki Kahani* (The Love Story) and posted to a film company in Bombay but, sadly without any success. Nazir Ahmad, a college student, was so carried away by Feroz Khan, the black robed hero of a 1974 movie, *Khotay Sikkay*, riding a white horse and galloping through the ravines and mountain valleys with a Kishore Kumar number, *Jeevan mai tu darna nahi sar neecha kabi karna nahi,* playing in the background, that after watching the movie he announced that the first thing he would do after securing a job "is to buy a white horse and ride to my office".

The publicity of upcoming and ongoing movies in itself was an entertainment. The *Palladium Cinema* had its own innovative style of doing it. At the stroke of 9.30 in the morning, two men holding a large hoarding with a poster of the film, followed by a band of pipers and a drummer, led by Band Master Mohammad Rajab, would start from the cinema and march through the streets of Srinagar. Javed Azar recalls that so accurate was the timing of the Band that mothers would rush children to school at the first beat of the drum. Some youth carrying placards with images and names of actors of the movie beautifully calligraphed by painter Assadullah Wani, would also join the Band as Mama Gasha's bagpipe played tunes of popular movie songs. Amused children followed the Band as it walked through the city and returned to the *Palladium* by the time the first show was about to start. At the ticket window, while police constables would fail to control the crowd, a hugely built Mohammad Ismail, staffer of the *Palladium*, would appear on the scene and feverishly use his cane or leather belt on the ticket seeking throng causing a commotion during which weak hearted and the 'respectable' would fall into the hands of 'Blackers' who illegally sold tickets at a high price. Each cinema hall had its own group of 'Blackers' who invariably worked under the oversight, if not with the blessings, of the cinema management and local police unit.

In later years, cinema owners would hire *tongas* to publicize new arrivals and show timings. A *tonga* with mounted colourful film hoardings and a drummer inside taking rounds of the city roads was a common sight in Srinagar up to mid-1970s when plying of *tongas* in the city was prohibited. Handbills were distributed to draw people's attention to new releases and show timings. Newspaper columns were also used for the publicity of films. Many newspapers like the *Aftab* and the *Srinagar Times* published weekly film pages. Prominent journalist, Yusuf Jameel, edited *Aftab's* film page for several years, besides editing its Islamic page on Fridays. Film hoardings were also installed over shop fronts in busy markets and in lieu of that a shop owner was given a weekly free pass to the movie. From very early days of cinema in Kashmir, many government officers and influential citizens would demand and get free passes. They included journalists. In 1936, the Cinema Reform Association asked the government to issue orders that "no State employee should avail free passes at Cinema houses."[329] Certain elements would resort to blackmail to secure free cinema passes. On 4 November 1940, the weekly *Desh* accused the *Palladium Cinema* of 'mismanagement, black marketing of tickets, misbehaviour of gate keepers with cinema-goers and overcrowding in the cinema'. Next week, the newspaper carried another piece lambasting the management for screening 'third class and immoral movies' and appealed the government to take action against the cinema management. An explanation was sought from the cinema management and the Manager Kashmir Talkies Ltd. informed the government that the allegations, made in the newspaper, were false and an attempt at coercion. He accused the Editor *Desh* of demanding free passes "which he had been availing for four months"[330] and was insisting for more free passes "for his staff and relatives" which was not possible for the cinema management to do.

Many college and school going boys would often bunk classes to watch movies in nearby cinema halls. Head Master Ghulam Ali Shaheed Salmani would, in the middle of a film show, quietly enter the *Broadway Cinema* with a torch in his hand and catch hold of unsuspecting boys of his High School Badimagh and pull them out of the theatre. Master Niranjan Nath Wanchoo alias *Nerre Kak* of the adjacent Sanatan Dharam Pratap Sabha High School would do a similar act at the *Palladium Cinema*. On 11 May 1936, the Kashmir Students Union headed by Janki Nath Zutshi passed a resolution seeking concession in cinema tickets for students and appointment of a few poor students against some emolument for identification of bonafide students at the cinema halls.[331] There was this section of people, mostly young men, unable to buy tickets, which was seen eves dropping at the closed doors of cinema halls enjoying the sound track of a movie. The State Government also held free film shows at public parks, schools and Panchayat Ghars for the entertainment and education of the people. A mobile film unit of the State Information Department, equipped with a projector and a screen, would go to different places in cities and villages to hold a film show carrying a social message. The movies screened during 1960s included *Do Aankhein Barah Haath, Jagriti, Dosti, Do Bheegah Zameen, Mirza Ghalib, Kabuli Wala, Chaar Darvaish* and *Boot Polish*. Newsreels on subjects of sanitation, small savings and elementary education were also screened for general awareness.

For its lush meadows, white mountain peaks, brimming streams and beautiful gardens, Kashmir was always Bollywood's favourite locale. During the decades of 1960s and 70s, in particular, film units would make a beeline for shooting in the Valley. The earliest known arrival of a film unit in Kashmir dates back to 1944. That year, the Taj Mahal Film Company, Bombay arrived at the fall to shoot scenes of its movie, *Begum*, featuring Ashok Kumar as a shepherd and Naseem alias *Pari Chehra* or the Fairy-Face, as a village damsel.[332] The movie, an adaptation of a short story by Sadat Hassan Mantoo, was laid in the countryside and snows of Kashmir. The crew of the film company comprised Director Sushil Mazumdar, Assistant Director Prabha Mitra, General Manger Samuel Ibrahim, Cameramen Kapadia and Ahmadullah, Sound Recordist Naik, Make-up Director Belcha Parera and Art Director Majeed. The music of the film was by Ghulam Haider.

The first scene was short at the *Kabutar Khana*, Gagribal inside the Dal Lake. Other sequences were filmed at Gulmarg, the Weir at Chhatabal, Kokar Bazar and Hari Singh High Street. One of the significant aspects of the shooting was that an educated Kashmiri girl, whose name was withheld, also acted in the film. At the Weir, she was filmed crossing the Jhelum and carrying under her arm a willow basket while a man was chasing her. On the other side of the river, a group of children ran after her forcing her to take shelter in a poor man's hut. In another scene, Prabha Mitra was filmed walking through Kokar Bazaar. Another shot of her was taken at the Huzoori Bagh. The crew also shot snowfall at Gulmarg. The Taj Mahal Film Company was so impressed with the acting of the Kashmiri girl that she was invited to permanently join the film line.[333] A film journal refuted the rumour that the film company had actually engaged a Kashmiri Pandit boy to do the female role. The boy, it clarified, had served with the film company as a *coolie* for a few days.[334] The promo of the film published in the *Tribune* on 5 March 1946 gave out the cast of the movie which included Misra, a very common female name then in Kashmir, who, in all probability, was the 'educated Kashmiri girl'. The Taj Mahal Company was asked to first send the filmed scenes to J&K Board of Censors for approval before the release of the film in and outside Jammu & Kashmir. The consignment of the film shots was charged custom duty of ₹ 16 and *annas* four by the Maharaja's Government.[335]

Jammu & Kashmir had its own Cinematographic Act promulgated in 1933, and the Board of Censors to keep a watch on movies being screened in the cinema halls. The Board consisted of the Chief Secretary as the Chairman, the provincial Governors, the Senior Superintendents of Police, Srinagar and Jammu and two non-official members, one from each province.[336] The Publicity Officer of the government acted as Secretary to the Board. Prominent bureaucrat turned politician and the first Kashmiri Muslim graduate, Khawaja Ghulam Ahmad Ashai, served as Secretary of the Board for several years. Others who held the position included S.L. Koul and G.D. Sharma. In 1939, one of the two nominated members of the Board of Censors was Khwaja Abdur Rahim Banday,[337] Custodian of the Holy Relic at the Hazratbal Shrine. In 1940, the government rejected a Srinagar Municipality passed resolution seeking to appoint a Provincial Censor Board comprising officers of the Municipality.

The resolution claimed that the officers of the Municipality were "responsible for the good moral conduct of the citizens ever since cinema halls have come into existence within the municipal limits".[338] Later, the Municipal Committee passed another resolution demanding representation in the Board.

The authority of issuing licenses under the Cinematograph Act vested in the Board of Censors was transferred to respective District Magistrates in 1943-44.[339] The Board of Censors was active till as late as 1960s when autonomy of the State was steadily eroded. No film imported from British India even if certified by other Boards of Censors like that of Punjab, Bombay or Calcutta was allowed to be screened without the State Board of Censors first viewing it and issuing a no-objection certificate. The Boards of Film Censors of different states would exchange information about certification or ban on a movie. The Boards were very sensitive to ethically distasteful scenes and portrayal of the British Empire in a negative frame. The movie *Damaged Lives* was denied permission for the suggestion of nudity by showing "a married couple in bed". Likewise, the movie *Gunga Din* was refused certification for portraying a British Sergeant "kicking a thug" and killing him while he was "at prayer in a temple".[340] In an unusual step, the British Resident in Srinagar wrote a letter to the Prime Minister of Jammu & Kashmir on 14 November 1939 requesting him to "ensure that this film is not exhibited in the Jammu and Kashmir State as the exhibition of the film of this nature is particularly undesirable in present circumstances [when the World War II was going on]".[341] Consequently, the cinema halls in the State were instructed not to screen the film. The iconic war film, *All Quiet on the Western Front* also was not allowed to be screened for being an "anti-war propaganda".

Some vigilantes would caution the Board of Censors against screening of a film likely to hurt sentiments of the people. The *Sudarshan* published from Jammu asked the Board to ban exhibition of a freshly released movie, *Dnyaneshwar* as "it hurt sentiments of Hindus by showing a buffalo delivering Vedic sermons".[342] In 1939, the Punjab Board of Censors shared with its Jammu & Kashmir counterpart a list of 132 movies it had uncertified between 1922 and 1936 and banned for screening. The cinema halls had to also exhibit propaganda films or newsreels known as Advisory or Information Films like *Frontline Air Force, Indian News Parade, Conquest of Germany, Workers and War Front, School for Farmers, Tube Well, Musical Instruments of India,* and *Workers' Weekend.*[343] After 1947, the newsreels were produced by the Films Division of India and distributed among cinemas for exhibition before each film show.

The two decades of 1960s and 1970s will always be remembered as the period when Bollywood used to the fullest the beauty of Kashmir for producing super hit films, mostly in the genre of melodramas. One such movie that instantly comes to mind is *Junglee* (1961) that inspired industrialist Ratan Tata to visit Kashmir along with 17 of his college friends.[344] Other movies include, *Kashmir ki Kali* (1964), *Jab Jab Phool Khile, Aarzoo, Jaanwar* (1965), *Do Badan* (1966), *Hamraz, Pathar ke Sanam* (1967), *Ek Phool Do Maali* (1969), *Aan Milo Sajna, Kab Kyon aur Kahan, Geet* (1970), *Bobby* (1973), *Roti, Aap ki Kasam* (1973) and *Kabhie Kabhie* (1976). *Betaab*, a 1980 movie, was shot in a valley in Pahalgam which came to be known after the film as the Betaab Valley. *Silsila* (1981) was another major hit shot in Kashmir. At one point in time in 1983-84, there were over four hundred film units active in Kashmir.[345] At times, there were 10-12 film shootings going on simultaneously at different locations in the Valley.[346] Pahalgam, Gulmarg and the Mughal Gardens in Srinagar were Bollywood's favourite locations.

Sometimes, during shooting of a film peculiar situation would arise like enthusiastic onlookers becoming unmanageable for a film crew, or a fan in order to meet or take a picture with a film star creating a scene. An interesting anecdote is narrated about the shooting of *Roti* in Pahalgam where actor Rajesh Khanna, who was then on the zenith of fame, had misbehaved with a local guy, Aziz Nartcur. The aggrieved person approached a prominent local man, a *zaildar*, who, not knowing enough about Khanna, confronted him on behalf of the guy and demanded to know why he had manhandled him. Unable to understand what the *zaildar* was saying in Kashmiri, Khanna in his trademark filmy style responded, "*Hamai to kuch bolna nahi aata*" (I cannot speak [Kashmiri]). Irritated, the *zaildar* retorted: "*Hata ma kar yim zanane warr*" (O, you! Stop behaving like a woman). When he was told by some onlooker that the film actor cannot speak Kashmiri, the *zaildar* shot back, "*Yeli ba zaildar aesith koshur bole amis kus prah chhu*" (When I, a *Zaildar*, can converse in Kashmiri why he can't?)

For a long time after the eruption of militancy and ban on cinema halls, film shooting in Kashmir suffered disruption. It were only few films, mostly on the subject of militancy, like *Mission Kashmir*, that were shot under tight security during 1990s. Other films with the same theme subsequently picturized in Kashmir and accused of furthering the State Narrative include *Dil Se, Lakshya, Sikandar and Shaury.* In recent years, some movies partly or substantially shot in Kashmir on subjects other than militancy include *Highway*, *Yeh Jawani Hai Diwani, Jab Tak Hai Jaan*, *Student of the Year*, *Saat Khoon Maaf*, *Rockstar*, *Lamhay* and *Yahaan*.

From Bakhshi Ghulam Mohammad to Omar Abdullah, politicians in power in Kashmir have always tried to woo Bollywood to visit and shoot in Kashmir. Some had developed close relation with film actors and actresses. Dr. Farooq Abdullah, for one, was known to have a warm rapport with movie stars and producers. He was reportedly offered a role by noted film producer B.R. Chopra opposite actress Salma Agha. A day before he was ousted from power on 2 July 1984 in the wake of revolt by a group of his legislators, he was pillion-driving actress Shabana Azmi on his motorcycle at Gulmarg. In 1960s, there was uproar about an alleged incident involving a leading film actress and some local politician. The matter was also raised in the State Legislative Assembly where a Member sought to know from the government the identity of the person involved. On 23 March 1964, participating in the discussion on grants for the Home Ministry, legislator Shiv Charan Gupta spoke about deteriorating law and order situation and chastity of women being "violated". Addressing the Chair, Gupta said, "I want to know the person who brought film actress Bina Rai here and where did she stay for that long period? The members who are not seated in treasury benches now, but were so previously, will suffer, rather are suffering, for such wicked and moral depravity."[347]

The allegations of misrepresentation of Kashmir by Bollywood are not new. For long, it has stereotyped Kashmiris. In a Hindi movie, Kashmir is either all about tourism without which its people would starve, or terrorism. There is no grey area. Earlier, if they were boat people or small time handicraft traders ever dying for a tourist to run their kitchen, now they are either gun wielding terrorists or a collection of unfaithful people, sponsored by a neighbouring country and ever disrespectful of India. The 2014 movie, *Haider,* co-written by a Kashmiri author and journalist, Basharat Peer, was an exception that avoided Indian nationalist narrative and portrayed the tragic human cost of the Kashmir Conflict, disappearances, torture and extrajudicial killings. One of the most talked about movies on Kashmir made recently, and shot in the Valley, *Haider* won several awards. Starring Shaid Kapoor and Tabu in lead roles, the film is a modern-day adaptation of William Shakespeare's tragedy, Hamlet, and an adaptation of Basharat Peer's *Curfewed Night*, set amidst Kashmir in turmoil. Director of the film, Vishal Bhardwaj, told the Indian Express on 27 October 2014 that it was "the first film where we see Kashmir from the inside. I don't think we have made a mainstream film about the issue."

People wedded to tradition and cultural values have often spoken about negative impact of films on Kashmir society. Apart from opposing the opening of new cinema halls—the *Naz Cinema* was not allowed operation for a long time—newspaper columns were used to express anguish over 'bad influence' of movies, especially on young generation. Opposition was also voiced against 'wrong depiction' of Kashmir and its people. When film *Begum* was screened in a Srinagar theatre in 1947, the *Kashmir* in a column titled, *Ye Kashmiriyun ki Gairat,* castigated the movie for "portraying Kashmiri women in a bad light".[348] The conservative society did not take very kindly the image of a Kashmiri girl openly romancing with a young boy. The newspaper alleged that the movie depicted Kashmiris as "more uncivilized than the African Negroes".[349] The newspaper alleged that the movie challenged self-esteem of the people, and demanded the Film Censor Board of the State to ban it, recalling that Shouri Film Pictures had earlier made a similar film which was banned in the State after the Editor *Martand*, Prem Nath Kanna, led a campaign against it. On 21 September 1939, Dr. Balram Das moved a resolution in the *Praja Sabha* recommending that "boys and girls between the ages of five and 18 be prohibited from attending the Cinema."[350] Rejecting the resolution, Prime Minister Gopalaswami Ayyangar argued that in modern times there were several films necessary for the education of children and if certain kind of cinema films has to be shut out then it should be prohibited for all people irrespective of their age.

During 1970s, when cinema and television had made deep inroads into the culture of Kashmir, voices of concern were raised on weakening social norms. Women going to cinema in a large number were specifically targeted. It was during this period that Molvi Mohammad Sultan, nicknamed the *Slacks Molvi,* with a cane in his hand would appear on the Maulana Azad Road to admonish and chase college girls away for wearing slacks, a skin tight leg-wear. This happened for several days before he was taken into custody by the police. Poet and educationist, Ghulam Ali Shaheed Salmani, captured the public mood against 'erosion of social values' in his long poem, *Naev Bochhi* (New Appetite) whose opening stanza reads:

> *Naev bochhi laejmetch az chhi zamanas waqtan bronh kun kor parwaaz*
> *Mael karaan az neichvein paelish kori chhi bawaan majen raaz*
> *Hayihik parde wudith geyi London zulfan duh dith geyi maikraaz*
> *Gare chha akh woen kus kati tchhandoan, Neelam kaale te subhan Naaz*
>
> (The world is struck by a new hunger; the times have moved ahead
> A father shoe-shines son's boots; mother confides in her daughter

Veils of modesty have flied to London; scissors have chopped-of toupee
Too many homes, where would one look out for someone,
It is today the *Neelam*, tomorrow the *Naaz*)

In 1989, amid rising wave of armed insurgency, a militant outfit, *Allah Tigers*, issued a warning to the owners of liquor shops and cinema halls to immediately wind up their businesses in Kashmir. The outfit's chief, Pir Nooruddin alias Air Marshal Noor Khan, attacked some liquor shops in the city, seizing and destroying crates of liquor. There were also bomb blasts targeting some cinema halls. Amid scare and serious security threat, all the cinema houses closed down on 1 January 1990. Nine years later, the Jammu & Kashmir Government gave huge monetary incentives to the owners for reopening their cinema halls. The government was desperate to sell the reopening of the cinemas as Kashmir's return to normalcy. Three cinema halls—*Broadway, Neelam* and *Regal*—reopened albeit for a brief time. The reopening of the cinema halls did not evoke much response. People were scared of visiting a movie theatre despite tight security arrangements. On 24 September 1999, the *Regal Cinema* reopened with a Sunny Deol and Mahima Chowdhary starrer, *Pyar Koyi Khel Nahi* when a grenade was thrown at the cinema, killing at least one person and injuring many. The cinema hall downed its shutters. Later, ownership of the *Regal Cinema* changed hands and the new owner pulled down the building to pave way for construction of a shopping complex. The *Broadway Cinema* located in a high security zone, was the first after the *Regal Cinema* to shut down. The cinema hall has since been demolished and a new commercial complex built on the site. The *Neelam Cinema* remained functional for some time but ultimately closed down during the widespread civil unrest in 2010.

Since then, it is curtains down for cinema halls in Kashmir.

7
Kashmir to Ka'ba

In olden times, travel from Kashmir to Makkah was arduous and time consuming. Very few people would embark upon the pilgrimage due to tough journey and poor economic condition. Some resolute and devout people, though, would undertake the journey on foot travelling through Afghanistan, Iran and Iraq. Haji Ali Joo Katju of Nalbandpora was one such pilgrim from Kashmir who was known to have travelled to Makkah on foot few hundred years ago. Like him, Noor Shah Qadri of Dangarpora, Eidgah in Srinagar travelled on foot to perform Haj in the distant past. About 80 years back, Mohammad Sultan from central Kashmir village of Chhatargam also achieved this feat and returned after a long time. Yet another pedestrian pilgrim was Abdur Rehman, later *Imam* of a local mosque at Zampa Kadal, who had performed Haj in 1930s. He had stayed in Medinah for ten years, worked as a sweeper there and returned to Kashmir in 1948 along with migrating Muslim Tibetans.[351]

There are many interesting stories of old times about people from Kashmir going on the Haj pilgrimage and coming back after years. If a pilgrim did not return in a year or two he was presumed dead and the family would perform his last rites in absentia. In certain cases, a 'dead pilgrim' would suddenly come home walking one day. Mohammad Rajab Saqqa of Breyikujen in Srinagar returned years after his last rites had been performed. His family members were pleasantly shocked to see him alive. It looks like that many people who went for Haj preferred to settle down in the holy land. Nawab Mustafa Khan Shaifta, Urdu poet and a contemporary of Mirza Ghalib, who left for

Haj on 2 March 1839, mentions Kashmiris among the people of "different countries who have settled down in Makkah."[352]

For a long time, sea voyage remained the main mode of travel for South-Asian Haj pilgrims. A century ago, the embarkation points for sea-route pilgrims were Karachi and Calcutta (Kolkata). Bombay (Mumbai) was added later. Pilgrims from Kashmir would take the Karachi route and arrive there by travelling through Punjab. This practice continued till the Partition of India in 1947. The road distance between Srinagar and Karachi was 611 km less than between Srinagar and Bombay and Karachi was 589 nautical miles closer to Jeddah than Bombay. The pilgrims carried no passports. Their travel document was a Pilgrim Pass issued by the concerned Deputy Commissioner or by the Port Haj Committee against a payment of ₹ 8, if the pilgrim failed to bring it from hometown.[353] Likewise, if a pilgrim was not inoculated at the place of his origin, he was vaccinated by a doctor of the Karachi Municipality before boarding a ship.

In 1936, an official communiqué on sailing schedule of pilgrims' ships was issued in Srinagar for the guidance of Haj pilgrims. The communiqué provided information on three ships named S.S. Jehangir, S.S. Islami and S.S. Alavi, owned by Messrs Turner, Morison and Company Ltd. operating from Bombay and Karachi.[354] As given out in an advertisement issued by the Mughal Line (The Bombay and Persia Steam Navigation Co. Ltd.) in 1937, there were other Haj pilgrim ships like S.S. Rehmani, S.S. Akbar and S.S. Rizwani operating from the two port cities.[355] During the sea voyage, pilgrims were supplied with cooked food as cooking on board by passengers was strictly prohibited. A pilgrim was supplied with morning tea, breakfast, luncheon, afternoon tea and dinner. Unlike first and second class passengers, deck pilgrims were required to express at the time of buying their tickets preference between rice and *chapati* and whether they would have dry fish with vegetable dish.

Articles of food were also made available to pilgrims on payment of extra charges. A fowl with gravy cost one rupee and seven annas each, mutton korma and kofta three annas a plate, biryani seven annas a plate and a shaami kebab nine pies each. A boiled egg was sold at an anna and six pies, fried egg two annas and three pies, curry and rice six annas per plate, rice one anna and six pies a plate, *halwa* (pudding) three annas a plate and tea without milk nine pies a cup and with milk an anna.[356] A cup of coffee with milk cost two annas. An orange was sold at one anna and six pies and an apple at two annas. It may be in place to recall that before 1957 when India shifted to decimalized currency, 16 annas would make a rupee and 12 pies an anna. All cooks and attendants employed on board the ship were Muslims. Deck pilgrims had to provide their own plates, cups and other receptacles in which food was served. Water from 'No-waste taps' was allowed to be taken in a day four times of two hours duration each. The official communiqué on the sailing schedule for Haj pilgrims was refused to be published in Kashmir by the *Martand* and the *Kashmir Times* unless the government issued it as paid advertisement. The return fare with food charged by Messrs Turner, Morison and Company Ltd. from Karachi and Bombay was ₹ 602 and ₹ 626 for the first class pilgrims, ₹ 427 and ₹ 451 for the second class pilgrims and ₹ 172 and ₹ 178 for the deck pilgrims, respectively. The Mughal Line (The Bombay & Persia Steam Navigation Co. Ltd.) information brochure of 1937 shows a uniform increase of ₹ 2 and anna four in the fare of all classes.[357] The return air fare from Bombay to Jeddah was ₹ 1500.[358]

Post-1947, Haj pilgrims from Kashmir would leave and return together on a single day. They travelled in buses from Srinagar to Pathankot, a surface distance of 427 kms. From there, they would board train to Bombay and then sail to Jeddah. Till few decades back, the number of women pilgrims from Kashmir was fewer. The situation has changed and their number is steadily increasing. The number of women pilgrims performing Haj through the aegis of the State Haj Committee was 2549 in 2015; 2644 in 2016; 3332 in 2017 and 3745 in 2018. At one point in time, women in Kashmir were reluctant to submit their photographs for travel documents as taking a lady's picture did not carry social approval. In 1937, Amir Gul Khan from Anantnag tehsil submitted an application to the Governor of Kashmir seeking passport for his mother, Gul Bibi, wife of Sarwar Khan Pathan to go on Haj pilgrimage with two other women who had already obtained travel documents and were now "anxiously waiting" for her.[359] Khan was asked to produce a photograph of his mother to complete formalities. In response, he informed the Governor that her mother was a "*pardah nisheen aurat*" (veil observing lady) and since taking picture of a woman was not allowed in the family, he cannot submit her photograph. "Attested documents would be submitted, nevertheless", he pleaded.

There was a time during 1950s-60s when *muallims* from Saudi Arabia would come to Kashmir to book accommodation for Haj pilgrims in Makkah and Medinah. A *muallim*, literally meaning a teacher, was a Saudi national who owned residential property in the two holy cities and rented it out to the pilgrims with provision for food also. He would also act as pilgrims' guide. One such *muallim*, Zainul Aabideen, had cultivated quite an influence in the Valley. He would arrive ahead of the Haj time and register prospective pilgrims. To ensure maximum publicity, he distributed leaflets at important shrines and mosques.

The departure and return of Haj pilgrims used to be an occasion of festivity in Kashmir. Pilgrims were taken in processions from their homes to the Tourist Reception Centre amid shouting of religious slogans. Enthusiastic children in large numbers joined these processions to raise and respond slogans at a full pitch. Women of the family and neighbourhood would shower candies on a pilgrim once he stepped out of his home. In cases where family members could afford they travelled to Pathankot to bid a pilgrim adieu there. Festivity was also observed in villages and towns of Kashmir at the time of bidding farewell to and receiving Haj pilgrims. On the return of pilgrims, welcome arches were erected and a feast held by their families for relatives and neighbours. Immediate relatives would also invite the pilgrim to sumptuous meals before he left for Haj. In 1972, the Jammu Railway Station was commissioned and the rail travel for a Haj pilgrim from Kashmir began from there instead of Pathankot.

Till recently, Kashmiri pilgrims would take with them rice, dried vegetables, mixed spice cakes, chili and turmeric powder, salt, dried fish, green tea leaves and pickle to have homely food while being away from home. Some chronic smokers also carried tobacco and *hookahs* with them. Mercifully, that practice has stopped now. The pilgrims carried light bedding and a large steel trunk filled with clothes and food items, which they watched over all the time. During return journey, the steel trunk would carry different gifts for family members and relatives which generally included dates, beads, praying rugs, pieces of dry soil of Medinah believed to have curing properties, perfume, pocket and wrist watches, *kamkhwab* cloth, kohl, umbrellas, transistor cum tape recorders and video cassette recorders (VCRs). Unlike now when only five liters per pilgrim are allowed, there was no limit prescribed for carrying *Zamzam* water and pilgrims would bring large canisters of the holy water.

Earlier, on their journey to Makkah, pilgrims would reach Bombay weeks before sail. The wait could extend for as long as 20 days during which time formalities were completed and tickets booked. A long queue was seen at the booking centre and since most of the pilgrims were illiterate or modestly literate, filling of forms and other formalities took long time to complete. Most of the pilgrims in the queue would return to the Saboo Sidiq Musafir Khana, named after a philanthropist who died at a young age of 26, to come again next day. The process would continue till all passengers were booked and the ship was ready for sail. Departure time printed on the ticket meant nothing as no ship ever left Bombay without postponing its departure several times and, in certain cases, pilgrims were made to wait longer than a month. In 1994, when the last ship carrying Haj pilgrims sailed from Bombay, the total number of pilgrims from all over India, taking both air and sea route, was 25,685. Of these, 4650 had opted for sea travel.[360]

Communication system being very primitive with near non-existent telephony, a pilgrim would be in touch with his family only through a letter which took weeks, if not months, to reach its destination. In the age of mobile telephony and social networking applications like the *Whatsapp* and *IMO* where a pilgrim even relays live to family and friends his circumambulation of the Ka'ba or paying obeisance at the Green Dome in Medinah, it is difficult to imagine today that pilgrims would virtually go incommunicado for months. In certain cases, communication received by the family would cause grief and anguish when the sender had meant to convey good news. In early 1970s, after long wait at Bombay when the day of departure finally arrived, Dost Mohammad of Uri sent a two-word telegram—"Sailing today"—to his home. The telegram received by the family read "Ailing today".[361] The news caused concern and anguish at home. A member of the family was rushed to Bombay to take care of the sick pilgrim. When the person arrived in the port city he came to know that Dost Mohammad, as other pilgrims, had since departed for Jeddah.

In 1957, new rules were laid down for facilitation of Haj pilgrims. The shipping companies were asked to publish the tentative departure schedule six to nine months in advance and the final schedule at least 15 days ahead of the departure.[362] Bookings were ordered to be started with the publication of the tentative schedule. The pilgrims were directed to provide all personal details with their applications. An amount of ₹ 100 was to be deposited with the application in the case of each adult and ₹ 50 in the case of a minor pilgrim. The pilgrims were asked to book their luggage at the Tourist Reception Centre a day before their departure and, on the day of leaving, reach the Polo Ground early in the morning from where they had to board buses and set out for the holy journey. Pilgrims arriving in Bombay without booking their seats were required to register themselves with shipping companies as intending pilgrims on a payment of fee of ₹ 10 and attach their photograph with their application. Pilgrims who had already booked their seats were required to buy their tickets at least three days before their ship left the Bombay port.

According to a government notification issued in 1958, the departure of Haj pilgrims from Srinagar that year was scheduled for 29 May.[363] They were advised to deposit their luggage with Mohammad Yusuf Rafiqi, Haj Clerk, at the Tourist Reception Centre on 28 May between 10 A.M. and 4 P.M. and reach the Polo Ground at 6.30 A.M. the next day. They were also advised to report at the office of the Chief Secretariat, Political

Department, Shergarhi on 25 May to pay the balance fare of ship, bus and rail.[364] The notification was issued by the Secretary Haj Committee, Dwarika Nath. The sea-route pilgrims travelling in cabin or first class were required to submit Income Tax certificate at the time of buying a ticket and could carry with them currency up to ₹ 3400. The deck class passengers were exempted from Income Tax certificate and the currency limit for them was ₹ 2400.[365]

Fazil Kashmiri, poet and a teacher by profession who later rose to the heights of literary fame, was one of the 141 pilgrims, including 25 women, from Kashmir who performed Haj in 1958.[366] There were two infants also in the group. On 29 May which happened to be a Thursday, the pilgrims reached the Tourist Reception Centre early in the morning where a large number of people, including relatives, acquaintances and keen onlookers, from different parts of Kashmir had assembled to see them off.[367] The pilgrims were garlanded. At 8.15 A.M. when the buses started moving, the air was rent with slogans. People stood in two rows to pave way for the moving buses and waived at the pilgrims, praying for their safe journey, sound health and successful completion of the pilgrimage. The caravan of pilgrim buses reached Anantnag at 10 A.M. and Qazigund at 10.30 A.M. Haji Mohammad Amin, an employee of the recently constituted State Haj Committee, accompanied the pilgrims.[368] Enroute, groups of enthusiastic people were waiting for them along the road under heavy showers. They greeted them and, in reverence, kissed their hands. The pilgrims reached Jammu by 7 P.M. and stayed for the night in a traveler's inn at Talab Khatikan. Next day, they were taken in a procession to the bus stand where they boarded buses for Pathankot. They spent the night at the Pathankot Railway Station and the train chugged off at 5.30 in the morning. During the train journey, many pilgrims cooked their food. On their arrival at Bombay on 2 June, the pilgrims were received, among others, by Haji Ghulam Ahmad Pardesi Kashmiri, a Bombay based Kashmiri trader. From the Railway Station, they were taken to Saboo Sidiq Musafir Khana, the halting place for pilgrims in the port city, where they stayed till 9 June. During their halt at Bombay, the pilgrims purchased umbrellas, *ahram* (unstitched cloth worn by pilgrims during the five days of Haj), dry milk, hand operated fans, charcoal, beads, buckets and fruit.

After luggage check and customs clearance, the pilgrims sailed for Jeddah on 9 June in S.S. Rizwani captained by B.M.J. Macklanahan. Most of the pilgrims travelling by sea for the first time felt bouts of nausea and some vomited out their breakfast. During sea journey, a pilgrim was served morning tea with biscuit, lunch and dinner each comprising a plateful of mutton or vegetable, pickle and *dal*, and tea and pudding in the afternoon. By 13 June, the pilgrims recovered from sea sickness. Congregational prayers were held five times a day after *adhan* was said on a microphone. Later, *muallims* would deliver religious sermons explaining various elements of the Haj and how to perform those. The ship arrived at the port of Aden at the crack of dawn on 16 June and the pilgrims had the first sight of sea shore and the barren mountain-line of the city after a week since their departure from Bombay. The ship halted at the port for six hours during which the pilgrims were not allowed to disembark. Here, fresh drinking water was loaded in the ship and many small boats filled with merchandise came near the ship to sell goods to the pilgrims. At the port of Aden, pilgrims posted letters to their families in Kashmir.

Three days after their departure from Aden, the pilgrims arrived in Jeddah on 19 June. Describing the city of those days, Fazil writes [translation]:

> This is Jeddah. A dazzling city sits here on the sea shore with houses like those in Bombay. Not a single house is *kacha*; all are built in solid masonry. The buildings are 8-9 stories high. The roads are wide and metalled on which hundreds of cars move one after the other. The *ikkas* and *tongas* are not in use here. However, the donkey-driven *chhakras* are available everywhere for hire. A *chhakra* driver usually sits on the back of donkey that pulls it. The fare of the *chhakra* is higher than that of an exquisite motor taxi. Like in Lal Chowk where *tongas* move around here and there in search of passengers, superb motor cars run around in Jeddah to lift

> passengers. All the markets in the city look ambulant.[369] ...In Hedjaz, Coca Cola is available in sealed bottles. It is like a black coloured soda water and tastes very sweet. It saves a Haji from heat and thirst. It is very useful and chilly. You can drink it as much as you want. A bottle costs a little over half a Riyal.[370]

The pilgrims arrived in Makkah at midnight. After performing Haj, they left for Jeddah to proceed to Medinah—some by bus, some by motor taxi and a few like Fazil by air. On return, he and 24 of his batch mates sailed from Jeddah in S.S. Muzaffari and after 12 days of voyage reached Bombay on 1 August. Others returned by S.S. Rizwani. On 6 August, Fazil reached home. Later, he came up with a useful and comprehensive Urdu language Haj Guide, *Tasveer-i-Haj*, with interesting details of the travel and hand drawn sketches. He considered ₹ 1500 sufficient for moderate expenses of the pilgrimage and gave point to point expenditure on transport from Srinagar to Makkah and Medinah, and back. Goods costing more than ₹ 500 carried by a returning pilgrim were subjected to custom duty at Bombay. Within this limit, a pilgrim could bring home one wrist and pocket watch each, a fountain pen, a Gramophone, toys, *Zamzam* water, utensils, pictures of holy places, religious books for personal use, soil of Medinah, medicines for personal use costing not more than ₹ 30, personal bedding, four to six silk or cotton shawls, 42 yards of *zamzam*-washed cloth, beads costing up to ₹ 25, dates, a camera costing up to ₹ 75, a bicycle, a sewing machine, a traveler's type writer, 100 cigarettes, 25 cigars, 250 *bidis*, half a pound tobacco, a cigarette case, a binocular and three praying mats including a used one. Import of gold was banned and a violator was arrested and prosecuted. In 1957, some pilgrims had been jailed for committing this offence.[371] Compared to 12 days in 1958 when Fazil performed Haj, the sea journey in 1967 took only 8 days. In all, it would take a pilgrim from Kashmir about three months to return from the holy pilgrimage. Pir Abdul Gani, Editor Weekly *Dilair*, who performed Haj in 1967, left his home in Sopore on 2 January. His sea journey from Bombay began during the intervening night of 17 and 18 January and the ship reached Jeddah on 26

January. After performing the Haj, the return sail from Jeddah started on 31 March and culminated at Bombay on 8 April. Gani reached home on 11 April.

A positive trend observed in recent years is that a large number of people prefer to perform Haj in young age as compared to earlier times when only aged and often physically weak people embarked upon the pilgrimage. A person would think of performing Haj only after he had retired from service or business, built a house, financially settled his children, married them off and had now no gainful work to do. It was then that his family members, friends or acquaintances would persuade him to go for Haj. Many who had never ventured out of the Valley were scared of sea or air travel. Some years back, one such pilgrim when his plane had a rough flight due to bad weather sank in his seat, frightened and sweating, and was head murmuring, "*Noshi kaer saezish*", meaning that his daughter-in-law who had insisted on his going for Haj had actually conspired to get him killed in an air crash! Some aged pilgrims would nurse the desire to die and be buried in the holy land. Any pilgrim passing away there was considered very fortunate. Yet his family members would mourn and grieve on receiving the news of his demise.

On his return from the holy pilgrimage, a *haji* would narrate for months and years anecdotes, spiritual experiences and travel stories. There always were eager and interested listeners. Habibullah Wani of Sonawar who had performed Haj during 1960s narrated tales of the pilgrimage over a long period of time at a local saloon and people would wait for him to take them on a virtual journey to the holy land. In many cases, Haji became the surname of a person and his family after his return from Haj. There is to this day a family at Chhatargam, a central Kashmir village, with the surname Haji whose one of the members had performed Haj eight decades ago. Ramzan Haji of Sonawar had never undertaken the pilgrimage. His grandfather or great grandfather had. Hence the surname!

Makkah and Medinah being the cities of reverence for Muslims across the world, some pilgrims removed their footwear while walking through streets and passages Prophet Muhammad (peace be upon him) is believed to have set his feet on. In early 1960s, when Ghulam Nabi Naqash of Malik Sahab, Safa Kadal returned from the pilgrimage, his neighbours were shocked to see his feet in bad shape—wide cracks in his heels and eyes sunken deep into sockets. When Haji Mohammad Jamal, a senior neighbour, asked the reason of his run down condition, Naqash told him that on his arrival at Jeddah he had thrown his slippers into the sea and travelled barefoot through Makkah and Medinah. Some pilgrims had pleasant encounters that they would have never imagined. Habibullah Panzoo from Naid Kadal in old Srinagar city who performed Haj in 1966 could not have asked for more when, to his great joy, he met Mirwaiz Molvi Mohammad Yusuf Shah there. After enquiring from Panzoo about his place of residence the Mirwaiz placed his family and told him how he had relished sumptuous food, especially the dish of spinach, many a time at his home. A diehard follower of the Mirwaiz who like thousands others had not reconciled to his separation as he was living in exile in Muzaffarabad since 1947, could not control his emotions and cried, "*Ba haz lagai balayi*" (I will sacrifice my life for you).

8

Changing Place Names

On 24 October 2018, the Jammu & Kashmir Government inaugurated in Srinagar a multi-storey library building named after the third generation Dogra ruler, Pratap Singh. Here was a former autocrat who is remembered in Kashmir for all the wrong reasons and the government dedicated to his memory a multi-crore Libraries' Complex to deify him 71 years after his dynasty's rule was abolished. The building does not house only the 19th-century SPS Library named after him which was shifted here from the SPS Museum building. At least three other public libraries of Kashmir—the very rich Research Library (Hazratbal) whose collection includes 5824 rare manuscripts in different languages and scripts including Sanskrit, Persian, Arabic, Balti, Hindi, Sharda, and Kashmiri, the City Centre Library (Karan Nagar) and the District Library Srinagar (Habba Kadal)—were amalgamated with the SPS Library and housed in the new building. The official handout released on the occasion mentioned the collection of the newly inaugurated SPS Library as "more than one lakh and fifty thousand books" which, in fact, is the total collection of the four public libraries. The government's decision to name the building and four libraries after Pratap Singh is irrespective of local sentiment and the fact that a proposal to name the building after an illustrious son of Kashmir was already with the government.

On 10 August 2011, Director Libraries & Research, Jammu & Kashmir sent to the government a proposal for naming the upcoming building after "some very distinguished personality of Kashmir in the field of literature and academics".[372] The letter identified the 16th-century scholar, author and poet Shaikh

Yaqoob Sarfi, as the person after whom the building should be named, given his "enormous contribution to learning and scholarship and to honour this illustrious son of Kashmir". Sarfi, it may be recalled, occupies a place of prominence in the history of medieval Kashmir and had acquired international reputation for his scholarship. He had also set up a huge personal library in Srinagar. The proposal was referred to the government committee on naming of public buildings and roads where it was pointed out that since the building was still under construction a decision would be taken after its completion. Maulana Anwar Shah Kashmiri, the unrivalled 20th-century Islamic scholar, was another name proposed for the Libraries' Complex.

In the meanwhile, the building was thrown open without the originally approved art gallery, auditorium, exhibition hall, internet café and researchers' cabins—facilities, as was intended, to make it a meeting place of cultural and intellectual offerings on the pattern of the India International Centre, New Delhi. The government showed haste in merging four major public libraries of Srinagar into one and name them after the late ruler of Jammu & Kashmir who was accused of practicing discrimination against a particular community."[373]

That brings us face to face with a more serious issue of changing place names—a favourite tool in the hands of unpopular regimes and men at the helm of affairs to distort history. Kashmir is not new to distortion and change in its place names. It is an old story. The very name 'Kashmir' is a misnomer, never accepted by natives as the name of their land. A Kashmiri calls it Kasheer, and himself and his language as Koshur instead of Kashmir, Kashmiri people and Kashmiri language, respectively. However, we are told of Kashap Rishi, a mythical character who lived for "thousands of years and spent, at least, one millennium in overpowering and eliminating demon Jaladbav"[374] who devoured human beings. Rishi also drained the water of the *Satisar* and made the place suitable for human habitation. An extension of this account is that the name Kashmir is a combination of two words '*Ka*' and '*Smira*' meaning 'a water body evaporated by the force of wind, resulting in the emergence of land mass' thus known as '*Kasmir*' or '*Kashmir*'. What is of importance, however, is that Kashmiri language recognizes the land by the name *Kasheer*, which according to scholar and author, Prof. Margoob Banihali is "a single word and not a blend of two words contrary to *Kashap-mar* and *Ka-smira*".[375] He refers to a 'universal principle' of a place and its people getting their names from the language originated from and spoken in that place, like German (a particular language), German (an individual or race speaking German language), Germany (land of German speaking people); French (a particular language), French (an individual or race speaking French language), France (land of French speaking people); English (a particular language), English (an individual or race speaking English language), England (land of English speaking people); and Nepali (a particular language), Nepali (an individual or race speaking Nepali language), Nepal (land of Nepali speaking people). Applying this principle to *Kasheer*, we have Koshur (a particular language), Koshur (an individual or race speaking Koshur language), Kasheer (land of Koshur speaking people).

An old and iconic place in Kashmir several times subjected to name change is the famous hill in Srinagar crowned with an ancient stone temple. In recent years, a section of the people have alleged that the hill's name was 'Islamized' from *Shankaracharya* to *Takht-i-Sulaiman* or *Koh-i-Sulaiman*. Historical evidence, however, does not corroborate the allegation. The name of the hill and the temple on its summit as *Takht-i-Sulaiman* predates by centuries its now officially used name, *Shankaracharya*. Does that mean *Takht-i-Sulaiman* was its original name? Certainly not. Such presumption would be erroneous, for this name is not available in history prior to Muslim rule over Kashmir, except in a legend about Prophet Solomon or Sulaiman visiting Kashmir and delivering its people of the great inundation. The name of the hill and the temple as *Shankaracharya* is relatively a recent development. The 12th-century chronicler and author of *Rajatarangini*, Kalhana, mentions the hill as *Gopa* and the shrine on its summit as *Gopadari*.[376] He assigns this name to the hill on the premise that the temple on its summit was constructed by Gopaditya whom he identifies as a ruler of ancient Kashmir. Before Kalhana, however, Pandit Ratnagar, narrating the visit of Sandhiman (Solomon) and his descent on the hill, mentions its name as *Jeetlark*.[377] So, those who say that the name of the hill was changed from *Shankaracharya* to *Takht-i-Sulaiman* are in the wrong. That brings to the fore the fact that the hill was known by different names in different periods of time, of which, at least, two—*Jeetlark* and *Gopa*—are recorded in history. The latest name change is from *Takht-i-Sulaiman* to *Shankaracharya*, not the vice versa, and it happened during the last years of the Sikh rule (1819-46).[378] For long, this name change did not find public acceptance. One could observe this from writings of foreign travellers or men in employment of the Dogra rulers, and archival papers which mention the hill as *Takht-i-Sulaiman*. It was only post-1947 when the new name was officially popularized.

In recent years, we have often come across allegations that place names in Kashmir have been Islamized, especially since the eruption of militancy in late 1989, to erase its Hindu past. In support of the allegation, the often-quoted instance one comes across is Islamabad, a South Kashmir town, said to have been originally known as Anantnag. The allegation, however, does not sit comfortably with history. The town bears the name of Islamabad since it was founded during the Mughal rule over Kashmir. Islam Khan, one of the governors of Aurangzeb (1658-1707 AD), had laid out a garden here for the pleasure of the king. The latter named the place as Islamabad after the governor. More than two centuries later, the town was rechristened as Anantnag during the Dogra rule (1846-1947 AD). We do not have any historical evidence to suggest that a town with its name as Anantnag existed in ancient Kashmir. The 6th-7th century *Nilmatapurana* or the 12th-century *Rajatarangini* do not mention any place or shrine with this name. Aurel Stein who minutely studied ancient texts including the *mahatmyas* while translating and writing annotations on the *Rajatarangini*, finds in them no *tirtha* by the name of Anantnag, the supposed shrine after which the town might have gotten its name. "Of the town, however," he writes, "I cannot find any old notice, and it is in all probability, as its Mohammadan name implies, a later foundation."[379] That Anantnag as the name of the town in south Kashmir is not traceable in history earlier to the Dogra rule is further corroborated by a Memorandum submitted by the then *Mirwaiz* of Kashmir, Molvi Mohammad Yusuf Shah, to Maharaja Hari Singh in 1941 where he points out rechristening of Islamabad as Anantnag. The *Mirwaiz* writes:

> Sir, you can very well imagine what we feel when Islamabad is changed into Anantnag, Hindi names are allotted to Palaces, Aga Syed Hussain and General Samandar Khan, etc. are converted to 'Thakur Hussain' and 'Thakur Samandar Khan', the legislative body is called '*Praja Sabha*' and its members '*Sad*', and all possible efforts are being made to popularize Hindi and Devnagri Script.[380]

In spite of the Dogra Government changing and patronizing its name, the town continued to be mentioned as Islamabad in official maps and correspondence. Even the then high ranking officials in the Government of India referred to it as such. One such instance is a letter written to Maharaja Pratap Singh by Sir B. Blood, Lieutenant General Punjab Forces who was in Kashmir in 1905. On his way to Achhabal in south Kashmir for game shooting, he wrote a letter to the Maharaja from 'Islamabad' on 16 October thanking him "for your kind arrangements for our visit" and "looking forward to the pleasure of seeing you again at Jammu on the occasion of H.R.H. the Prince of Wales's visit to you in December."[381]

Notwithstanding a strong historical background to the contrary, there was always official pressure on people to use Anantnag instead of Islamabad, as the name of the south Kashmir town. During 1960s and 70s, the State Government bullied private transporters to use Anantnag as destination name on Islamabad bound buses but the Kashmir Motor Drivers' Association refused to succumb to the pressure. The Association forced to drop Islamabad as the name of the town, replaced it with Khannbal, a place little distance short of the main town of Islamabad. However, the Government Transport buses had no such option. During early years of militancy and crackdown across the Valley, passengers who would say 'Islamabad' in response to a query on their destination or residential place were often thrashed.

Gulmarg, the famous hill station in north Kashmir, is another place about which one comes across allegations, mostly in on-line literature, that its name *Gauri Marg* (Path of Gauri) was changed by the 16th century ruler of Kashmir, Yusuf Shah Chak, to Gul Marg. The suggestion belies poor acquaintance with the local language and history. The name Gulmarg is a combination of two Persian words *gul* and *marg*. The former means *flower* and the latter *a meadow*. Together, the two mean the 'Meadow of Flowers' which the place is literally known to be for its rich flora, especially wild flowers. Mughal ruler Jahangir is known to have collected 21 different varieties of flowers here. The two words are also used in Kashmiri language and literature to convey the same meanings. The *Kaeshir Dictionary* (Kashmiri Dictionary) gives the meaning of *gul* as *posh* (flower); an imprint of flowers made on a cloth, etc.; *gul pholean* means coming into flower, *gul rukhsaar* means flower-face or beautiful.[382] Famous Kashmiri poet, Mehjoor's verse: '*Ha gulo tohi ma sa wuchhwan yaar myon*' (O flowers! Did you spot my beloved?), sums it up. The dictionary offers the meaning of *marg* as '*balas pethe kani sotur gaase meadaan*' (a highland meadow); *nai* (pasture).[383] Poets and writers of Kashmiri language have used the word to convey the same meaning. A verse of leading local poet of the 20th century, Dina Nath Nadim, in praise of Kashmir's beauty is a good example. He says, '*Sone seind sangar, rope koh maale, marge te baal chhi poshi posh*' (The peaks wear gold, the mountains are garlands of silver, the meadows and the hills are carpeted with flowers). There are several other hill stations in Kashmir like Sonamarg (Meadow of Gold) and Yusmarg (Meadow of Yus—short form of *yusman* or jasmine) named after different elements of nature rather than religious or mythical characters. No ancient narrative on Kashmir history, it may be recalled, identifies any place by the name of *Gauri Marg*.

Kashmiris as a people have generally exhibited lack of concern over changes or distortion in their place names or corrupting these to suit others' phonetic convenience. Such cultural distortion has received public approval by silence. One could understand a place name getting corrupted where it was difficult for a non-local ruler or visitor to pronounce it but where is the need for distorting Varmul to Baramulla, Panpar to Pampore, Pulwom to Pulwama, Vejibror to Bijbihara, Kopwor to Kupwara, Badgom to Budgam, Tulmul to Tulmula, Nayut to Nowhatta, Razay Kadal to Rajouri Kadal, Sovur to Soura, Nov Kadal to Nawa Kadal and Buchhwor to Buchhwara *et al.*, especially when Kashmiris in their speech use these names in their original form. The difficulty of the people from outside Kashmir in pronouncing Tsar-i-Sharief correctly should be no reason to distort the name of this revered town to Charar-i-Sharief. It is still better that some people, not versant with local language, mispronounce the name than change or distort it in official record. Every place name has a history behind it that needs to be preserved. Some years back, the daily *Greater Kashmir* had taken an initiative of using Varmul, instead of Baramulla, as the original name of an important north Kashmir town and district. The initiative, however, did not last long.

Rechristening villages for their awful names like Gyuer (faintness) to Noorpora (abode of light) in Tral or Gohpur (abode of cow dung) to Goharpur (abode of jewels) in Budgam district is a welcome step. It is also fine to name a new settlement after a politician irrespective of local aversion, like Indira Nagar in Srinagar. But the same cannot be said about renaming places or distorting their names with political or religious import. Such attempts are an assault to history and culture of a people and tantamount to snatching the identity of a place. Here, we take up only three places in the neighbourhood of each other within Srinagar district, whose names have been distorted in recent years, sadly, with official approval. These are Shivpora, Ram Munshi Bagh and Pantha Chowk.

Beginning with Shivpora, the locality is settled in the loop of the Jhelum River between Batwara and Sonawar. One recalls that it was known as Shopore, rhyming with Sopore. In old revenue record, like *Intikhab-i-Jamabandi* and state subject certificates, for instance of Mohammad Maqbool Wani issued on 19 January 1949, the place is recorded as 'Shopara'. The first recorded settlers of the 'village' are 'Wanis', followed by 'Bhats'. If one checks with any +70 year old resident of the area he will confirm its name as Shopore. The Census Report of India, 1941, Vol XXII, Jammu & Kashmir, Part III, on village tables and housing statistics, unambiguously mentions at page number 354 the place as 'Sho Pora'. The Report is an authentic official document to know the original name of the locality. The census was conducted during the reign of Maharaja Hari Singh and the report was printed under the supervision of J. Sharma, Superintendent, Ranbir Government Press, Jammu in 1943.

As regards Ram Munshi Bagh, the area was a large tract of open land, part of which was later converted into a cricket stadium, situated between the Amar Singh Club and the All Saints Church, at Sonawar on the right bank of the Jhelum. The land was known and entered in official records as Munshi Bagh, after a Munshi in the Dogra Darbar who enjoyed holding rights on the land. At the eastern end of the stadium is located a police station which was previously a *thana* known as Thana Munshi Bagh. One fine morning—somewhere during late 1970-early 1980s—there appeared a signboard on the building of the police station declaring its name as Police Station Ram Munshi Bagh. Nobody knows who enforced the change in the name of the place and why but it soon attained official recognition. Today, if you read or hear about the stadium or the police station, you will come across the name of the place as Ram Munshi Bagh.

Old records of the police station, if there was any left after the great deluge of 2014, would establish that the place was known as Munshi Bagh. However, there are enough archival documents available to confirm this. The Census Report of 1941 (page No. 354), referred to in the preceding, is one such document. Here are more: In 1915, the Pratap Singh Government published 'Report of the Committee on Grant of Land for Building Purposes', listing the beneficiaries with localities where land was allotted to them. Appendix 'K' of the Report at page number xlii mentions, in sequence, persons from serial number 1 to 14 who were allotted land in different pockets of Sonawar. At serial number 4 figures Aziz Din Kausa son of Kh. Samad Shah who was allotted '1 acre 7 kanals and

10 marlas' of land at 'Munshi Bagh'. The allotment followed communication from the Chief Minister under No. 2022 dated 25 June 1906.

Another supporting document is a letter written from his summer camp at Gulmarg by the British Resident to the government in Kashmir on 22 July 1904 wherein he conveys the Residency's "no objection to repairs to the roof of the shrine of Sayid Sahib, situated in Munshi Bagh, Srinagar". The shrine is located on the road separating Munshi Bagh from the shrine premises. Another documentary evidence is the 'List of Permanent European Residents in Kashmir' updated and published by the Hari Singh Government in 1937. At page number 2 of the List figures Mrs. H. Bromley whose residential address is recorded as "H.B. [House Boat on the Jhelum] 818, Opposite Munshi Bagh". At page number 5 figure Mrs. Houstan with residential address as "H.B. 261, Munshi Bagh", Mrs. A.H. Jonston, "H.B. 112, Munshi Bagh", Miss A.E. Johnson, "Bunglow No. 21, Munshi Bagh", Mrs. and Miss Lambert, "Munshi Bagh", and, at page number 7, Dr. and Mrs. E.F. Neve, "Munshi Bagh". In 1914, during a meeting of the Revenue Officers a decision was taken about "Plantation in Munshi Bagh"[384] which, again, points to the original name of the place.

Lastly, we take up Pantha Chowk, the name used to identify a locality situated between Beswan Hill and River Jhelum at km 8.8 on the Srinagar-Jammu Highway. It is important to note that the word 'chowk' is a post-1947 addition to the vocabulary of a Kashmiri after Srinagar's city centre, Amira Kadal, was renamed as Lal Chowk. The name Pantha Chowk began circulating in early 1990s and, as in other cases, quickly received official endorsement. Before this, the place was known as Pantchhokh which is a corrupted form of Paan Chhokh literally meaning 'a gust of water'. In old revenue record, the place is indeed mentioned as 'Paani Chhokh", a name apparently derived from its location on a river bank. It would be of interest to note that the names of two other places—Panpar and Pandrethan, literally meaning 'abode of water' and 'a place from where water can be seen', respectively—in its immediate up and downstream, also point to a connection with their location on the river bank. The syllable '*Pa'n*', Kashmiri equivalent of 'water', like *Pa'n Tsadar* (cascade of water or waterfall), is the basic part of "the string of [the three] identical place names".[385]

About the place name Pantchhokh, there is an anecdote from local folklore related to the trudges of the 14th-century saint and poet, Sheikh Nooruddin Wali, across Kashmir. The legend has it that when he reached this place and enquired of its name, he was told that the place is named Pantchhokh upon which the Sheikh in rhyme with the name, purportedly exclaimed, '*Koren dokh, noshan sokh*' (Daughters [of this place are] distressed and daughters-in-law happy). The name of the place as Pantchhokh, however, is evidenced from record. One can refer to a file from the Archives Repository Srinagar pertaining to the year Samvat 1993-94, corresponding to 1937-38 AD. The subject of the file from the office of the then Governor of Kashmir bearing number 258 (Part 1st), is 'R/S to Pantchokh-Khonmoh Road.' It is about instructions of the government on repair of this stretch of road in anticipation of Maharaja Hari Singh's visit to Tral for game shooting. Another important proof comes from a file, again, resting in the Archives Repository Srinagar bearing number 729 related to the year Samvat 1969 corresponding to 1933 AD. The file carries details of amount outstanding against various villages on account of *maalia*. At serial number 239 is listed village 'Pant Chhokh' with an outstanding of ₹ 1139 and paise six. It may not be too long before some enthusiastic etymologist comes up with linkage between Pant and the place, citing in his support the existence of G.B. Pant Children Hospital located 5.6 km downstream, foundation of which was laid in 1989.

In recent memory, a name change people have resisted was in 1973 when the Mir Qasim Government attempted to rechristen the Government College for Women, Maulana Azad Road as Jawaharlal Nehru Memorial College for Women. On 5 November that year, a function to announce the name change was organized at the college where the guest of honour was Sheikh Mohammad Abdullah who was then inching close to wrap up a deal with Nehru's daughter, Prime Minister Indira Gandhi, for his return to power two decades after his unceremonious sack in 1953. However, a fierce protest by students, during which Abdullah had to make a hasty retreat from the college gate, foiled the government plan. For the first time, slogans were raised against the 'most popular leader' of Kashmir and his retreating car was hit by several stones hurled by agitating students.[386]

9

Story of an Uptown Quarter

Shortly before his flight to Jammu in October 1947, Maharaja Hari Singh was known to have toyed with the idea of converting Sonawar, a quarter in uptown Srinagar, into a lake to accord a unique peculiarity to his palace, *Talay Manzil*, literally meaning the Abode of Luck, of sitting between two lakes, the other being the famed Dal Lake. There was a wetland at the eastern-southeaster extremity of Sonawar close to the meeting necks of the two hills of *Takht-i-Sulaiman* or *Shankaracharya* and *Beaswan*, visited by thousands of migratory birds every winter, which the Maharaja sought to expand and turn into an artificial lake. Unfortunately for him, Hari Singh could not hold on to his throne long enough to realize his dream and had to leave his Abode of Luck, as well as Kashmir, in haste to save his life in the face of the Tribal Attack. The wetland has since been filled and converted into a residential colony.

Literally meaning the Alcove of Gold, Sonawar is the civil lines of Srinagar, the capital city of Kashmir. It is nestled between the *Takht-i-Sulaiman* and the Jhelum River, four kilometers to the east of the city center. The area extends from the Burn Hall School adjacent to the mausoleum of Sayyid Yaqoob, popularly known as Sayyid Sahib's Ziarat, in the west to the erstwhile Broadway cinema, few hundred meters short of Batwara market, in the east. Once comprising three segments of Sonawar, Palpora and Bonamsar, it has since expanded eastward with the addition of new settlements like Iqbal Colony, Indira Nagar and Dar Mohalla on the either side of the Srinagar-Jammu Highway that runs through the area.

The story of Sonawar is old but it is difficult to say how old. We find a mention of Gopa Agrahar (Gupkar), an important segment of Sonawar and a foothill stretch from the office of the United Nations Military Observers Group for India and Pakistan (UNMOGIP) to the *Talay Manzil*, in a 12th-century text. We are told, Gopaditya, a king of ancient Kashmir, brought Brahmans from outside Kashmir and settled them there.[387] He granted them *agrahars* or dwelling units at the foothill. The place came to be known as Gopa Agrahar after the name of the hill at whose feet it is located. Over a period of time, the name Gopa Agrahar got corrupted to Gupkar. For Aurel Stein, the 19th-century explorer, Gupkar was "a considerable village"[388] while Walter Lawrence, Settlement Commissioner of Kashmir during the Dogra rule, too records Sonawar as a "village" as late as in 1895. On 1 April 1938, Maharaja Hari Singh, through his Command No. 93, defined the limits of the Badami Bagh Cantonment which included Sonawar, Bonamsar and Palpora. All civilian constructions were banned and repairs of existing buildings allowed only with prior permission of the Cantonment Magistrate. Later, Bonamsar was transferred to Srinagar Municipality, now Municipal Corporation. People have unpleasant memories of that period when if somebody wanted so much as to drive a nail in the wall of his house the hammer was wrapped in a cloth lest its sound attract the attention of an official of the Cantonment Authority. People were scared of even mud-washing their modest dwellings. At one point in time, Khawaja Ali Mohammad raised this issue in the *Praja Sabha* seeking an answer from the government why the Military Department was "strictly prohibiting" inhabitants from building houses when several officers had constructed their bungalows there recently. In response, the government only gave assurance that the complaint would be forwarded to the Military Department.

Sonawar of yesteryears was a captivating landscape—dense groves of *chinars* and willows, a prominent hill with an ancient temple on its summit in the north and a calm and lazy Jhelum flowing in the south with a walking mall, the Bund, along its right bank, cycling on which was strictly prohibited. The Bund was a favourite track for morning and evening walkers and the elite who loved strolling along the river bank under the cool shade of the *chinars*. Downstream from Shopore above the curve of the Jhelum near the Bakhshis to the Zero Bridge, beautifully decorated houseboats were lined up along the river bank and with flower pots tastefully spread in the frontage and on the decks. Being somewhat away from the hustle and bustle of the city, Sonawar was thronged by foreign visitors who preferred staying in houseboats on the Jhelum here or pitched tents in open area along the river bank. The Jhelum's water was clean and potable. Those were the times when houseboats were not moored in the Dal Lake.

The families whose houseboats were moored at Sonawar included Chapris, Buddoos, Badyaris, Tundas, Kalwathoos, Siahs, Darazs, Kolos and Khars. The Chapris have a long history in houseboat industry. The family patriarch, Mohammad Ibrahim Chapri, had a houseboat named *Europe* as early as in 1872. From then onwards, the different houseboats they owned included *Lizard, Helen, Rowallan, Hiawatha, Haifa* and *Neil Armstrong*. Among the prominent visitors to their houseboats were Sir Alexander Bull, the then Governor of Canada, Zulfikar Ali Bhuttoo who as a student visited Kashmir, bird watcher Robert Filming, and Sushila Nair, Mahatma Gandhi's close aide. Muhammad Ali Jinnah also visited the Chapris and had tea there. So did film actor Balraj Sahni. Other houseboats included *Miss England* of Kalwathoos, *Dawn, and Merry Dawn* of Tundas, *Prince of Kashmir* of Siahs, *Ritz* of Badyaris and *Catherine* of Kolos. Kashmir's first double-storey houseboat, *Viceroy,* also was moored at Sonawar. British scholar, and archaeologist, Percy Brown, is said to have stayed in the *Catherine*. Legendary film actor Dilip Kumar too has stayed in a houseboat of Kolos. Houseboat *Star of Zanjibar* was owned by an African. There was another houseboat of J.J. Flaycart, former British naval officer nicknamed as *Kokar Sahab* for raring chickens and selling eggs. He stamped each egg with the date it was laid, and had several hencoops on the river bank. An English lady, Miss O'Connell who always ate fish in the breakfast, had obtained on lease a building and some houseboats which she rented out to foreign tourists. Another European lady living on a houseboat of Patloos was known as *Cook Meem.*

In 1937, the Dogra Government published a list of over 150 'Permanent European Residents in Kashmir' along with their residential addresses.[389] Among those who had taken residences in different pockets of Sonawar included Dr. and Mrs. E.F. Neve, Mr. and Mrs. D.G. Cockburn, Ms. Cockburn, Ms. Douglas, Mrs. Freeman, Mrs. H.B. Houstan, Ms. L. Hughes, Mrs. Jones, Mrs. A.H. Jonston, Ms. A.E. Johnson, Mrs. and Ms. Lambert, Ms. Macleod, Ms. W. Malcom, Lt. Col. and Mrs. Marshal, General McCrea, Lt. Col. J.C.S. Oxley, Lady M. Roberts, Mrs. R.L. Sevenoaks, Mrs. H.B. Stuart, Mr. and Mrs. F.R.B. Spencer, R.D. Spencer, Mrs. C. Tennant, Mrs. M.C. Wall, Mrs. Walton, and Col and Ms. A.E. Ward.

During the Dogra rule, the expanse of open area along the course of the Jhelum for which Sonawar was known, and also mentioned in official record, as Sonawar Bagh, was used as a camping site by visiting English officers and entourage of *rajas* and *nawabs*. Senior resident Ghulam Mohammad Bhat recalls that a part of the area which now holds the Army's Holiday Home was also used for celebration of Maharaja Hari Singh's birthday where, after a public reception, he would ride a large State boat known as *paranda* for a river procession downstream to Chhatabal. Across the road, a large open field known as *Looel Bagh,* later taken over by the Army, was the playground where youth of the area played football and cricket. It was also the venue for a major entertainment event in 1965 when Farooq Khan exhibited his skills of non-stop week-long cycling—eating, bathing, changing clothes and performing different stunts while driving his bicycle on a defined circular track.[390] During the event, Mohammad Subhan alias Subil Bachhe recited Maulana Zafar Ali Khan's famous *naat* '*Wo shama ujaala jis ne kiya chalees baras tak garoon mai*' (The candle that lit up the darkness of the caves for forty years) before crossing over to Muzaffarabad where he later attained stardom as a singer. Inspired by Farooq Khan, a resident of Sonawar named Ali Mohammad Malik announced that he could also achieve this feat. The stage was set at the Bhagtuhund Bagh and Malik began weeklong non-stop cycling amid fanfare. Unfortunately, however, on the very next day the poor guy suffered urine blockage, fell seriously ill and had to be removed to a hospital.

The Sonawar Bazaar was a modest market with shops having a humble stock of provisions unlike today when these are filled with merchandise. Till 1960s, there were few grocery shops, two mutton shops, one or two vegetable shops, a pharmacist's shop, a cloth shop, a mustard oil shop, two bakery shops, a cobbler's shop and a cycle repair shop. Abdul Aziz Rather was a prominent shopkeeper and the postal address of everybody in the area. Each letter in Sonawar would arrive "care of shopkeeper Abdul Aziz Rather". In 1960s, he successfully fought election of the Cantonment Board. The celebration of his victory was an event long remembered by people of Sonawar.

Abdul Khaliq Hajam, or *Woste Khaeliq* as he was known, possessed sharp wit and understanding of current affairs. His saloon was the busiest meeting place where local and international politics was heatedly debated by senior citizens of the locality and the Kashmir problem resolved on daily basis by *hukka* smoking participants. Tragically, he fell victim to a bomb blast at Lal Chowk where he had gone to sharpen his shaving razors. Syed Hussain Shah Madni was a gentleman shopkeeper who commanded respect. Children would buy candies from his shop and addressed him as *Pir*. He wore a *Rumi* cap and an elegant look. Janki Nath Saproo's was among the earliest photographer shops of Srinagar situated close to the Madni's. Akbar Mir's bakery, especially puffs, cream rolls, ginger biscuits and pastries, was a class of its own, both in quality and taste. Mir's bakery shop was run by a green turbaned Habibullah, a thorough gentleman who lived in the shop and, one day, breathed his last there. Jia Lal, the pharmacist, had *har marz ki dawa* (medicine for every pain) when it came to small medical emergencies. He was a cricket lover and introduced the game in Sonawar by encouraging local youth to participate in matches he organized at the *Looel Bagh*. Wali Mohammad Bhat, Mohammad Kamal Sofi, Amiruddin the butcher, Ghulam Qadir Lone, Abdul Khaliq Dandru, Ghulam Rasool Bhat, Abdul

Gani Wani, Abdul Khaliq Wani and Ghulam Mohiuddin Gaani were other shopkeepers who had made the Bazaar a lively place.

There were mischievous people also ever present in the Bazaar who did pranks, mostly with passersby. If one day it was directing a stranger to a cobbler, instead of a barber, for a haircut, the next day it was dropping few embers in a sack of dried cow dung strapped to the back of a village man going to the city to sell it as fuel. The poor guy after marching a few hundred yards would suddenly feel heat and, to his shock, observe fire raging over his shoulders while shopkeepers and shoppers amused themselves at his expense. One day, a man was passing through the Bazaar with a newly purchased calf when he stopped at a shop to rest a while. He tied the young animal with the shop front and sat to have few puffs of *hookah* that the shopkeeper had offered to him. Some other people came and stood in front of the shop, obstructing his view. Few minutes later, the shopkeeper asked him where he was heading for with a stray dog. "What dog?" he asked in astonishment and the shopkeeper pointed to the animal. Good Heavens! There actually was a fat dog with a rope round its neck tied to the shop front. The man nearly fainted. It so happened that while he was busy with *hookah* someone untied the calf, pushed it into a side alley and replaced it with a nearby resting lethargic dog.

The Bazaar had a peculiarity of always hosting a *majzoob* or *moat* and when one left the area another would take his place. People believed that they were spiritual guardians of the area and were posted and transferred like the government does in case of its employees. So, between 1940s and 1990s, we had in succession Subhan Moat, Nabir Moat, Pathan Moat, Mohiuddin Saeb, Noor Moat, Gande Aelve, Habbe Moat and Oblah Saeb. Subhan Moat would wear a thick coating of mud on his head and plant Iris leaves in it. He passed away on 21 *Rajab* 1372 *Hijri* corresponding to 6 April 1953 and lies buried in the premises of Sayyid Yaqoob's shrine. During the Indo-Pak War of 1971, Habbe Moat was Sonawar's resident *majzoob* and caused traffic jams on the highway during his frequent spells of *wajd*. At one point in time, a lady *majzoob*, Jaane Maetch, graced the Bazaar. Her favourite line was a movie number '*Man dolay mera tan dolay meray dil ka geya qaraar re*' that she often sang loudly. Around 1989, when Kashmir was in turmoil, a non-local ascetic appeared in the Bazaar and became its permanent feature for many years. He spent chilling and snowy days and nights on a shop front literally without any shred of fabric on his body. Nobody knew his name or where he had come from. One day, in a rare tranquil mood he told Sheikh Nazir Ahmad, a local resident, that his name was Tauqir Ali Khan and was earlier engaged in manufacture of aluminium utensils. He belonged to some north Indian state, most probably Uttar Pradesh. One day, he quietly disappeared and since then Sonawar Bazaar did not have any permanent ascetic although some would occasionally pass through the market. Hassan Sahib and Bakht Sahib were Sonawar's two spiritual healers, much sought after by people seeking divine blessings to recover from ailments or cope with difficult circumstances. The former was also the *Imam* of Palpora mosque.

In 1953, after the dismissal and arrest of Prime Minister Sheikh Mohammad Abdullah, a people's agitation broke out in the Valley leading to several deaths by police firing on protesters. The Sonawar Bazaar also witnessed protests, sloganeering and painting of pro-Abdullah graffiti on the highway. Army was called out and the scene was captured by a photographer of the famous US journal, *Life*. Several people were arrested and languished in jail for a long time. In later years, Sonawar Bazaar was at least twice the scene of violence resulting in some casualties. In the first case in 1973, when a procession taken out against the blasphemous content of a publication titled *The Book of Knowledge* descended on the UNMOGIP office and a protester climbed the high steel flag post to pull down the UN flag, police contingent led by the Superintendent of Police, Ghulam Rasool Kirmani shot at him and fired indiscriminately at the mob injuring many. In another case, on 23 January 1990, a protest demonstration was going on at Sonawar against the killing of 55 persons at Gaw Kadal two days back when a senior official of the UNMOGIP with army guards passed through. On seeing the UN vehicle the protesters raised slogans and the panicky guards opened direct fire on them killing five persons.

People were generally simple and modest. The prominent among them included centurion Mohammad Sidiq Parray who lived through the reign of the last two Dogra rulers and was a witness to 100 years of Kashmir's turbulent history, Abdul Gaffar Chapri and his son, Mohammad Iqbal Chapri who were frontline houseboat owners of Kashmir and were victimized for their political views which ran counter to the politics of the National Conference, Umar Bhat, Mohammad Sidiq Wani, Abdus Samad Bhat, Mohammad Ahssan Bhat, Wali Mohammad Bhat, Haji Habibullah Wani, Mohammad Sidiq Dar and Abdus Samad Mir.[391] Some well-known people who came from different parts of the city or elsewhere and settled at Sonawar, especially during 1940-60s, include former Prime Minister of Jammu & Kashmir, Bakhshi Ghulam Mohammad and his siblings, former Chief Minister, Dr. Farooq Abdullah, former Indian Ambassador to the then USSR, Durga Prasad Dhar, Chief Justice of Jammu & Kashmir High Court for about 20 years, Justice Janki Nath Wazir, eye specialist Dr. Mathura Das, social activist and an Indira Gandhi lookalike, Mrs. Khosla and her famous broadcaster daughter, Uma Khosla or *Nikki Aapa* as she was known, dentist Dr. S.L. Soni, businessman Tirath Ram Amla, founder of Kashmir's first cinema hall, Bhai Anant Singh Gauri, historian S.S. Gregan, former bureaucrat Ghulam Nabi (Nabji), Prof. Syed Ali Shah Masdar, playwright Ali Mohammad Lone and former President College Teachers' Association, Prof. Laiq Ahmad Quraishi. The Bhats, living on the river bank, is a family known for administrators, doctors and academics among its progeny. Also known by the sobriquet of *Guzarwan* (The Octroi People) for once administering an octroi post outsourced by the Dogra Government, one of the family members, Mohammad Subhan Bhat, possessed fair knowledge of astrology and had written a manuscript on the subject during the early 20th century.

Ghulam Qadir Sheikh was the *sehar khan* of the area whose loud call—*Waqt-e-Sahar* (It is time to have pre-dawn meal)—awoke devotees during the fasting month of *Ramadan*. Due to a serious ailment that hindered his free movement during his last years, he would take a round of the area on a horse back and wake people up by ringing a bell. Several persons in the area were identified by their sobriquets rather than their real names. Some nicknames were borrowed from world leaders or famous personalities. Thus, there were a Kennedy, a Dixon and a Tshombe at Sonawar whose real names were hardly known to anybody beyond their family and close friends.

To the ordinary inhabitants of old Srinagar, Sonawar was not a familiar place until 1965 when the Broadway cinema was opened and it caught their attention. In 1970s, when a public meeting of the then *Mirwaiz of Kashmir*, Molvi Mohammad Farooq scheduled at the Municipal Park near the Polo Ground, was dispersed by police after resorting to cane charge and firing tear smoke canisters the followers of the *Mirwaiz* took to their heels and few, with gasping breath, reached Sonawar. Unaware of the area and in utter desperation, one of them told others, "*Taavan ha pyov, aes ha waet Udhampur*" (We are damned, for we have reached Udhampur (the garrison town, 274 km south of Srinagar)). At one point in time, the buses of Government Transport Undertaking, the predecessor of the State Road Transport Corporation, would ply to Batwara via the Gupkar road skipping the Sonawar Bazaar, a routine later abandoned. The fare from Sonawar to Lal Chowk, the city center, was 15 paise. Till late 1960s, vehicular traffic on the now busy highway running through the Bazaar was sparse. A motor car or a passenger bus would pass through the Bazaar after a long pause. Bicycles and *tongas* plying on the road were more in number than the moving vehicles.

The landmark sites and institutions situated at Sonawar include, besides the shrine of Sayyid Yaqoob and the office of UNMOGIP, State Guest Houses (East and West), Circuit House, Burn Hall School, Woodlands House School, All Saints Church, G.B. Pant Children Hospital, Kashmir Nursing Home, Sher-i-Kashmir Cricket Stadium, Institution of Engineers and Amar Singh Club. Most of the State's top bureaucracy and ministers also live at Sonawar.

The mausoleum of Hazrat Sayyid Yaqoob is a popular shrine visited by a large number of people. The spiritual personality is one among hundreds of Central-Asian preachers who came to Kashmir during the 14th-17th century to propagate Islam. Legend has it that Sayyid Yaqoob had come to Kashmir along with six siblings, together known as Seven Sayyids. One of them is identified as buried within the army cantonment at Badami Bagh and the other at the Emporium Gardens. Strange though it sounds, one does not find Sayyid Yaqoob's mention among the 1,000 odd saints whose lives were documented by historians Hassan Khoihami and Mohammad Azam Dedmari. Mulla Ahmad Bin Abdus Saboor Kashmiri's *Khawariqus Salikeen* mentions Sayyid Yaqoob as "a spiritual personality of higher achievement and a disciple of Baba Dawood Khaki"[392] who in turn was a prominent follower of Kashmir's patron saint, Sheikh Hamzah Makhdoom. The reference is too sketchy to conclusively suggest that it is about the saint buried at Sonawar. The annual *urs* at the shrine is observed on 17 *Rabi-ul-Thani*. In 1914, the caretakers of the shrine, Umar Bhat son of Jala Bhat of Palpora and Ahad Mahazan son of Khizir Mahazan of Drugjan approached the government for repairs of the shrine which was then in a modest state. Sonawar being a restricted area, the application was forwarded on 23 June to the British Resident in Kashmir who conveyed his 'no-objection' to the repairs of the shrine on 22 July 1914.[393] Consequent to this, Bhat and Mahazan were allowed to undertake repairs. There is this legend passed on from one generation to another about a leopard visiting the shrine on Thursdays to pay obeisance. However, no one is ever known to have seen a wild cat at the shrine. The portion of the shrine over the grave of the saint is without roof and efforts made earlier to cover it are believed to have failed. A spacious mosque was built within the shrine precincts recently and many under-threat 'mainstream' politicians find it safe to offer Friday and Eid prayers there. Other shrines at Sonawar include *Shurayar Mandir* on the right bank of the Jhelum and the tomb of Sayyid Kamal ud Din Sahib in the interiors of Sonawar.

The Gilania Middle School, established in late 1930s, was the pride of Sonawar and played an important role in promotion of education in the area. The school was established by Pir Mohammad Maqbool Gilani, hereditary administrator of the shrine of Sayyid Abdul Qadir Jeelani at Khanyar in Srinagar. Head Master Ghulam Hassan Shah's stewardship soon saw the institution attaining excellence and competing with the city's famous Christian Missionary School in quality of education, discipline, cleanliness and extra-curricular activities. Only a few schools could match its reputation as a provider of quality education. Besides setting high standards in education, punctuality, hygiene, seminars, elocution competitions, sports and staging plays were the hallmark of the Gilania Middle School. A number of ex-students of the school made a mark as doctors, engineers, bureaucrats, lawyers, writers and artists. The school was taken over by the government in 1950s and later upgraded, first, as a Lower High School and, later, High School. A reading room located on the sideways of the highway established by the Cantonment Board also contributed to the dissemination of news and information in the area. Some years ago, the reading room was demolished to pave way for construction of an abattoir.

There are many buildings and spaces at Sonawar linked to the history of Kashmir. Of these, the office of the UNMOGIP, ever since its establishment in 1949, has drawn large political processions of people on different occasions. On 1 March 1990, a million protesters marched to the office. The Amar Singh Club, a vibrant social spot in the past, was built by Hari Singh in 1933 and named after his father. It is the first club of Jammu & Kashmir. During his last visit to Kashmir, Muhammad Ali Jinnah attended a reception party here on 28 May 1944. He also attended a reception at the Club hosted by Kashmir's Old Boys' Association of Aligarh Muslim University. A dreaded interrogation center named Red-16 was located at Gupkar where during 1960s-70s separatist leaders and political activists were incarcerated and allegedly tortured. During 1990s, another infamous 'interrogation cum torture centre' was set up few hundred yards from the Red-16 and was known as Papa 2. It is now the residence of a former Chief Minister of Jammu & Kashmir.

The Sher-i-Kashmir Cricket Stadium, formerly the Munshi Bagh, is the ground on which cricket in Kashmir was born—

literally. Here, both Pratap Singh and Hari Singh are known to have tried their hand at the bat. About the former, it is said that if his bat touched the ball a fielder instead of stopping would kick it towards the boundary and spectators cheered the Maharaja for hitting a four. The stadium has hosted many Ranji Trophy matches between the teams of Jammu & Kashmir and Punjab, Haryana, Delhi, Railways and the Services. On 13 October 1983, a cricket match—the first international game at the Stadium—played between India and West Indies—turned into huge embarrassment for the government when spectators booed home team while clapping and bucking up the visiting team that won the match. Following the incident, the Stadium was withdrawn from international itinerary until 9 September 1986 when a match was played between India and Australia under heavy security. No international cricket match has been played in the Stadium since. For the last couple of years, the main ceremonial functions of 26 January and 15 August are held here instead of the Bakshi Stadium located few kms away.

Maharaja Pratap Singh had set up at Gupkar a wine manufactory named Gupkar Distillery. During the year 1892-93, as many as 6,093 bottles valuing at ₹ 20,939 were manufactured.[394] During 1911, a total of 228 bottles of Gupkar made wines were exported to British India. However, the Annual Administrative Report of Samvat 1970 (1911 AD) shows a sharp fall from 312 gallons to 86 gallons in the sale of liquors and wines manufactured at the Distillery between the years 1911 and 1914 in view of which the manufactory was abolished in the year 1913-14.[395] The stock was gradually disposed of. For a long time, the Superintendent of the Wine Manufactory and State Vineyards was one A.M. Peychaud.

Another prominent building at the Gupkar was the Masonic Lodge or *Jadu Ghar* (The House of Magic) as the locals called it. On 25 July 1904, W. Mitchell, First Master of the Lodge, wrote to the British Resident in Kashmir that the Grand Lodge of Freemasons in England had acceded to a request "to found a Lodge in Srinagar which was styled No. 3043 on the roll of England with the very appropriate name of Takht-i-Suleman."[396] The Resident recommended to the

Kashmir Government allotment of land on the slopes of the hill and, on 3 November 1904, the Jammu & Kashmir State Council allotted 47,250 square feet land for construction of the Masonic Lodge.[397] There was always an element of curiosity in the minds of local people about the building as nobody other than the Freemasons who assembled there once or twice in a week, notably on Tuesdays, were allowed entry. Abdul Samad Mir, a local resident, was the caretaker of the Lodge who, as Merajuddin Bhat, another local resident, recalls, wore butler's uniform when weekly meetings were held there. Late Master Abdul Aziz had seen "a few human skeletons hanging on the walls" of the building—reason perhaps for the Lodge also being named as *Jadu Ghar*. The premises of the Lodge was used as *Charse Takyi* or cannabis smokers' situate for many years. The Dogra administration liberally allotted large tracts of land to its favourite people especially non-Kashmiris from the Punjab. The beneficiaries who included government officials built residential houses on the allotted land. Many of them received big chunks of land at Sonawar including Bonamsar and Munshi Bagh.[398]

In 1938, Hari Singh's Government issued a notification for acquisition of about 20 kanals of land at Sonawar for a Parsee cemetery.[399] This notwithstanding that we do not find any significant population of Parsees living in Kashmir during the recent or medieval period save some "Parsi priests who were living as community in sects and sub-sects during the 17th century"[400] or individual businessmen like Pestonjee who had a huge commercial building on the Bund near the Head Post Office. The land under survey numbers 794 *min* and 795 *min* situated on the right bank of the Jhelum behind (now non-existent) *Broadway Cinema* was held by one Mrs. Salil Chatterji of Calcutta, under *wasidari* (lease). There is on record considerable correspondence between the Kashmir Government and Mrs. Chatterji. The latter objected to the conversion of a portion of the land possessed by her under lease into a cemetery and expressed "grave apprehension" that it "will seriously affect the value of my estate."[401] On 18 November 1939, the Governor of Kashmir invited B.N. Pestonji, Trustee Parsee Anjuman, Srinagar for discussion on the issue and, four days later, Pestonji gave a written undertaking that the "plot when granted will in no case be used by Parsees (the trustee of whose *Anjuman* I am) for a cemetery but used as a garden and built upon only in case permission is granted by the Cantonment authorities."[402] In the meanwhile, there arose some disagreement between the Revenue Department and the Special Land Acquisition Officer following which the notification was cancelled.

Sonawar was one of the worst flood-hit areas of Srinagar in 2014 and remained submerged for about three weeks. Other calamities visiting the area include severe inundation during the flood of 1950 when the right bank of Jhelum breached at Batwara, and a major fire incident in 1956 when 50-60 residential houses were reduced to ashes.

10

Of Prices and Fares

During one's childhood, when elders at home talked about prices of essential commodities prevalent during their own youth that they referred to as *prone zamane* (old times), one's reaction would be of disbelief. Although their *prone zamane* was only 40 or 50 years backwards in time but the stories they told would bring it into one's mind as an ancient age. By what they narrated, one felt that commodities were literally given away free. So cheap were their prices, or so one thought. Imagine a sheep selling for half a rupee! A family had traded a flock of 150 sheep for ₹ 75 following the death of the sole caretaker of the herd.

Going back in time, incredible though it may sound, prices of commodities were non-existent in Kashmir. Andrew Wingate who joined as Settlement Officer in the Valley in 1887, points this out in his preliminary settlement report.[403] His successor, Walter Lawrence, observes that "money prices did not exist".[404] Salaries were paid in grain, including to the army and civil officials. Lawrence himself was asked to take oil-seeds in payment of his salary and that of his staff. Pertinently, oil-seeds were considered as an appreciated currency in comparison to maize and *singhara-nuts* which were regarded as a depreciated medium.[405] Private individuals also paid wages of their domestic servants in grain. Silver played a subsidiary part in the business.[406]

Coins, weights and measures prevalent in old Kashmir were different than those now in use. To give an idea of how these compared with the present metric system, 1 *seer* was equivalent to 0.93 kg, 1 *maund* to 37.32 kg, 1 *trak* to 5 seer, 16 *traks* to 1 *kharwar*, 1 *kharwar* to 80 *seer*, 1 pound to 0.453 kg, 1 *pao* to ¼ of a *seer*, 1 *chhatank* to 1/8 of a *seer* and 1 *tola* to 10 gm. A *gaz* was equivalent to 0.91 meter. A rupee was made of 16 *annas,* and an *anna* of 4 *paise.*

Most of the trade was conducted through barter system. Until recently, buying commodities of daily use from a local shopkeeper against domestic produce like eggs or grain was a common practice in villages of Kashmir. Commodities exported were traded in value with those imported. Statistics of 1870-72 reveal that per *maund* cost of honey was ₹ 20, saffron (first quality) ₹ 800 and (second quality) ₹ 140, rice ₹ 5, *moong* (pulse) ₹ 8, barley ₹ 1.4, barley meal (*sattu*) ₹ 1.6, ghee ₹ 26, tobacco ₹ 20, paper ₹ 1, woolen sheets ₹ 5 and coloured blanket ₹ 5. A sword was sold at ₹ 10 and a gun and a horse at ₹ 40 each.[407] Between 1887 and 1894, prices of village commodities had risen appreciably. The price of woolen blanket shot up from ₹ 3 to ₹ 4 and of walnut from ₹ 3 to ₹ 7 a *kharwar*. A rupee which earlier fetched 4 *seers* of *ghee* bought back 3 or 2.5 *seers* only. The price of a pony increased by ₹ 10 to ₹ 15, and that of a bullock showed a steady rise of one rupee per year. Likewise, wool earlier sold at 2 *seers* a rupee, fetched one and a half *seer* only.[408]

At the dawn of the 20th century, Major Swinburne and his wife, Jane, were in Kashmir for six months and their expenses on food, wine, cigarettes and washing were £ 72.7 and on hire of boats, tents and equipment £ 17.6. In 1905, it may be recalled a Pound sterling was equivalent to 19.98 Indian rupees.[409]

A look at the Annual Trade Reports from 1900 to 1923 throws up interesting figures with respect to prices of different commodities. In 1900, a *maund* of almonds was exported from Kashmir to Punjab at the rate of ₹ 20, potato at ₹ 2.50 and apples and pears at ₹ 5. A year earlier as well as a year later, a *maund* of rice was exported at the rate of ₹ 2, raw silk at ₹ 600 and raw wool including *Pashm* at ₹ 40. In 1902, export rate of a *maund* of raw cotton was ₹ 3.62, of cattle hides ₹ 18, of *ghee* ₹ 23.19 and of tobacco and snuff ₹ 33.94. In 1916-17, a *maund* of wheat was exported at the rate of ₹ 8 and pulses at ₹ 2.15. In 1922-23, a *maund* of walnut was exported at the rate ₹ 5.40 and *ghee* at ₹ 47.70.

As regards prices of staple food grains in 1911, the quantity per rupee by *seer* was wheat 14, barley 25, maize 28, moong 15, oil 2 and paddy 33.[410] Next year, rice was sold 14 seers and gram 5.5 seers a rupee.[411] A communication sent in 1918 by the Superintendent of Zanana Hospital, Srinagar, Ms. Kovanghan to the Governor of Kashmir tells us that rice was sold in Srinagar at ₹ 7 a *maund* and an equal weight of paddy at ₹ 2. The hospital had purchased for its patients food grains from a private contractor but because of poor quality "the supply had to be thrown away".[412] Kovanghan then approached the Governor for supply of 100 *kharwars* of paddy.

Dr. Arthur Neve, Surgeon to the Kashmir Medical Mission, who lived in the Valley for many years, published *The Tourist's Guide to Kashmir, Ladakh, Skardo & C.* during 1923 wherein he lists prices of food items prevalent in those days. He writes that in Srinagar prices tend to rise in summer season and because of scarcity many articles were expensive in winter. According to him, good mutton was usually sold about *seer* a rupee. "In the Districts", he writes, "if a sheep is killed, the meat might be taken at 5 *seers* a rupee."[413] A good sized fowl was sold at a rupee and small sized ones two at a rupee. The price of a duck in the city was 8 *annas* in winter and 12 *annas* to a rupee in summer. A goose was sold at ₹ 2 to 3. Fish was available at 4 to 6 *annas* a *seer*. The price of eggs varied from season to season and when plentiful, these were sold 6 to 8 *annas* a dozen. A rupee would fetch 6 *seers* of milk in the city and 10 *seers* in the higher grazing grounds. Local vegetables like turnip, carrot, vegetable marrow, tomato and peas were "very cheap".[414] The English kind vegetables were sold "8 to 10 *annas* a dali [basket] from the public garden near the [SPS] Library."[415] Potatoes were sold 16 *seers* a rupee or more in the places they were grown in summer.

The prices of local fruit were less than those of the European variety and were sold at higher prices at Gulmarg than in the city. Kashmiri apples were sold at ₹ 1.8 per 100 while the best European was available at 4 to 7 *annas* a dozen. The local pears were sold at 8 to 10 *annas* per 100, melons 6 to 10 *annas* each depending on the size and season, grapes 6 to 10 *annas* a *seer*, apricots and peaches 4 *annas* a *seer*, cherries 8 to 12 *annas* a *seer* and raspberries 4 to 8 *annas* a *seer*.[416] In food grains, *basmati* rice was sold 3 to 4 *seers* a rupee, white rice 7 *seers* a rupee, wheat 8 to 10 *seers* a rupee, atta 6 *seers* a rupee, barley 12 to 14 *seers* a rupee, dal (pulses) 5 *seers* a rupee. Ghee was sold to *seer* a rupee, butter (table) ₹ 1.8 per lb and (cooking) ₹ 1 per lb, raisins 1 *seer* a rupee, currants to 1 *seer* a rupee, country oil 2 *seers* a rupee and sweet oil 1 seer rupee. Bread was sold 8 loaves a rupee while the same amount would fetch 32 Pampori *rotis*.[417] A bag of 5 *seers* of sugar was sold at ₹ 3 to four, depending on the quality while the rates constantly fluctuated. If purchased in bulk, sugar was available at 10 *annas* a *seer*. The superior quality kerosene oil was sold at ₹ 15 per box of two tins and No. 2 at ₹ 13.[418] Neve also acquaints us with the rate of tinning of kitchen utensils which cost 1 to 2 *annas* each utensil. A houseboat could be rented for ₹ 40 a month exclusive of boatman to ₹ 600 for the season. Two *maunds* of firewood were sold at 1 rupee. The list of official rates of commodities was pasted in the Library verandah at Srinagar and changed fortnightly in the season.

A 1931-born Ghulam Mohammad Bhat recalls that during his childhood a *seer* of rice was sold at 1 rupee, mutton at 8 *annas*, and onion and potato 1 *anna* each. People generally lived from hand to mouth. Once, Bhat reminisces, he went to Mahda Joo, a vegetable seller of his locality, for purchase of onions and potatoes for an *anna* each, the shopkeeper asked him, "*Tohi kya az padshah mizaj heiu?*" (How come you are in royal mood today?)

In 1939, the Kashmir Government invited tenders for supply of food items to frontier areas. In response, Amir Lone of Gurais (misspelled and mispronounced as Gurez) offered the lowest rates at potatoes 16 *seers* a rupee, flour 10 *seers* a rupee, poultry (large) 10 *annas* and 9 *paise* a bird, poultry (ordinary) 5 *ananas* and 6 *paise* a bird, eggs 3 *annas* and 3 *paise* a dozen, and mutton 8 *annas* a *seer*.

To calm down people's continued unrest following Sheikh Mohammad Abdullah's unceremonious overthrow as Prime Minister in 1953, the government supplied food grains to consumers on subsidized rates. Up to 30 June 1959, rice, wheat and maize were provided at 3 *seers* a rupee. On 1 July, the rate was changed to 2½ *seers* a rupee. The rate of paddy was increased from ₹ 12 to ₹ 16 a *kharwar*.[419]

From the *Travel Guide to Kashmir*, an official pamphlet published in 1955, we get a fair idea of market prices of different articles during mid-1950s. Depending on the quality, rice was sold at ₹ 12 to ₹ 20 per *maund*, atta at ₹ 8 to ₹ 10 per *seer* and sugar at ₹ 1 to ₹ 1.8 per *seer*.[420] A *seer* each of mutton, fish and milk was sold at ₹ 2 and *annas* 4 to ₹ 2 and *annas* 12, ₹ 1 to ₹ 2 and *annas* 8 to *annas* 12, respectively. A fowl was sold at ₹ 2 to ₹ 4 depending on the size, a duck at ₹ 3 to ₹ 5 and a goose at ₹ 6 to ₹ 8. A *seer* of salt cost *annas* 3 and *paise* 6 to *annas* 4. A *seer* of tomato was sold at *annas* 4 to 6, peas green *annas* 8 to 12, turnip *annas* 2 to 4, cabbages *annas* 4 to 8, brinjals and beans *annas* 4 each, cauliflower *annas* 8 to 12, green chili *annas* 5 to 8, onions *annas* 4 to 8, potato *annas* 3 to 6, and radish *annas* 3 to 6.[421] The per *seer* price of fruit was apples (Ambri) ₹ 1 to 2, pears *annas* 12 to ₹ 1, melons *annas* 8 to 12, apricots (green) *annas* 12 and grapes ₹ 1 to ₹ 1.8. A *seer* of butter was sold at ₹ 3 and a *seer* of *moong dal* at *annas* 6 to 9. A gallon of petrol cost 3 rupees, 14 *annas* and 6 *paise*. Big size bread (double-roti) was sold at *annas* 8 and small size *annas* 6. A pound of biscuits of sorts and pastry was sold at ₹ 2 each and cake plain and ice-cake ₹ 2 and *annas* 4 each. A *seer* of country-oil was sold at ₹ 2.[422]

When one looks back at prices of commodities during one's own childhood which would mean 1960s, the feeling of disbelief is no less. It seems unbelievable that in 1963 a liter of petrol was sold at 72 *paise*. Likewise, in 1971, a *masala dosa* and a cup of coffee cost 50 paise each.

A notebook and some loose handwritten papers of Mohammad Ahssan Bhat[423] who had this good habit of writing down expenditure, especially incurred on special occasions like *Eid* and marriages, provides enough clues on market prices in Kashmir during 1960s. When he reconstructed his house at Sonawar in 1963, the per cubic feet of *deodar* (cider) was sold at ₹ 7 and *annas* 8, *kairoo* (pine) at ₹ 6 and *annas* 2 and *budloo* (fir) at ₹ 4 and *annas* 4. To give an idea about water transportation charges, 170 cubic feet of timber was transported from Barbar Shah Ghat upstream to Sonawar Ghat on labour charges of ₹ 20.[424] The sawing charges of a log of 74 cft *kail* were ₹ 37. Fired bricks of first grade quality were available at ₹ 92 per thousand. According to a receipt issued to Bhat on 3 September 1963 and signed by Syed Abdur Rashid Qadri, clerk at the brick kiln of Haji Sidiq Mir Lasjan, ₹ 736 were charged for supply of "8000 *khisht ha rekhta darja-e-awwal*" (8000 fired bricks of first grade quality).

During those times when LPG and induction heaters were unknown and power heaters were used by only a small section of population, firewood was the main source of fuel used to light up a hearth locally known as *daan*, for cooking food. A *maund* of *hatab* was sold at ₹ 4 and willow at ₹ 2 and *annas* 8. The walnut wood, used to warm *hamams*, cost ₹ 3 a *maund*.

In 1966, a *tola* of gold cost ₹ 170 and making charges were ₹ 6 per *tola*. A *Pashmina Dussa* (long male shawl) cost ₹ 372.50. A Roamer wrist watch cost ₹ 135, a *gaz* of *shaneel* ₹ 12, a suit length of Kashmir cloth ₹ 60, of Kanjivaram and Wash-n-Wear ₹ 75 each. Sangam was available at ₹ 9 a meter, Plush ₹ 18.37 and Crepe plain ₹ 4. A *gaz* of *khaddar* was sold at ₹ 2, Night Cloth at ₹ 2.5 and Poplin ₹ 1.60. A Banarasi *dupatta* cost ₹ 35. The sewing charges of a lady's suit of Kashmir cloth were ₹ 5 and of a silken suit ₹ 3.50. For a *pheran*, the stitching charges were ₹ 1.50. A *jagar* cost ₹ 7 and *annas* 8.

A *tola* of saffron was sold at ₹ 20. A *seer* of milk and curd cost ₹ 1 and *annas* 6, and ₹ 1 and *annas* 10, respectively. A *seer* of red chili powder cost ₹ 3, turmeric powder ₹ 2.70, *suji* ₹ 1, onion 50 *paise*, sugar ₹ 1.6, garlic 50 *paise*, cinnamon ₹ 16, and clove, dry ginger and cooking oil ₹ 4 each. A *chhatank* of *zeerah* (cumin) was sold at ₹ 2 and *annas* 8 and a *pao* of raisins for ₹ 2.5. Mutton, *desi* fowl and fish cost ₹ 5, ₹ 5.25, and *annas* 12 a *seer* each, respectively. A fat duck cost ₹ 8, a bundle of *nadru* (lotus stem) for ₹ 1 and *annas* 4, and a *seer* of tobacco for ₹ 2.50.

Copper utensils were popular for cooking and serving food. A *thale baan* weighing 950 gram cost ₹ 21, a *tooer* weighing a kilogram ₹ 14, a small size *tooer* ₹ 4 and *annas* 2, *trae'm* ₹ 22, *naer* ₹ 17, *deechiwaer* ₹ 40 and a spoon ₹ 1.50. A ceramic tea-set was purchased at ₹ 20, a cup at 90 *paise*, a fountain pen at ₹ 2.25 and jute-mat at ₹ 9 a *gaz*. In 1967, a Kashmiri *tchot* and *tchchwor* (kinds of bread eaten with tea in the morning and afternoon, respectively) was sold at 5 *paise* (small size) and 10 *paise* (big size) each, respectively. A puff, a rough cake, a pastry and a queen cake cost 20 *paise* each. One pound of plain cake cost ₹ 2.50. In 1968, the queen cake was dearer by 5 *paise*.

In 1969, a *seer* of mutton was sold at ₹ 6 and potatoes 50 *paise*. In 1970, a kilogram of cooking oil (then measured by kilogram not liter) was sold at ₹ 5.25, tea leaves (salt tea) at ₹ 10, turmeric powder at ₹ 7, Dalda *ghee* at ₹ 6.50, *sonth* at ₹ 8 and *badyan* at ₹ 7. A packet of Glucose-D (250 gm) cost ₹ 1.10. By mid-1970s, a kg of mutton was sold at ₹ 14 and sugar at ₹ 3 and *annas* 10. Wild onion cost ₹ 4 a kg. On special occasions like marriage, an economically modest family would give the bride or the bridegroom *guli myooth* or *vartaav* anywhere between ₹ 1 to ₹ 20. Children would receive an *anna* or *duaani* (two annas) as *eidi* on the festival of *Eid*.

As regards the modes of transport and passenger fares prevalent during old times, Al-Beruni (973-1050 AD) writes that "the inhabitants of Kashmir are pedestrians; they have no riding animals or elephants. The noble among them ride in palankins [palanquins], called *katt* [*khaat*], carried on the shoulders of men".[425] Al-Beruni's account may not be the whole truth for the fact that elephant fossils of prehistoric era have been discovered in Kashmir in 1931 and 2000. It is possible that the animal specie had disappeared in the event of some topographic and, the resultant, climatic change. Water transport, however, was known to ancient Kashmir. A 12th century chronicle informs us of "the coming and going of ships [on the *Vitasta* that] gave splendour to the river".[426] In the medieval Kashmir we know of the river being used as the prime mode of transportation of goods and people. Zainul Aabideen, the 15th century ruler of Kashmir, is known to have taken boat rides and Mughal ruler, Akbar, has visited places travelling on the Jhelum in a boat. For Frederic Drew, the Jhelum was "the great highway of Kashmir" and "much used for navigation."[427]

During 1890s, a *doonga* with crew of four persons was available on a monthly rent of ₹ 20, a kitchen boat with crew of three men on ₹ 15 and a *shikara* with crew of one person on ₹ 1. If the boats were taken out of Srinagar then ration money at the rate of *annas* 4 per crewman per month was payable.[428] River travel from Srinagar to Baramulla in an A-class boat would cost *annas* 8, to Islamabad *annas* 10, and to Awantipore *annas* 6. Boat travel from Srinagar to Ganderbal and Bandipore cost ₹ 1 and *annas* 4, and ₹ 2, respectively.[429]

Travel between Kashmir and British India, was undertaken on the Jhelum Valley Road also known as the Srinagar-Rawalpindi Road—inaugurated in 1890—first through *ekkas* and *tongas* and, later, through lorries and motor cars. A Mail Tonga from Srinagar to Murree charged ₹ 37, a Special Tonga for three passengers ₹ 110 and a Special family Tonga for three adults and two children ₹ 145.[430] A Phaeton for three passengers and 12 *seer* luggage charged ₹ 175. An *ekka* was hired on ₹ 18. The fare in all cases was exclusive of toll.

For travel by bus, lorry or car, passenger fare varied from season to season, up journey and down journey and one mode of transport to another. During 1930s, between April and July, per passenger bus and lorry fare from Srinagar to Rawalpindi was ₹ 3 to ₹ 5 and from Rawalpindi to Srinagar ₹ 7 to ₹ 10.[431] Between August and November, the fare for up journey remained the same while for down journey it was ₹ 5 to 8. A full bus or a lorry charged ₹ 20 to ₹ 25 from Srinagar to Rawalpindi and ₹ 115 to ₹ 120 in the reverse direction, between August and November. In a shared motor car, per seat was charged at ₹ 5 to ₹ 6 from Srinagar to Rawalpindi between April and July and ₹ 20 to ₹ 25 between August and November. From Rawalpindi to Srinagar, the charges were ₹ 20 to ₹ 25 and ₹ 15 to ₹ 20, respectively. A full motor car charged ₹ 10 to ₹ 15 from Srinagar to Rawalpindi between April and July, and ₹ 40 to ₹ 45 between August and November. For up journey, the full motor car charges were ₹ 60 to ₹ 70 between April and July and ₹ 50 to ₹ 60 between August and November. Earlier, in 1922, Chaman Motor Car Service charged ₹ 34 and *annas* 10 per passenger from Rawalpindi to Srinagar. Prior to 1947, bus fare between Muzaffarabad and Srinagar was "twelve *annas*, which was later increased to one rupee."[432] Among different bus services plying on the route, the prominent were the Nanda Bus Service and the Allied Chirag Din. There were separate seats for men and women. Married couples were allowed to sit together.[433]

The Jhelum Valley Road was closed in the aftermath of armed hostilities over Kashmir between India and Pakistan in 1947. However, six decades later on 7 April 2005, the road was reopened for the divided Kashmiri families living on the either side of the Line of Control (LoC), and some limited trade. The bus service and trade between Srinagar and Muzaffarabad was suspended in August 2019 when the Government of India scrapped Article 370 of the Indian Constitution guaranteeing special status to Jammu & Kashmir, and placed strict restrictions on communication and movement of people.

During mid-1950s, three types of *tongas*—1st class, 2nd class and 3rd class—were used to ferry passengers in Srinagar whose rates for full day of nine hours was ₹ 10, ₹ 7 and ₹ 5, respectively, and for half day of five hours ₹ 5, ₹ 3.8 and ₹ 2.8, respectively.[434] A 1st and 2nd class *tonga* carried four passengers and a 3rd class three passengers. A full *tonga* from Amira Kadal to Cheshma Shahi, a distance of eight kms, and back was hired for ₹ 4 (1st class), ₹ 3 (2nd class) and ₹ 2 (3rd class). The hire-rates for Nishat and back were ₹ 5 and *annas* 4, ₹ 4 and ₹ 3, respectively, for Shalimar ₹ 6 and *annas* 8, ₹ 4 and *annas* 8 and ₹ 3 and *annas* 8, respectively, for Harwan and back ₹ 7, ₹ 6 and ₹ 5, respectively, and for Naseem Bagh, Nigeen and Hazratbal and back ₹ 4, ₹ 3 and ₹ 2, respectively. Within the city, for all stations including Zaina Kadal, Rainawari, Maidanpora, Razay Kadal, Chhatabal and Batwara the hire-rate was *annas* 4 for 1st and

2nd class *tonga* and *annas* 3 for 3rd class *tonga*. From Maisuma to Rainawari (via Munawarabad), Rambagh and Bagat Barzula the hire-rate for 1st and 2nd class *tongas* was *annas* 4 each.[435]

The Government Transport Undertaking-run passenger buses charged ₹ 1 per seat each from Srinagar to Shopian, Islamabad (Anantnag), Sopore and Baramulla, ₹ 1.4 to Bandipore, Handwara and Kulgam, ₹ 1 and *annas* 8 to Kupwara and ₹ 1 and *annas* 12 to Uri. A regular 'City Bus Service' was plying in Srinagar city and Cantonment area from different places at the rate of *annas* 2 per seat. Regular bus services to tourist destinations were also operated. For a return trip to Mughal Gardens in Srinagar, ₹ 2 and *annas* 8 were charged per seat, for Pahalgam ₹ 5 per single seat and ₹ 8 per return seat, for Verinag via Achhabal ₹ 10 per return seat, for Sonamarg ₹ 8 per return seat and for Tangmarg ₹ 2 per single seat and ₹ 3 and *annas* 8 per return seat. During those years, Tangmarg to Gulmarg, a distance of four miles, was covered by ponies.

During 1970s, the per passenger fare from Lal Chowk—the city center—to different destinations like Zainakadal, Nawa Kadal, Safa Kadal, Rainawari and Batwara was 20 *paise*, and to Sonawar 15 *paise*. From mid-1970s, when Sheikh Mohammad Abdullah returned to power and revised passenger fare structure, to 1980, the per-seat bus fare from Srinagar to Baramulla was ₹ 2 and *paise* 30, Sopore ₹ 2 and *paise* 20, Handwara ₹ 3 and *paise* 30, Tangmarg ₹ 1 and *paise* 75, Kupwara ₹ 3 and *paise* 90, Sumbal ₹ 1 and *paise* 25, Bandipore ₹ 2 and *paise* 45, Budgam *paise* 50, Tsar-i-Sharief ₹ 1 and *paise* 40, Ganderbal ₹ 1, Kangan ₹ 1 and *paise* 75, Sonamarg ₹ 4 and *paise* 20, Tral ₹ 1 and *paise* 75, Anantnag ₹ 2 and *paise* 45, Pahalgam ₹ 4 and *paise* 55, Pulwama ₹ 1 and *paise* 45, Kulgam ₹ 3 and *paise* 20, Khrew ₹ 1, Pakherpora ₹ 2, Uri ₹ 4 and *paise* 5 and Khag ₹ 1 and *paise* 80. Per passenger fare from Srinagar to Jammu was ₹ 28 and *paise* 50 for A-Class, and ₹ 22 for B-Class buses, and from Srinagar to Leh ₹ 65 and ₹ 48 and *paise* 50, respectively.[436] The B-Class bus fare for Kargil was ₹ 23 and *paise* 50, Doda ₹ 16, Bhaderwah ₹ 18 and *paise* 50, Reasi ₹ 22 and *paise* 50 and Ramban ₹ 12 and *paise* 50. As regards tourist destinations, the return A-Class and Super Deluxe bus fares for Pahalgam, Gulmarg, Aharbal and Sonamarg were ₹ 20 and *paise* 50 and ₹ 23, respectively. A return trip to the Mughal Gardens by A-Class and Super Deluxe was charged at ₹ 8 and ₹ 9 and *paise* 50 per seat, respectively. In January 1981, passenger fares were revised and marginally increased. During early 1980s, air-fare from Srinagar to Jammu was ₹ 330 and from Srinagar to Leh ₹ 335.[437]

11

Romance with Rumours

17 January 2016 brought with it horror, chaos and worst confusion to Kashmir. Thousands of panic-stricken parents poured on the streets of Srinagar and other towns to make it to the nearest hospital for a medical checkup of their children after someone spread a rumour on social media that few infants had died soon after being administered polio drops. The rumour was false but it did the trick its originator had intended. It started on social networking sites, with *WhatsApp* and mobile phone calls doing the rest. "Within hours, streets choked with cars, auto-rickshaws, jeeps, load carriers and buses carrying weeping mothers and their babies."[438] Special messages were broadcast through radio and television asking people not to panic but nothing seemed working. Kashmir had been gripped by panic.

One recalls a similar scene during mid-1960s when in Srinagar word spread like wildfire that a mysterious gang in the name of vaccination was drawing blood out of the veins of children in schools. The anguished parents ran towards educational institutions. Mothers turned sprinters running towards schools to look for their children and bring them home. The chaos caused in the city was terrible and died down only when the rumour turned out to be a prank.

Generally speaking, Kashmiris love rumours and exaggeration. They tend to derive amusement out of overstatement. If they like a person they make him divine and if they dislike someone they make him look like a devil's sibling. If a small adversity befalls them, it is no less than a *qayamat*. Newspaper reports often describe an incident of a couple of deaths or property loss as *qayamat-i-sugra*. A small misfortune is a *toofaan*. Likewise, you often come across people with small or inconsequential achievements mentioned as 'world famous', 'globally acclaimed' and the like.

Rumour mongering in Kashmir has remained a favourite pastime of the idle since very old times. They make a mulberry tree out of a gourd plant (*Alle kulis tulle kul banavun*). Phrases like *Khabr-i-Zaina Kadal* or the adage *Gayi ho gayi ho Zaina Kadle* speak about their fascination for rumours. To Aurel Stein who translated Kalhana's *Rajatarangini* into English, Kashmir capital has always been a hotbed of "political gossip and fertile nursery of false and often amusingly absurd rumours."[439] Strolling down to the city bridges and the *ghats* on the river bank, he notes, one would always watch small crowds eagerly gathering around news-fabricators who were always found in these localities. Walter Lawrence believes that half the stories to the discredit of Kashmir and its inhabitants were due to the fertile imagination of a particular community in the Valley, who like the Irish car-driver told quaint scandals of Kashmir and its ruler.[440]

Towards the end of 19th century, a frightful creature, like a great cat, was rumoured to have struck the city. While nobody had actually seen the creature it was believed to be coming out of the Jhelum to visit homes at night and tear people apart. The rumour spread dread across Kashmir and nobody ventured out after the day fall. Likewise, during the time educationist Tyndale Biscoe was in Kashmir, a terrible beast was rumoured to inhabit the Jhelum one summer. Frightening stories about it were making rounds in Srinagar and no one dared to bathe in the river for a month. When, after the summer vacations, students returned to school dirty and unclean, Biscoe persuaded 130 boys of his school to leap into the Jhelum from Amira Kadal, and swim right through the city to Safa Kadal "so that this beast might burst itself with swallowing so many boys and thus would save the city".[441] The bridges and banks and the roofs of the houses were crowded with people to see what would happen. "Nothing did happen and next day city was washing itself once more, for the bogey was slain"[442], recalls Biscoe in his book *Kashmir in Sunlight and Shade.*

In the olden times, the legend has it that a woman in a Kashmir village delivered a baby boy with a slightly dark complexion. A lady neighbour visited the mother and the infant and, on return, told one of her acquaintances that the woman had given birth to a black coloured boy. The second woman then took the news to her friends telling them that a jet black skinned baby was born to the lady. Everybody who heard and forwarded the news added extra black tinge to the boy's skin. One lady described the baby as black as a crow. The news kept on circulating in the village until one woman announced that the lady had given birth to a crow. That drew people in scores to see the new born creature.

Not to speak of a moron or a heartless dealer-in-gossip taking people for a ride and deriving sadistic pleasure out of their torment, even journalists have not spared people of this horror game in the past. In 1935, for instance, the *Kashmir Times* published a news report, quoting Robert Macfield, a non-existent eminent geologist, warning that the *Takht-i-Sulaiman* or the *Shankaracharya Hill* will erupt between July 15 and August 15. The news report cautioned that the areas immediately surrounding the hill within a distance of two miles will be in very great danger and it is probable that the shock will change the physical configuration of the whole area and that Srinagar will be flooded by latent fountains existing underground. As expected, the news created widespread panic and migration of people to safer places until another newspaper, *The Civil & Military Gazette*, described the news as a cruel joke and the *Kashmir Times*' idea of April Fool. The dread caused by this rumour keeps visiting people periodically even now, although geologists have ruled out any possibility of the hill ever erupting.

It is difficult to conclusively identify the reasons for Kashmiris generally being rumour lovers. However, there are geographical, historical and cultural aspects that can be attributed to the birth and evolution of this trait in them. Geographically, as we know, the Valley was landlocked and even today inclement weather for a few days cuts it off from the rest of the world.

Consider the situation hundreds of years ago when the land was isolated and winters were harsh and long. Added to it, the long subjugation and oppression had left people with few or no means of free expression or entertainment. In such a gloomy and depressing atmosphere, they devised their own ways to keep themselves in good humour and fight melancholic conditions. One such medium was *tarr* or fabrication of news, and rumour. They weaved fantastic stories to laugh out loud at their despair and misfortune and successfully used rumour mongering for political purposes. Political leadership often used it to mount pressure on the powers that be. During the concluding days of the Dogra rule, the popularity of Sheikh Mohammad Abdullah skyrocketed through a widespread rumour that his name was found naturally imprinted on tree leaves. People across the Valley took it as gospel. Recalling the development, Pir Mohammad Afzal Makhdoomi writes [translation]:

> On the same day [28 July 1933], a rumour was floated at Safa Kadal that the name *Sher-i-Kashmir* was seen naturally imprinted on tree leaves. The fact was that fallen mulberry leaves had, due to certain disease, developed a pattern of lines that resembled words *Sher-i-Kashmir*. As the rumour got wings, people in hordes thronged to see the development. Next day, everywhere *Sher-i-Kashmir* was observed written on the leaves with an addition of *zindabad* [long live]. I myself observed inscription of this slogan at a jeweller's shop. When this jeweller was probed about the truth behind the inscription he poured droplets of acid on mulberry leaves to make an impression of *Sher-i-Kashmir Zindabad*. The man distributed these leaves as a blessing and described it as Heaven's endorsement of *Sher-i-Kashmir*. Some people bought these leaves and took to different villages. This continued for weeks.[443]

The incident was planned to show the supporters of Mirwaiz Mohammad Yusuf Shah, an adversary of Abdullah, down. There was another rumour that Abdullah, incarcerated as he was then in the Hari Parbat Fort at Srinagar, was thrown in boiling oil but came out of it unharmed. These rumours grew a halo around the image of the leader who had taken up fight against an autocratic rule. Once in 1930s, the middle-rung leadership, in order to test how widespread their word of mouth can go, circulated that a female leopard had delivered three cubs at the entry of the city's *Jama Masjid* and within no time hundreds of people thronged the mosque to have a glimpse of the baby leopards. Many swore that they actually saw the cubs.

In a superstitious society, rumour mongers circulate, without much effort, frightening stories like monsters and celestial bodies visiting villages and taking away children. During the 2014 deluge, rumours made rounds in the Valley that hundreds of bodies were floating on flood waters and many prominent doctors were washed away by the swollen Jhelum across the Line of Control.

History

12

Sir Mohammad Iqbal: The Untold Story

Soon after G.E.C. Wakefield had been replaced as Prime Minister of Jammu & Kashmir with a wily Hari Kishen Koul following the carnage of 13 July 1931 at the Srinagar Central Jail, a Lahore-based advocate, Amar Nath Chona, in a letter addressed to Mirza Zafar Ali Khan, a recently appointed minister in Kashmir Government, informed him that Sir Mohammad Iqbal wanted to become a minister of the Kashmir Government and had approached the Governor of Punjab for a recommendation. Mirza, a former judge of the Lahore High Court had been picked by Maharaja Hari Singh as his Home Minister to "show his desire to meet the reasonable demands of the Muslims"[444] in the wake of their widespread disenchantment and anguish against his discriminatory regime.

Sir Mohammad Iqbal, widely known as Allama Iqbal, was a Lahore-based barrister, philosopher and a prominent poet of Urdu and Persian languages of the pre-partitioned India. His ancestors had migrated from Kashmir to Sialkot in Punjab where he was born on 9 November 1877. He had a strong emotional bond with the land of his forefathers. He visited Kashmir only once in 1924 but his heart ached for the land and its people for the plight they suffered under a prolonged autocratic rule. They were in shackles and trampled by the boots of injustice and bigotry. Thirty-one years prior to Iqbal's birth, a Hindu Rajput dynasty from Jammu had, in the most obnoxious manner, assumed power when in 1846 the East India Company dislodged the Sikhs and sold Kashmir to Gulab Singh. The majority population, toiling and sweating to fill the coffers of the State, was denied a life of dignity and oppressed and robbed to the last penny through fleecing taxation. Iqbal's heart beat for Kashmir and its broken people, a feeling amply reflected in his poetry. *Tod us dast-e-jafa kaish ko yarab jis ne Rooh-e-aazadi-e-Kashmir ko pamaal* kiya (O' God! Break the hand of oppression that razed the soul of Kashmir's freedom), he beseeched the Almighty, and engaged himself in creating awareness about the suffering of Kashmiris by voicing for their basic human and economic rights. He was in the forefront of the Kashmir Committee spearheading awareness about Kashmir, held meetings, addressed gatherings, and wrote verses. His activism, apart from his poetry for which he was adulated by Muslims across boundaries, earned him love and respect of Kashmiris in great measure, which they have sustained generations down. At the same time, it earned him enmity of Kashmir's ruling class and its apologists. He was criticized, vilified and even banned from visiting Kashmir.

Advocate Chona's four-page letter, accessed by this author, begins with an expression of gratitude for the "regard" Mirza as a Judge of His Majesty's Court of Judicature used to show to him and in view of which he felt obliged to disclose the "substance" of a conversation he had with the Governor of Punjab, Sir Geoffrey de Montmorency. The undated letter originating from Edwards Road, Lahore, speaks of Chona's meeting with the Governor at the Government Guest House "yesterday".[445] The conversation, Mirza is informed, was about Kashmir which "will interest you somewhat and will make you acquainted with the reason why 'the Muslim Outlook' [newspaper] and other persons who are at the bottom of the agitation against the Kashmir State are adversely criticizing your appointment as Minister of the Government of His Highness the Maharaja of Kashmir and Jammu."

After giving a resume of what allegedly transpired between him and the Governor, Chona drops a bombshell. He quotes de Montmorency as telling him that Allama Iqbal had come up to him for a minister-ship in Kashmir. "His Excellency told me that Sir Mohammad Iqbal had approached him for recommendation for being appointed as a Minister of the Kashmir State and being disappointed in his desire to secure the job had put himself at the head of the agitation", Chona informed Mirza.

The Advocate's claim was not an isolated allegation. There was some talk going on in a section of the Press in the Punjab about Allama Iqbal eyeing for minister-ship in Kashmir at a time when he was accused of mentoring the anti-Maharaja sentiment in the Valley. One newspaper went a step further and claimed that he wanted to become the Prime Minister of Kashmir. Another, hinting at him, wrote that a prominent leader of British India had applied for a post in the Kashmir Government.

Being the most influential Muslim voice in the British India, Iqbal's word carried weight. The supporters of autocracy saw in him a threat to the throne of Kashmir's Hindu ruler. A smear campaign was launched against him in the Punjab-based Press. He was accused of prompting Kashmiri Muslims and creating disaffection against the government. Motives were attached to his stand on Kashmir. Newspapers that had no qualms about siding with an oppressive regime circulated all kinds of stories to show him in bad light. A Kashmiri journalist going by the name of Gwasha Lal Koul fabricated a story about Iqbal instigating people to overthrow the Maharaja. The story was widely circulated. Koul claimed to be present at the residence of Iqbal in Lahore where "several suggestions to bring down the Kashmir Government were discussed." A Lahore-based newspaper in one of its special issues prominently published the purported contents of the alleged meeting, describing Iqbal's residence as "A hub of conspiracy".[446] Koul accused Iqbal of advocating public disorder in Kashmir at such a scale where rebellion would be inevitable.[447] Abdul Majid Saalik, Editor *Inqilab*, who Koul claimed took him to Iqbal's residence, rejected his narration of the meeting as "dishonesty and mischief of the extreme order" and an "absolute lie".[448]

Around this time, whatever was happening in the Valley was highlighted by the Punjab-based newspapers divided into two sections of the Hindu Press and the Muslim Press, with the former supporting the Kashmir Government and the latter promoting the cause of Kashmiri people. Besides, criticising Kashmir's majority community for seeking equality with minorities in matters of basic human and economic rights, the so-called Hindu Press castigated their leaders and sympathizers within and outside Kashmir. Iqbal, in particular, became a target of vilification and rumours. The *Kaisri* accused him of harbouring political ambitions. The newspaper alleged that Iqbal wanted to become the Prime Minister of Kashmir. The insinuation was that since he did not succeed in getting a ministerial berth in Hari Singh's Government, he was now spreading hatred against it and instigating Kashmiri Muslims against their Hindu ruler. The accusation was carried forward by the *Tribune*. On 26 August 1931, the widely circulated daily carried an article by G.S. Raghavan in which the author, without mentioning any name, wrote that the intentions of some personalities were revealed by the fact that during the Kashmir Agitation a prominent leader of British India had applied for a certain post in the Kashmir Government. Coming as it did soon after the *Kaisri* report, the hint was unambiguous. Raghavan was one among those journalists who in the backdrop of the Kashmir Agitation had taken upon themselves the task of defending the perpetrator and slandering the victim. He also visited and stayed in Srinagar for some time and filed stories from there, prompting some fellow journalists back in Punjab to ask who had sponsored him.

At a massive public rally, attended by 50,000 people, held in support of Kashmiris and presided over by Iqbal at Lahore on 14 August 1931, one speaker, Syed Mohsin Hassan Shah alluded to various rumours spread by newspapers against the Muslim leaders who had come out in solidarity with the people of Kashmir. He specifically referred to the *Kaisri* claiming that Iqbal craved for the Prime Minister's job in Kashmir while he (Syed Mohsin Shah) wanted to become a judge. In his address, Iqbal rejected the allegation and, referring to the Maharaja of Kashmir, declared, "*Mai aise haakim ki wazarat pe la'anat bhejta huni*" [I imprecate the ministry of such a ruler].[449]

Later, when Abdul Majid Saalik asked him who was the prominent Muslim leader Raghavan had mentioned as having applied for a post in the Kashmir Government, Iqbal replied that he could not say who the author had in mind but since a newspaper had already named him and since it was possible that somebody will be misled by Raghvan's words, he vehemently refutes this rumour. He recalled that he had categorically said at the Kashmir Day public meeting that he imprecates such a ministry. "I have never applied even for positions higher than this ministry. Moreover, I am a Member of the Kashmir Committee which wants reforms in the system of governance in Kashmir. Being a Member of this Committee, I consider it dishonesty and betrayal of trust to do such a thing",[450] he told Saalik. Significantly, after Iqbal publicly refuted the allegation, nobody came forward with any proof to the contrary.

Advocate Amar Nath Chona's letter to Mirza Zafar Ali Khan appears to be an extension and amplification of the allegation against Iqbal. Its contents more than establish this premise. The letter clearly identifies the Advocate with the pro-Kashmir Government sentiment. Showing off his proximity with the Governor of Punjab, Chona writes that he impressed upon him the need for the British Government to "publicly disapprove of the Kashmir agitation" and declare it "an act of unfriendliness against an ally of the Empire". He wrote:

> "I called His Excellency's attention in [sic] the virulent speeches that were made on 14th August by some so-called responsible people against the person of His Highness the Maharaja [Hari Singh] and suggested Government's taking action under the Princes Protection Act. I told His Excellency further that if *jathas* were permitted to be formed in and started from British territory that would be clearly an act of unfriendliness towards the [Kashmir] State on part of British Government and that would have very serious consequences and would complicate matters."

It may be in place to recall that after the 13 July carnage and subsequent crackdown on people in Kashmir, agitated groups of *Ahrars* from Punjab sneaked into the State territory from Jammu to show solidarity with protesting Kashmiris.

The letter further quotes Governor de Montmorency assuring Chona that the British Government were "certainly friendly towards the [Kashmir] State" and that "the persons who were at the bottom of the agitation had their own axe to grind." It is here that the Advocate then reveals to Mirza that the Governor confided in him that Iqbal had approached him for a recommendation for being appointed a Minister in Kashmir and that due to his failure in seeking the desired job he was now in the vanguard of the Kashmir Agitation. He informs Mirza that the Governor had asked from some Muslim gentlemen at Amritsar in what spirit would they take it if the Marhattas in neighbouring territories were to carry out an agitation against the Nizam of Hyderabad. The Governor, Chona adds, remarked that the speeches made in Lahore [by Iqbal and others] "were violent".[451]

Did Governor de Montmorency actually tell Amar Nath Chona that Iqbal had sought his recommendation for a Minister's post? While we do not have any evidence to suggest that he did or did not, the Advocate himself puts to question the contents of his letter when he advises Mirza to use the information he had given to him but ensure that his name was not mentioned. "You can make use of the information mentioned in the letter but I don't wish my name to be made public. You can certainly inform His Highness the Maharaja and the Prime Minister Raja Hari Kishen Koul of what I have stated", Chona writes and expresses confidence that "you will be serving the Government of His Highness the Maharaja in the same manner in which you served the Lahore High Court."

Before winding up his letter and informing Mirza that he is going to Simla "on a private business" where he wishes to avail himself an opportunity to meet the members of the Punjab Government and the Government of India "to nip the allegation against the Kashmir Government in the bud otherwise it will have very serious repercussions throughout India", Advocate

Chona makes a reference to Sir Shadi Lal, Chief Justice of the Lahore High Court between 1920 and 1934. He writes:

> It is a curious coincidence that in Sir Shadi Lal you had a very capable person as Chief Justice with whom you cooperated with loyalty and in Raja Hari Kishen Kaul you have got a most capable administration [sic] who, I doubt not, will set everything in Kashmir right and with whom you will cooperate just as you did in Lahore.[452]

The warm references to Sir Shadi Lal and Hari Kishen Koul in Advocate Chona's letter make it somewhat easy for a reader to place the context of his views on Iqbal and Kashmir. Justice Lal's 'special' relationship with Iqbal is a matter of record. In 1925, he played a 'dirty trick' to deny Barrister Iqbal a berth on the Lahore High Court Bench and gleefully narrated to 'Babuji', his friend and father of writer Ved Mehta, how he had "cooked the goose of two Punjabi Muslims"[453]—Iqbal and Khan Bahadur Shahnawaz—whom the Governor was considering for a vacancy of a Muslim Judge. When Babuji told him that he had made a grave mistake as both were "prominent Muslims and well qualified", he shot back, "Let Iqbal and Shah Nawaz cut each other's throats. Punjabi Muslims deserve each other."[454] It is a different matter that Iqbal and Shah Nawaz were best of pals and their friendship lasted till the former's demise in 1938. "Both had understood Sir Shadi Lal very well",[455] recounts Javed Iqbal, son and biographer of Allama Iqbal, who writes about an earlier incident when his father declined Lal's offer of recommending him for the title of *Khan Bahadur*. "I have no desire for any title. Please don't take this trouble",[456] Iqbal had told him. Javed counts the former Chief Justice of Lahore High Court among those "communalist Hindus of Punjab who could not stand the progress of any competent Muslim" and who though outwardly Iqbal's admirers, lost no opportunity to "poison the ears of English officers against him".[457] It is also important to recall Sir Shadi Lal's proximity with the Kashmir Darbar. He had been visiting Kashmir where Gulmarg seemed to be his favourite place for holidaying, and enjoyed full official hospitality. An urgent telegram sent by Maharaja Pratap Singh to Michael Adam Nedou, owner of the Nedous Hotel at Gulmarg, on 20 August 1905 speaks about Lal's closeness with Dogra rulers. Singh wrote:

> L. Shadi Lal, Bar-at-Law coming to Gulmarg tomorrow morning. Please accommodate him in Palace or Diwan Sahib's quarters and see to his all comforts. He shall be provided with everything free of charge. You are personally responsible for his comforts.[458]

As for Advocate Chona's optimism about Prime Minister Hari Kishen Koul 'setting everything right in Kashmir', the man in whom it was said "Machiavelli and Kautilya were combined",[459] failed to suppress the mass movement through machinations, force and intimidation, including that notorious threat he held out at Kashmiri leadership: "You do not know who I am. I will lock your mosques and snatch your freedom to pray and fast. I had made hell the lives of Akali Sikhs in Nankana. They would shudder on hearing my name."[460] Within a year, however, he was unceremoniously sacked by Maharaja Hari Singh and replaced with Colonel E.J.D. Colvin.

Coming back to Advocate Chona's letter, it is intriguing to observe that he wanted Minister Mirza to keep his name secret while information passed on by him was shared with Maharaja Hari Singh and his Prime Minister. Certainly, the letter would have endeared him to the Maharaja as a selfless person who was persuading the British Government to openly come out in his support in a time of crisis. It could have earned him Hari Singh's pleasure and many a worldly favour. At the same time, with Chief Justice Sir Shadi Lal being around, Iqbal would not be in a position to cause any harm to him if the letter was leaked. So, what was it that he was afraid of? The only explanation that comes to mind is that Chona did not want Governor Sir Geoffrey de Montmorency to get the whiff of what he had quoted him as saying.

Iqbal's Brahman Cousins

Iqbal was very proud of his roots in Kashmir. Like the majority of Kashmiri Muslims, his ancestors from a Kashmiri Brahman *gotra* Sapru, had converted from *Shaivite* Hinduism to Islam. Iqbal's taking pride in his Kashmiri origin is generally explained as his being proud about his Brahman ancestry. However, his son, Javed Iqbal, has a different opinion. He believes that the renounced beliefs carry no importance in the personal life of an individual and that their influence dissolves after a generation or a half. "Iqbal's ancestors", he argues, "had accepted Islam about four hundred and fifty years before his birth. Hence, what pride can Iqbal feel about his Brahman pedigree?"[461] For Javed, his father's verses pointing to the Brahman lineage actually carry sarcastic reference to the infighting of the Muslims in politics and the irony that if there was anyone informed about the secrets of Islam or its bright future it was a *Brahman zaadah* (scion of the Brahman), the reference being to himself.[462]

Be that as it may, Iqbal's acclamation of his Brahman cousins has attained proverbial status. His tribute to their qualities is extraordinary and could serve as the community's best PR statement. The *Javed Nama* contains verses overflowing with admiration of the *Brahman zaadgaan-e-zindah dil* or the 'Scions of the Brahmans with vibrant hearts'. Says Iqbal:

A'an Brahman zaadganan-e-zindah dil
Laleh-e-ahmar zi rooye sha'n khajil
Tez been-o-pukhta kaar-o-sakht kosh
Az nigah-e-sha'n farang andar kharosh
Asl-e-sha'n az khaake-e-daamangeer ma'st
Matla-e-ein akhtara'n Kashmir ma'st

(Those scions of Brahmans with vibrant hearts, their glowing cheeks put the red tulip to shame. Keen of eye, mature and strenuous in action, their very glance puts Europe into commotion. Their origin is from this protesting soil of ours, the rising place of these stars is our Kashmir.)

In *Payam-i-Mashriq*, Iqbal sang praises of a Brahman maiden's beauty like no poet could do:

Dukhtarey Brahmaney lala rukhey saman barey
Cheshm barooy-e-oo kusha, baaz ba khawaishtan digar
(A Brahman maiden, rose-cheeked and jasmine-bodied;
Cast your eye on her and turn it backwards upon yourself)

Unfortunately, however, Iqbal's warmth towards Kashmiri Pandits is one sided. The 'vibrant hearts' did not feel obliged to reciprocate. Widely recognised as a learned and educated community, its scholars many of whom were well versant with Persian and Urdu, the languages of Iqbal's poetry, simply ignored him.

During Iqbal's life time, Sir Tej Bahadur Sapru, a Kashmiri origin Brahman, was an honourable exception who had publicly expressed his liking for Iqbal. Sapru, who shared his family name with Iqbal, was not only warm towards him but also openly came out in his support when the latter was sought to be dismissed as a poet for the Muslims only. Sapru had read and appreciated Iqbal's poetry. When Rabindranath Tagore was awarded Nobel Prize questions were raised why Iqbal was ignored. The Western media then argued that Tagore was a humanist and a Universalist while Iqbal was the poet for Muslims. Rebutting the argument, Sapru said that Iqbal was a Universalist. "If Kalidas who wrote *Shakuntalam* is a Universalist, then Iqbal too is a Universalist",[463] he wrote. He justified Iqbal's voicing of Muslim concerns in the backdrop of the community being relatively voiceless compared to other communities.

In Jawaharlal Nehru, though Iqbal had another Kashmiri Brahman admirer but his praise of the poet was a garment on the body of criticism he did on his vision as the one who influenced the Muslim sentiment in British India. Ironically, Nehru, besides Sapru and some others, is believed to be one of those Kashmiri Brahmans who was in Iqbal's mind when he wrote those eulogising 'Scions of the Brahmans' verses. Nehru appears in two minds while expressing his opinion about Iqbal and, in fact, ends up giving him a left-handed compliment. In the *Discovery of India*, he presents himself as an admirer of Iqbal and his 'fine poetry' and greatly pleased "to feel that he liked me and had a good opinion of me." He recognises Iqbal as "a poet, an intellectual and a philosopher" but hastens to emphasise his "affiliations to the old feudal order." For him, Iqbal failed to influence the masses who were "hardly affected by him", and he was "very far from being a mass leader."[464] At the same time, however, he admits Iqbal's popularity "due to his having fulfilled a need when the Moslem mind was searching for some anchor to hold on to."[465] It is not difficult to see through Nehru's words a veiled attempt to establish Iqbal as a failure in his vision of Pakistan.

Nehru invokes Edward Thompson to suggest that Iqbal believed that creation of Pakistan "would be injurious to India as a whole and to Muslims specially."[466] He writes that Iqbal's "whole outlook on life does not fit in with the subsequent developments of the idea of Pakistan or division of India."[467] Thompson, it may be added, had twisted Iqbal's words to give an entirely different meaning to what he had told him. Iqbal had written to him that personally he believed that merger of the Muslim provinces in the north-west of India would be beneficial for England, India and Islam but he quoted him as saying that the proposal of Pakistan would be detrimental for British Government, Hindus and the Muslims. Iqbal wrote to him that as President of the Muslim Conference it is his duty to support separation of Sindh but Thompson put into his mouth words to the effect that as President of the Muslim League it was his responsibility to support the proposal for [creation of] Pakistan.[468] Nehru also wrote three articles in the *Modern Review*, Calcutta to counter Iqbal's views on the Ahmadis and the finality of the Prophethood.[469] In response, Iqbal wrote an exhaustive piece to justify his and the Muslim point of view on the subject in which he also had a dig at Nehru:

> It is obvious that for an Indian nationalist whose political idealism has destroyed his sense of recognition of the truth will not tolerate birth of the feeling of right to self determination in the hearts of the Muslims of the north-west India.[470]

Iqbal's support for Muslim sentiments and for Muhammad Ali Jinnah was not to the liking of the leadership of the Indian National Congress. He was blamed to have fathered the notion of dismembering the country, and labelled as "one of the most dangerous sponsors of Islamic hegemony."[471] Despite this, there is no dearth of Hindu scholars or writers who studied and extensively wrote about Iqbal and his poetry. Jagan Nath Azad,

Tara Chand Rastogi, Gopi Chand Narang, Maalik Ram and Kali Das Gupta Raza are some of the many big names among Hindu scholars that instantly come to mind. The lovers of Iqbal's poetry are in no less number in a Hindu-majority India than they are in a Muslim-majority Pakistan. There is also a whole body of literature on Iqbal written by Muslims of Kashmir and Kashmiri-origin Muslims among whom Khalifa Abdul Hakeem, Akbar Hyderi, Dr. G.R. Malik, Hamidi Kashmiri, Ghulam Nabi Khayal, Mohammad Din Fauq and Mohammad Amin Andrabi are in the forefront.

On the other hand, the Kashmiri Pandit scholarship has refused to look towards Iqbal. No writer or poet from the community considered him or his poetry for study. Ratan Nath Sarshar, Brij Naraian Chakbast and Daya Shankar Naseem who made it big in Urdu literature could have paid a return compliment to him. Nand Lal Koul Talib, with command over Persian and Urdu languages, wrote a book on Ghalib but felt no desire to write about an equally, if not more, renowned poet from his own land. Jia Lal Koul and many other community writers could not see beyond Lall Ded, the 14th century Kashmiri mystic poetess. An article or reference on Iqbal here and there by an odd Pandit writer [Moti Lal Saqi's *Iqbal Aur Bhagwat Geeta*] is all that is forthcoming if one searches for any literary work on Iqbal by Kashmiri Pandit scholars and writers.

Sixty-six years after Iqbal's demise, a Kashmiri Pandit author and Urdu teacher by profession, Premi Romani, made a humble attempt to break this community tradition by coming up with a book, *Iqbal Aur Jadeed Urdu Shairi* [Iqbal and Modern Urdu Poetry] in 2004. Romani thus has the distinction of being the only among Iqbal's Brahman cousins to write a book about his poetry. The great literary contribution of Iqbal that attracts scholars from world over, has failed to tempt them to write about it. It is intriguing to see a community which basks in the tradition of learning and scholarship ignoring an eminent poet coming from their own stock.

Why does Iqbal not invoke interest in the Kashmiri Brahman scholars and writers? There can be three reasons for their indifference towards him. First, his transformation from a nationalist poet [remember his poems like *Tarana-e-Hindi* (with that opening line *Saare jahan se accha Hindustan hamara*), *Ram, Himala, Swami Ram Teerath*] to an advocate of pan-Islamic unity [*Neel ke saahil se lekar ta ba khaak-e-Kashgar Aik hun Muslim haram ki pasbani ke liye* (From the banks of the Nile to the land of Kashgar, let the Muslims unite to guard the Grand Mosque)]. This transformation was negatively viewed by Hindus in general and their leadership in particular. Second, Iqbal was seen as the brain behind the division of India and the creation of Pakistan, although many scholars do not agree with this notion and argue that Iqbal's highlighting the Muslim identity in British India was misunderstood as his advocating a separate country for Indian Muslims. Third, his support for the cause of Kashmiri Muslims against autocracy did not generally go well with its adherents. Of the three, the last proved the main irritant for Kashmiri Pandits. Iqbal's stand on Kashmir situation in the aftermath of the 13 July 1931 carnage earned him disfavour from and virtual rejection by his very own *Brahman zaadgaan-e-zindah dil*. A historian among them even attempted to scandalise his ancestry.

A Kashmiri journalist turned historian, Pandit Gwasha Lal Koul, deposed against Iqbal before the Riots Enquiry Committee, constituted by the Kashmir Government after the July 13 incident. He alleged that Iqbal was instigating Kashmiris to overthrow Maharaja Hari Singh. He told the Committee that he had gone to the residence of Iqbal where several suggestions to overthrow the Kashmir Government were discussed. The allegation was picked and widely circulated by a section the Lahore-based Press. The weekly *Guru Ghantal*, in its special '*Kashmir Number*' published the contents of the purported meeting of Gwasha Lal with Iqbal under the caption: 'Dr. Iqbal's Mansion: A hub of Conspiracy—How a plot was hatched at Lahore against Kashmir Government.' The newspaper wrote:

> Journalist Mr. Gwasha Lal, BA has revealed before the Kashmir Enquiry Committee a very dangerous conspiracy to overthrow the Kashmir Government wherein he said, "I had gone to Lahore to attend the

meeting of the Kashmir Committee. [I] attended the public meeting. After that I was taken to the office of the Inquilab newspaper. There, I met Mr. Saalik. Then we went to the residence of Dr. Iqbal where suggestions to overthrow the Kashmir Government were discussed."[472]

The newspaper reproduced the purported conversation in which Abdul Majid Saalik, Editor *Inquilab*, was allegedly present. In the purported conversation Iqbal was accused of advocating public disorder in Kashmir at such a scale that it would lead to rebellion. The alleged conversation, in fact, was an attempt at discrediting an influential pro-Kashmiri voice in British India.

Abdul Majid Saalik who was quoted in the deposition as having escorted Gwasha Lal to Iqbal's residence refuted the allegation. In a press statement, the Editor *Inquilab* said that a Hindu youth whose name he did not remember had come to his office along with a group of Muslims from Jammu and expressed his desire to meet Iqbal. He said that he took them to Iqbal's residence where issues pertaining to Kashmir were discussed but to say that the *Allama* advocated public disorder and rebellion is dishonesty and mischief of an extreme order. Saalik published a rejoinder in his newspaper which was carried by some other newspapers also. He wrote:

> On the contrary, he [Iqbal] said that the Dogras have no reason to start a movement in Kashmir as they have their own government there. As regards Kashmiri Pandits and the Muslims they should foster unity and fight for their rights so that the matter remains between the ruler and his subjects and nobody gets an opportunity to make it a Hindu-Muslim issue. Beyond this, whatever has been said is absolute lie.[473]

Koul's deposition before the Riots Enquiry Committee turned out to be an attempt by an individual who was alleged to be on the right side of the Dogra rule, to remain in its good books. During the recording of witnesses, a witness described him as a "*riyakaar*" who was on the payroll of a minister in the Kashmir Government.[474] Majid stated that Koul had himself confided in him about receiving money from the minister. An internally circulated government report also accused him of receiving money from "one or the other Minister of the time" and being "opposed to the setting up of a responsible government in the State."[475]

About four decades later, R.K. Parimu, a Kashmiri historian, tried to scandalize the ancestry of Iqbal by identifying an alleged Pandit embezzler in Kashmir's revenue department during the Afghans rule as his grandfather. In his book, *A History of Muslim Rule in Kashmir (1320-1819)* published in 1969, Parimu wrote that in 1939-40 he came across a paper in the Persian documents of the State Archives, Jammu according to which one Sahaz Ram Sapru who was incharge of revenue during the governorship of Azim Khan had held the revenue in arrears having expended the money on his personal expenses including marriages in the family. When the embezzlement was discovered, Sahaz Ram admitted his guilt. He was offered death or conversion to Islam as penalty. The Pandit, according to Parimu, accepted Islam but at the same time requested that as Muslim he would not like to live in Kashmir, upon which he was allowed to settle in Sialkot. Parimu quotes Hassan Khoihami, a 19th-century Kashmiri historian, to claim that Azim Khan had sent Sahaz Sapru to Kabul to escort his wealth and family in 1818-19 wherefrom he must have gone to Sialkot.

Parimu's observation is reproduced in the works of some other writers, notably Khushwant Singh. In his article, *Iqbal's Hindu Relations*,[476] Singh reproduced embezzlement story but with a changed name. In his account, Parimu's Sahaz Ram Sapru becomes Rattan Lal Sapru. Singh attributes the narration of the story to Syeda Hamid. One does not know where from Hamid had lifted it but in the ultimate analysis Singh, a writer of high calibre, ended up producing a poor piece in which at one place he writes that the Sapru family shifted to Srinagar where Iqbal and most of his cousins were born but ten sentences later, says that Iqbal was born in Sialkot on 9 November 1877. An argument based on wrong information could not go any worse.

Parimu's linking of the alleged embezzlement with Iqbal's ancestor is gibberish. He has committed intellectual dishonesty by naming the revenue collector under Azim Khan's governorship as

Sahaz Ram Sapru when the official's name was Sahaj Ram Dhar, as recorded by Hassan whom Parimu quotes as his source.[477] Presenting Sahaz Ram Sapru, the alleged embezeller, about whom Parimu purportedly found a paper in the State Archives, with Sahaj Ram Dhar, the *Madarulmiaham* of Governor Azim Khan is an apology of scholarship. Even if Parimu's claim of finding the document is taken at face value the two are different persons. Hassan's Sahaj Ram Dhar was sent by Azim Khan to Kabul with his fortune and family when he was recalled by his minister brother Wazir Mohammad Khan, to assist him in the discharge of his duties as a minister after he had lost eyesight.[478] Efforts to locate the purported paper from the State Archives, whose index number Parimu has failed to mention even when he claims to have organised and listed the Persian record of the Archives Department, did not succeed. None of the index registers of the Persian record mentions this paper.

Iqbal's grandfather's name was Sheikh Mohammad Rafiq, not Sahaz Ram Sapru as Parimu would like us to believe. He ran a cloth shop in Sialkot. The family had converted to Islam about four hundred and fifty years before Iqbal's birth. Parimu's attempt to scandalize Iqbal's ancestry, thus, falls apart.

13
The Temple Agitation

Less than two months after the Jammu & Kashmir Muslim Conference was dissolved to replace it with a secular Jammu & Kashmir National Conference, Kashmir witnessed a major agitation in August 1939. Launched by its minority Kashmiri Pandit community against an attempt by the Maharaja Hari Singh Government controlled Dharmarth Department (now Dharmarth Trust), the agitation was against the takeover of the Durga Nag Temple in Srinagar. The agitation engaged angry protesters and police for several days, resulting in stone pelting, cane-charge, injuries to and arrest of many protestors, and litigation. It was second major outpouring against the government by Kashmiri Pandits in seven years after the Roti Agitation of 1932 when the community lock, stock and barrel hit the streets of Srinagar to safeguard its monopoly over government employment in the wake of the Glancy Commission Report. The Commission had conceded some demands of the Muslim majority population in matters of employment and education.

The Dharmarth Department was established by the founder of Dogra rule, Maharaja Gulab Singh, in 1846 for "erecting and maintaining temples, *dharmshalas* and *shivalas*."[479] In Kashmir several old and recently built temples were taken over by the Dharmarth Department which was provided for by the government like its other departments, besides by raising donations and different kinds of taxes. The Muslim peasants had to pay a certain tax known as *shitra shahi,* which went to the Dharmarth Department but they could not claim any help from the fund.[480]

The dispute over the Durga Nag Temple arose on the death of a non-local priest, Mahant Shiv Ratangir, also known as Mahant Shivrattnanad Saraswati, who had taken seat at the site during the rule of Maharaja Pratap Singh (1885-1925) and later built a temple and a dwelling unit on the land. Following his death on 31 July 1939, the Dharmarth Department, assisted by the government, tried to take control of the temple. The attempt was resisted by Kashmiri Pandits. The showdown continued for several days during which the Pandits took out massive processions, boycotted work in government departments, pelted stones on police and held sit-ins in the temple premises where community leaders made speeches against the temple takeover. The Pandit students of S.P. College, S.P. School and Government High School bunked classes and joined processions.

The Durga Nag Temple situated at the western extremity of Sonawar near the Burn Hall School in uptown Srinagar serves as the first stopover of the annual *Amarnath Chhari* procession after its departure from Dashnami Akhara, Budshah Chowk. It is a 20th-century shrine even as some accounts like the *Koshur Encyclopedia* (1989) and INTACH's *Cultural Resource Mapping of Srinagar City* (2010) give an idea of its very old origin which is not correct. The latter, without quoting source, gives its age as 'Approx. 285 years'[481] implying that it was constructed somewhere during the Mughal Rule over Kashmir. The temple is not mentioned in any of the old historical account on Kashmir including the *Nilamata Purana* (7th-8th century) and the *Rajatarangini* (12th century). Khuihami's *Tareekh-i-Kashmir* (19th century), Stein's *Ancient Geography of Kashmir* (20th century) and Anand Koul's *The Geography of Jammu & Kashmir* (20th century) also do not make any mention of the temple. The affairs of the temple and its properties are administered by the *Shri 1108 Jagatguru Shankaracharya Sharda Peeth Durga Nag Trust*, known in short as Durga Nag Trust, established in 1939. Over a period of time, the Trust has leased out on rent the temple land to different people who have raised hotels and commercial complexes over it. Several lessees, according to General Manager R.L. Bhan, are Muslims. "At least, 15 employees of the Trust are also Muslims."[482]

During the reign of Pratap Singh—a staunch Hindu ruler who religiously performed rituals, patronized priests, attended annual congregations at Hindu holy sites like Banaras (now Varanasi) in north-India and liberally donated money to Hindu shrines and organizations—Mahant Shiv Ratangir lodged himself in the foot of Rustum Garhi, the spur of the Shankaracharya hill spotting the second largest Muslim cemetery of Kashmir known as Malateng which also has a locality by this name in its midst. The cemetery has an exclusive enclosure, *Mazar-i-Sho'ra*, overhanging the temple premises, where prominent Persian poets of yore including Shah Abul Fateh, Tugrai Mashhadi, Qazi Abul Qasim, Mohammad Jan Qudsi, Mohammad Quli Saleem, and Mirza Abu Talib Kaleem who had come from Iran and other cities of central Asia, lay buried.[483]

Mahant Ratangir served as the *pujari* of the Shankaracharya temple. Senior resident of Sonawar, Mohammad Siddiq Parray (1907-2013), recalls that the *pujari* "would go up the [Shankaracharya] hill in the morning and climb down in the evening to retreat to his hut at Durga Nag."[484] In 1936, the Mahant Shiv Ratangir, also known as Swami Shankaracharya of Sharda Peeth Kashmir, had cabled from Multan his resignation from the *Gaddi of Shankaracharya* to Prime Minister of Jammu & Kashmir requesting him to forward it to the Maharaja for acceptance.[485] The Mahant's resignation was a reaction to, what he alleged, the "highhandedness of police" against his two servants one of whom had died in custody, in a case of theft at Durga Nag while the real culprit was not apprehended.[486] In response, the Political Secretary assured the Mahant of enquiry by Inspector General of Police, and told him that nothing would be gained by sending telegrams to the Prime Minister.

Residents of Malteng knew Mahant Shiv Ratangir as *Shiv Saad*. *Saad* is a Kashmiri synonym of *Sadhu* or mendicant. Although there exists no dispute over it, they claim the ownership of the land to be controversial. The temple management refutes this claim. Farooq Ahmad, 68, *Numberdar* of the area, recalls his late father narrating his own grandfather, Sultan Akhoon's account that prior to the arrival of the Mahant, the land was part of the Muslim community property categorized as '*Maqboozai*

Ahl-i-Islam'.[487] Historian Molvi Mohammad Shah Sa'dat (1880-1953) writes that Ratangir occupied a portion of the cemetery.[488] The President, Durga Nag Trust, Vijay Bakaya, however, asserts that there was no controversy over the ownership of the land.[489]

The *misel-i-haqqiyat*, based on the first revised land settlement executed in Samwat 1977, corresponding to 1921 AD, records the status of the land, and the kind of soil, which includes a spring, walls, path, willow grove, slope, rocky soil, constructions, human settlement, etc. The land spread over both sides of the road running in front of the temple, comprises 55 kanals and 3 marlas under survey numbers 7, 11, 174/1, 173/1, 13 and 18 under village Bonamsar, is entered in the name of 'Shankara Swamiji [Shankaracharya] Temple, village Kothi Bagh under the auspices of Mahant Shiv Ratangir, *Chela* Kalyangir'. Significantly, there is no mention of any temple existing on the land in 1921. The *Jama Bandi* of Samvat 1987-88 (1931-32 AD) and Samvat 1991-92 (1935-36 AD) also does not record any temple at the site which means that it was constructed somewhere between 1935-36 and 1939.

Immediately after the death of Mahant Ratangir who was buried in the temple premises where his *samadhi* was built, Kashmiri Pandits put forward a community member as the caretaker of the temple, asserting that the deceased priest had constituted a Trust and transferred to it the management of the Durga Nag Temple and its property. The Mahant was said to have constituted the Trust on 20 *Ashad* 1996 (corresponding to 4 July 1939) with Rai Bahadur Pandit Manmohan Lal Langar, Wazir Tej Ram, Kanwar Harnam Chand, Pandit Amar Nath Kak, Chandrajoo Advocate, Janardhan Teng and Sarwanand Channa as its Trustees. The Kashmiri Pandits sought control of the temple premises and denied the Dharmarth Department any right over the property. On the other hand, the Dharmarth Department claimed the temple premises as the property of the Shankaracharya temple, which, like many other Hindu shrines in Kashmir, was under its control, and the deceased Mahant was working as an appointee of the Maharaja like his predecessors. The President, Dharmarth Council, Wazir Tej Ram described the late Mahant as a "Manager only" of the Dharmarth Department who "could not evidently create any such Trust".[490] However, before the Kashmiri Pandits could take control of the temple and its property the Dharmarth Department swung into action and a team of its officials, assisted by police and other senior civil officers, reached the venue to take charge of the temple premises. A confrontation ensued between the two sides on 1 August which developed into a major agitation. The police physically stopped agitators to take control of the temple.

The Maharaja's Government took the side of the Dharmarth Department against the Kashmiri Pandits. On 1 August 1939, the Governor and District Magistrate (DM), Kashmir, Baldev Singh Pathania, warned the Senior Superintendent of Police (SSP), Baldev Singh Samyal, of certain persons out to create trouble, and asking him to take proper action and "ensure that there is no breach of peace nor should irresponsible persons be allowed to create fuss or interfere with the Dharmarth arrangements."[491] The DM's missive followed a letter to him written by Wazir Tej Ram the same day. The DM informed the SSP that the new Mahant would be appointed in due course by the Dharmarth Department which will, in the meanwhile, make arrangements to look after the property. He was asked to provide police protection to the Dharmath employees in looking after the temple property. The government accused the Sanatan Dharam Yuvak Sabha, an organisation of Kashmiri Pandit community, of instigating people and warned any person presenting himself as a Trustee of the late Mahant or claiming any connection with him. In a separate letter, Pathania assured Tej Ram of police arrangements to ward off any interference by "irresponsible persons."[492] For the government, these irresponsible persons were "well-known Kashmir Leaders, some Pleaders and some Government pensioners...trying to create some fuss in connection with the Durga Nag Temple and the property of Shri Shankaracharya temple."[493] The government rejected their claim over the property and challenged them to go to the court of law and establish their case.

In the afternoon of 1 August, when the officials of the Dharmarth Department arrived at the Durga Nag Temple to take possession of the premises, they were confronted by protesters who had assembled there in hundreds. They had occupied the premises and blocked every entrance, resulting in a fight between the two sides. Senior civil and police officers who arrived at the scene, found the *Mohtamim* of *Dharmarth*, Sant Ram, injured and "lying almost unconscious."[494] Efforts to disperse the gathering peacefully failed and the protesters, gaining more numbers, showed defiance and shouted slogans at which point the police swung into action. Two of, what the government called "the ring leaders," Shiv Narain Fotedar, President Yuvak Sabha, and Pandit Kashap Bandhu, were arrested, which further infuriated the mob that resorted to throwing at police "stones, brickbats, empty bottles, window panes and all other sorts of things",[495] which the government alleged had been collected previously. The police resorted to cane-charge and managed to clear the outer obstruction under the shower of stones.

As the police and the magistracy entered the outermost compound they were greeted with more resistance and stone pelting. The protesting Pandits had filled the compound to the brim and many had lain on the ground to block passage. Hundreds more had occupied vintage points towards the graveyard on the hill side end. They heavily pelted at the police, the magistracy and the Dharmarth officials, and managed to stop them for a while. The latter, twice lifted bodily by the mob, were rescued by the police. The whole premises including the verandah of the temple was strewn with stones and brickbats. Among the injured were the Additional District Magistrate, Superintendent of Police (CID) and a large number of police personnel including Inspectors and Sub-Inspectors. Eight protestors also were injured. The protesting mob tried to take out a mock funeral procession by placing a man on a *charpoy*. However, the 'dead' man ran away when police intervened. At least, 32 protestors including Fotedar and Bandhu were arrested.[496] The protestors withdrew from the scene at 9.30 P.M.

The retreating mob formed itself into a procession and proceeded to Sheetal Nath, the Pandit bastion, via the Nedous Hotel Road. Enroute, they pelted stones at the car of the District Magistrate in which the Inspector General of Police was also travelling, and broke its glass pane. They shouted slogans against the officials of the government. At Sheetal Nath, a protest meeting was held which was addressed by Pandit leaders including Amar Nath Kak, Janardhan Teng, Prem Nath Kanna, Shambu Nath Dhar, Sri Kant Chaku and Jigiasu. Resolutions were passed condemning the police action and the Dharmarth Department. It was decided that a group of five *satyagrahis* would daily court arrest. As a mark of protest, Kak announced his resignation from the Dharmarth Council, a government body. The speakers exhorted Pandit shopkeepers to down their shutters, Pandit students to abstain from classes and the community members to hold protest demonstrations.

On 3 August, a large procession, comprised mostly of college and school students, led by Amar Nath Kak and four other *satyagrahis*, was taken out from Sheetal Nath which proceeded towards Durga Nag. The protesters squatted on the road from Drugjan Bridge to the Durga Nag Temple and blocked traffic. The government alleged that they 'abused' the District Magistrate and other civil and police officers and pelted stones at them causing injuries to five policemen. The police cane charged the protesters some of whom in panic jumped into the nearby Tsunt Kol, an outflow channel of the Dal Lake. They were rescued by Muslim boatmen.[497] Three protesters were arrested. The protesters alleged that Shiv Narain Fotedar was dragged and beaten and many of them including a "well-known Pandit lady", namely Mathra Devi alias *Mata Ji*, were thrashed. The police rejected the allegation as a "malicious lie."[498]

On 4 August, Raghunath Vaishnavi, a liberal Kashmiri Pandit leader who later earned the sobriquet of *Pakistani Pandit*, addressed a public meeting at Chota Bazar Temple and later led a procession, mostly of students, to Durga Nag. The procession shouted slogans including 'Kashmir for Kashmiris', which a police report found "the only objectionable slogan."[499] Vaishnavi was accused of making "a very objectionable and exciting speech"[500] and was taken into custody under section 107/151 Cr.P.C. "so that he may not have an opportunity of further inciting the already excited mob."[501] Rashid Taseer, journalist and author of the four-volume *Tehrik-i-Hurriyat-i-*

Kashmir writes that Vaishnavi spoke on Hindu-Muslim unity and citizen's rights.[502]

At one point, there was this rumour making rounds in the city that the *samadhi* of the late Mahant was being removed from the temple premises. A poster was issued by the Pandits in which the government was accused of working hand in glove with the Dharmarth Department. It alleged that the District Magistrate had hosted a meeting at his residence in which the SSP, the Additional District Magistrate and the Dharmarth Officer, Pandit Thakur Dass participated. This infuriated the Pandits and the District Magistrate had to issue a denial on 8 August and ask the Publicity Department to contradict the rumour.[503] In another development, Ishar Singh Gorkha, an employee of the Dharmarth Department and four other Sikh *chowkidars* of Dharmarth resigned and left the temple premises. Singh was garlanded by the agitating Pandits.

The highlight of the agitation was participation in it by a large number of Kashmiri Pandit students and government employees. The government took a serious view of it. The intelligence reports identified employees, pensioners and students, and also pin-pointed government officials, including some holding high and responsible positions, whose wards were taking part in the agitation and slogan shouting against the government. The names included Surendernath Kak, son of Chief Secretary R.C. Kak, causing embarrassing situation for the senior-most bureaucrat in the government who would have already been in a tight spot as his elder brother, Amar Nath Kak, was the frontline leader of the agitation. Reacting to this, Kak, on the basis of his son's account, wrote to the District Magistrate that he had never joined any procession or attended any meeting. Only on one occasion, he added, his son had gone to Durga Nag to meet his uncle, Amar Nath Kak, when there was no meeting or procession going on there. He also wrote that his son was not a student of any educational institution in Srinagar and that his inclusion in the list was a case of mistaken identity.[504] However, on enquiry, the five Foot Constables, all Kashmiri Pandits, who had prepared the list of students, reiterated that they had seen Surendernath Kak taking part in processions along with college students even before 5 August and that they "knew him to be the son of Pt. Ram Chand[ra] Kak Chief Secretary."[505] The Governor of Kashmir, who also held the post of District Magistrate, had his own awkward moment when an official in his office, Shamlal, was also reported for taking part in the agitation. In response, the DM wrote to the Chief Secretary that he would deal with the concerned official and remarked that the Durga Nag agitation "is not to my mind purely religious. There must be other motives behind it."[506] However, he did not spell out those motives. A case of mistaken identity concerned the Wazir Wazarat Muzaffarabad whose cousin, Somnath Ambardar, was identified as his son. The Heads of educational institutions were asked to take action against students joining processions. Chief Secretary Kak issued a circular asking all Heads of Departments to ask their subordinates to exercise influence on their wards and ensure that they did not take part in the agitation. Some Kashmiri Pandits were reported to have collected funds at Maharajganj for carrying forward the agitation.

On 5 August 1939, a large procession comprising about 3000 people was taken out from Sheetal Nath which passed through Ganpatyar and Maisuma and reached Durga Nag. The protesters were shouting different slogans including *Inqilab Zindabad* (Long Live the Revolution). In the afternoon, Pandit Thakur Das managed to have Amar Nath Kak and his associates, who were on *satyagrah*, evicted from the rooms they had occupied in the temple premises a day earlier. In the process, Kak and Janardhan Teng received some injuries which the government dismissed as 'scratches.' As the news of the two leaders getting injured by the Dharmath employees spread in the city, protest demonstrations were held in different parts of Srinagar. Chief Secretary Kak visited his indisposed elder brother, Amar Nath Kak, at the Durga Nag Temple and stayed with him for about two hours.[507] Next day, another procession was taken out from Sheetal Nath. The protesters were carrying placards denouncing breaking of locks of "Durga Nag, our holy temple" and "dragging of our injured men to jail." On 9 August, another rumour about a protester, Vedah Ram of Chandpora,

Shalimar in a state of delicate health being kicked by Inspector Baldev Singh caused tension and spontaneous demonstrations in different parts of the city including Rainawari. The police said Ram, a former police constable, was not of sound mental health and had fainted due to heat and fatigue.

Meanwhile, several prominent people visited Amar Nath Kak in the temple premises including Shiv Nivas Shah, President Dogra Sabha, Jammu, Editor, the *Ranbir*, Jammu, Mulk Raj Saraf, Commissioner Srinagar Municipality, Ahsan Ullah, Ghulam Mohiuddin Hamdani alias Zohra and Prem Singh of Gurdwara Maharajganj. It was feared by the government that Sikhs might as well join the agitation and District Magistrate Kashmir on 9 August wrote to the Wazir Wazarat, Baramulla asking him to send for some responsible Sikhs and counsel them not to "jump in an affair with which they have no concern."[508] At a *dewan* held at Baramulla, the Sikhs had expressed solidarity with the agitating Kashmiri Pandits. At the Durga Nag Temple premises, few more people including Lala Shiv Ram Gupta, Editor *Amar*, Jammu, Advocate M. Assadullah, Satpal Vakil and college professors J.L. Koul and Sham Lal Dhar met Amar Nath Kak in an effort to diffuse the situation. In the meanwhile, protest demonstrations continued to be held in the city. On 9 August, the government issued an order prescribing routes and time for taking out and terminating processions. A procession was taken out from Durgeshwar Dal Temple which passed through Ban Mohalla, Fateh Kadal, Khanqah-i-Mohalla, Bohri Kadal, Malaratta, Nowhatta, Bahuddin Sahib, Bachhi Darwaza and Devi Angan.

The protesters received a shot in the arm when on 9 August the President of newly launched Jammu & Kashmir National Conference, Sheikh Mohammad Abdullah, extended his support to them. Abdullah was addressing a public meeting held under the auspices of his party at the Naqashband Sahib's shrine in downtown Srinagar. Referring to the ongoing Durga Nag agitation, he expressed sympathy with the Kashmiri Pandits and asked the audience to pray for them. He said that the dispute was neither religious nor political[509] but between two sides of the same community and the government should remain neutral and resolve the matter early.[510] Only two months back, Abdullah had dissolved the Jammu & Kashmir Muslim Conference, the largest political party of the Muslims of Jammu & Kashmir established seven years ago, and replaced it with secular Jammu & Kashmir National Conference to woo Kashmiri Pandits into its fold. On 15 August, the National Conference held a meeting at Gankhan, a downtown locality, where support to Kashmiri Pandits was reiterated. Pandit leader Jia Lal Kilam told the audience that Kashmiri Pandits have joined the National Conference and that if the Durga Nag issue demanded sacrifice he would be the first to offer it.[511]

Journalists and others who met Amar Nath Kak on 9 August were M.A. Sabir, Mulk Raj Saraf, Baldev Prasad Sharma, Pir Maqbool Shah Khanyari and Pandit Bhim Sein. Next day, another group of people including Ghulam Mohammad Sadiq, Pandit Niranjan Nath Kak, Pandit Niranjan Nath Dhar, journalist Radha Kishen Kak, Sudharshan Karihaloo, Janki Nath Sapru and Gan Lal Vakil had a meeting with Kak in the temple premises. The meeting of groups of people from different walks of life with Kak continued for several days. Meanwhile, the efforts by the Yuvak Sabha to persuade the Progressive Party of the Kashmiri Pandits to join the agitation did not materialize. The later did not show any enthusiasm.

Protest meetings were held also outside Srinagar in towns like Sopore and Baramulla. On 5 August, Yuvak Sabha held a meeting at Reshapir Temple at Sopore during which it was decided that a *jatha* of 17 persons would be sent every week to Srinagar to join protest marches to Durga Nag. On the same day, a protest meeting convened by Jagar Nath Chogtu, Secretary Pratap Temple Sabha, was held by Kashmiri Pandits in a temple premises at Gulmarg. The meeting, presided over by Charanjit Lal, Advocate from Peshawar, passed a resolution asking the government to restore the management of the Durga Nag Temple to the representatives of the late Mahanat Ratangir pending the settlement of the dispute by the court. At Rainawari in Srinagar, Kashmiri Pandits rented a house to hold meetings in connection with the ongoing agitation and prepare *jathas* and named the house as *Satyagrahi Aashram*.[512]

Amid standoff between the agitating Pandits and the Dharmarth Department, Raja Narender Nath, a Lahore-based Kashmiri origin leader, arrived in Srinagar on 13 August to negotiate a settlement. He was given authority and confidence by the Kashmir Pandits to enter into negotiations with the other side. Nath visited Durga Nag and met Amar Nath Kak. Next day, he addressed a public meeting at Sheetal Nath and told the audience that Kak and Fotedar had given him "full authority to regulate and control the present movement."[513] A resolution was passed reposing full confidence in Nath. The agitating Pandits were optimistic that he would be able to bring about an amicable solution to the dispute. It was rumoured that he had met the Prime Minister who reportedly told him that the Durga Nag Temple will be handed over to Kashmiri Pandits. However, Nath did not succeed in hammering out a solution. As days passed, the agitation seemed losing steam. The volume of protest demonstrations slowly started dwindling from thousands to hundreds. By 16 August, the government had the feedback that protesters were "tired of the present movement and were discussing this amongst themselves."[514] Pandit shopkeepers who had downed their shutters in protest were reported selling articles whenever they got opportunity to make sales.

The standoff on the Durga Nag Temple issue continued for days until the leaders of the agitation sent several letters to the government declaring that "the agitation had been withdrawn for all time and requesting amnesty for all those punished for taking part in it."[515] The government was informed that the Pandit community had moved the court of law for a decision on the temple dispute. The case was filed under Section 145 Cr.P.C. The signatories to the letters included Amar Nath Kak, Janardhan Teng, Shambu Nath Dhar, Janki Nath Koul, Sri Kant Chaku, P. Kannaw and S.L. Kannaw. On 18 August 1939, the government ordered general amnesty for all under-trial prisoners and those convicted and sentenced in connection with the agitation.[516] The District Magistrate Kashmir asked the Public Prosecutor to withdraw all the prosecutions whether for substantial offences or under security sections pending in the courts. The fines imposed on convicted persons were refunded and students penalized for taking part in the agitation were let go. During the agitation, 634 persons were arrested among whom 422 were convicted under different sections of law and 24 discharged.[517] In all, 68 police personnel suffered injuries while controlling the mob.[518]

The case to decide the title of the Durga Nag Temple and its property was heard by Judge Nila Kant Hak. An interesting development took place in the court when the *Mohtamim* of *Dharmarth* gave a statement that the Dharmarth Department had nothing to do with the Durga Nag Temple and that it was the property of late Swami Shri Rattnanand. He stated that the Dharmarth Department was not in possession of the Durga Nag Asthapan and that it was the property of "Jagat Guru Swami Shiv Rattnanand."[519] The development put the government and the Dharmarth Department in an awkward position and the Governor and District Magistrate Kashmir asked the Dharmarth Council to take disciplinary action against "such a disloyal employee of the Dharmarth Department."[520] After several hearings, the court decided the case in favour of the Kashmiri Pandits. Maharaja Hari Singh was not pleased with the judgment and conveyed this through Prime Minister Gopalaswami Ayyangar to Chief Justice of Jammu & Kashmir High Court, Justice Masood Hassan. The Chief Justice returned the royal message with a candid comment that the court was free of pressure and expedience, and if the Dharmarth Department felt that the ends of justice were not met it could go in for appeal against the judgment which it did.[521] However, the High Court upheld the judgment of the lower court, ending the dispute over the Durga Nag Temple property. It goes without saying that Maharaja Hari Singh took the court verdict in a stride and, notwithstanding his overriding powers, did not try to overturn it.

Although the Kashmiri Pandits won the battle for Durga Nag Temple against Maharaja Hari Singh's Dharmarth Department in 1939, the community does not see favourably its many temples and shrines in Kashmir still being under the control of the Dharmarth Trust headed by the late Maharaja's son, Dr. Karan Singh. They demand creation of a Shrine

Board and handing over to it 12 temples including those of Shankaracharya, Khirbhawani, Hari Parbat and Khrew to take their care and utilize the money generated from these shrines.[522] The Prem Nath Bhat Memorial Trust (PNBMT), one of the organizations representing Kashmiri Pandits, is pitching for Temples and Shrines Bill to "pass the control of shrines and temples from the elite to the ordinary people and clear the way for the creation of an elected board that will manage places of worship on behalf of the people."[523] The Dharmarth Trust and its strong support base in Jammu are vehemently opposed to such an idea.

14
Through the Dogra Rule

Raining Stones and Snakes

Kashmir is known in history as a place of natural and unusual calamities. Earthquakes, famines, epidemics, floods and fires have been frequent visitors to the Valley. But ever heard of stones and snakes falling from the sky? Strange though it may sound, the official records describe two such incidents occurring in south Kashmir over a century ago.

In 1912, when Pratap Singh, an exceedingly superstitious person, was the ruler of Kashmir, a strange incident was reported from a village in Shopian in south Kashmir. People were shocked and shaken to the core on seeing, what was described as, stones falling from the Heaven. The natives interpreted it as a frightening sign of the coming events. As the news of falling stones reached the Palace in Srinagar, an anxious Pratap Singh asked for spiritual interpretation of the incident. Pandit Jagdeshji, the Palace priest, was approached and asked if the falling of stones bore any bad luck for the Maharaja and, if it did, he might as well ward it off by offering special prayers. Funds were ordered to be placed at his disposal for meeting the expenditure on performing the *puja*. The priest marshaled his knowledge and spirituality to decipher the incident for his master and came up with an interpretation that Pratap Singh would have least wanted to hear.

Unlike in the case of the Roman Emperor Maximillian who convened his council to find out meaning of the fallen celestial matter in 1492 AD and was told that it was a good omen for his wars against the French and the Turks, the Pandit told the

Maharaja's Chief Minister that the incident forebode drought for the country and trouble for the ruler.[524] However, he had the remedy too up in his sleeves and suggested certain religious ceremonies to be performed so that bad effects of the incident were neutralised. The Pandit presented a handwritten three-page list of the ceremonies to be performed including a *yag* for the appeasement of gods of Moon, Sun, Wind and Indra; gold, food and a white horse to be given away as a *sankalp* and 43 items required for performing *puja*. The items that he listed with an estimated cost of ₹ 500 were as varied as silk cloth, clay of seven colours, thread of five colours, flour, coconut, golden idols of Sun, Moon, Indra and Varuna (Hindu gods), cut pieces of cloth, five types of leaves, flowers, incense sticks, sandalwood, betel nut, oil, ghee, rice, fruits, cardamom, wood, grass mat and an umbrella.[525]

The Chief Minister recommended to the Maharaja the sanction for provision of ₹ 500 from the 'Foreign Miscellaneous' account head which was granted with the instructions that "Pandit Jagdeshji may be deputed to have the ceremonies performed in a proper manner under the proposed (Dharamarth) supervision".[526] The order was signed by Pratap Singh on 15 April 1912. About two months subsequent to the issue of this order, on 10 June 1912, the Superintendent Dharamarth informed the Secretary to the Chief Minister:

> The proposed ceremonies for the appeasement of deities are being performed through Pandit Jagdeshji and a report will be submitted to you when the said ceremonies are accomplished.[527]

Pandit Jagdeshji submitted his report, along with vouchers of expenditure on 5 *Har* 1969 *Bikrimi* corresponding to 17 June 1912, about the conclusion of the ceremonies at Shergarhi, Srinagar which, he wrote, were successfully held "in accordance with the *shastras* and "with the high fortune" of the Maharaja".[528]

The rained stones that disturbed Pratap Singh were parts of a meteorite, rocks from space that continually fall to the Earth's surface and give an insight into the material the solar system is formed of. As records indicate, four pieces of a meteorite were recovered from the site in Shopian, two of which are now among the prized collection of the SPS Museum, Srinagar. The objects were received in the Museum from the Superintendent of Police, Kashmir Province on 25 May 1912, sixteen days ahead of the instructions from the Chief Minister's office that the objects be sent to the local museum for display.[529] The other two pieces were given, one each, to the then British Resident in Kashmir, Mr. Frasin and the Prince of Wales College, now Gandhi Memorial Science College, Jammu.[530] However, a model of the meteorite is in the museum of the Geology Department of the institution. No record about the actual object is available.

The place where the pieces of the meteorite fell is the Nadigam plateau, about 3 to 4 kilometers from the Shopian town.[531] Local people had described it as *sang baaran* which had also created craters on the plateau. The Muslims of the area offered special prayers to seek Allah's mercy in the wake of the scary incident.[532] The fall, accompanied by a thunderstorm, appears to have happened in late March or first week of April 1912 as the first official communication from the Palace, Jammu addressed to the Chief Minister is dated 6 April 1912. In the communication, Pratap Singh refers to the reports that he had heard about the "very inauspicious" occurrence in Kashmir in the form of "the fall of stones from above (Heaven)" and issued instructions that "ceremonies as may be dictated by the *shastras* should be performed".[533]

The Shopian meteorite is one among the 1085 falls of various sizes and weight around the world documented up to December 2009 and listed in the widely used databases, most of which have specimens in modern collections. The meteorite is classified as Group H and Petrologic type 6 and is also represented in the collection of the Natural History Museum, London.[534] The Museum entry records the weight of the meteorite as 5 kilograms. The study of meteorites reveals interesting information. Based on their composition, the meteorites are divided into three categories of Iron meteorites, Stony-iron meteorites and Stony meteorites. The overwhelming 94.5% of the documented 1085 meteorites including the Shopian meteorite belong to the last category. The Shopian meteorite fall occurred during 1901-20, the period when the world witnessed the third highest number of 118 documented meteorites and the highest ever recorded in any single continent during any given period of 20 years since 1800 AD. The world-wide highest two numbers of meteorite fall of 161 and 123 relate to the periods 1921-40 and 1961-80.

Though meteorites have not been generally known to cause destruction to life, the crash of a Boeing 747 aircraft from New York to Rome in 1996 was talked about as being the possible result of a meteorite strike. The two pilots of another plane flying in the vicinity had reported that they suddenly saw in the distance a strong and intense flash of white light which followed a descending and vertical trajectory and broke in six seconds. Eyewitness account also spoke of a streak in the sky just before the crash.[535]

People across the globe are known to have different beliefs about meteorites or shooting stars. While most of them consider these as bad omens, some like ancient Greeks held meteorites as objects of reverence. Many Greek and Roman temples enshrined rocks that had reportedly fallen from the Heaven. Instances of meteorite worship have been noted from Europe, Asia, Africa, and the Americas. The situations in which meteorites have been found at the Hopewell Mounds in the United States suggest that they were worshipped. "Few natural objects have more generally been worshipped by the human race than meteorites. From the dawn of history to the present there has probably never been a day when there was not being carried on somewhere upon the globe the worship of a 'sky stone'".[536] A shooting star crossing the night sky is a breathtaking scene with a degree of romance attached to it. Many people, especially in the West, wish on seeing such a spectacle. In some traditions it represents a sign of someone's death.

Notwithstanding the superstition associated with meteorites, Kashmir did not see any perceptible change in the fate of its unfortunate people or fluctuation of luck of their ruler in 1912 or the years in its immediate trail. The year, though, saw a flood taking place in the Valley which was far less in intensity and destruction than some of the worst preceding it. An unrelated tragic incident, however, took place continents away resulting in the death of 1503 passengers when the Titanic sank in the Atlantic Ocean in the wee hours of 15 April 1912, incidentally the day when the Maharaja sanctioned expenditure for performing ceremonies to ward-off the evil effects of the meteorite. No one could have blamed the shipwreck on the Shopian meteorite as the news of the tragedy must have reached the Valley, or of the meteorite travelling outside of it, in years given the status of communications then.

That nothing bad or untoward happened to Pratap Singh following the Shopian meteorite must have elevated Pandit Jagdeshji in his estimation, for he was soon summoned to interpret for the ruler another worrisome incident happening in yet another south Kashmir village. Two years after the Shopian meteorite fall, people in Kulgam Tehsil were stricken by dread when in 1914 AD, as official record puts it, snakes rained with snow in the village. The Pandit interpreted the "fall of snakes from the Heaven" as an indication of war breaking out "on the spot where snakes, fishes, etc. fall from above". He submitted an estimate amounting to ₹ 338 and *anna* 1 for performing *shanti puja* to "pacify the evil effects of the fall of snakes with snow".[537] The Dharamarth Department was asked to provide funds for the ceremonies which declined to do so, citing religious scruples that its money could not be used for this purpose. The Maharaja then asked his Chief Minister to arrange funds for the *puja*.

It might be of interest to the reader to know that in very olden times when Kashmir was ruled by Marhan Dev and Kaman Dev, the two siblings who are said to have shared the country between themselves, a huge python is reported to have fallen with torrential rain. Kaman Dev was debauch and ruthless who ruled Kamraz (north Kashmir) and made lives of his subjects hell. People in large numbers migrated from Kamraz to Marhan Dev's dominion, Maraz (south Kashmir), to escape torture. The incident was followed by appearance of a *dumdaar sitarah*, considered to be a bad omen, announcing the wrath of God.[538] Torrential rains and flood that followed brought havoc to life and property. During heavy rains, a huge python fell from the sky at Chakdar. The reptile was active for two days and, after death, we are told, its body lasted for a year.[539]

A Forlorn Pandit

During the reign of Gulab Singh (1846-57), two Christian missionaries came to Kashmir on a reconnoitering task in 1854 AD to assess the field for their activities. Rev. Robert Clark and Colonel Martin found the first Dogra ruler quite willing to allow them to preach in Kashmir for which he had his own argument. The Maharaja observed:

> My subjects in Kashmir are very bad. I am sure that no one can do them any harm. I am rather curious to see whether the *Padre Sahibs* [emphasis intended] can do them any good.[540]

One could not have expected a better opinion of his subjects from a ruler who had attained the throne through the foulest transactions in the history of the mankind.[541]

In 1864 AD, Clark founded the Kashmir Medical Mission in Srinagar under the aegis of the Church Missionary Society. Incidentally, he was one of the three Englishmen including Rev. T.R. Wade and the then British Resident against whom some local people later allegedly performed witchcraft to get rid of them.[542]

Next year, Dr. W.J. Elmslie came to Srinagar and started his medical work. He introduced the use of chloroform and, therefore, painless surgery in Kashmir. His successors carried on his work after his demise and Dr. Arthur Neve arrived in Srinagar in 1882. Two years earlier, educational work had been started by Rev. J.H. Knowels which was further developed by, now famous, Rev. C.E. Tyndale Biscoe in 1890 and beyond.

Did the Christian missionaries come to Kashmir for providing health and education facilities only or was the social service a cover up for engineering conversions?

"Among the depressed classes there are unlimited openings for Christian teachers. The door is wide open"[543], wrote Ernest Neve, brother of Arthur Neve, about Kashmir and groups of people accessible for Christian teaching. Indeed, Kashmir was the land of depressed population during the Dogra rule. Side by side with imparting modern education and medically treating the sick, the missionaries did the job they knew the best—preaching Christianity. In 1926, more than 3300 Gospels were sold in Kashmir to patients and their friends.[544] This we have straight from Ernest Neve. "If our methods are sound and our lives at all adequately emphasize our teaching, there should be no room for doubts as to results"[545], he wrote about the sale of the Gospels. What else would one understand by 'results' other than conversions?

Known for their good work in education and health sectors, the Christian missionaries have often courted controversy in Kashmir for their alleged trespass into the area other than of their pronounced activity. Ever since their arrival in the Himalayan Valley, there have been allegations against the Christian missionaries of converting people by the lure of money. On several occasions, there have been protests against their role and at times things have turned unpleasant. As recently as in 2012, there erupted a huge controversy about their role in Kashmir and the alleged conversion of a large number of youth at their hands. A video appeared on the YouTube in October 2011 showing baptism of some Muslim youth at the All Saints Church in Srinagar resulting in huge public uproar and resentment.

Four Pastors, C.M. Khanna, Gayoor Massi, Chandra Kanta and Jim Borst, were accused of luring Muslims to Christianity. Police in Srinagar filed a criminal complaint against Pastor Khanna for promotion of religious enmity by conversions. He was arrested and spent 40 days in jail before granted bail by a court. While the Grand Mufti of Kashmir 'ordered' expulsion of the four Pastors from Kashmir, the Chief Cleric of Kashmir, *Mirwaiz* Umar Farooq, condemned the Christian missionaries for "clandestinely enforcing conversions in Kashmir in lieu of money and other privileges."[546]

The complaints of conversion by allurement against the Christian missionaries in Kashmir are not new. While some could be exaggerated not all can be dismissed as untrue. A few years back, media reports suggested that there was a sharp increase in the number of neo-Christians in the Valley even as there were over a dozen Christian missions and churches, based in the U.S., Germany, the Netherlands and Switzerland, operating in Jammu & Kashmir. Pastor Khanna landed up in jail for allegations against him which were serious[547] but there have been famous missionaries like Dr. Arthur Neve and pioneer of modern education in Kashmir, C.E. Tyndale Biscoe, who in the past also faced allegations of enticing people to Christianity.

In March 1915, a complaint was made to the then ruler, Maharaja Pratap Singh, by a self-acclaimed 'forlorn Kashmiri Pandit', Gulab Ram Gigu, against the two Englishmen for allegedly converting his son, Madho Bhan, to Christianity. Gigu wrote a long petition and managed to deliver it to the ruler in person. The petition began with a lament:

> I am a forlorn Kashmiri Pandit, and approach your Highness' presence in the extreme anguish of my heart, and beg to lay before your Highness the tortures and troubles to which I have been put to.[548]

Gigu alleged that he had sent his son to the Christian Mission School, Srinagar where Tyndale Biscoe wanted to convert him to Christianity along with two other boys. He accused him of deception by saying that he would teach medicine to Madho and pay him ten rupees per month. Dr. Arthur Neve engaged Madho in the Mission Hospital Srinagar on the promised monthly pay and Gigu had no objection, as "there were many Hindus serving there".[549] On 15 March, Madho left his home in the morning telling his mother that she should not expect him back tonight. When he did not return the second day Gigu was alarmed. He went to all his relatives to look out for his son but found him nowhere. At this time, he heard that Dr. Arthur Neve had taken Madho to the Plains and had converted him to Christianity.

Distraught, Gigu along with his brother and Madho's father-in-law went to see Ernest Neve, brother of Arthur Neve, and enquire about his son. He was told that Madho had gone "to learn" with Dr. Arthur Neve and will not return as he was ill-treated at home. "What pain did he experience at our hands", asked Gigu of Ernest Neve, adding, "You pay him rupees ten per month, the clothes he has on cost ₹ 50".[550]

Ernest Neve, Gigu alleged, did not share with him the address of his brother and told him if he wanted to write a letter to his son he must hand that over to him which he will post himself. Gigu wrote a letter to Dr. Arthur Neve requesting him to "return me my son within eight days" or else "I would be compelled to go to Jammu Railway Station to lay case at the feet of His Excellency the Viceroy". "I would take along with myself my brother, Madho Bhan's young wife and her parents", he wrote and handed the letter over to Ernest Neve. He did not get any reply. Then he sent a registered letter which also remained unanswered.

Gigu then approached the Maharaja for taking "pity on our deplorable condition and the helpless state of the poor and forlorn Hindu girl [Madho's wife], who cannot remarry according to the Hindu laws, and for the sake of God to direct Dr. A. Neve to send my son back to me". He informed the Maharaja that he had stopped to personally go to Ernest Neve as he was followed by a large majority of Hindu population who demanded justice and feared that if he went to Neve the latter might accuse him of causing a "riot or rebellion".[551]

Pratap Singh marked the representation to his Chief Minister in whose presence it had been submitted to the Maharaja. He had also discussed the matter with him and called for a report as to "how the matter stands". On 28 April 1915, Ernest Neve was asked by the Governor of Kashmir to give his version of the story. He wrote back, "Like the German War Reports Gulab Ram Gigu's petition is a skilful mixture of falsehood and truth".[552]

According to Neve, Madho Bhan was indeed a student of Mission School at one time and subsequently on the staff of the Mission Hospital where he was trained as a dresser and assistant in the pathological laboratory and also passed the first aid examination of the St. Johns Ambulance Society. He alleged that Madho was ill treated at home for "he was enquiring into the Truth of the Christian Religion".[553] He further stated that when his doctor brother was leaving Kashmir for the Punjab for hospital inspection duty before going to the War, Madho Bhan expressed his desire to accompany him and did not inform his relatives about leaving Kashmir lest they prevent him and subject him to ill treatment. Ernest Neve's argument was that Madho was of age and responsible for his own actions and that he had made a statement on affidavit before a Magistrate at Amritsar as to his reasons for wishing to leave Kashmir. He accompanied Dr. Arthur Neve to Lahore and subsequently went to Agra from where his friends received his letters and his uncle went there to "forcibly" bring him back.

The reply of Ernest Neve was submitted to Pratap Singh who disposed the file. The matter rested there.

The petition of Gulab Ram Gigu is a part of the State archival record. The handwritten petition addressed to the Maharaja is an emotional read:

> Your Highness, I am a forlorn Kashmiri Pandit, and approach Your Highness' presence in the extreme anguish of my heart, and beg to lay before Your Highness the tortures and troubles to which I have been put to. I had sent my son to Church Mission High School, Srinagar to be educated. I had no knowledge that this would result in my dire destruction. It is three years now that it was rumoured in the city that Mr. Biscoe wished to convert three Hindu boys to Christianity hooking them with the bait of decent and fair salaries. My son Madho Bhan too was included in those three boys. He (Madho Bhan) was deceived and Mr. Biscoe was informed of the fact. Mr. Biscoe in turn deceived us, he never meant to convert Hindu boys but would teach him the practice medicine and would pay ten rupees per month. Accordingly Dr. Neve paid him ₹ 10/- per month and he worked in the Mission Hospital Srinagar. I consented and did not raise any objection thinking that there were many Hindus working there.
>
> On the first March 1915 my son went to the Hospital early in the morning as was usual with him. He told his mother that she need not expect him back tonight as he would probably stay at her sister's house for the

night. Then in the evening of second day too he did not come. I felt anxious and went to the Mission Hospital to look after him and find out the cause of his yesterday's absence from home. I could find nothing there. I set a search at foot at all the relations but to no purpose. Then it was rumoured that Dr. Neve has taken Madho Bhan along with him to the Plains and has converted him to Christianity. I, my brother and Madho Bhan's father-in-law, we all three then went to Dr. Ernest Neve. He was at his meals and we were asked to wait when we sent word to him. He came out after he finished dinner and we enquired of him as to the whereabouts of Madho Bhan. He replied that he has gone with Dr. A. Neve. We asked him, will he come back with Dr. Sahib. He replied "No. He has gone to learn. He wishes to be free. You illtreated and troubled him." I said, "What troubles did he experience at our hands. Think sir for a moment, you paid him rupees ten per month the clothes he had on cost ₹ 50/-. He was our darling, and we loved him better than ourselves." Dr. Sahib still persisted and said, "No you troubled him". I replied, "What you say is not true. Who troubles and illtreats his son and what sympathy can you Englishmen have with him—a Kashmiri[?]". He replied, "No you may go he will not come". We then asked him about his address. He said, "If you have to write anything to him, you may give it to me, and I shall post it myself after having written the address upon it." In the evening we sent a letter to Dr. A. Neve through Mr. E. Neve, [in] which I requested him to return me my son within eight days. I wrote therein that I would be compelled to go to the Jammu Railway Station to lay case at the feet of H.E. The Viceroy in the presence of Your Highness. I would take along with myself my brother, Madho Bhan's wife and her parents. We did not receive any reply to it. Then we sent a letter under registered cover to Dr. A. Neve and Dr. E. Neve but still we were unanswered.

We do not go to Dr. Neve personally now because we are followed by a large majority of Hindu population to demand justice. We fear, perhaps Dr. Neve may not accuse us of riot or rebellion.

We are obliged to request Your Highness to take pity on our deplorable condition, and into consideration, the helpless state of the poor and forlorn Hindu girl—his (Madho Bhan's) wife—who cannot remarry according to the Hindu laws, and for the sake of good to direct Dr. A. Neve to send my son back to me.[554]

At His Majesty's Service

Apart from using an iron fist to perpetuate its hold on people, autocracy sometimes also takes recourse to certain soft methods to achieve this objective. The Dogra regime at one point in time roped in Muslim clergy, through incentives including periodic cash doles, to generate kind feelings among the masses towards their rulers.

In a religiously minded society like Kashmir where the clergy commanded respect and obedience, the Dogra rulers tried to keep it on their right side. They annually distributed *khillats* among the *molvis* and *muftis*. The distribution of grants, however, was subject to specific condition of loyalty and devotion to the 'Throne and Person of His Highness the Maharaja Bahadur'. Strange as it may sound, when the masses in Kashmir were up against an autocratic and oppressive rule, many of their *molvis* were harvesting the fruits of loyalty to the oppressor. On *Eid-ul-Fitr*, the annual Muslim festival celebrated as thanksgiving on culmination of the fasting month of *Ramadan*, Pratap Singh and Hari Singh issued *khillats* valuing ₹ 203 and ₹ 255 and *Annas* 8 annually to the *molvis* and *muftis* of Jammu and Srinagar, respectively.

In return, the recepients who led prayers and delivered sermons to the faithful in mosques, would pledge, often in writing, their loyalty to the ruler. The grant would be stopped if the recipient was found violating the laid down condition. To ensure that the recepients did not violate the loyalty provision, a strict watch was kept on them and where a violation was reported the *khillat* was stopped. If there was delay in disbursement of the grant, the beneficiary *molvis* would make a written request to the government for its early release.

In 1922, the caretaker of the Srinagar's Jama Masjid, Mir Mohammad Abdullah Qadri Aalikadali, in a written representation made on 30 *Jaith* 1979 *Bikrimi*, corresponding to 20 June 1922, implored the *Aala Huzoor Faiz Ganjoor Bandagaan-i-Sri Sarkar Wala Madaar* (long salutations for the Maharaja, in this case Pratap Singh) to grant him a Pashmina shawl costing ₹ 60 that he would receive annually from him on the *urs-i-shareef* of Hazrat Miranji Sahib [Sikh and Dogra rulers of Kashmir reverentially called Hazrat Sheikh Abdul Qadir Jaeelani as Miranji]. The plea was made with the prayer, "May the Sun of the ruler's grandeur and majesty ever shine on the horizon of fortune and wealth". The petition was examined by the administration which found that a Pashmina *chadar* for the year was indeed due to the applicant and recommended the case to the concerned Member of the Council, Hari Singh, who approved the issuance of the shawl on 28 July 1922.

A communication from the Governor of Kashmir to the Minister-in-Waiting dated 1 *Magh* 1988 *Bikrimi*, corresponding to 21 January 1931, recommended the release of annual *khillats* in favour of some *molvis* in view of the fast approaching *Eid-ul-Fitr*. The report refers to one Molvi Zia-ud-Din of Dukan-i-Sangeen as being reported against by the Deputy Inspector General of Police for his son, Jalaluddin, taking part in the agitation of 1931. Jalal had also served a jail term in this connection. Molvi Zia was a recipient of the grant from the Darbar. The participation of his son in an anti-government agitation would mean for him the stoppage of annual grant but he had his own argument to avoid the punishment.

The Governor had called Molvi Zia to explain his position. Zia told him that while it was true that his son was an active leader of the movement but he did not share his ideas on this count. "*Aise mamlaat mai apnay farzand ke saath mera ilhaq nahi*" (On this issue, I have no agreement with my son), was his answer. He also informed the Governor that his son was now taking very little part in the movement.

The Governor's report clarified that there was no complaint against any other *molvi* or *mufti* of taking part in the ongoing mass movement and recommended the release of *khillat* in their favour. In case of Molvi Zia, the report said that if rules permit he may also be considered for the *khillat*. The report further said that since Molvi Sa'd-ud-Din and Aman Ullah of Wazapora had expired, their descendants may be considered for the grant. Outside the list of would-be-beneficiaries, the report also mentioned Pir Mohammad Shah, *Imam Masjid* Paristan, Uri and Abdur Rehman, *Imam Masjid* Muzaffarabad as having taken part in the "current agitation".

Before his demise in 1925, Pratap Singh had ordered that *khillats* should be granted in accordance with past practice to those persons only who had not taken any part in the agitation of 1924.[555] The matter was submitted to Hari Singh, the new Maharaja, for his orders. The Governor of Kashmir's report said that other than *Mirwaizs* Ahmad Ullah and Ahmad Ullah Hamdani, no *molvi* or *mufti* to whom *khillat* was granted had taken part in the agitation. The foreign secretary to the Maharaja recommended to him the grant of *khillat* except in the case of the two *mirwaizs* for taking part in the agitation.

A communication from the Minister-in-Waiting, Colonel Nawab, on 1 February 1932, mentioned, besides the son of Molvi Zia-ud-Din, Molvi Mohammad Ishaq, the *Imam of Eidain*, and Yaqub Ali of Lahore Party as having taken part "in the recent disturbances" and suggested to the Prime Minister that *khillats* to them be stopped. Prime Minister Hari Kishen Koul forwarded the case to the Maharaja with the recommendation that since Molvi Mohammad Ishaq had been taking an active part in the Ahrar Agitation he should, therefore, "in my opinion not be granted a *khillat* this time. *Khillats* may be granted to the others." Hari Singh approved the recommendation.

The recipients of *khillat* in 1931 included 27 *molvis* and *imams* of Kashmir including siblings in some cases. A list of that year gives details of the amount of grant given to each of the beneficiary. The recipients were a virtual 'Who is Who' of the then Srinagar city's clergy. The list included Khawaja Abdur Rahim [Banday], caretaker of Hazratbal shrine, Molvi Ghulam

Mohammad, Imam of Khanqah-i-Moalla, Molvi Ghulam Ahmad, Imam of Hazratbal and Molvi Ghulam Mehmood, Imam of Jama Masjid and Idgah. The highest amount of individual grant was ₹ 30 given to Molvi Rafi-ud-Din and Abdul Gani, sons of Molvi Sa'd-ud-Din of Wazapora and the lowest of ₹ 4 and *Annas* 8 to Molvi Aziz Bangi and Molvi Najm-ud-Din, sons of Salam-ud-Din, and Ahmad Baba, son of Gani Baba, all residents of Jama Masjid. The *Imams* of Jama Masjid, Hazratbal and Khanqah-i-Moalla received a grant of ₹ 11 each.

The recepients of *khillats* in *Samvat* 1887 corresponding to 1931 AD were Molvi Rafi-ud-Din and Abdul Gani sons of Molvi Sa'd-ud-Din, residents of Wazapora ₹ 30; Khawaja Abdur Rahim, Caretaker Hazratbal shrine ₹ 22; Molvi Sharaeef-ud-Din, resident of Wazapora ₹ 22; Pir Ghulam Rasool Qamri, son of Pir Abdullah Shah Qamri, resident of Shergarhi ₹ 21; Molvi Nizam-ud-Din, resident of Jama Masjid ₹ 11; Molvi Zia-ud-Din and Molvi Mohi-ud-Din, residents of Dukan Sangeen ₹ 11; Molvi Zia-ud-Din, Mohammad Yusuf and Najm-ud-Din, residents of Dukan-i-Sangeen ₹ 11; Molvi Ghulam Mohammad, Imam Khanqah-i-Moalla ₹ 11; Molvi Salam-ud-Din, resident of Jama Masjid ₹ 11; Molvi Sa'd-ud-Din, resident of Khawaja Bazar ₹ 11; Molvi Mohi-ud-Din, resident of Wazapora ₹ 11; Molvi Mohammad Shah, resident of Nowhatta ₹ 11; Molvi Ghulam Ahmad, Imam Hazratbal ₹ 11; Molvi Mohammad Jawad, resident of Khanqah-i-Sokhta ₹ 11; Molvi Ghulam Mehmood, Imam of Jama Masjid and Idgah ₹ 11; Molvi Aziz Bangi and Molvi Najm-ud-Din, sons of Salam-ud-Din and Ahmad Baba son of Gani Baba, all residents of Jama Masjid ₹ 4 and *Annas* 8; Molvi Amir-ud-Din and Azim-ud-Din, heirs of Molvi Ali Shah, residents of Ishan Sahab, Zaina Kadal ₹ 7 and *annas* 8; Molvi Shareef-ud-Din, resident of Wazapora ₹ 7 and *Annas* 8; Molvi Mohammad Amin, son of Molvi Aman Ullah, resident of Wazapora ₹ 7 and *Annas* 8; and Molvi Hassan Shah Zeerak, resident of Srinagar (presently Islamabad) ₹ 12 and *Annas* 8.

Passport for Begging

Kashmir has always attracted people of varied interests. Scholars, preachers, traders, poets and solace seekers have been coming here since ages. These interactions have immensely contributed towards the rich culture and heritage that Kashmir has evolved into over the centuries. In recent years, however, a different breed of people has been arriving in hordes during summers. These are panhandlers who swarm its city centers, busy traffic junctions, eateries and markets.

Begging being an old profession is borne out by numerous proverbs available in different languages spoken across the world. Some of these are very interesting and full of wisdom. Yet, some teach a trick or two of the trade like this Arabian maxim which says that a beggar should only beg at large gates. The Dutch believe that a beggar's estate lies in all lands. The Germans say that beggars breed and rich men feed. The Portuguese feel that a beggar's wallet is never full. The Danish adage that one beggar likes not that another had two wallets, speaks about jealousy that, like in any activity, is common among competitors.

The steady annual arrival of beggars in Kashmir began somewhere in the early 1970s when in almost every public transport bus you would bump into a non-local lady abruptly bursting into a melancholic song, *Insaan jaan kar bhi kuch bhi samajh na aaya, yeh hai maka'n paraya* (Alas! as a human being you do not appreciate that this world is a temporary abode) and then stretching her hand before every seated and standing passenger for alms. Another category would distribute hand bills certifying the extreme destitute status of the distributor and making a fervent appeal for monetary help. The new-age arrivals are mostly children of both sexes who would simply not let you go unless you doled out some money. Compared to these, their local cousins were never such harpies. From these will-not-leave-you panhandlers to the Internet beggars, the profession has now entered into an age of technology. Nowadays, e-beggars set up websites and beg from their drawing rooms.

Panhandling in Kashmir, as perhaps elsewhere, is a lucrative vocation for its practitioners. Some years back, a news report suggested that there were 4,500 non-local and local beggars active in and around Srinagar city earning at an average

₹ 300 each.[556] It estimated that the beggar industry in the Valley annually generated ₹ 42 crore.[557] Long before it had turned into a paradise for beggars, the Valley, for well over two centuries, remained a cursed land for its inhabitants. Unless one was from the ruling or the privileged class, life of an inhabitant always envied death. Taxes and exactions imposed by the rulers and the inhuman methods employed by their heartless officials to recover taxes from the subjects had transformed a flourishing valley into the land of deprivation. In the 18th and 19th century, people flocked out of Kashmir through the inhospitable and rugged mountain treks to seek respite from torture and forced impoverishment.

With this backdrop stretching over to the early part of the 20th century, begging in the Valley too suffered recession. As is natural, a taker must find a giver but the system-inflicted impoverishment had not left many givers in the land. The terrible situation forced a group of over half a dozen people in north Kashmir to seek passports to go to a foreign country for —imagine what—begging. The year was 1927 AD. The last of the Dogra rulers, Hari Singh, had been two years on the throne.

In Gori Akarhal, a village of Uri in north Kashmir, eight members of a family submitted an application to the *Wazir-i-Wazarat* of Baramulla district requesting him for issuance of passports to them for going to Afghanistan for begging. The applicants, Aziz Shah, Gul Shah, Jabar Shah, Hayat Shah, Mukhat Shah, Khazir Shah, Wahid Shah and Ahad Shah were "professional beggars of Baramulla side".[558]

The application remained in cold storage of the subordinate offices for seven years. All this while, the Shahs must have run from pillar to post to make the file move forward until it reached the Governor of Kashmir Province. The request for passports left the Maharaja's Government in a quandary as it involved a sensitive issue of foreign relations that could trigger resentment of a neighbouring country. The *Wazir-i-Wazarat*, on his part, had recommended issuance of passports. The Governor too sided with the opinion of his subordinate district officer and found nothing objectionable in doing so. He even went a step further in expressing that, "Formerly beggars had no such restriction of having passports with them".[559]

The Governor's comment indirectly referred to a situation where desperate people had been moving out of Kashmir even for seeking alms. Towards the close of the 19th century, Walter Ropert Lawrence, the then Settlement Commissioner in Kashmir, had enumerated 24,673 beggars and their dependents in the Valley.[560] Looking at Kashmir's total population of 200,000 in 1835 AD "to which number it had been reduced in 20 years from 800,000 by oppression and the awful dispensation of earthquake, pestilence and famine",[561] the beggars comprised an enormous 12.33% of the population.

On 24 September 1934, the Governor forwarded the passport case to the Political Secretary to Maharaja's Government who felt that issuance of passports to the applicants might affect diplomatic relations with Afghanistan. He submitted the case to the Maharaja for orders with observations that "there would have been no objection ordinarily but the fact that they are going to Afghanistan as professional beggars may be resented by the Afghan Government."[562]

Maharaja Hari Singh was in no mood to antagonize his neighbour. On 29 September 1934, he returned the file with instructions to consult the British Resident in Kashmir. The Resident, Lt. Col. L.E. Lang, was approached through a communication from the Political Branch of the Prime Minister's Office. The letter, dated 6 October 1934, said that His Highness' Government had received application from certain professional beggars for passports to Afghanistan. It informed Lang of the local authorities having no objection to the grant of passports but "before I send formal recommendation in their favour I would be much obliged if you could kindly let me know whether there would be any objection on the part of the Afghan Government to our doing so."[563]

The Resident did not offer personal comments. Not taking the responsibility of a possible diplomatic showdown on his shoulders, Langer, in his wisdom referred the matter to his Government back in Delhi. The Government of India thought it unpleasant to issue passports to the Shahs in view of their stated profession. The Viceroy's Government communicated its view to the Resident. On 13 November 1934, the Resident wrote back to Prime Minister Lt. Colonel E.J.D. Colvin:

> The Government of India to whom the matter was referred intimate that in view of the profession of the applicants they do not on the present information think it desirable to create the impression that they are anxious to unload them on a neighbouring country, and consider that passports should be withheld.[564]

The matter was set at rest on 24 November 1934 by the Prime Minister's Office through a communication to the Governor of Kashmir informing him that "in view of the profession of the applicants, the Honourable Prime Minister does not consider it advisable to recommend their application to the Residency for grant of passports for Afghanistan".[565] "The original enclosures are returned", the letter added with a mention of these being 57 leaves and copies of photographs.

The Shahs of Akarhal were, thus, deprived of an opportunity to go to Afghanistan for engaging in a profession despised by all but its practitioners.

A Rasputin Guru

At the time of the Partition of India, Maharaja Hari Singh was known to be in favour of independence of Jammu & Kashmir instead of joining the dominion of either India or Pakistan. It has been argued that he was opposed to communal politics of the Muslim League and equally loathed the Indian National Congress for its propinquity with his nemesis, Sheikh Mohammad Abdullah. Was that the only reason behind his aspiration to see Jammu & Kashmir as an independent country or was there something more to it?

Hari Singh's desire to rule a sovereign country once the British had departed from India was deep rooted and independent of his alleged aversion to Jawaharlal Nehru and Muhammad Ali Jinnah. His idea of independence "was not a democratic country where people would be powerful but a monarchy where he himself would wield absolute power."[566] He was feudal at heart and not happily disposed to British suzerainty. In fact, the ruling dynasty had a longing for total independence ever since the overbearing British interference into the affairs of the largest Princely State. The diminution of Maharaja Pratap Singh, Hari Singh's predecessor and uncle, to a show-piece ruler after his alleged hobnobbing with the Czar of Russia had not gone well with the dynasty. The departure of the British from the subcontinent was an opportunity for Hari Singh to realize his long cherished dream and he wanted to seize this opportunity.

When the British paramountcy lapsed and India and Pakistan became sovereign countries, Hari Singh saw independence as an active option. He grabbed the opportunity and refused to listen to Nehru, Mountbatten and Jinnah until he was forced by circumstances and individuals into signing the Instrument of Accession after remaining ruler of an independent country for two months. It may be recalled that the Maharaja had 'several talks' with Mountbatten who had arrived in Srinagar on 18 June 1947. During these talks, Hari Singh, as he later wrote to the President of India (see Appendix III), the Governor General of India, explaining the situation with plans and maps, had advised the ruler of Jammu & Kashmir to acceded to Pakistan, assuring him that doing so would not be regarded as an unfriendly act by the Government of India. He even offered an assurance to this effect by the newly created States Department.

There were quite a few people, apart from Prime Minister Ram Chandra Kak, who had fuelled Hari Singh's desire to be an absolute ruler of an independent country. Among them, *Rajguru* Swami Sant Dev was the foremost. He was a non-state subject about whose native place nothing is known even as it was believed by some that he had been planted in the palace by the British Government.[567] He had arrived in Jammu & Kashmir during the time of Maharaja Pratap Singh who, being a very superstitious person, had assembled a number of Hindu *swamis*, astrologers and *gurus* around his court.

The Swami had convinced Hari Singh that luck was smiling at him and that he would become the sovereign of "an extended kingdom sweeping down to Lahore."[568] This had stoked the desire of the Maharaja to remain independent rather than joining

India or Pakistan at the time of the Partition. He believed that he could build a new kingdom which some called 'Dogristan'[569] and had 'at great cost' prepared a new crown of diamonds and emeralds for his coronation as ruler of this new kingdom.[570]

A tall, handsome and well-built pink-complexioned man even in his advanced age which he would actually never reveal, the Swami was known as the Rasputin of the Court of Kashmir[571] who loved the company of women and took opium regularly. Rasputin was a Russian faith-healer who exercised significant influence on Czar Nicolas II and his wife, Alexandra Feodorovna, and was considered to be responsible for their downfall. The Swami was a prototype of the present day 'god-men' who exercise considerable influence over the minds of some of the top politicians of India[572]—*ala* Dhirendra Brahmachari. The royal ladies would visit him for his *darshan*.[573] Once, he was reported against by a British woman, Mrs. Berk who lived nearby, for making passes to her young daughters upon which he was asked to leave the State for some time.[574]

The Swami had risen to the position of *Rajguru* during Pratap Singh's rule and was rumoured to have great spiritual powers. He used his position to ensure a firm grip on the Maharaja who, in turn, gave him full state protocol. The Maharaja would issue orders under his own signatures instructing authorities to make special arrangements for the Swami whenever he visited some place. Addressed in official communications as Swami Sant Dev Ji Maharaj, when he reached Jammu on May 14, 1925, Pratap Singh issued an order a day earlier for a motor car to "meet him at the Railway Station"[575] and when he visited Achhabal that year the Maharaja directed his Foreign Department to "make all arrangements for *Farash Khana* and *Farashes* as in the past" for the Swami.[576]

On the demise of Pratap Singh in 1925, fortunes of Swami Sant Dev changed for the worse. An agnostic Hari Singh, after ascending the throne, banished from his presence the *swamis* and *gurus*, including Sant Dev, collected by his uncle although as the spiritual guide of the predecessor Maharaja he had sanctioned life-time monthly *mukarari* of ₹ 300 in his favour on December 5, 1925.[577] After about two decades, Sant Dev made a mysterious comeback in 1944 and, by 1946, had firmly ensconced himself again as the *Rajguru*. He was installed by Hari Singh in the Cheshmashahi Guest House[578] or the present Raj Bhawan, originally built by the Maharaja for his consort, Maharani Tara Devi. From May 1946 until October 1947, he was always in residence in various houses within the palace compound in Srinagar.[579] Meanwhile, Tara Devi, the "warm and gregarious"[580] fourth wife of Hari Singh and the only to bear him an heir, had taken full control of the palace affairs since 1945. She was under the "overpowering influence"[581] of the Swami who used this proximity to extend his influence on Hari Singh. The Maharaja, to the amazement of everyone including his son, became a devout disciple of the Swami, sat on the ground before him for long hours and never smoked in his presence. He also gave him many gifts and amenities, including costly silk robes and a car.[582]

The dream of Hari Singh to rule a sovereign and independent Jammu & Kashmir was, however, shattered by subsequent developments which saw him acceding to India following visits by Mahatma Gandhi and other senior Congress leaders, besides mentoring by RSS Chief, Madhav Sadashiv Golwalkar, who was specially flown to Srinagar on October 18, 1947 by Indian Home Minister, Vallabhbhai Patel, to persuade Hari Singh to acceded to India.[583]

The Tribal Attack on Kashmir dramatically changed the situation, forcing the Maharaja to flee from Srinagar. When the convoy reached Kud, 100 kms from Jammu, a cream coloured car joined the procession. Seated in the car was *Rajguru* Swami Sant Dev Maharaj whose miraculous powers, recalls Maharaja Hari Singh's son, Karan Singh, with sarcasm, did not include facing the Tribals.

As the curtains on Hari Singh's dream of independent Jammu & Kashmir were drawn, he "had come to realize that the Swami's pretensions to great occult powers were somewhat over-rated, and his old scepticism had begun to reassert itself."[584] Subsequently, he had released himself from the influence of Swami Sant Dev. The Swami, a strong supporter of the RSS in

Jammu & Kashmir,[585] was one among many influential persons close to the palace accused of instigating anti-Muslim violence in Jammu in 1947.

Hari Singh remained a titular Maharaja of Jammu & Kashmir up to 1949 when he was forced by Government of India to abdicate in favour of his son, Karan Singh, and asked to leave Jammu & Kashmir along with his wife. He shifted to Bombay and died a sad man there on April 26, 1961, separated, as he was, from his wife who, after leaving Jammu, had returned to her native place in Himachal Pradesh.

Kashmir in Shimla

The 13 July 1931 carnage at Srinagar saw groups and individuals outside the Valley rallying around the people of Kashmir. The support came primarily from the Muslims of British India, especially from the Punjab. The first development was the formation of Kashmir Committee at Shimla[586], barely a week after the incident. Sir Mohammad Iqbal was the main force behind mobilizing support for Kashmir. The Committee comprised prominent leaders including Sir Zafrullah Khan, Khawaja Hassan Nizami, Maulana Hasrat Mohani, Mirza Bashiruddin Mehmood, Hassan Shaheed Suharwardy, etc. who belonged to different parts of India from Peshawar to Calcutta.

The Conference at Shimla spelt out its objectives to help Kashmiris in securing elementary rights of humanity. It decided to build pressure on the Government of India for achieving this objective, and also to acquaint the ruler of Kashmir with the 'real affairs of his State'. It asked for appointment of an independent commission of inquiry into the Kashmir affairs and sought a new interpretation of the Treaty of Amritsar which had deprived Kashmiris of their proprietary rights. The Committee decided to put this demand before the British Parliament and make affairs in Kashmir known to the world by writing books and widely circulating those in England.[587] The Kashmir Committee tried to open dialogue with the Maharaja of Kashmir and send a deputation to Srinagar which he did not agree to. Dismayed by his response, the Committee in order to create awareness in India about Kashmir, decided to observe 14 August as the Kashmir Day.[588]

The success of the Kashmir Day could be measured by the fact that it did not restrict to the Punjab but was also observed in other cities of India like Delhi, Surat, Gorakhpur, Bombay, Calcutta and, of course, Shimla, where the Kashmir Committee was founded. Processions and public meetings were held at all these places in support of political and religious rights of the Kashmiri Muslims. This was the first time that they heard loud supportive voices from outside their State. A significant aspect of outpouring of support for Kashmir within India was the distance its majority community maintained from it. On the Kashmir Day, a massive public meeting was held at Lahore. Observing this indifference, Iqbal said that the Muslims of India could no longer remain indifferent to the plight of their Kashmiri brethren, and were determined to carry on their agitation until their grievances were addressed.[589]

Shimla, thus, held the distinction of bringing together a large section of people of India in support of Kashmir in its hour of suffering. The city besides hosting the meeting at which the Kashmir Committee was constituted, witnessed a large procession on 24 July 1931 taken out to condemn the 'atrocities against Kashmiris'. The procession passed through Ganj Maidan, Ganj Road and Cart Road and, in the evening, culminated at the Jama Masjid. Molvi Zia-ud-Din and Abdul Gani were in the vanguard of the procession that raised slogans like *Shaheed ki jo moat hai woh quom ki hayaat hai* (Blood of martyrs is the charity of the Nation), *Zulm Murdabad* (Death to oppression), *Zaalim Sarkar Murdabad* (Death to oppressive government), *Kashmiri Sarkar Murdabad* (Death to Kashmir Government), *Islam Zindabad* (Long live Islam) and *Musalmaan-i-Kashmir Zindabad* (Long live Muslims of Kashmir).[590] One Ferozuddin of Lahore addressed the procession at four different places and castigated the Kashmir Government for its "oppression against its Muslim subjects". He claimed that the atrocities suffered by Kashmiris were inexpressible, and described the rulers in Kashmir as "devils" for opening fire on innocent and unarmed people in Srinagar as "an act of meanness".[591]

In the evening, a public meeting was held at the Jama Masjid of Shimla. The meeting presided over by Khan Bahadur Mian Rahim Bakhsh, began at 10.15 p.m. An intelligence diary, submitted to the Prime Minister of Jammu & Kashmir on 29 August 1931 by his Inspector General of Police, reported that the meeting passed the following resolution:

> This public meeting of the Muslims of Simla expresses deep indignation over the *zulm* perpetrated upon the Muslims of Kashmir and that its consequences will be ultimately injurious for the Kashmir State.[592]

The mover of the resolution made a fiery speech alluding to making, for long, representations against the "tyranny" in Kashmir and the decision now to fight to the finish. He said that until Kashmir was freed from oppression no rest would be taken nor others allowed doing so. He then referred to the killings at the Central Jail Srinagar and refusal of the Kashmir Government to allow medical aid to the injured. He said that if the Viceroy of India and the Secretary of State for India had appointed an independent inquiry commission into the affairs of Kashmir the facts would have come to light. The speaker countered the Maharaja of Kashmir's assertion that outsiders had no right to interfere in the internal affairs of his State, arguing that "the Muslims of the world were like one body". He warned that the responsibility would squarely lay at the door of the Kashmir Darbar and the Government of India if, out of frustration on the refusal of the Kashmir Government to take the right steps, they did anything untoward.

The public meeting, which lasted till midnight, was addressed by several other speakers including Mohammad Umar, Abdul Gani, M. Ziaullah, M. Ahmad Hussain, M. Zakaullah and Khan Bahadur Mian Rahim Bakhsh. They dismissed the inquiry commission appointed by the Kashmir Darbar to enquire into the July 13 incident and demanded an independent inquiry. The meeting also resolved to raise funds for relief of the victims of the carnage. In spilling of blood in Srinagar, the speakers drew parallels with the incident of Karbala.[593] One speaker dismissed the allegation of Kashmir Government that the killed men had invaded the Central Jail Srinagar and snatched arms from the soldiers.

Twenty days later on the Kashmir Day, Shimla again reverberated with voices and slogans in support of Kashmir. A public meeting was held under the chairmanship of *Imam* Syed Hussain during which three resolutions were passed.[594] The resolutions demanded appointment of an independent body to inquire into the events related to the 13 July killings, allowing a barrister from outside Jammu & Kashmir to defend the cases pending in connection with the riots, justice to Muslim subjects, abolition of all such rules as were hostile to Islam, complete freedom of religion and social, economic and political progress of the Muslim subjects, recognition to the proprietary rights of land for Muslim *Zamindars* and distribution of State services and a share in the ministry to the State's majority community in proportion to their population. The allegation levelled by a section of the press that the Muslims wanted to capture Hindu states one after the other, was dismissed through a resolution.

Years later when India was partitioned in 1947, Kashmir became a bone of contention between India and Pakistan. The issue went to the United Nations and the two countries also fought wars over the territory. Following the 1971 Indo-Pak War in which Pakistan suffered defeat and dismemberment, losing her eastern wing, Shimla became the venue of a summit meeting between the two countries where an accord known as the Simla Agreement was signed on 2 July 1972.[595] The two countries agreed to bilaterally resolve the Kashmir problem, closing the option of international mediation.

Death of A Sarai

The Mughal rulers' romance with Kashmir is a well-documented story. What singles them out from other conquerors is that their intervention with nature in Kashmir was an add-on, rather than tampering with it. They preferred laying out awesome gardens to raising huge structures. From Akbar down to Aurangzeb, the Mughal kings in Kashmir chose to pitch tents instead of erecting palaces for their summer sojourns. Wherever they constructed buildings these were elegant in architecture and did not occupy much space. Of these, the *sarais* or resting places they constructed along the famous Mughal Road used by them to enter and leave Kashmir, bespeak the grandeur and majesty with which their caravans travelled into the Valley.

One such monument is the Aliabad Sarai perched in the Pir Panjal mountain range in whose lap traverses the Mughal Road. A *sarai* is believed to have been first constructed here by Akbar who annexed Kashmir in 1586 AD and visited the Valley, at least, three times. But the present structure was built by Shahjahan's Governor of Kashmir, Ali Mardan Khan, after whose name a quarter in the Srinagar city is known as Bagh-e-Ali Mardan Khan. The Mughal Governor is said to have constructed seven *sarais* on the Mughal Road between Kashmir and Rajouri-Poonch across the Pir Panjal.

The Aliabad Sarai, sitting on the banks of a stream, 32 kms from the north Kashmir town of Shopian, has served as an important stopover for the Mughal journeys into the Valley where the caravans took rest and royalty refreshed before proceeding further on their passage. The *sarai* has served as a shelter for travellers who set out on an arduous journey through mountain gorges and rocky track. A square construction facing south, it is a typical Mughal architecture raised of boulders and bricks in red lime mortar. The *sarai* must be witness to many a travel story and royal romances. It is an Archaeological Survey of India protected monument, now in a wretched condition, serving as a shelter to migratory shepherds and their cattle with its courtyard having turned into a cesspool. During the peak of militancy in Kashmir started in 1989, the *sarai* was used by para-military forces as a camp till 2002.

The cessation of the Mughal supremacy over Kashmir saw gradual decline in the importance of the Aliabad Sarai. Construction of alternate motorable roads via Uri and Banihal Pass in 1890 AD and 1916 AD, respectively, further robbed the Mughal Road of its significance as the main route of travel to and from Kashmir. However, the road continued to be a foot traveller's preferred short distance route to the Valley, especially for the nomadic shepherd community of *Bakarwals* during their annual crossover to Kashmir pastures.

In 1934, the Aliabad Sarai was at the center of an interesting squabble between the police stations of Uri and Poonch, then an autonomous principality, over the escape of two criminals from custody. The tiff ultimately culminated in the conversion of the famous Mughal monument into a police lock up. The Poonch police accused their Uri counterparts of being accomplice of the criminals and facilitating their escape.[596] The prisoners had broken into a house in village Bagh, now on the other side of the Line of Control, and fled to Uri with stolen property. There were allegations and counter allegations from both sides during which the absence of a *hawalat* between Poonch and Uri, as being the main reason for in-custody escape by criminals, was in sharp focus. Movement of escorted prisoners, between the two areas on opposite sides of the Panjal barrier, for investigation or trial was a routine matter those days and many a time during the 35 mile hard foot journey, with no resting facilities or lock-ups en-route, the prisoners would make good their escape from an exhausted policeman's custody.

During the intervening night of 8 and 9 *Sawan* 1991 *Bikrimi* (corresponding to 21 and 22 July 1934), three robbers broke into the house of Dafadar Sher Mohammad in village *chowki* under Police Station Bagh, Poonch and decamped with property of "considerable value".[597] The description of the culprits as given by the lone inmate of the house, led the Poonch police to conclude that they had come from Uri and Garhi areas. Two constables, Nawab Khan and Mohammad Amir Khan, were sent to search and arrest the culprits. On their way, at Chakothi, the Head Constable of the local Police Station informed them that the description of one of the accused matched with a notorious character, Samundar Shah alias Mithu Shah of Kandi Shahdara village in Uri. Acting on the information, Constable Nawab Khan set out for Mithu Shah's village and found him among a group of people talking with Head Constable Abdul Majid Khan of Police Station Uri. Mithu was wearing a *zari kulah*, one of the articles stolen from Dafadar's house in Poonch. Before he could be apprehended, the accused sensed trouble and ran away from the spot. However, he was chased and arrested.

Mithu admitted to the offence and named his two accomplices in the crime. A substantial portion of the stolen property was recovered. One of the accomplices, Kalu, was also nabbed subsequently. The two accused were kept in judicial lock-up and, later, under police custody, sent to Poonch when extradition warrant was received from the Poonch court. On their way, at Bhedi, the accused escaped from police custody. Meantime, the third accused, Safdar, also was apprehended and handed over to Poonch police which alleged complicity of Uri police in the escape of Mithu and Kalu at Bhedi as also in the former's fleeing from Kandi Shahdara earlier.

The accusation was endorsed at the highest level through a communication sent by *Wazir* of Poonch, Feroz Chand, on 4 February 1935 to the Superintendent of Police, Baramulla. The communication alleged that the Uri police sympathized with the accused, made false entries and did not keep them in police lock-up. Worse, it accused, the Sub-Inspector and the Sergeant of the Uri Police Station of receiving some of the stolen property as graft. In yet another communication addressed to the Revenue Minister in the Maharaja's Government on 1 April 1935, Feroz Chand dismissed the Uri police's claim that Mithu and Kalu escaped from their custody at Bhedi and alleged that they were let off by the escorting policemen.

The serious allegations levelled by Poonch authorities were internally investigated by Police and the enquiry report of the Assistant Superintendent of Police (ASP), Muzaffarabad termed these as "based on hearsay and circumstantial evidence."[598] The report averred that since Poonch police could not recover the stolen property in full and whatever recovery was made was made by the Uri police, the former, in order to conceal its failure, had levelled wild allegations against the latter. The ASP equated the Poonch police with a bad workman quarrelling with his tools. However, the fact that the Uri police dismissed from service its two policemen who accompanied the accused when they escaped at Bhedi fizzled out its stand.

The Inspector General of Police, Kashmir endorsing the ASP's report, in a communication to the Government on 26 September 1935, shifted focus to a different point—asking the *Wazir* of Poonch to make provision of a *hawalat* at Aliabad Sarai by making necessary additions and alterations in it or by constructing a new one there. Following the prisoners' escape, a suggestion had been made earlier to construct a guard hut at Aliabad which was turned down by the *Wazir* of Poonch citing three buildings—the Rest House at Bhedi, the Sarai at Aliabad and a side police station at Kahuta—located between Poonch and Uri where "prisoners can easily be accommodated while passing the bridle path."[599] The Kashmir Police held on to the *Wazir's* suggestion and asked for the conversion of the Aliabad Sarai into a lock-up.

The Poonch Principality did not show any sign of urgency in converting the Mughal monument into a police lock-up until several reminders were sent from the government. It was after more than four years and the matter having been "included in the list of cases pending since long"[600] that the *Wazir* of Poonch, in response to a letter of the Revenue Minister dated 2 December 1935, wrote back on 28 February 1940 that the "work for the conversion of a room of Aliabad Sarai into a *havalat* has been taken in hand."[601]

Thus, the imposing Aliabad Sarai that hosted the Mughal kings and members of royalty started playing home to criminals and outlaws. The transition was the saddest part in the turn of fortune of an iconic monument.

A Wounded Prime Minister

In the afternoon of 29 August 1938, Prime Minister Narasimha Gopalaswami Ayyangar was returning from office to his residence in Srinagar when his car was attacked by a crowd of agitating men and women at Amirakadal, the city center. Ayyangar, accompanied by Home Minister and another colleague, was injured. While fleeing from the scene his car ran over a protester and grievously injured him. The crowd was protesting against the arrest of Sheikh Mohammad Abdullah and other political leaders who had made speeches against the government at Hazratbal on the previous day.

The trouble in Srinagar had started soon after rejection of an appeal by the High Court against conviction of Raja Mohammad

Akbar Khan, then a senior Muslim Conference leader from Mirpur, in a case of sedition. Earlier on 16 June 1938, Khan had been sentenced to 3 years rigorous imprisonment and a fine of ₹ 100 by the Sessions Court for making, what the court termed, a seditious speech at Jammu in 1937. The rejection of appeal by the High Court was followed by series of incidents—demonstrations, fiery speeches, slogan shouting and stone pelting by people, and, in return, arrests, cane-charging and firing by the police—resulting in some fatal casualties. Besides a host of prominent political leaders, over a thousand people were taken into custody.[602] The arrest of Sheikh Mohammad Abdullah added fuel to the fire. For weeks, Srinagar was on the boil. All major towns of Kashmir including Anantnag, Baramulla, Sopore, Ganderbal and Bandipore witnessed public demonstrations and government reprisal. Poonch and Jammu too were rocked by protests and punitive police action.

The Jammu & Kashmir Muslim Conference was still a united house although process of its dissolution and replacement by a 'nationalist and secular' party had long been set in motion. Abdullah, focused on political conversion of the party, was not able to gather majority support within its ranks. Raja Mohammad Akbar Khan was in the forefront of, what he believed, broad-basing the Muslim Conference by bringing non-Muslims into its fold. A public meeting—the last by the united Muslim Conference in the winter capital—was held at Eidgah Jammu in June 1937 where Khan moved a resolution to convert the Jammu & Kashmir Muslim Conference into the Jammu & Kashmir National Conference. The resolution failed due to strong opposition, leaving Khan in a sour mood in which he made a fiery speech against the Dogra rule. "*Meri awaz chalees laakh logun ki awaz hai jo Hari Singh ke mehhalaat se takrakar unhain paash paash kardegi* (My voice is the voice of four million people [of Jammu & Kashmir] which will strike against the palaces of Hari Singh and raze them to the ground)", Khan roared.[603] A case of sedition, first in Jammu & Kashmir against a political leader, was filed against him under Section 124-A in the court of Sessions Judge Jammu, Haveli Ram Malhotra, who sentenced him to imprisonment with fine.

An appeal was filed in the High Court against Khan's conviction. Dr. Mohammad Alam, a prominent lawyer of Lahore nicknamed as *Dr. Lota* for shifting loyalty from the Muslim League to the Unionist Party to the Majlis-i-Ahrar, appeared for Khan. The Court maintained the conviction but reduced the sentence to 18 months rigorous imprisonment and fine to ₹ 25. Khan's colleague in the Muslim Conference, Allah Rakha Sagar, made a sarcastic versified comment on the rejection of the appeal: *Mirpur ke Mujahid Akbar baat kartay thay iddiaa karke Appeal bhi mustarad huee baat bhi khoyi iltija karkay* (The struggler Akbar of Mirpur whose words carried conviction lost both his appeal and face by making a request for reversal of his conviction).[604] Senior politician and writer, Krishen Dev Sethi, however, asserts that Khan was not in favour of filing an appeal and Sagar's sarcasm, as he later wrote, was directed against Sheikh Mohammad Abdullah who had decided to move the High Court against Khan's conviction.[605]

By the time the order of dismissal of appeal came, Abdullah in anticipation of dissolution of the Muslim Conference, had since warmed up to Kashmir's non-Muslim leaders like Prem Nath Bazaz, Jia Lal Kilam, Kashyap Bandhu and Budh Singh who joined the protest meetings held in support of Khan. During these meetings, speeches were made whose anti-autocracy contents, the government alleged, were "untrue and scurrilous things".[606] People defied law and the judgment of the High Court and repeated passages from Khan's speech "from place to place and incessantly".[607] The government responded with banning, for one month, processions and public meetings within the municipal limits and issuing notices to some leaders against their being bound over for good behaviour under Section 108 of the Criminal Procedure Code. The measures had no effect on the ground.

Two days after 26 August 1938 when the District Magistrate issued prohibitory orders, a public meeting was held outside the city limits at Hazratbal where speeches against the government were made and people "incited to defy the law openly".[608] The speakers, besides Abdullah, included Prem Nath Bazaz, Kashyap Bandu, Jia Lal Kilam, Mohammad Sayeed Masoodi and

Ghulam Mohammad Sadiq.[609] Next day, on 29 August, defying prohibitory orders, a public meeting jointly attended by the leaders of the Muslim Conference and the minority community was held at Maisuma. Police swung into action and arrested Sheikh Mohammad Abdullah, Budh Singh, Kashyap Bandu, Mohammad Sayeed Masoodi, Ghulam Mohammad Sadiq, Ali Mohammad[610] and Ghulam Mohiuddin Hamdani. The arrests were followed by protest demonstrations and shutdown in the city. Traffic at Amira Kadal was impeded.

In the afternoon, amid disturbances at the city center, Prime Minister Ayyangar, accompanied by Home Minister Abdus Samad Khan and Minister-in-Waiting Nawab Khusru Jung, left his office for home. When his car reached Amira Kadal market it was mobbed by agitating people who pelted stones at the vehicle and broke its glasses. Ayyangar sustained injuries by shattered glass. His car sped away from the scene but in the process ran over a protester, Mohammad Rajab, dragged him on for about 500 feet until an Englishman stopped his car in the middle of the road to obstruct passage to the Prime Minister's vehicle and bring it to a halt. Rajab was seriously injured and sustained a 2 inch deep and 25 inch long wound.[611] Admitted to the Mission Hospital in a critical condition, he survived but suffered a permanent limp.

The government blamed it on "a mob of goondas, urchins and some women"[612] that attacked the Prime Minister's vehicle, "broke the glasses and caused damage to the mudguard and other parts of the car with stones which were flung at the car.... The Prime Minister himself received a shower of splintered glass all over his person but luckily escaped any substantial injury."[613] About the Prime Minister's car running over a protester and seriously injuring him, the official press release explained it away thus:

> A number of them [protesters] tried to stop the car and force it back and one of them apparently got on to the bumper in front of the radiator and, in trying thereby to hold on to the moving car, got entangled therein. The car however proceeded on its way but the man clinging to the bumper being not visible to the driver or the

> inmates of the car was dragged on for some distance. He sustained severe injuries which are being attended to in the Mission Hospital.[614]

In the evening, another protest meeting was held at the Dhanjibhoy Adda, a *tonga* station near the Polo Ground opposite the building named after its Parsi owner, Dhanjibhoy, where more speeches were made and more people arrested. In all, 65 persons were taken into custody on 29 August. As is the wont of all repressive regimes, Maharaja Hari Singh's Government dismissed the public anger as "engineered by a small clique and that the vast majority of the members of all communities condemn them without reserve and desire that this exhibition of lawlessness should be put down with a firm hand as quickly as possible."[615] Notwithstanding the government crackdown, protests continued and business remained affected especially in the city center with people holding demonstrations and shouting slogans. Passage to any vehicle carrying a government officer was particularly obstructed.

In different parts of the city, funeral processions and parades of wounded people allegedly killed or injured in cane charge by police were taken out. The government, however, said no person was injured or killed as "no can charge of any magnitude was made". The police claimed that in one case a dispersed procession left the 'dead body' on the road and when the blanket covering it was removed it turned out to be "a bundle of grass" with red colour sprinkled over the bier. "The bundle and the blanket", the government claimed, "is with the police."[616] Similarly, "a so-called wounded person on receiving a poke from a policeman jumped off the bier and took to his heels", it added. The government continued with arresting people. It alleged that *goondas* in the city were responsible for drilling boys for the processions. Overnight, two persons were arrested for allegedly attempting to burn the Nawakadal, a wooden bridge over the Jhelum in old city.

Angry demonstrators pelted stones at police and army in different parts of Srinagar. The situation seemed turning difficult for the government when the District Magistrate issued a stern warning that "throwing of stones on the military or the police might result in the latter firing on the persons throwing stones and if the people persisted in stone throwing, punitive police would be imposed on the Mohallas concerned."[617] Punitive action was also threatened against localities where shouting of slogans occurred. One of the notable features of the protests was the strike by *tongas* which then were the main mode of transport in the city. The government admitted that the strike had caused inconvenience to visitors. In Baramulla, protesters attacked and injured the Wazir (Deputy Commissioner) of Baramulla and the Superintendent of Police.[618] The government's helplessness was manifest in the President Srinagar Municipal Committee's warning to his Mohalla Officers (Wardens) that they would be held responsible for "controlling the batches of unruly boys who move about in the streets and lanes shouting slogans."[619] They were forced to take the responsibility of maintaining peace in their respective areas and in the event of their failure, provide lists of the parents of delinquent boys to the government.

On 31 August, seven leaders arrested two days ago were sentenced to different periods of imprisonment and fine. Sheikh Mohammad Abdullah (mentioned in official press notes as Mohammad Abdullah Sheikh or Mohammad Abdullah only), Budh Singh, Kashyap Bandu, Mohammad Sayeed (Masoodi) and Ghulam Mohammad Sadiq were sentenced to six months imprisonment and a fine of ₹ 25 each. Ali Mohammad was sentenced to six months imprisonment and a fine of ₹ 20 while Ghulam Mohiuddin received a sentence of one month's imprisonment.[620] During the day, 47 persons were arrested from different parts of the city.[621] Other leaders like Chowdhary Ghulam Abbas, Prem Nath Bazaz, Mirza Afzal Beg and Jia Lal Kilam were also arrested at different places and on different dates.

As the agitation gained momentum, a printed poster titled 'National Demands' with ten prominent leaders from Muslim, Hindu and Sikh communities as signatories, was "broadcast and published in various parts of the country"[622] declaring the movement as "nation-wide" and all classes of the people "participating in it with the fullest consciousness of the issues it involves."[623] The poster described the ultimate goal of the movement "to bring about complete change in the social and political outlook of the people and to achieve a Responsible Government under the aegis of the Maharaja."[624] The publication and circulation of the poster, wrote Bazaz, "proved to be a signal for measuring the swords between the fighters for Kashmir's freedom on the one side and the alien and autocratic Dogra rule on the other."[625] The government felt that the poster could reinforce the ongoing agitation. In a press communiqué issued the next day, among other things, it blamed "Mohammad Abdullah Sheikh and his associates"[626] of committing offence under Section 124-A and repeating passages from Raja Akbar Khan's seditious speech from public platforms at different places and timings, and carrying on a vilification campaign.

On 2 September, one person was reported to have died due to police action at Maisuma on the previous evening. His body, refused by people to be handed over to the police for postmortem, was kept at the *Khanqah-i-Moalla*, the largest hospice in Kashmir built in the 14th century. The government denied that he died due to police action, for the "only injury on his body was an abrasion on the skull which according to the doctor would not cause death".[627] However, it did not give out the cause of his demise. Later, the body was taken in a procession for burial. Besides earlier branding protesters as *goondas* and urchins, the government, reacting on the incident, blamed the protest demonstration at Dhanjibhoy Adda and stone pelting at Maisuma on the previous evening on "a mob of Muslims" and "rowdies of Maisuma Mohalla".[628] It claimed that 21 policemen received injuries, some of serious nature. At Soura, birthplace of Abdullah, a police party was attacked with stones, injuring some of them including a Head Constable. The attackers then "took to their boats and concealed themselves in the islands of the [nearby] Anchar Lake"[629] leaving the police clueless about their location. Two days later, it claimed 8 persons involved in the incident were arrested. For days, the *Khanqah-i-Moalla* remained center of large protests and speeches against the government. The *Statesman* reported that college and school students had joined the ongoing agitation in Srinagar.[630]

Reports of police high-handedness kept pouring in from different parts of the Valley. There were allegations that victims injured in police action were denied treatment in hospitals, residents of Maisuma and Gaw Kadal were looted by police, and repression on women was committed at Ganderbal leading to the death of a pregnant woman. These allegations formed consistent part of speeches made from public platforms. The government rejected the allegations as "gross and malicious lies."[631] In an atmosphere of protests, slogan shouting, police action and the resultant chaos, several rumours were afloat in the city keeping the government on tenterhooks. At times, it had to issue press communiqués to deny rumours. On 4 September, it rebutted a report seeking to circulate an impression that government had failed to control the situation and Kashmir's Governor and Senior Superintendent of Police had been transferred out.

After completing six months imprisonment, Abdullah was released on 28 February 1939. By this time, ground for conversion of the Muslim Conference had been cleared. Pertinently, when political leaders were arrested during the 1938 agitation, Abbas and Budh Singh were lodged in the Reasi Jail where the latter brought the former, previously a critic of the move, around on the issue of conversion of the Muslim Conference.[632]

The Snooping Resident

On 30 September 1938, a foreigner on his arrival in Srinagar checked in at the Nedous Hotel, a crow flight of three minutes from the Maharaja's Palace. Soon, he was joined by a non-local guest and the two had one-on-one meeting in room number 67. The local Administration, still grappling with the after-shocks of the horrifying political tremor jolting Kashmir seven years back in 1931, was intrigued. The arrival of the person, of whose physical features not many were known to be coming to the Valley, seemed beyond a normal visit. Political developments as a spin-off to the July 13 incident had filled the atmosphere with suspicion and the Maharaja's Government, working under the hawk's eye of the British Resident, would, obviously, not take any risk.

The visit caused alarm at the highest level of British supervision over Kashmir which had earlier accused the Maharaja's predecessor and uncle of hobnobbing with Russia and divested him of his powers, only to be restored some years later. The Residency asked the Kashmir Darbar to keep an inconspicuous watch over the movement of the foreigner and his guest. The visitor who had checked in at the Nedous Hotel was a Japanese citizen, H. Sago, and the guest who called on him was Achambi Lal, proprietor of Achamba Trading Corporation, a business concern in Srinagar. Before his meeting with Sago, Achambi had a rendezvous with some Yarkandis in his office the same day. He had invited several of them and among those who arrived four were Gaffur Jan Haji, Karim Jan Haji, Mohi-ud-Din Haji and Ahmad Jan Haji. Concerned by the developments, the Resident sought a report from the Kashmir Government. His Extra Assistant wrote to the Chief Secretary, Political Department, Pandit Ram Chandra Kak, asking him to keep an inconspicuous watch on the two and inform the Residency in case anything of interest was observed. The operative part of the letter reads:

> I am desired to request that steps may kindly be taken to keep an unobtrusive watch over the movements of Sago and Achambi Lal and that anything of interest that may come to light be communicated to this Residency.[633]

The communication was passed on to the Inspector General of Police for taking necessary action and reporting back. By the time the Police Chief received the letter, Sago had left Kashmir. He had stayed in the hotel for nine days and checked out on April 9. The intelligence gathering officials went out to sniff the motive of his visit and meeting with Achambi. The latter's movement, however, remained under constant watch.

What came out of the police investigation showed that the Resident was gratuitously alarmed and had seen a mountain in a molehill. The meeting between Sago and Achambi had no political overtone. Achambi was a whole-sale dealer in *namda* and was in constant touch with Yarkandi traders putting up at Safa Kadal in the old Srinagar city. Historically, the Yarkandis were the merchants who arrived via Silk Road in the Valley with goods from Central Asia and returned with Kashmir products. A market had been set up at Safa Kadal in Srinagar where business of import and export items was conducted. They were all known to have performed *haj* and were, hence, called *hajis*. There is still a shelter house located on the left bank of the Jhelum at Safa Kadal known as Yarkand Sarai.

The investigation conducted by the Senior Superintendent of Police revealed that Achambi Lal had been persuading Yarkandi traders to import Japanese goods. His persuasion was based on the argument that these were durable and cheap. The meetings he had on 30 September with Sago and Hajis were purely business related but were wrongly read by an over-sensitive Resident as fraught with political implications, obliging the Government to investigate.

Was the Residency keeping a constant watch on the movement of non-British foreigners in Kashmir and was it scary of their presence in the Valley? Apparently, there is no material evidence to suggest that. However, the pro-active institution of the Resident was constantly meddling with the affairs of the State. The Resident's missive to the Chief Secretary on Sago's visit showed that this pro-active stance was taken even on routine matters. It also spoke negatively of the State Administration as waiting for instructions from the Residency even in ordinary matters like keeping surveillance on the activities of visitors in the Valley.

An earlier development relating to the visit of an important political figure of India to Kashmir in 1927 had resulted in a huge embarrassment for Maharaja Hari Singh to whom this piece of vital information was not passed on by his administration. The Maharaja had come to know about the visit through a newspaper report.[634] Post-1931, the Resident's interest in local affairs seemed to have been sharpened. He would want from the government to be constantly posted with the situation. If, for some reason, he was out of the city he would ask from the Prime Minister to send a messenger to him in case any emergency occurred that required the Government of India to be informed.[635]

Following the Treaty of Amritsar, the Government of India had been ruing the absence of a provision in the Treaty allowing its direct involvement in the affairs of Kashmir and was looking for an opportunity. Its attempts were not to materialize any time soon. However, in due course of time, all political and commercial dealings with Central Asia, China and Tibet were taken over by the British and with the appointment of Political Agent in Gilgit and Joint Commissioner in Ladakh, the foreign relations of Kashmir with the countries on its north and north-west borders came under full domination of the British Raj.[636]

The Raj was apprehensive of Russian intentions towards India and its incursions in Central Asia had pressed the panic button. The expansionist forays of the Kashmir Darbar in Chilas, Ponial, Yasin, Hunza and Nagar that were looked at by the British as facilitation for Kashmir intrigues with Kabul and Moscow had added to the anxiety. The strategic importance of Kashmir had dawned upon them as also the need for a political Resident in Srinagar. In 1851, an Officer on Special Duty was appointed by the Government of India in Kashmir for summer months without any political duty.[637] A window of opportunity for the appointment of Resident in Kashmir was opened by the likelihood of Pratap Singh, the meek and timid eldest son of Maharaja Ranbir Singh, succeeding his father who was now on the deathbed. The new Maharaja, who ascended the throne in 1885, suffered intrigues by his own siblings, one of whom was the pretender and had been recommended by his father to succeed him. However, Governor General Lord Ripon, before demitting office, had decided in favour of Pratap Singh along with the appointment of a Resident in Kashmir.[638] The Resident's appointment was announced on 25 September 1885 with the formal proclamation of Pratap Singh as the ruler of Jammu & Kashmir, thirteen days after the death of Ranbir Singh.

Sir Oliver St. John became the first Resident in Kashmir. Although Governor General Lord Dufferin had assured an upset Maharaja that the Resident would assist him with friendly advice only but Sir Jhon did not mince words about what was to unfold. He told an emissary of the Maharaja that he would leave all the active work of administration to the Darbar but he should be informed of any matter in detail, which he thought proper to know. He would give advice, if asked for, and if he thought proper he would also give advice on his own, which was to be obeyed.[639] The appointment of the Resident opened doors for active British interference in political and administrative affairs of Jammu & Kashmir. The subsequent events saw Pratap Singh facing charges of conspiracy with the Czar of Russia. The new Resident, Colonel Nisbet, claimed to be in possession of letters that the Maharaja had purportedly written to the Czar and the Maharaja's own brother, Amar Singh, testified that the handwriting was of Pratap Singh.[640] Nisbet also accused Pratap Singh as "timid and very superstitious man at the mercy of a set of unscrupulous scoundrels who plunder the State" and recommended to the Foreign Secretary, Government of India, "the practical setting aside of the Maharaja's authority."[641] Much as the Maharaja protested that the letters were forged and written in Dogri, a language which only a fool would think he could be writing in to the Czar, the Resident succeeded in extracting voluntary resignation from him by virtue of which he relinquished all powers. In 1889, the administration was entrusted to a State Council comprising his two brothers and an officer nominated by the Government of India.

For the next 16 years, the State Council, with the Resident actually calling the shots, ruled Jammu & Kashmir as Maharaja Pratap Singh was relegated to the sidelines. He was left to make emotional and pathetic representations to the Raj for restoration of his powers which evoked a sympathetic response only in 1905 when powers were restored to him. Some English friends in the Government of India were sympathetic to Pratap Singh and apparently pushed through restoration of his powers. One such person was Arthur Oliver Villiers, Baron Ampthill and Governor of Madras to whom an obliged Singh addressed a letter of thanks on 16 August 1905 in which he wrote:

> I have received an intimation from Government of India that the Secretary of State has sanctioned the proposal of the Government to invest me with extended powers of administration; and that His Excellency the Viceroy would confer them in person at a ceremonial Darbar to

> be held for the purpose about the middle of October. My heart feels full of gratitude and indebtedness to Your Excellency at this prospect, for verily it is merely due to the keen interest Your Excellency took in my affairs and the promptness with which the matter was pushed through by Your Excellency that we now see the plant bear the desired fruit.[642]

On 26 October 1905, Lord Curzon visited Jammu and restored powers to Pratap Singh at a specially held ceremony and on 10 November, beholden Pratap Singh wrote an emotional letter to Arthur Baron, pouring out his heart in gratitude. He wrote:

> I should have written this letter earlier and I hope Your Excellency will not consider me ungrateful owning to this delay that has unavoidably taken place. I sent Your Excellency a telegram the other day, which I hope has reached you before this. My feelings of heartfelt indebtedness and sincere gratitude to Your Excellency for all the great kindness in being the chief instrument for my restoration to powers are beyond expression. My innermost heart prays for Your Excellency's long life, happiness and every success and prosperity in life.
>
> His Excellency Lord Curzon, Viceroy and Governor General of India has been exceedingly kind and gracious to me. The Ceremonial Darbar to restore me to powers was held on the 26th of October last; and although Your Excellency was not gracing the Darbar on the occasion by your presence yet I felt as if the whole Darbar was being inspired with Your Excellency's kind and good wishes and the great interest Your Excellency has always been pleased to evince in me and my State.
>
> I am exceedingly delighted to find in the papers that Your Excellency will also be present at Bombay to say good bye to His Excellency Lord Curzon, the Viceroy and it will afford me a chance of meeting my benefactor and sincere friend and well wisher, I mean Your Excellency. I am also going to Bombay and hope to reach there on the 16th November.[643]

Such a helpless Maharaja who and whose family ruled Kashmir as tyrants for 101 years!

An Embarrassed Maharaja

In 1935, Sheikh Mohammad Abdullah and Pandit Prem Nath Bazaz had jointly started an Urdu newspaper, *Hamdard*, from Srinagar. However, the two soon fell apart. Subsequently, the newspaper was solely owned and edited by Bazaz. In 1943, the newspaper published an interview of noted industrialist Jehangir Ratanji Dadabhoy Tata, popularly known as JRD Tata, who was then in Kashmir on a short holiday. It quoted JRD as criticizing Kashmir Government for the State's backwardness and pitiable condition of its people. He was also reported to have denounced the State's policy of land ownership. The strictures, as these came from a leading industrialist and father of civil aviation in British India, were highly embarrassing for the ruler and his government. The interview stirred up a hornets' nest as Maharaja Hari Singh was not happy over its contents. He asked his Prime Minister for action against the newspaper beyond 'mere warning.' The Editor of the newspaper had to apologize for "wrong" reporting while JRD admitted it was "imprudent for him" to give the interview to a reporter he did not know.

The timing of the interview was crucial. The majority population of Kashmir had risen against an unsympathetic autocratic rule. The National Conference and the Muslim Conference were in the vanguard of a mass movement fighting for the basic rights of people. The media in India, mostly based in Punjab, was divided into pro and anti-Maharaja camps. The former defended Hari Singh's regime and measures it took to quell protesting masses while the latter highlighted the plight of a subjugated people.

The JRD interview was a serious indictment of the Maharaja and his government, second such by a non-local highly influential personality. Earlier, Hari Singh's Bengali Prime Minister, Albion Banerji, reacting to the plight of Kashmiris, had resigned in 1929 with these famous parting words:

> Jammu and Kashmir State is labouring under many disadvantages, with a large Mohammedan population absolutely illiterate, labouring under poverty and very low economic conditions of living in the villages, and practically governed like dumb driven cattle. There is no touch between the government and the people, no suitable opportunity for representing grievances.... The administration has, at present, no or little sympathy with people's wants and grievances.[644]

The Press in Kashmir was still in its infancy and among the few newspapers published from Srinagar, *Hamdard* enjoyed a fair amount of respect and credibility among its readers. The publication of an interview critical of the Maharaja's Government and its policies by a prominent British Indian would mean vindication of the Muslim Press of the Punjab. The Kashmir Government felt awkward. On 17 May 1943, Prime Minister Maharaj Singh asked his Government's Publicity Officer, Shankar Lal Koul, to visit JRD at the Guest House and show him the newspaper clipping of his interview. In a hand-written note, the Prime Minister wrote to Koul:

> There was a cutting in one of the local newspapers which I saw today purporting to give an interview with Mr. R.D. Tata. The latter denies some of the statements attributed to him. Can you please see Mr. R.D. Tata (Iqbal Masjid Guest House) and if you have the cutting show it to him. He is leaving for Bombay by plane at 6.30 A.M. tomorrow morning. Kindly speak to me tomorrow.[645]

The Publicity Officer met JRD the same day and the latter issued a rejoinder in the form of a 4-page handwritten letter addressed to Koul wherein he regretted that the "few words" he had said were "grossly distorted" and that words he never uttered were put in his mouth in an attempt to make him appear critical of the State and its policies. He claimed to have in fact expressed enthusiasm in the scenic beauties of Kashmir and offered his help in building up tourist traffic and influx of money into the State. He denied having found the condition of the people of the State pitiable. He also denied expressing the opinion that the State was industrially backward or that he criticized the policy of land ownership. JRD described himself as a "sincere admirer of this beautiful land and a friend of His Highness (the Maharaja) and of a number of State officials" to emphasize that the last thing he would do was to criticize the State in an interview with, what he labeled as, "an obscure and evidently unscrupulous newspaper." The letter dated 17 May 1943 and written on the official stationery with the State emblem reads:

> My attention has been drawn to an article appearing in the "Hamdard" of Srinagar dated 14th May which purports to report an interview given by me to a representative of the paper. I much regret to find that the few words I did say have been grossly distorted and words that I never uttered are put in my mouth, the whole object being apparently to make me appear critical of the State and of the policies of the State. In actual fact my few remarks to the reporter were quite the reverse of critical! I expressed enthusiasm over the scenic beauties and wonders of the State and said it rivalled the finest one could find elsewhere in the world including Switzerland. I said I would be happy if it was found possible after the [World] War for my firm to help in building up still further the Tourist traffic of the State and thus in helping to increase further the influx of money into the State and therefore the prosperity of the people of the State. It is of course absolutely untrue to say that I found the condition of the people of the State "pitiable". This is pure fabrication. Nor did I express the opinion that the State was industrially backwards. Finally, I certainly did not criticize the policy of the government in the matter of land ownership. I am sorry that the courtesy I showed to the reporter by agreeing to see him for a few minutes and by exchanging a few polite words with him instead of refusing outright to see him, has been taken advantage of by this newspaper, in a most dishonest manner, to suit some selfish motive of theirs which, as far as I can see, is to find by hook or by crook some support for their criticisms of the government. As a sincere admirer of this beautiful country and a friend of His Highness and of

> a number of State officials and as the guest of the State the last thing I surely would do would be to criticize the State in an interview with an obscure and evidently unscrupulous newspaper. You may by all means make use of what I have said in this letter in any way you or the government may think fit.[646]

Next day, on the basis of JRD's letter, the Publicity Department of the Government issued a handout, a copy of which was endorsed to JRD on his Bombay address as he had left Srinagar in the morning. The handout was published by the *Hamdard* on 19 May. It was also carried by the Government Gazette of 27 May 1943 which caught the attention of Hari Singh. Apparently not satisfied with the publication of the rebuttal alone, he sent a signed Note to the Prime Minister on 8 June asking him to "let me know what action you have already taken, or propose to take, against the Editor and Publisher of the *Hamdard* for concocting and publishing such a gross distortion and misrepresentation of Mr. J.R.D. Tata's conversation with him. In a case like this a mere warning is not sufficient."[647]

Following the Maharaja's missive, Bazaz was summoned by the Chief Secretary to his office and asked to express his "sincere regret" for, what he was told, "gross misrepresentation of Mr. Tata's conversation with his reporter." Bazaz expressed regret and published an apology in his newspaper under the heading, "The report was wrong". After mentioning the publication of the interview and JRD's rebuttal to it, he wrote:

> We published the [Government] press communiqué in the issue of the Hamdard dated the 19th May along with a brief statement from our reporter. But we did not express our personal opinion. We are now pained to learn that the report of our reporter was wrong and Mr. Tata did not utter these words. We are extremely sorry for having published this wrong report.[648]

Prime Minister Maharaj Singh informed Hari Singh about Bazaz's published apology with the hope that "His Highness will consider this to be sufficient". He referred to his conversation with JRD and the latter telling him that "it was imprudent for him to give any interview to a local reporter without knowing anything about the man."[649] An otherwise infuriated Maharaja felt convinced and disposed of the matter.

Maharaj Singh, a Christian by faith, was appointed Prime Minister after the exit of his predecessor, Gopalaswami Ayyangar, in 1943. Ayyangar was the architect of a huge controversy resulting out of the government order changing the script of the official language of Jammu & Kashmir from Persian to Devnagri and polarizing people on religious grounds. It was said then that Muhammad Ali Jinnah had made a complaint to the Viceroy of India against Ayyangar for playing a mischief in the State politics after which His Majesty's Government dropped a hint to the Maharaja Hari Singh leading to Ayyangar's ouster.[650] Bazaz shows warmth towards Maharaj Singh who had given him the permission—Ayyangar had refused—to convert his weekly newspaper into a daily. Without mentioning the Prime Minister's role in saving him from a severe action in the interview controversy, Bazaz writes about his sympathetic approach towards the State press by refusing to penalize a journal even "when told to do so by the Maharaja himself."[651] Maharaj Singh served as Prime Minister only for a short period of three months and seven days before he resigned on 26 July 1943 when Hari Singh resented his wife's humanitarian gesture of donating her blood to a needy poor Kashmiri village girl at a hospital in Srinagar. The Maharaja sent word to him that the Prime Minister and his wife should not mix with the common people.[652] In response, Maharaj Singh resigned and left Kashmir.

15

A Bowl of History

Gulmarg, the famous meadow and tourist destination in Kashmir nestled in the foothills of the Panjal Range, holds a rich history in its bowl. From the 16th century when Kashmir's last native Muslim ruler, Yusuf Shah Chak, is believed to have discovered the place and named it Gulmarg meaning the Meadow of Flowers, to the last Hindu ruler, Hari Singh, the *Queen of Hills* has attracted kings and dignitaries, besides hordes of ordinary visitors that arrive here from all over the world. Bewitched by its charm, Chak is said to have frequented the meadow with his poetess queen, Habba Khatoon. An equally romantic Mughal ruler of medieval India, Jahangir, and his celebrated wife, Nur Jehan, too were smitten by the beauty of the meadow. During a picnic, they pitched their tents at the end of a stream flowing through the bowl.[653] The king also collected 21 different kinds of flowers from the meadow.

Chak and Jahangir were not the only ones besotted by Gulmarg. There is no count of souls who have felt ecstasy in the lap of the meadow. Travellers, explorers and writers have sung songs of its loveliness. Godfrey Thomas Vigne (1801-63), for one, describes Gulmarg as:

> a lovely spot on the downs of the Panjal flat; green, open, and perfumed with wild flowers; the snowy peaks sloping gently upwards from its extremities, and the valley itself extended beneath it; whilst the scenic disposition of its woods and glades, watered by a stream that winds through its whole length from north-west to south-east, is so highly picturesque, that little is wanting but a

> mansion and a herd of deer to compete its resemblance to an English park.[654]

Explorer, army officer, author and former British Resident in Kashmir, Sir Francis Younghusband (1863-1942), found in the world "no place like Gulmarg".[655] After giving an account of the beauty of the place, he adds:

> [T]here is the further attraction in the Gulmarg scenery that it is ever changing—now clear and suffused in brilliant sunlight, now the battle-ground of monsoon storms, and now again streaked with soft fleecy vapours and bathed in haze and colour. No two days are alike, and each point of view discloses some new loveliness.[656]

C.G. Bruce, in her book, *Peeps at Many Lands: Kashmir* draws an elaborate picture of how Gulmarg of yesteryears looked like:

> Here are the race-course, polo ground, golf links, and tennis courts. Here are the church, post and telegraph offices, ballroom and club, library and native shops, while endless wooden huts are dotted about the turfy slopes. They are built chiefly by English people. The season lasts from June to September, though some people go up as early as the end of April and stay over the first of November; but there is an early and heavy snowfall, and the huts are half buried in snow during the winter months when the place is deserted. Undulating downs, with fir trees in clumps, bubbling streams, and, lower down towards the plains, a ridge of pines, make a charming selection of sites for the little chalets, while a protecting screen of dense forest covers the hills which slope up to the mountains behind. Kilanmarg [Khilanmarg] is another of these upland meadows. And the great Tosh Maidan spreads its extensive downs for miles. Gulmarg is the holiday centre now for Northern India, and the goal of many a globe-trotter as well as those whose professional lives are fixed in India. With just as great joy as the Mogul emperors and their entourage sought Kashmir do Englishmen on leave, and ladies with children, order their tongas and set their faces to Gulmarg. Too much Eastern sun is not appreciated

> even by Easterns themselves, far less by people who exclaim when the thermometer reaches 80°. Gulmarg is the summer residence of the Maharajah and his nobles, of the British Resident, and of Kashmir bigwigs. It is a fine sanatorium, and social sports such as are dear to English men and women can be enjoyed.[657]

At the dawn of the 20th century, Gulmarg was pristine and unfilled. In summers, European visitors, bitten by scorching heat in the Plains, would flock to this "resort of six or seven hundred visitors every summer."[658] In the words of Christian missionary, Ernest Fredric Neve, who spent several years in Kashmir, "After the middle of June a great exodus occurs to Gulmarg, the season of which lasts about the middle of September. During these three months Gulmarg is a gay Anglo-Indian hill station."[659] Unlike today, when a veritable township has emerged within the bowl[660], there were "the Maharaj's Palace, a Residency, a hotel with a theatre and ball room, post office, telegraph office, club, and more than a hundred huts built and owned by Europeans."[661] For sports activities, there were golf links, two polo grounds, a cricket ground, four tennis courts, and two croquet grounds.[662] The huts were mostly outside the bowl in forest area and scattered even to higher reaches like the Khilanmarg. Still, Younghusband quotes those who knew it in the old days to be now "spoilt."[663] In 1928, Maharaja Hari Singh also felt Gulmarg was too congested and decided to stop its overfilling.

Journalist Sat Pal Sahni (1922-2010), who was in Gulmarg on 3 September 1939 when the World War II broke out, gives us a closer view of Gulmarg of 1930s and 1940s:

> [M]ore British spent their summer in Gulmarg than in Srinagar. They would stay in huts and for short stay in the Nedous Hotel. The hotel was also functional in a number of huts, only the dining hall was common. The Club House which had a large two storied wooden structure was the centre of most of the activities of visitors. The ground floor had a large sized dance hall. There were 2, 3 and 4-bedroom huts available on three or five year lease at an annual rent of ₹ 500-800. The

> shops at Gulmarg dealing with medicines, toiletries, wine belonged to Kashmiri Pandits, while those of tailoring, barber saloons, shoe smiths, leather goods and gunsmiths belonged to the Muslims. A photographer and chemist shop belonged to W. Lambert of Srinagar but his entire staff at the shops was Kashmiri. Gulmarg was the Golfer's Paradise. Horse-racing and polo was also played here. Polo matches were staged twice a week. Gulmarg provided to the Britishers their kind of life. There was no ban on *shikar* provided one had a license. The common *shikars* were black bear, birds, partridge, fowls, etc. Three to four Golf championships were held in a season. There used to be an annual bawl-dancing competition at the Club. In winters Gulmarg was the Ski capital of India. Maharaja Hari Singh visited Gulmarg only on special occasions. He took many steps to promote tourism and develop Gulmarg as a tourist resort. The Tourist Department, then known as the Visitors Bureau, was established in India first time by him in 1928. In the same year, the Ski Club of India was also started at Gulmarg. There was a piped water supply from springs for tourists. Labourers would bring daily chopped wood pieces from forests for fuel purposes.[664]

Among the significant landmark sites of Gulmarg are the Gulmarg Golf Club and Golf Course, the Nedous Hotel, St. Mary Church, Mohineshwar Shivalaya and the Gulmarg Gondola. The St. Mary's Church was built in 1902, Shri Mohineshwar Shivalaya, also known as the Rani Temple, was constructed by Mohini Bai Sisodia, wife of Maharaja Hari Singh, in 1915, and the Gulmarg Gondola was started in 1998 and subsequently extended to the Afarwat Peak (4200 meters) in 2005.

Gulmarg and Golf

The Gulmarg Golf Club was founded in 1881 by Sir Naville Chamberlain (1856-1944), a British Army Officer and former Military Secretary to the Kashmir Government, with a modest 6-hole golf course, now developed into 18-hole international championship course. It is the world's highest green golf-course at an altitude of 2650 meters. Between 1901 and 1947, the Gulmarg Golf Club was "a reflection of British life and organisation and of eventful golfing seasons filled with glittering club dances, dinners and festivity". At one time, there were three golf courses—the Upper Course, the Lower Course and the Rabbit's Course—simultaneously in use. The Club regularly hosted different golf championships from as early as 1901. The oldest of these was the Mens Amateur Championship of Northern India which was held from 1901 to 1947 regularly with only 3 year's interruption between 1914 and 1916 due to the outbreak of the World War I. The first winner of the Championship was Capt. John Hill, an army officer from the 15 Sikhs who became the first Honourary Secretary of the Gulmarg Golf Club in 1902. Of the total 44 events, the Championship was won 38 times by the Europeans. The first non-European winner, I.S. Malik, won the championship in 1923. The tournament played last time in 1947 was won by Lt. Col. W.R. Howson. The highest number of times any individual won the tournament was H.S. Malik who emerged as winner in 1926, 1928 and 1930. Alongside the men's championship, the Ladies Amateur Championship of Northern India was also held between 1901 and 1947. The first winner of the tournament was Mrs. R.C. Plowden. Mrs. J.L.F. Taylor held the distinction of winning the tournament a record five times, including three consecutive wins in 1938, 1939 and 1940. Among other golf tournaments played at Gulmarg, the Duncan Vase was started in 1918, the Nedou Cup in 1921, the Holkar Cup in 1945, the Calcutta Challenge Trophy in 1965 and the Sher-i-Kashmir Open Golf Trophy in 1983.

On 2 December 1939, the Gulmarg Club was completely gutted in a fire incident. The Club Committee wanted to make a temporary club ready by 1 June 1940 and import the required articles from India as these were not available locally. The Committee Chairman, Lt. Col. J.L.R. Weir, writing from Baroda House, New Delhi on 17 January 1940 directly to the Prime Minister of Kashmir, highlighted the importance of the Club as "a magnet for visitors to Gulmarg."[665] Weir asked for exemption from customs duty the import of articles and wrote:

> Such a concession would be of infinite benefit to us as it would help us to maintain the high standards for which the Gulmarg Club is noted. It would also, as you will realize, be of value to the state by ensuring a large number of visitors in Gulmarg.[666]

The request, however, did not evoke the sentiment Weir had aimed to arouse. The Inspector General, Customs and Excise opined that to accede to the request would "create a precedent likely to afford encouragement to others to come in with similar requests which might place the government in an awkward position".[667] He went against the request as there was no such instance of granting such concession to any private institution. The opinion of the Inspector General, Customs and Excise, carried the day and a terse reply was sent to Weir on 4 February 1940:

> To grant the request in the case of the Gulmarg Club would create a very bad precedent. It cannot be contended that the kind of people for whom the Club would cater and from whom recoveries will have to be made for meeting all the expenditure incurred by the Club are so badly off in worldly goods as to justify a concession of this nature.[668]

In 1948, the Club building was again destroyed by fire and golfing activity suffered a severe setback for 5 years until the Jammu & Kashmir Government reconstructed the Club House in 1953. However, by then, the Lower Course and the Rabbit's Course had been given up, retaining only the Upper Course where now stands the 18-hole Gulmarg Golf Course.

The First Hotel

The Nedous, one of the foremost landmark sites of Gulmarg, is the first hotel in the meadow. It was established in 1888 by Michael Adam Nedou who came from Dubrovnik, now in Croatia, and opened hotels in Lahore and Kashmir. His son, Michael Henry Nedou, also known as Harry Nedou, converted to Islam and married a local Muslim Gujjar girl, Mir Jan. The couple had only one child, Akbar Jahan, who was married to Kashmir's popular leader, Sheikh Mohammad Abdullah in 1933. The hotel, surrounded by green golf course and captivating view of Mount Apharwat, gives its guests 'the best of our heritage' and a 'Home away from home' experience.[669] An old promotional printed piece issued in the name of M. Nedou & Sons, informs readers that the Nedous Hotel "is open from 15th May to 30th September annually, and is fitted throughout with Electric Light. There are large spacious Public Rooms including a Billiard Room which is fitted with a first class Billiard Table."[670]

The Nedous, mentioned in old archival papers as the Gulmarg Hotel, was given on lease to Michael Adam Nedou by the Kashmir Government on an annual rent of ₹ 500. According to the terms of the lease, Nedou was responsible for keeping the building in a proper state of repairs and was allowed ₹ 144 on account of the pay of two *chowkidars*. He was liable to make good any loss to the building caused due to his or his servants' negligence.[671] The original term of the lease had ended on 30 May 1898 and no fresh lease had been executed. In 1901, when the renewal of the lease came up, the State Engineer found that the rent charged from Nedou was far low than permitted by the existing rules. The rules provided for 15% of the total cost of the building to be charged as annual rent which, as the cost of the building then amounted to ₹ 26,000, would be ₹ 3,900. The Engineer was also of the opinion that Nedou should pay the two *chowkidars* out of his own pocket. He also rejected Nedou's plea for a loan of ₹ 10,000 and free grant of 20 trees for rebuilding a block of the hotel.[672] The government felt that the State had shown 'sufficient consideration to Mr. Nedou during the past and, now, that the Hotel has been placed on sound footing' there was no reason for charging rent lower than other buildings at Gulmarg. On 4 April 1903, Nedou wrote a long letter to Raja Amar Singh, Vice-Chairman State Council, on the subject of enhancement of rent and the state of his hotels, an excerpt of which reads:

> In fixing the rent to be paid for the Gulmarg Hotel, I would venture to state generally, that when I first undertook to open a hotel in Gulmarg and subsequently at Srinagar I had to invest a large amount of capital

> in furnishing and stocking them and had to accept a heavy risk as to the future of an enterprise, the profits of which were by no means assured in as much as, in those days at any rate, visitors to Kashmir went there to combine pleasure with economy and were not inclined to patronize more or less expensive hotels. In the early years of the Gulmarg Hotel, the profits were exceedingly small, while the Srinagar Hotel brought in nothing for the two first years, while I had to pay the rent. Last year, it brought in a small income. Just as I am beginning to make headway in my enterprise and reap the benefit of my outlay and heavy labour, it is proposed to raise the rent of the Gulmarg Hotel to an almost prohibitive figure.[673]

Nedou pleaded that since the tourist season was short and his two hotels at Gulmarg and Srinagar were not making any big profit the decision of the State Council to enhance rent of the Gulmarg Hotel be reconsidered. However, the government turned down the request and fixed rent at ₹ 2000 per annum. Besides hotel business, the Nedou father-son duo, Adam and Henry, engaged themselves in other business activities. While the senior Nedou did construction and repair works also, the junior Nedou ran a pony and cart service between Tangmarg and Gulmarg. For years, the Maharaja's huts and palaces at Gulmarg were repaired by senior Nedou and according to the State Engineer, M. Field, "this has been found to work better than interference by the P.W.D. [Public Works Department] and as His Highness also desires to continue this arrangement."[674] In one of the letters, Nedou complained that his previous year's payment on account of repair work had not been released to him.

Transport Service

At the dawn of the 20th century, Kashmir like most parts of the world did not have motorized surface transport. The means of public transportation were *tongas, ekkas*, block-carts and *dandis*. Travel by riding on the back of a *coolie* was also prevalent. The means of civil transport were supplied through a revenue officer or a *chaudhri*. Transport agencies were set up at important stations along a particular road whose in-charge, on requisition, supplied the required number of ponies, *tongas* or bullock-carts and *coolies*. The cart road from Srinagar to Tangmarg, halting point 12 km short of Gulmarg, was completed by 1900.[675] On 13 May 1901, the Kashmir Darbar opened *ekka* and bullock-cart service between Srinagar and Tangmarg in addition to the *tonga* service already established. Consequently, the Transport Agencies supplying baggage and riding ponies at Baramulla and Magam were abolished. The up-journey to Gulmarg was covered by riding ponies and *dandis*, or on foot.

The Residency had asked the government in 1900 to keep a fleet of 50 baggage ponies, 25 riding ponies, 25 *kahars* and 100 *coolies* at Gulmarg and Tangmarg stations. Given the figures of preceding 3 years, the average annual traveller inflow to Gulmarg was 477 and average per year transport supplied was 1724 *coolies*, 450 luggage ponies and 163 riding ponies.[676] The figures suggest that most of the visitors did not use riding ponies for upward journey to Gulmarg. It may be recalled that Gulmarg then was an exclusive summer tourist destination for European visitors.

In 1904, Messrs Dhanjibhoi & Sons were given the contract for supply of transport between Srinagar and Gulmarg. The contract was extended for 1905 and 1906 also. The Agency agreed to supply carts, *ekkas,* ponies, *coolies* and *kahars* for the distance between Srinagar and Tangmarg and vice versa at the following rates:

> Open bullock country carts carrying 10 *maunds* at the uniform rate of ₹ 6 throughout the season (1 May-30 September); *ekkas* at the uniform rate of ₹ 3 and *annas* 8; riding ponies at ₹ 1; load or baggage pony at *annas* 12; *coolie* at *annas* 6; and a *kahar* at *annas* 9.[677] The contractor was required to ensure at Tangmarg or Gulmarg the minimum number of *coolies*, baggage and riding ponies at 25, 10 and 10, respectively. Fifty percent of hire was to be paid in advance and with 72 hours notice for all classes of transport. A Tonga Booking Office was set up in a hut at Gulmarg by Dhanjibhoi & Sons.

By August 1906, the Srinagar-Gulmarg road had been metalled. In 1907, while the contract for *tongas* and *coolies* was accorded to Messrs Dhanjibhoi and Sons, that of *ekkas* and carts went to another contractor, Chaudhri Sher Singh. According to an order signed by Maharaja Pratap Singh on 18 July 1908, the contract for supply of ponies, *coolies* and carts between Tangmarg and Gulmarg for the year 1908 was given to the Imperial Carrying Co. from Rawalpindi, and that of *ekkas* and carts between Srinagar and Tangmarg to Chaudhri Sher Singh.[678] In 1910, the contract for Tangmarg-Gulmarg section was given to Raj Mohammad of Ferozpur who, as Governor Kashmir reported to the State Council, was a front man for Henry Nedou and served only as his agent. Next year, also the contract went to Nedou who had been carrying on this work for the past 12 years. The contract for Srinagar-Tangmarg section was allotted to Kanshi Shah and Sukh Dayal.

Lady Curzon's Visit

Among the early 20th century visitors to Gulmarg was Mary Curzon, wife of Viceroy and Governor General of India, Lord George Curzon, who visited Kashmir in 1902 and stayed here during her full 10-day long stay in the Valley.[679] The Kashmir Government was on its toes to make her stay comfortable and elaborate programme was chalked out to ensure that the Imperial Guest enjoyed her stay in the Valley. It had even planned to disallow Amarnath pilgrims halt at Mattan, one of the important traditional haltage points of the pilgrimage, to avoid clash of the visit and the pilgrimage. Lady Curzon left Simla, the summer capital of British India, on 1 August and travelling on the Jhelum Valley Road reached Gulmarg on 6 August where she camped till 16 August and returned to Simla from there. Her entourage included, besides her staff, two *ayas* and 10 native servants. She was received at Kohala, the State boundary by Dewan Daya Kishen Koul, Maharaja Pratap Singh's private secretary.

When Lady Curzon arrived in Kashmir, Maharaja Pratap Singh was nursing his wounds after having been forced to relinquish powers in 1889, and was making passionate pleas with her husband, the Viceroy and Governor General of India, for restoration of his position. In her visit, Singh saw an opportunity to win Lord Curzon over to his side. The Kashmir Government had expected that Lady Curzon would visit other parts of the Valley and, accordingly drew up an elaborate programme including a shooting expedition, river journey, and cleanliness of possible stopover venues at Shadipore, Manasbal, Achhabal and Martand. Roads leading to the possible places of her visit were also ordered to be repaired. Besides a visit to the Mughal Gardens, an exhibition of handicrafts to be visited by Lady Curzon was also planned at the Museum at Lal Mandi. At each stopover of the royal entourage from Kohala, government officials were required to be in attendance. Messrs Dhanjibhoi & Co was assigned the task of providing transport including *tongas*, *ekkas* and *dandis* for the visiting guests and the accompanying officials. A *baghi* was to come from the Maharaja's Palace. Since the probable time of her visit to Kashmir coincided with the annual Amarnath pilgrimage, the government took special care that the two did not clash with each other.

Raja Amar Singh, brother of Maharaja Pratap Singh, who, as Vice President of the powerful State Council, was calling the shots after the latter had been divested of powers by the Government of India, wrote to the Resident in Kashmir, Louis W. Done:

> [I]t is not desirable that the pilgrimage should camp at the same place where Her Excellency's halts are proposed to be made. There are grave reasons for avoiding such a coincidence which need not be gone into here. It would be difficult perhaps to arrange that Her Excellency should return from the visit to Verinag before the pilgrimage starts from Srinagar and the best plan therefore to adopt would be that Her Excellency should leave Srinagar for Anantnag after the pilgrimage have left Martand on their way to Amarnath by the 13th August 1902. Special arrangements for cleanliness and conservancy of the stages where the pilgrimage is to halt will be made under the immediate supervision

> of the Assistant Surgeon under the formal control of the Chief Medical Officer. The question of the return of the pilgrims from Amarnath need not be discussed as the number coming back via Martand and Anantnag is small and they do not reach Martand till 22nd August 1902. Even then the pilgrims can be ordered not to stop either at Mattan which is more than can be done while pilgrims are on their way to Amarnath. Most of them are s*adhus* who are not at all amenable to control, nor can such control be on religious grounds exercised as to clash with the vested privileges.[680]

The Viceroy of India between 1936 and 1944, Victor Alexander John Hope, known as Lord Linlithgow, and his wife, Doreen Maud Milner, visited Gulmarg on 18 October 1936 and had lunch at the Maharaja's Palace there. The couple also went for shooting at Tral where the Viceroy shot a *hangul* and Lady Linlithgow a leopard and a bear.[681] The two political stalwarts of the United India, Pandit Jawaharlal Nehru and Muhammad Ali Jinnah, who later ruled independent countries of India and Pakistan, respectively, have also holidayed at Gulmarg. Among other prominent visitors to Gulmarg are the Central Asian explorer, Sir Aurel Stein, Indonesian Vice President, Adam Malik and former President and Prime Ministers of India, Neelam Sanjiva Reddy, and Indira Gandhi and Inder Kumar Gujral.

Cricket at Gulmarg

Strange though it may sound, cricket and polo were also played at Gulmarg in the early years of the 20th century. Maharaja Pratap Singh was "a real patron of cricket" and had collected in his cricket team some "finest bowlers and batsmen in India at that time".[682] He was a short statured man and looked comic in his attire while on the field. He wore a false sense of himself as a fine batsman. The 'mixture of sense and non-sense', as Viceroy Lord Curzon called him, could not sense that fielders were making fun of him as a batsman. He was known to carry his *hookah* to the playground and take breaks from the field to return to the pavillion and have a puff or two. Diwan Jarmani Dass draws a comic picture of Pratap Singh at the wicket:

> The Maharaja of Kashmir was a small sized man almost a dwarf, and he wore oversized Kashmiri pagri (head dress) which made him look comic. He used to wear tight trousers with long coat and had large pearl hear-rings in his ears. He was convinced that he was a great batsman and in each and every match played against him, the Maharaja used to score the highest.
>
> Whenever the Maharaja came to bat, the bowler would bowl his slowest and generally away from the stumps. The Maharaja would touch the ball with his bat and the fielders, instead of fielding properly, would kick the ball till it reached the boundary line, and if the ball was still short of the boundary line, the fielder at the other end would kick it till it covered the point. The Maharaja thus made several boundary hits all along the field. It was indeed comic and amusing to see the Maharaja play cricket.... The Maharaja could not detect that the fielders were making fun of him by kicking the ball to reach the boundary or that the ball was not sent straight to hit the wicket. Even when the ball came towards the wickt by mistake the Umpire took good care to call it a 'no ball'. Though the Maharaja himself was a poor batsman, his team consisted of the finest bowlers and batsmen in India at that time.[683]

Pratap Singh, it seems, took time to go for practice. In a letter to educationist Tyndale Biscoe on 18 June 1906, he regretted his inability to instantly reply his letter as when it reached him he was preparing to go for a practice session to keep himself fit to play a match later.[684] He did practice sessions with an Englishman named S.G. McNamara of the Sericulture Department whom he gifted a bat out of his own collection. In another letter to Major J.L. Rose, Inspecting Officer, Kashmir Imperial Service Troops, written on 25 June 1906, he informed him that after the new Resident would arrive in the Residency he himself will be at the cricket ground and claimed doing practice sessions regularly.[685]

With an inflated sense of a 'fine batsman', Pratap Singh laid out a cricket field at Gulmarg in 1906 to play the 'Gentleman's Game' there with the Englishmen. He gave ₹ 300 for laying the ground and asked the Public Works Department to assist Major Rose. There was a proposal to lay a second polo ground at Gulmarg, the idea, however, was later dropped in favour of converting the earmarked land into a cricket ground. On 15 July 1906, Major Rose informed Pratap Singh that he had started the work and hoped to make the ground ready in a month's time. "I am relaying the portion selected for a pitch in places where the ground is uneven, cutting the turf into very large pieces, leveling the ground underneath, and then replacing it. In the out-field I am doing the same thing only not so carefully where there are deep dips in the ground"[686], he wrote. Rose also intimated Singh that several good cricketers were coming up to Gulmarg and "we should have no difficulty in producing a European XI."[687] The archival material of the period shows that Pratap Singh was taking extra ordinary interest in the cricket ground at Gulmarg and kept on seeking updates through letters and telegrams to Rose and others.

On 10 August 1906, Rose again wrote to Pratap Singh from Gulmarg:

> Although the pitch is not put yet it is fit for play. We played a match in the outside of it yesterday. The outfielding is very rough and very few coolies are working so the progress made is slow. I spoke to the Naib Tehsildar about it, who showed me a telegram he had received from you and he says it was very difficult to get coolies on account of the harvest being now on.[688]

In a 7-page hand-written letter, Rose informed the Maharaja about several events scheduled at Gulmarg in the 'next week' and how he intended to fit in cricket matches so that the two do not clash with each other. During 14 to 18 August, cricket matches were scheduled with a mix of polo match on 15 and a horse show on 16 and 18. Four days between 19 and 22 August were left "vacant". Rose informed the Maharaja that "the wicket yesterday played fairly well, but the ball hung a little and bumped now and then" and if trouble was taken with it "we might have an excellent ground and pitch next year." The letter further reads:

> The Resident and I leave at 6 A.M. on the 14th for Baramulla. I have not heard whether Mela Ram's XI is coming up or not—perhaps as the pitch is not very good it is hardly worth his coming, anyhow we should give Your Highness' XI a very good match but it is difficult to get any practice as golf, tennis, etc. monopolises the time of the players. I hope the matches are arranged.[689]

The playing field had no pavillion and Rose requested Pratap Singh to send up tents for accommodation of the spectators and players. He also made a requisition to him for balls, wicket keeping gloves and bats "as we have nearly run out of these and I doubt whether those I am ordering will arrive in time." The Major made an interesting offer to the Maharaja if the latter also decided to play a match. He writes:

> If we get all the best players to play it is quite possible that I shall not play myself as there are many younger and probably better players than myself. I have been thinking that perhaps Your Highness might open the match by playing few balls. I would not ask you to field as not being accustomed to fielding and the ground being rough it is not very pleasant work and rather dangerous. If Your Highness feels inclined to take part in the game I would ask Sir Francis[690] to take the same position on our side, we will play 12 a side but have only 11 on the field.[691]

In his reply the next day, Pratap Singh wrote to Major Rose:

> I am glad to know that the ground has become somewhat better now and a match can be played on it. I have ordered R.D. Pande, P.A. to private secretary, to arrange for everything which is necessary and he will bring up to Gulmarg necessary material, etc. I have read your proposed programme, but I think it will be better to have cricket match on vacant days, for I think cricket play for half days will not be very interesting and one match should be continued for 2 or 3 days till it is finished. You must play in the cricket match because I am sure without yourself the game will not be interesting. My private secretary Rai Sahib Dewan Daya Kishen Koul

> will return back (sic) to Srinagar tomorrow. As regards my taking part in the match I will decide when I come up to Gulmarg, but at the same time I thank you for your kind suggestion.[692]

As everything was in place, Major Rose informed the Maharaja that in view of his visit to Gilgit he would not be able to take part in the cricket matches "as it is absolutely impossible to finish all my work and make my arrangements for Gilgit and send my baggage off on Wednesday if I am occupied for the whole 2 days at cricket."[693] He promised to "get a better batsman than myself to take my place". Pratap Singh who was already in Gulmarg for the matches on 20 August was not happy on receiving this information. He decided to play the second match of the series scheduled in the meadow.

In late October 1906, Pratap Singh also organized cricket matches at Srinagar and invited British officers, posted at far off places, like Lieutenant H. Russell of Royal Artillery who came from Peshawar in the North West Frontier Province.

Animal Care

In 1923, Captain P. Grey, a British soldier on vacation in Kashmir, visited Pahalgam[694] and requisitioned ponies including luggage and riding ponies. The visitor was appalled to see the precarious condition of the pack animals. On August 2, he sent a two-page letter, written with a pencil, to the British Resident in Kashmir wherein he shared the painful condition of suffering animals, and sought his assistance to stop cruelty to them. Grey wrote:

> Of the eight luggage ponies, three were so lame to walk even without a load and two others had enormous gulls under the saddles at least five inches in diameter and an inch deep. In one case, the bonny ridge of the backbone was protruding. Of the riding ponies, one was too lame to proceed at all. From the surprise manifested by the contractor when I rejected these animals, I cannot but feel sure that visitors do not pay much attention to this pain.[695]

Grey felt that an appeal and some strong deterrent for the contractor might assist matters and alleviate the sufferings of these poor beasts. Through the letter, he sought the Resident's assistance. A month later, precisely on September 7, 1923, another foreigner, Mrs. K. Geary Dyer camping at the Chinar Bagh in Srinagar, wrote to the Resident:

> Whilst passing the village of Bren on the Shalimar road last evening, I found a horse with (apparently) a broken pelvis moving in the direction of the village under conditions which must have been sheer torture. I stopped my car and enquired from villagers the following information:
>
> The horse was once the property of Col. Dennis and is now in the possession of his late [former] servant Hamid Wani; who lives in this village (Bren). Some two months ago, the animal met with an accident and same has been allowed to continue living under this wretched condition throughout this period. I earnestly request that you will take immediate action to have the animal inspected, and if incurable, destroyed and in the interest of prevention of cruelty to animals, I feel sure that you will also make an example of the owner.[696]

On 23 June 1924, several residents and visitors in Gulmarg held a meeting and decided to approach the government with a view to have the Prevention of Cruelty to Animals Regulation, Samvat 1969, extended to Gulmarg and Srinagar. The Secretary of the Royal Society for the Prevention of Cruelty to Animals, Mrs. P. Thomson-Glover, wrote to the Resident the same day. She conveyed to him decisions taken in the meeting including starting a branch of the Society for Gulmarg and Srinagar, and sought permission of the Darbar to appoint an Inspector to help in bringing to notice cases of cruelty and to assist in the prosecution of the offender.

The Resident, Sir Jhon Wood, on 30 June 1924, sent a letter to the Foreign Member of the State Council, Hari Singh, who was soon to don the mantle of Maharaja, informing him that a number of cases of gross cruelty to pack animals have been brought to his notice, and endorsed the decisions taken in the Gulmarg meeting. Subsequent communications between the Residency and the Darbar resulted in the State Council meeting in Srinagar on 20 September 1924 and approving the extension of the Regulation to Gulmarg. The Council refused starting of a branch of the Royal Society for Prevention of Cruelty to Animals at Gulmarg and Srinagar as it believed there was already "arrangement for prevention of cruelty to animals in Kashmir".[697]

A year later, on 21 September 1925, the State Council accepted the recommendations of the Re-organization Commission made during its meeting at Srinagar on June 24, 1925. It accorded sanction to the provision of funds for the construction of a suitable hospital at Srinagar and a shed at Gulmarg for the treatment and accommodation of sick animals, besides grant of a monthly allowance of ₹ 10 to the Inspector at Tangmarg for attending to the work at Gulmarg, appointment of a *chowkidar* on a monthly consolidated pay of ₹ 12 and formation of a local society to assist the Darbar officers in measures taken for prevention of cruelty to animals. The Public Works Minister was asked to furnish estimates of cost of the hospital at Srinagar and a shed at Gulmarg.

Up to August 1925, neither the Inspector had started work at Gulmarg nor was the *chowkidar* appointed. H.R. Cobbold, Secretary and Honourary Treasurer, Suffering Animals Fund Kashmir, through a letter, informed the Resident about it who forwarded it to the Foreign Secretary to the Maharaja, to "know how the matters stand".[698] In 1927, Hari Singh, who by now had ascended the throne, approved construction of sick Animals' Shed and Veterinary Dispensary.

The Suffering Animals Fund in Kashmir passed several resolutions in 1926, 1927 and 1928 regarding cruelty to animals and making recommendations to the Darbar. In 1931, the Fund observed that without an animal hospital and medicines, the movement would not be far reaching enough to do much good. It further noted that the offences under the Prevention of Cruelty to Animals Regulation were on the increase. The Fund argued that not only *tonga* ponies but the pack ponies and bullocks which are mercilessly beaten and ill-treated on the roads also need protection.

As a result of continued pressure from the European activists, veterinary dispensaries were established in Kashmir and by the end of 1930's, there were 12 dispensaries—six named as 'road dispensaries' were located on the Jhelum Valley Road and Banihal Cart Road for treatment of transport animals and to prevent entry of the disease into the State from the Punjab.[699] A small veterinary hospital was built at Gulmarg close to the Club, and a permanent Veterinary Assistant was appointed to deal with all cases, including dogs of visitors to Gulmarg.[700]

In 1935, the *Civil & Military Gazette* in one of its stories observed the good impact of the Suffereing Animals Fund on the condition of ponies in Gulmarg:

> His Highness the Maharaja and the Government gave every assistance and the improvement which began to be noticed at once in the condition of Gulmarg ponies has been steadily maintained. Branches have been operated in Srinagar and other parts of Kashmir. Pony shows are held every season and the owners have begun to take a real pride in their animals. A lame of sore-backed "tat" [*Tatoo* or pony] is a rarity nowadays, as the owner realizes that he has only to take the animal to the hospital to obtain free treatment.[701]

Café and Liquor

Mrs. M. Brown, Manager Café De Rose, Caterers and High Class Bakers and Confectioners, The Mall, Lahore in a letter to the Secretary of State, Kashmir written on 23 February 1925, asked for permission to open up a Café at Gulmarg for the season. The Chief Engineer, Roads & Buildings who was asked to give his opinion on the request, conveyed to the Revenue Minister his no-objection, arguing that it was "all in the interest of the trade and provides employment for local youth."[702]

The Member for Commerce and Industries, however, did not agree with the opinion of the Chief Engineer. He consulted officers of the Customs and Excise Department and on 4 September 1925, informed the government that "in the opinion of the Superintendent Customs and Excise there is no real demand for a licensed café at Gulmarg. Almost all the visitors (Europeans) are the members of the club and for those who are not there is the hotel."[703]

The opinion, however, did not carry weight and on 15 April 1926, the State Council accorded permission to Mrs. Brown to open a café at Gulmarg and to sell liquor on retail on the premises.[704]

Wild Flowers

Gulmarg has been known for its flora including wild flowers. Mughal king, Jahangir, as we have observed in the preceding, had collected 21 varieties of wild flowers here. In 1927, Maharaja Hari Singh desired measures to be taken for the protection of wild flora in Gulmarg. Consequent to the ruler's instructions, the Chief Conservator of Forests was asked to propose rules. He proposed an additional Section (4A) to be incorporated in the Forest Regulations of S. 1970. The additional Section provided:

> No ferns or wild flowers shall be uprooted without the written permission of the Divisional Forest Officer and no one shall be permitted to trade in or to offer for sale any ferns or wild flowering plants.[705]

The Member for Commerce & Industries proposed deletion of the words 'without written permission of the Divisional Forest Officer' and substitution of 'wild flowering plants' by 'wild flower'. The Judicial Minister concurred and the proposed amendments were approved by the Maharaja on May 18, 1927. The new rule was notified and included in the Visitors' Rules.

No More Constructions

The Chief Justice of the Punjab High Court of Judicature, Rai Bahadur Sir Shadi Lal, wanted to construct an annex at Gulmarg in the corner of hut number 225-C under his occupation since 1920. On 22 August 1928, he wrote to the Foreign and Political Minister seeking permission. The file, after going through different administrative channels, reached Maharaja Hari Singh. The Maharaja declined permission and, in his own handwriting, recorded on the file: "Construction of further buildings at Gulmarg should not be allowed as the place is already too congested".[706]

Justice Lal had pleaded that several individuals occupying C-type huts had been allowed to build annexes but Hari Singh passed a firm order: "No more constructions at Gulmarg". That was 93 years ago when Gulmarg had only one hotel, the Nedous, and a hundred or so huts for the European tourists—all on the periphery of the bowl.

The Europeans were granted lease to construct huts at Gulmarg and many of them would sublet accommodation and take fellow visitors as paying guests. The subletting of huts was approved by the Maharaja himself after a Memorandum was submitted to him. As per the Rule 35 of the Visitors' Rules, the Residency would forward to the Maharaja the requests of hut owners to take in paying guests. Most of such requests came from English ladies who routinely took paying guests as a commercial activity. In 1927, for instance, the Resident forwarded such requests of Miss B. Chesney, Mrs. E.J. Cole, Mrs. E. Davis and Mrs. K. Meares.[707]

The Kashmir Darbar did not like the indulgence of the Residency in the matter. Accordingly, on 23 August 1923, the State Council, through a resolution, directed "that persons desiring to take in paying guests should in future apply direct to the Home Minister of Council who should consult the Superintending Surgeon and accord sanction if there is no objection under Rule 5 Section VII of Gulmarg Building Site Rules".[708] The Council further directed that the Foreign Minister be requested to communicate this resolution to the Residency Office and that the Home Minister should have it printed and sent to all owners of huts.

The Resident could not easily digest the dilution of his authority and tried to have the decision reversed. He referred to "many complaints"[709] received by his office regarding bad management of some boarding establishments and argued that only those establishments which were well conducted would be recommended by the Resident. He also invoked the 7 July 1923 conversation with the Foreign Member of the State Council regarding the Darbar agreeing 'not to modify any of Visitors' Rules without the Resident's concurrence' and requested for reconsideration of the order. However, his plea was not accepted. On 23 December 1923, the Council ordered alteration in the Rule 35 by omitting the words "Such sanction being applied for through the Resident in Kashmir" asserting that "according of permission for the maintenance of Boarding Houses was a matter which concerned the State alone".[710]

During the reign of Pratap Singh, the Visitors' Rules remained unaltered. However, two years after his death when Hari Singh was in the saddle, a note was submitted on 27 May 1927, to the new Maharaja by his Foreign Minister who wrote that "the Rules need revision and applications should be received by the Government direct; but as [of] this year, the procedure hitherto followed has been adopted and the season is advancing, I suggest that the applications may be disposed of according to the recommendations of our local officer."[711]

On 5 June 1927, the Minister-in-Waiting informed the Foreign Minister that his suggestion was accepted by the Maharaja for the season 1927 only and conveyed the latter's directions that a complete report in the matter may be submitted for his commands in consultation with the Public Works Minister who was asked to submit proposals regarding delegation of powers in this behalf. The issue of delegation of power to grant permission to take in paying guests in huts in Gulmarg was finally approved by Hari Singh on 2 February 1929.

The Boarding establishments at Gulmarg virtually developed into actual hotels as each boarding house took some six to eight huts and accommodated as many as 40 to 70 paying guests. This was objected to, as loss to their business, by Messrs M. Nedous & Sons who ran a hotel there.[712] Their objection was that conversion of boarding establishments into veritable hotels was infringement of their agreement with the government which gave monopoly of hotel business in Gulmarg to them to ensure that a good hotel is run for the convenience of the visitors. The Nedous' complaint pointed out that, in the past, these boarding houses kept to reasonable numbers, but now they were going beyond limits and each year finds them increasing their numbers of boarders by taking more huts. The Nedous argued that since they pay big rent for their Gulmarg Hotel, the boarding houses now existing and those that appear annually should be restricted to the numbers that they take in. The letter of Nedous gave the names of individuals running these boarding houses as Mrs. Baines, Miss O'Connor, Mrs. Gatmell, Miss Christie, Mrs. K. Byrne and Mrs. Amesbury.[713]

On 15 December 1933, Home Minister, Wajahat Hussain, wrote to the Chief Engineer that the six ladies "should be informed that they will not be permitted to take more than four or five guests each. They should be told that the State has given total monopoly to Messrs Nedous and Sons, and it would be an infringement of one of the conditions of agreement with them, if boarding houses were permitted to take paying guests in unrestricted numbers".[714]

At one point in time, government huts at Gulmarg were not in much demand and visitors preferred to stay in private accommodation. The decline in interest of the visitors in the government accommodation was due to its poor facilities and upkeep. An idea of this fact is reflected from a letter written by the Finance Minister to the Home Minister on 20 September 1933. The Minister, quoting the Director Visitors' Bureau's report, observed that the chief reason why government huts remained vacant in the season was that they were not furnished and provided with cookery, cutlery, glass and lamps. In the following year, the situation remained the same as was reflected from this letter of 28 April 1934 written by the Director Visitors Bureau to the Finance Minister:

> I understand that most of these huts are still vacant. From the enquiries received from the visitors I could find that the Government huts are not taken by the visitors owing to the fact that they are unfurnished and are available on lease for a very short period while the private huts are furnished and could be had by the visitors for several years together. The visitors might prefer to have the government huts as the rates or rent are comparatively lesser than those of the private huts and would not I think also mind to furnish the huts

> themselves and maintain a good condition provided they could be leased to them for a longer period.[715]

The Director Visitors' Bureau then proposed to have the huts leased for a period of at least 10 years and a communiqué issued by the government to the effect for the information of prospective visitors to Kashmir through various prominent newspapers.

Dhobee Ghat

On 24 October 1928, the Residency Surgeon, Lt. Col. F. Stevenson, visited Gulmarg and observed some 30 workmen engaged in building a channel to take water from the main stream which flowed through the length of the *marg* at a level just above the second green of the lower course.[716] He followed the channel and found it would round the quarry, beneath Col. Sutherland's Hut and round up the Leopard's Valley towards the Circular Road. Next day, he sent a report to the Resident informing him that the channel was being taken off the main stream for irrigation purposes and from sanitary point of view, the *dhobees* should have a sufficient supply of clean water for washing in. The Resident took up the matter with the government.

The Sanitary Inspector who had accompanied the Surgeon had, in the previous year, raised objection to the building of the channel and stopped the ongoing work. From a sanitary point of view, the Surgeon observed very unsatisfactory arrangements for *dhobees* of Gulmarg. He found that the water in which clothes were washed was "practically liquid sewage".[717] The Surgeon desired the State authorities to make suitable arrangement for washermen to wash in clean water. Stevenson suggested that the "plenty of overflow water from the stream which supplies Gulmarg with drinking water" could be taken in a main pipe to the Dhobee Ghat requiring a mile of piping and small tanks made for *dhobees* to wash in.

Meanwhile, Director Medical Services, Kashmir, Col. J.H. Hugo, objected to the construction of water channel, arguing that it would "adversely affect the water supply at Gulmarg."[718]

His opinion was based on the report of the Chief Medical officer, Kashmir.

Concerned about unhygienic condition at their work place, the *dhobees* approached the Residency Surgeon and requested him to remove the Dhobee Ghat to some other convenient place. The letter signed by Abdullah Dhobee, Mohammad Dhobee, Aziza Dhobee, Ramzana Dhobee, etc. of Dhobee Ghat Gulmarg reads:

> With due respects we the washermen of Gulmarg most respectfully beg to approach your honour on the following lines with a strong hope to receive favourable consideration. The water we use for washing visitors' clothes is very dirty as it comes right up from the Gulmarg Bazaar and brings with it all dirty things in as much as some dead dogs are thrown in this drain in front of Mrs. Skinners Bungalow near Dhobee Ghat which has made the water so noxious and it has become very dirty and there is every danger of some atmosphere of some illness. Besides this, there is no arrangement of pipe for our drinking water although several petitions were submitted to Public Works Department duly supported by visitors for having a pipeline connected in the centre of Dhobee Ghat, but due to our bad luck no action has so far been taken.
>
> The present water has become so noxious that its smell has made it unbearable and we can use it neither for our drinking nor for washing clothes.
>
> We, therefore, earnestly request that you will graciously take early action to remove us this difficulty. If this *Ghat* was shifted to some other convenient place that will remove all this difficulty.
>
> Thanking you, sir, in anticipation.
>
> With due respects,
>
> Your most obedient servants.[719]

Since Gulmarg was populated mostly by the European visitors whose hygiene now was in question, the Resident, G.D. Ogilvie, on 6 July 1929, took up the issue with the government and sought an early action in, what he highlighted was, an "important matter which virtually concerns the health of the population of Gulmarg."[720] On 13 July 1929, the Director Medical Services also chipped in and wrote to the government:

> The question of a piped water supply to the Dhobee Ghat and Teelwanmarg was put up in 1921 and recommended as most urgent measure, the estimate prepared by the P.W. Department was for ₹ 2371. This was sanctioned but has never been forthcoming although the request was repeated. The estimate is now by P.W.D. Rules time expired. The Home Minister, His Highness' Govt. [Government] Jammu and Kashmir has recently directed the Chief Engineer, P.W. Department of His Highness' Government to include this work in his Urgency List for 1986-87.[721] So far as my recollection serves some Dhobee lines were constructed below the Divisional Engineer, J.V. Road's house at Gulmarg but the Dhobees would not use them preferring the present site. I am, however, enquiring about this and will let you know.[722]

The work was included in the Budget proposals for the year 1929.

Telephone Service

The need for a telephone connection at Gulmarg had been felt as early as in the first quarter of the 20th century when the government was approached for providing the facility at the hill station. In 1929, the Minister for Development, in a communication to one of his ministerial colleagues, stated that an estimate amounting to ₹ 14,925 had been sanctioned for construction of the Gulmarg-Srinagar Trunk Telephone Line. However, the work could not be carried out as no provision was made for it in that year's budget.[723]

Years later, in 1938, the Visitors' Bureau, predecessor of today's Department of Tourism, highlighted the "badly wanted" need for telephone service to Gulmarg, Nagin-Nasim Bagh area and to Pahalgam "not only in the interests of visitors to Kashmir but in the interests of local traders and of the administration itself."[724] Earlier, the Secretary Gulmarg Club had flagged the need of a telephonic connection with Srinagar. He had pointed out that such facility would increase tourist arrivals at Gulmarg. He wrote:

> To bring Gulmarg into telephonic communication with Srinagar and so with British India would make good a long felt want and would add considerably to the convenience and contentment of visitors to Gulmarg and probably add to the number of visitors there.[725]

By this time, the Electrical Department had already a line from Srinagar to Gulmarg and it was felt that there would be little difficulty or expense in connecting this line up with the exchange in Srinagar. Arguing for a telephone line as the "most urgent" necessity for Gulmarg, the Director Visitors' Bureau also proposed connectivity for two other important tourist spots in the Valley, Nagin-Nasim Bagh and Pahalgam. He suggested that, besides private connections that may be installed, a public call box be also installed at a central place in Gulmarg for the convenience of the general public. Likewise, he proposed public call boxes at Nagin-Nasim area and Pahalgam and a rate of 8 *Annas* per call in the first instance which could be revised "after some experience had been gained."[726]

The government did not agree to connect Pahalgam with Srinagar through telephone. Instead, Srinagar's telephone connectivity with different towns of the Valley was deemed more important. On August 20, 1938, the Prime Minister wrote to his Home Minister:

> The idea of connecting Pahalgam with Srinagar by Telephone is no doubt a commendable one but it seems to me that in the interest of the administration, the connection of Shopian, Kulgam, Pulwama and other Tehsil Headquarters with the District headquarters and Srinagar should have precedence.[727]

In the meanwhile, the Director Visitors' Bureau kept on pursuing the matter with the government. Ultimately, on 7 March 1939, he was informed that arrangements were being made to provide funds for the telephone connections for Gulmarg, Nagin-Nasim and Pahalgam, and its execution before the coming season.

Works relating to "installation of telephone connections between Srinagar-Gulmarg and Srinagar-Nagin-Nasim Bagh were ordered to be carried out before the ensuing season with funds provided for by re-appropriation."[728] An amount of ₹ 18,100, re-appropriated from the sanctioned grant for flume renovation works at the Mohora power house,[729] was transferred to take up lay telephone communication lines between Srinagar and Gulmarg and Srinagar and Nagin-Nasim Bagh. On 31 March 1939, the Secretary, Srinagar Club, R.B. Langrishe was officially informed that "Nagin, Nasim and Gulmarg will be connected with telephone this year."[730]

Chaplain's Hut

The employees of the British Residency in Kashmir were provided rent-free hutment accommodation at Gulmarg. The Residency Chaplain of the St. Mary Church was allotted Hut No. 185-A. On 16 October 1930, the government withdrew Residency easements and informed the Resident that it proposed to henceforth charge rent on the Chaplain's Hut. The Resident communicated the decision to the Right Revered the Bishop of Lahore who supervised the Church at Gulmarg. Three years later, on 6 October 1933, the Residency informed Prime Minister E.J.D. Colvin that the Bishop had requested that the rent for 1933 on account of the Chaplain's Hut be waived off on the understanding that from 1934 it would be paid by the Church Committee at the annual rate of ₹ 277.

Earlier, the Bishop wrote to the Resident that "my predecessor appears to have taken no action in accordance with the Resident Ogilvie's letter."[731] The Bishop further wrote that he was informed by the Chaplain that he had no money to pay for rent of the hut that year and asked for waiving it off.

The case for waiving the rent from 16 October 1930 to the end of 1933 was submitted to the Prime Minister. Colvin, himself a Christian, felt embarrassed by the Chaplain's request and wrote on the file:

> I am a little ashamed of the Bishop's naïve suggestions but the case will have to go to HH [His Highness].[732]

The case was put up to Maharaja Hari Singh for his orders with Colvin's observation, "It is a bad principle to accept and the PM [Prime Minister] considers that we should politely press for payment." Hari Singh concurred with his Prime Minister and ordered that the "rent should not be waived."[733] Not to be discouraged, the Resident now raised the issue of overcharge and wrote back to the Prime Minister that the rent charged to all Residency buildings was 7% of the capital cost of the hut while in case of the Chaplain's Hut it had been charged at the rate of 9% of the capital cost. He requested that the rent be brought at par with the rest of the Residency buildings.

The matter was again put up to Hari Singh with a note from the Prime Minister that "the Chaplain's hut was originally included in the list of Residency buildings, but the Resident had intimated in his letter of 21 July 1930 that the question of payment of rent by the Chaplain for his hut at Gulmarg had no connection with Residency easements, and would be dealt with separately. "The Church Committee had also accepted this rate and there seems no reason to reduce the rent".[734] "I quite agree. No reduction should be allowed,"[735] wrote Hari Singh. Later, in the exchange of series of letters between the Resident and the Prime Minister, the former tried to drag the matter by asking whether the rent was chargeable per season or per calendar year and requesting that the balance amount may be allowed to be paid in instalments. Ultimately, the Church Committee paid ₹ 277 as rent for 1931, 1932 and 1933.

It may be interesting to recall the picture educationist Tyndale Biscoe had drawn of the Chaplain's Hut at Gulmarg in 1921. He writes:

> I shall never forget the chaplain's hut in heavy rain; there was no dry spot under the roof. The chaplain's wife had to sleep with mackintoshes over her bed and all the umbrellas that she could muster. She put the children to sleep under the bed, for that was the only spot where they could sleep in the dry.[736]

Biscoe also presents a picture of the Church which had changed into "a pretty stone building" from a very poor structure. He recalls:

> The church in the winter was used by the cowherds for their cattle, as it was the only hut besides the Residency and another which withstood the weight of the snow on the roof, as it was built in more solid fashion. It was a long barn like building, with a row of stout pine pillars down the centre supporting directly the ridge-pole of the roof, so every summer there had to be a good cleaning.[737]

Polo in the Meadow

Gulmarg, among other things, is known for one of the highest golf courses in the world but not many people know that at the start of the 20th century, polo was also played in the upland meadow. Francis Younghusband gives an idea of the game of polo at Gulmarg. He writes: "What is now the polo ground was then a swamp".[738] He refers to "a sufficient number of visitors" coming to Gulmarg to "supply subscriptions enough to make and keep up really good golf links, polo grounds, etc."[739]

Polo at Gulmarg was popular among the European visitors who mostly comprised British civil and military officers. However, the laying out of the Polo Ground at Srinagar by Maharaja Hari Singh turned out to be the death knell for the sport at Gulmarg. Singh was in no mood to let the prospects of polo in Srinagar to be upset by allowing the game to be now played at Gulmarg. He stopped it altogether. In early 1930s, some efforts were made by European lovers of polo to revive the sport at Gulmarg but the Maharaja refused approval to the proposal.

On 12 December 1930, Major D. Pott of the 6th Lancers, Sialkot wrote to the Resident, G.E.C. Wakefield (later Prime Minister), then camping at Jammu, "Will you be at home any time on Tuesday (December 17) afternoon. If so, may I come and see you? There is a suggestion of starting polo again in Gulmarg and I was appointed Hon. Sec. [Honourary Secretary] last summer provisionally. But before doing anything about it, I would like to consult you".[740]

On the proposed date, the Resident invited Pott over tea in the afternoon. After the meeting, Pott again wrote to Wakfield on 8 March 1931, informing him that he had consulted Anderson and Mobbay in Delhi to know their views. While the latter had told him that he was out of touch with polo in Srinagar, Anderson had agreed with Pott that "the fact of there being polo in Gulmarg would attract more players to Kashmir which would undoubtedly help the tournament in Srinagar".[741] In his letter to Wakfield, Pott wrote:

> It is possible that in July and August, a few players who would ordinarily have played in Srinagar might go to Gulmarg but I understand that at present the Srinagar grounds will hardly stand the number of Station Chukkers so that would not matter. I have not circulated any letter about polo in Gulmarg and it may be too late to do anything about it this year by the time we have heard HH's [His Highness'] views but if he smiles on it, I would have a try. I shall be very grateful if you could let me have a line as soon as you have been able to ascertain from HH.[742]

In response, the Resident, then camping at New Delhi, took up the matter with the Maharaja through the latter's Personal Secretary, Nawab Khusrao Jung. On 17 March 1931, Wakefield wrote to Jung who was away in France with Maharaja Hari Singh, where the latter's son and heir, Karan Singh, was born. The letter, sent on that address, reads:

> I told him (Pott) that I thought he or anybody else would be ill-advised to do any such thing without first consulting His Highness' wishes because His Highness has spent a great deal of money and time in developing Polo in Srinagar and it appeared to me to be a pity to dissipate polo by starting in Gulmarg. As you would see from Pott's letter, he appears to think that the starting of polo in Gulmarg would not affect polo in Srinagar. Will you kindly take His Highness' commands and let me know to enable me to give Major Pott a reply.[743]

Hari Singh did not take very kindly attempts by Pott to upset prospects of polo in Srinagar in which he had invested great deal of money and time. He thought that the best of arrangements had been established for the game in Srinagar, and refused to encourage playing polo at Gulmarg. In fact, he scoffed at Pott's official high ranking position to be any reason to let him "upset our plans and attempt things in Kashmir". On 7 April 1931, he wrote back to the Resident from Hotel Martinez in Cannes:

> I quite agree with you that considering all that we have done in developing amenities for Polo in Srinagar, it would completely upset Polo prospects in Srinagar and do no good in Gulmarg, if an attempt was made to resuscitate Polo in Gulmarg again. "In the interests of polo itself, if for nothing else, I should certainly squash this proposal and give no encouragement whatsoever and no facilities to it. The mere fact that Pott has been Military Secretary to the Governor of the Punjab is no reason why he should attempt to upset our plans and attempt things in Kashmir. If visitors desire to come up to Kashmir and enjoy a good season's polo, they can well do so by playing at Srinagar where we have established the best of arrangements in every possible way.[744]

In view of a clearcut "No" from Hari Singh, Wakfield explicitly communicated to Major Pott on 28 April 1931 that the Maharaja was not at all in favour of the proposal. However, Pott still did not give up his ambition. He wrote a long letter to the Minister-in-Waiting on 7 June 1931 arguing, though vainly, how the game of polo at Gulmarg would not adversely affect the sport at Srinagar. He wrote:

> I do not know how many polo players have gone to Srinagar this year but I think I am right in saying that there are many players who do find Srinagar rather hot in June and July, if they have to spend the remainder of the summer in the plain of India. My own opinion is that the really keen player who goes to Kashmir for polo only, will continue to play in Srinagar on account of the good grounds and higher standard of play. I think however that there are many others who would prefer to combine polo with golf in the cooler climate of Gulmarg. For amongst such players, Teams would certainly go to Srinagar to play in the Tournaments there. I think in this way that although there might be rather fewer visitors playing Station Chukkers in Srinagar, which might be an

> advantage, if there is any question of saving the grounds there would undoubtedly be more visitors teams for the tournaments.... I understand that His Highness thinks that Gulmarg is too high for ponies. I have however exceptional cases of ponies not playing as well there as in the plain but in the four or five years before the war when I was playing in Gulmarg I do not remember hearing of a case of "heart failure" or of any pony being injured. I shall be much obliged if you would show this letter to His Highness and ascertain his views on the subject.[745]

The Pott letter did not change Hari Singh's mind, nor evoked a response. Thus, the prospect of revival of polo at Gulmarg was laid to rest.

In 1939, Hari Singh was very enthusiastic about the Westchester Challenge Cup matches being played between the British and the American squads at the International Field, Meadow Brook in the United States. He spent $ 30,000 on purchase of four ponies which he gifted to the British squad for the big game. This, when majority of his subjects in Kashmir lived a life from hand to mouth. About the development *The New Yorker* wrote:

> The Maharaja of Kashmir, who is particularly enthusiastic about the coming matches, did'nt have any ponies that he thought were good enough to contribute, so he commissioned Jose Reynal to buy four of the best Argentines obtainable. These, named Flechilla, Figurina, Gold Leaf and Rosita, cost the Maharaja around $ 30,000, not counting shipping charges. He turned the ponies over to the British.[746]

A Broke Residency

Strange though it may sound, at one point in time, the British Resident in Kashmir did not have ₹ 213 to clear an outstanding on purchase of some furniture articles for his Gulmarg hut and had to write a letter of apology to the government for his inability to pay the balance amount. In 1933, the Residency in Srinagar wanted to purchase all the articles of furniture lying in its Gulmarg Hut, called the First Assistant Resident Hut. The total amount due was ₹ 1254 and *Annas* 2. The Residency had already paid ₹ 950 and, on 21 December 1933, the Resident, L.E. Lang, paid further sum of ₹ 91. However, he did not have enough money to pay the amount in full. In a letter of regret, he wrote to the Prime Minister, E.J.D. Colvin:

> I much regret my inability to pay the whole amount this year, failure to do so being due to the fact that the Government of India have only placed Rs 1041 at my disposal for the present. I trust that His Highness' Government will have no objection in the matter.[747]

The government agreed to the request but, on 13 January 1934, sent a word of advice to Lang that "requisition of such purchases are only received piecemeal which complicates accounts and delays their final adjustment."[748] However, a little less than three months later, the Resident expressed his inability to pay the balance amount of ₹ 213 and *Annas* 2, explaining his failure thus:

> The Government of India have for the year 1934-35 reduced the grant for the maintenance of furniture in the houses of this Residency, and consequently I am not now in a position to take over all the furniture and pay the balance of ₹ 213/2/- as previously intended.[749]

Lang had only ₹ 34 in his kitty which he sent to the Prime Minister saying that the articles of furniture costing the balance amount of ₹ 179 and *Annas* 2 will be returned to His Highness' Government as soon as the Gulmarg season reopens. The government could have easily remitted the meagre amount but chose against it. On 26 April 1934, the Prime Minister wrote to the Resident: "Please return the articles of furniture valuing ₹ 179/2/- to the Reception Department as soon as the Gulmarg season reopens."[750]

Observing a cold shoulder from the government, the Residency promised to return the furniture but complained that more money was charged than was actually payable against the purchase of the furniture.

The Killer Avalanche

In 1929, two British Army officers, Major Headow and Major Metcarp, established at Gulmarg the Ski Club of India—the first in the colonial India. The Club's maiden secretary was B.N. Pestonji. The inception of the Club heralded skiing as a sport in Kashmir. Among the first skiers in Gulmarg was John Hunt, again a British Army officer, who came here in 1931. Before leaving for Kashmir, he recalled the enthusiasm on the prospect of skiing thus:

> The early years following the First World War marked the beginning of downhill competitive skiing. At that time, British skiers led the world, and it was not long before enthusiasts serving in this outpost of the British Empire had found a centre for their sport: the Ski Club of India was formed at Gulmarg in 1929. But Pejanpathri, the pastoral highlands beyond the Khilan Marg [Khilanmarg], an 'empty quarter' known only to shepherds in summer, was still waiting to be explored. In January 1931, as a junior subaltern about to embark for service with the overseas battalion of my regiment, such a prospect was beyond my imagination. I was astonished, therefore, a few days before my departure for India, to receive a telegram from a brother officer who had preceded me a few months earlier, which read: 'BRING YOUR SKIS'. This was glad news indeed.[751]

A further peep into that period is allowed by Mohammad Ashraf, former Director General Tourism, Jammu & Kashmir who writes:

> Those days all ski competitions were held at Khilanmarg and the pony track was kept open throughout the winter. There were two major events, the Christmas and Easter Competitions. The famous British Sports Equipment Firm, the "Lilywhites" had introduced some trophies for various ski competitions. In fact one of the ski slopes above Khilanmarg is still called the "Lilywhite Slope". The attendance in the open competition held at Christmas in 1938 was over 500.[752]

In his write-up, Beyond *Gulmarg—Exploring the Pir Panjal in the Thirties*, Hunt talks about the mountain hut of the Ski Club of India situated high up on the Khilanmarg and close to the foot of the Christmas Gully.

In the first week of March 1936, there occurred a major tragedy at Khilanmarg when a heavy snow avalanche hit a hut and swept it away, killing three British Army officers and a hut *chowkidar.* The Military Officers from Rawalpindi Garrison, Lieutenant J.L. Nolan, Lieutenant A.R. Hingston and Second Lieutenant J.K.C.M. Graham, had slept in the hut after the day's skiing on the slopes. The officers had remained in Gulmarg after the spring meeting of the Ski Club of India. During the night, a major avalanche struck the hut and overwhelmed it along with the inmates.[753] As initial search operation failed, rescue teams were rushed from Srinagar. Eric Tyndale Biscoe of the C.M.S. School with a number of his senior boys, Dr. Marion Symthe, a lady doctor of the C.M.S. Zanana Hospital and F.D. Hartley, former Superintendent of Police, Calcutta formed a rescue party and reached Gulmarg.[754] The Governor of Kashmir, Raja Mohammad Afzal Khan, accompanied by Deputy Inspector General of Police arrived in Gulmarg and supervised rescue operations.

Towards the end of February, Gulmarg had experienced heavy snowfall disrupting all communications—telegraph, telephone, mails—and power supply. Both the transformers and telegraph lines between Baramulla and Rampur were swept away by snow drifts. An idea of the amount of snowfall could be gleaned from the fact that "the army of a hundred coolies who brought the Hotel gear from Gulmarg to Tangmarg on February 27 took four hours to make their way from the Hotel to the Gap—less than a mile over completely level country."[755] A massive army of four to five hundred *coolies* was engaged in rescue operation at the site of the ill-fated hut.[756] A report published in *The Civil & Military Gazette* detailed events leading to the tragedy:

> [A]t the termination of the Ski Club of India meeting at Gulmarg of February 27 Lieuts Nolan, Hingston and Graham remained in Gulmarg with the intention of living

> in the Khilan hut and making daily ski excursions in the vicinity, and possibly to Tosh Maidan [Tossa Maidan] and Lyanmarg. Nolan and Hingston decided to remain until about March 8 and Graham who had left his car at Tangmarg, intended leaving Kashmir on March 3. Nolan and Hingston's absence, therefore, gave no cause for anxiety in Srinagar, and Graham might easily have gone to Rawalpindi direct from Tangmarg. Remarks about the three young officers in Gulmarg having a pretty rough time were frequently heard but no suggestion of a tragedy entered the mind of anyone in Srinagar. Sufficient provisions were taken to the Khilan hut by the party, and the hut *chowkidar* was engaged as general servant. Before proceeding to Khilan the *chowkidar* made arrangements with his brother, who is also a *chowkidar* at Gulmarg, to send up food. The bad weather which compelled the Ski Club to close its meeting a day earlier than was intended continued for several days, culminating in a very heavy snowfall on the night of March 3 and 4. When the weather cleared the *chowkidar* went up to his brother, but could find no trace of the hut, and with the help of ten or a dozen *coolies* commenced digging on what he considered to be the position of the hut. He soon found his task too difficult with the small number of helpers available, so he decided to go to Srinagar to report the whole matter to Major Haddow.[757]

The rescue party dug out three bodies of the Army officers on 7 March. The wrist watch on one of the bodies had stopped at twelve o'clock. The bodies were clothed in ski kit with boots on. For several days, search for the body of the missing *chowkidar* continued which was finally recovered on 15 March.[758] On his last visit to Khilanmarg in 1935, John Hunt was delighted to meet "my friend", the deceased *chowkidar*. Years later, he wrote:

> One of the pleasures of that visit was my reunion with the old chowkidar. It was the last time I saw him, for the following year the new hut, strongly built and apparently safely sited, was overwhelmed by an avalanche, killing

> my friend and three army officers who were there on leave.[759]

The Publicity Department of the government was caught in an awkward position with the press reporters filing details of the rescue operation way ahead of it. The Department accused the concerned authorities of not apprising them of the developments when "the Press Correspondents at Srinagar knew more about what had happened and much earlier in time."[760] The March 1936 heavy snowfall and consequent avalanches caused widespread death and destruction in several areas of north-Kashmir.[761]

Municipal Laws

In 1937, some foreign visitors observed a public nuisance around Gulmarg and their activism over it resulted in the formulation of an important municipal law in Kashmir. That year, on 24 July, an alarmed Col G.S. Bocquet Redcot wrote to the Director Visitors Bureau:

> On the road up from Tangmarg advertisements are affixed to most trees; on arrival at the Residency Gap (fortunately the Resident does not often visit Gulmarg or he would have something to say) one's eyes are assailed by a battery of advertisements round the famous circular walk one is again inflicted by similar eye-sores. The Nanda Bus Coy: [Company] have gone so far as to paint their name on every large and conspicuous stone. Cannot something be done to restrain these vandals from defacing the country side? One cannot very well prohibit shopkeepers from disfiguring their own shop fronts, but no other advertisements should be allowed anywhere.[762]

Next day, another visitor, Mrs. J.L. Bond, staying in the Nedous Hotel, also took up the issue with the Director Visitors Bureau. She wrote to him:

> I am writing to ask you if you can do something to get rid of those dreadful and unsightly advertisements which are disfiguring the entrance to Gulmarg and all the road up to Tangmarg. Surely something can be done to forbid

> people even ruining the stones and rocks by painting on them.[763]

As the issue was agitated by foreign visitors, the government in Kashmir swung into action. On 12 August, the Finance Minister wrote to the Revenue Minister, K.N. Knox:

> Certain European visitors resent the painting of stones and trees, etc. in Gulmarg on account of business advertisements and some written complaints have also been received by the Director Visitors Bureau, copies of which are enclosed for your information. I shall be glad if you will kindly order the President of the Town Area Committee, Gulmarg to prohibit such advertisements in Gulmarg.[764]

Three months later, on 11 November, the Director Visitors Bureau wrote back to the Finance Minister:

> ...could you kindly press for suitable orders being issued to stop the nuisance and for all un-authorised advertisements being removed under the official action of the Town area Committee or the Executive Engineer Gulmarg.

The letters of Redcot and Bond resulted in the formulation of the Municipal Rules in 1939 which regulated posting of bills and advertisements and erection of notice boards, etc. The Bye-laws framed by the government banned un-authorised posting of bills and advertisements, fixed penalty for violators, spelt out exemptions and notified schedule of rates for erecting notice boards, overhanging projecting notice boards on streets, roads, lanes and river banks.

The Regal Cinema

Among the facilities and means of recreation available to visitors at Gulmarg during the first decade of the last century, Francis Younghusband mentions a theatre. In 1940s, the Bal siblings who had opened a cinema hall, the *Ragal,* in Srinagar also operated a small cinema hall at Gulmarg with the same name, which functioned only during summers. During winters, as Gulmarg closed down, the cinema hall would also wind up for six months only to reopen in May next. The theatre was a

Hollywood-movies-only facility. No Indian films were screened because the target audience were only the European. Movies were changed after every two days, screening quite a substantial number of films in a season. Printed leaflets detailing films to be screened during the coming month were circulated in advance, with change, if any, intimated to the Board of Film Censors. In 1943, due to heavy rains and chilly season, the cinema hall started on 22 May instead of the first day of the month. Some of the movies screened during that summer included *Springtime in Rockies, The War Against Mrs. Hardley, Eagle Squadron, Parachute Batallion, Forever Yours, Gold Rush, To the Shores of Tripoli, The Little Foxes, The Invaders, Day will Dawn, To Be or Not to Be, Jungle Book, Lady is Willing,* and *Moonlight in Havana*.

License for running the cinema hall was issued for six months and extended next year by the Board of Film Censors in consultation with electric and police departments and after an inspection of the hall. On 3 April 1943, Superintendent of Police, Baramulla inspected the Regal Cinema, Gulmarg and observed:

> The floor of the Cinema Hall has been made paces with stone masonary and has been cemented. About half of the walls have also been made of stone masonary and have been cemented as well. The cement at various places cracked due to severe winter and the Manager has stated that necessary repairs would be carried out within a couple of days. One outer wooden steps leading to the Cinema Hall require early repairs, which the Manager promised would be set right within a few days.[765]

Sometimes, no film show was held because of non-availability of a film print as happened on 22 June 1944 when the cinema hall was closed "since we have no picture in hand".[766] The cinema hall was situated near the Gulmarg Club. Due to disuse for years, the building collapsed under the weight of snow somewhere during 1970s, bringing to an end the story of cinema in Gulmarg.

Prime Minister Arrested

In 1953, Gulmarg saw Kashmir's tallest leader and the incumbent Prime Minister being woken up in the dead of the night, served with an order of his dismissal and arrest, and whisked away in a police jeep to Udhampur in Jammu province where he was imprisoned. On 8 August, Sheikh Mohammad Abdullah accompanied by his three Kashmiri Pandit aides arrived in Gulmarg to relax his worked out nerves and review some local development works. His wife, Akbar Jahan, and children were already there since they had left Srinagar hours before his departure.

Lately, Abdullah had run into serious differences with some of his cabinet colleagues who were acting at the behest of New Delhi. He was being accused of working for an independent Kashmir but the charge brought out for his dismissal was the claim that he had lost confidence of his cabinet. His friend and Prime Minister of India, Jawaharlal Nehru, had consented to his dismissal. The *Sadr-e-Riyasat*, Karan Singh, was in the loop. He had Abdullah's ministerial colleague, D.P. Dhar and Brigadier B.M. Koul working out minutest details of the coup. They were looking for an opportune moment to strike which was offered by Abdulla's leaving for Gulmarg.

In the afternoon, the Prime Minister left Srinagar where, at his back, all details had been tied up including informing the Army and discretely handling the media to disallow Abdullah "any opportunity to take his case to the streets".[767] Nehru's team in Srinagar had ensured that Abdullah did not get a whiff of what they were up to. Shortly before he left for Gulmarg on Saturday afternoon, Karan Singh had called him to his house where he was asked to settle issues with his colleagues at a cabinet meeting on Monday. As he boarded his vehicle to start for Gulmarg, he told his media officer, Baldev Prasad Sharma, "Hold the fort and tomorrow when journalist Durga Prasad arrives from Delhi bring him with you to Gulmarg".[768]

The temperature at Gulmarg had dipped due to heavy showers and Abdullah and family went to bed soon after dinner. In the wee hours, precisely 4.20 A.M., of 9 August, somebody violently knocked the door of the Prime Minister's bed room. Abdullah woke up to the knock, opened the door and found R.C. Raina, his Private Secretary, there who informed him that army had laid siege of the house and Superintendent of Police, L.D. Thakur, had come to arrest him. Thakur and an ADC to the *Sadr-e-Riyasat* entered the drawing room and handed over a sealed envelop to Abdullah which carried his dismissal and arrest orders. Another envelop given to him had a memorandum inside signed by his cabinet colleagues, Bakhshi Ghulam Mohammad, Shyam Lal Saraf and Girdharilal Dogra, declaring no-confidence in him as Prime Minister.

Sensing the gravity of the situation, Abdullah tried to argue with Thakur that *Sadr-e-Riyasat* had no constitutional authority to dismiss him but the time was over and he quietly surrendered, asking only for some time to say his morning prayers. Finally, at 9 A.M., he was driven to Udhampur to a long incarceration. The rest is history.

16
Dateline Kashmir

Journalism in Jammu and Kashmir is generally believed to have begun with the birth of weekly *Ranbir* at Jammu in 1924. For long, its printer, publisher and editor, Lala Mulk Raj Saraf, has been known as the *Baba-i-Sahafat* or the Father of Journalism in the State. However, long before the *Ranbir*, the first periodical—an 8-page news sheet—*Bidya Bilas*, was published from Jammu in 1867.[769] Ten years later, the *Dharam Darpan* was launched from there, followed by the *Jammu Gazette* in 1884.

From Kashmir, the first newspaper, *Tohfa-e-Kashmir* meaning the 'Gift of Kashmir' was started by Munshi Harmukh Rai in 1875. The 8-page weekly was published on Saturdays from Maharajganj, Srinagar and its editor was Jamna Prasad.[770] In 1896, Abdul Salam Rafiqi, a Kashmiri and an associate of the founder of the Aligarh Muslim University, Sir Syed Ahmad Khan, launched a monthly, *Ar-Rafiq*, from Srinagar.[771] The periodical was very critical of the autocratic rule, leaving Maharaja Pratap Singh fuming. Failing in winning him over, Singh banned *Ar-Rafiq* and exiled Rafiqi from Kashmir soon after publication of the second issue of the newspaper.

The first prominent newspaper of Kashmir, erroneously believed by many as the first ever published from the Valley, was the *Vitasta* launched by Prem Nath Bazaz in 1932.[772] Earlier, in 1904, Pratap Singh had frustrated an attempt by Mohammad Din Fauq to start a newspaper, *Kashir*, from Srinagar by denying him permission. The ruler was not prepared to even consider the request and asked his Prime Minister to issue an order forbidding even receiving of such an application in future.[773]

However, on 21 March 1923, when Saraf's application—third since 1921—was received, a minister convinced the reluctant Pratap Singh that a newspaper, in fact, would prove helpful for his government.[774]

The evolution of journalism in Jammu & Kashmir began during the rule of Hari Singh (1925-47). He allowed a large number of newspapers to be published from both Srinagar and Jammu. In 1942, when restrictions on freedom of press and platform were eased and 'the Press laws in the State were brought in line with those of British India', there were as many as 50 newspapers and periodicals published from Jammu & Kashmir.[775] In Kashmir, the *Vitasta*, survived only for a year but Bazaz's effort encouraged many others to take a plunge.

During 1930s-40s, newspapers published from Kashmir included *Jahangir* (1932), *Haqeeqat* (1932), R*ehbar* (1933), *Islam* (1934), *Sadaqat* (1934), *Islah* (1934), *Hamdard* (1935), *Martand* (1935), *Quomi Dard* (1935), *Kaisri* (1936), *Millat* (1936), *Tawheed* (1936), *Hidayat* (1937), *Vakil* (1937), *Khalid* (1938), *Albarq* (pre-'40), *Khidmat* (1940), *Khalsa Gazette* (1942), *Roshni* (1943), *Noor* (1946), *Jyoti* (1948), and *Kashmir* (1948). Around this period, some English newspapers like *Kashmir Times* (not the one founded by Ved Bhasin) 1934, and *Kashmir Chronicle* (1939) were also published. Most of these newspapers had a short life, some few months only. Although many newspapers in Kashmir had started publishing in 1930s, the plight of the people under an oppressive regime could not get highlighted through their columns for the fear of government reprisal. It was essentially the Urdu Press of Lahore that brought to the world the ground realities of Kashmir. Newspapers like *Inqilab, Paisa Akhbar*, *Alfaz* and *Siyasat* devoted their pages to Kashmir and quite often were banned entry into the Valley.

Pratap Singh had granted Mulk Raj Saraf permission to start the *Ranbir* with explicit direction to write on social and development issues only but Hari Singh was a little liberal than his uncle and predecessor in allowing publication of newspapers, although journalists under his rule did not enjoy much freedom in deciding on what to print. His Government's Publicity Department kept a watchful eye over what was being published. Editors were often summoned to the Publicity Department to impress upon them what material they should or should not publish, and if found flouting the government directives, they were reprimanded, blacklisted and, in serious cases, their guarantee was forfeited and registration of newspapers suspended. Material of interest to the government would be handed over to them for publication. During the World War II, material eulogizing the Allied Forces' achievements and denouncing the Nazi Germany, received from the Government of British India, was religiously circulated among the local newspapers for publication with compliance monitored periodically. Criticism of the Maharaja was not countenanced. Bad press against a government department or official was not taken kindly. News reports about misconduct of government officials were responded with filing of cases against concerned editors, instead of taking action against delinquent officials.

Strict surveillance by the government, however, did not stop newspapers from occasionally criticizing the functioning of its different organs or expressing views to its dislike. In 1930, the *Ranbir* was banned for reporting a protest march taken out in Jammu against the arrest of Mahatma Gandhi by the British Government. Likewise, in 1936 when Sheikh Mohammad Abdullah was arrested, newspapers in Srinagar stopped publication in the wake of a government directive to publish newspapers only with its permission. In 1941, the Editor *Rehnuma* was proceeded against in a court for violating government directive. The registration of two newspapers published from Poonch was withdrawn for failing to send two free copies to the Prime Minister. In 1943, Hari Singh asked his Prime Minister to take action "beyond mere warning" against the *Hamdard* for misquoting industrialist JRD Tata in an interview critical of the government. Bazaz, as was observed earlier, was summoned, reprimanded and asked to tender an apology which he duly published. On the intervention of a mild Prime Minister, Maharaj Singh, he was saved from an imminent severe action.

The first body of journalists in Kashmir, about which the earliest reference is available, was the Kashmir Journalists' Association. A meeting of the Association was held in Srinagar on 24 May 1937 under the president-ship of Mohammad

Sayeed Masoodi at the office of the daily *Hamdard* where members of the executive committee and the office bearers for the next year were elected. Pandit Shamboo Nath Koul was elected President while L. Ramsarandas Malhotra, Mohammad Sayeed Masoodi and Pir Mohammad Maqbool Baihaqi were elected as Vice President, General Secretary and Secretary, respectively.[776] Since the election was held for the 'next year', it is obvious that the Association had come into existence before May 1937, may be, in 1936 or even before that. Another body of newsmen named Kashmir Journalists' Federation was formed on 7 June 1937 to, what a newspaper report described "safeguard the rights and privileges of the local papers and the correspondents of newspapers published outside the State working in Kashmir."[777] The meeting to elect the journalists' body was held in a houseboat under the chairman-ship of H.L. Vohra, the Srinagar-based correspondent of the Civil & Military Gazette. The meeting was attended by the editors of the local newspapers including the *Martand*, the *Kashmir Times*, the *Vakil*, the *Albarq*, the *Islam*, the *Islah*, and the correspondents of the *Civil & Military Gazette*, the *Tribune*, the *Hindustan Times*, the *Amrita Bazar Patrika*, the *Times of India*, the *Milap*, the *Pratap* and the *Vir Bharat*. The meeting also adopted the constitution and aims and objectives of the Federation. The office-bearers elected included P.N. Kanna, Editor *Martand* (President), Abdul Ahad, Editor *Islah* (Vice-President), M.A. Sabir, Editor *Albarq* (Secretary) and S.N. Koul, Editor *Vakil* (Assistant Secretary and Treasurer). The Federation was decided to be affiliated with the Indian Journalists Association. Later, in 1941, a new set of office-bearers of the Kashmir Journalists' Federation was elected which included Janki Nath Zutshi, Baldev Prasad Sharma, Radha Krishen Kak, Mohammad Yusuf Qureshi, Sadruddin Mujahid and Harbans Singh Azad.[778] The first two gentlemen later headed the State's Publicity Department.

Regarding the first press conference held in the State, Sofi Mohiuddin, author of *Jammu Wa Kashmir Mai Urdu Sahafat* (Urdu Journalism in Jammu & Kashmir), who also edited weekly *Shahmir*, claims that it was held on 13 February 1944 at Jammu and addressed by Prime Minister B.N. Rau. Interestingly, prior to the press conference, journalists from Kashmir and Jammu held a meeting to devise strategy on presenting their issues before Rau. About two dozen journalists including Radha Krishen Kak and Balraj Puri, attended the press conference. Mohiuddin's claim on Rau's press conference being the first in Jammu & Kashmir is not correct. In fact, about two years before the Rau's presser, Sheikh Mohammad Abdullah had, at the height of the controversy generated by a decision of the government to change the script of official language from Persian to Devnagri, addressed a press conference at Jammu on 18 January 1942 where, among other things, he had declared that if the Indian National Congress decided Sanskrit to be the National language he would readily accept it for the State.[779] In Kashmir, among the earliest, if not the first, press conferences was the President, All India Muslim League, Muhammad Ali Jinnah's interaction with newsmen at Srinagar during his last visit to the Valley in 1944. Decades later, journalists Jagan Nath Sathu and Abdul Aziz Shora who had attended the presser would recall the event with much enthusiasm.

During Kashmir's resistance against autocracy, newspapers such as *Khidmat* and *Hamdard* played significant role in highlighting the plight of Kashmiris, and creating awareness on their demands for basic rights. After the termination of autocratic rule in 1947, the ground rules for newspapers were slightly changed for better with the incumbent governments adopting a policy of carrot and stick. Newspapers that did not toe its line were subjected to penalties including suspension of advertisement support.

Among the Urdu newspapers published from Kashmir during 1950s were *Apna Sansar*, *Nai Lehar*, *Naya Sansar, Jamhoor*, *Mashaal, Al-Haq*, *Azad, Funkar*, *Payam-i-Inqilab, Dehqan*, *Kashmir Samachar,* and *Mazdoor*. The rise of *Aftab* in 1958, however, proved a turning point in the development of vernacular journalism in Kashmir. The newspaper had its fingers on the pulse of the people and, over the years, its printer, publisher and editor, Sanaullah Bhat, introduced to Kashmir the latest offset printing technology, photo journalism and hiring national and international wire services. He had also the distinction of popularizing newspaper reading through hawking and home delivery. He also hired bright people to work on the desk and as reporters. For these achievements, he is referred to as the *Baba-i-Sahafat* in Kashmir. It was at the *Aftab* that this author earned in 1979 a byline, the first ever by a reporter in Kashmir, for a news story. The newspaper also introduced a daily poetic cartoon by him reflecting on current issues.

On 1 July 1964, the publication of weekly *Aayeena* heralded arrival of fearless journalism in Kashmir. Its editor, Shamim Ahmad Shamim, wrote very critical pieces against the incumbent governments. His columns, high in quality and strong in punch, were a treat to readers and earned equal appreciation within and outside Kashmir. On 18 June 1969, with the publication of the *Srinagar Times*, another important development happened with regard to growth of Urdu journalism in Kashmir. The newspaper through its daily cartoon by Bashir Ahmad Bashir achieved instant popularity and wide circulation, both among highly as well as marginally educated readers.

In 1970, noted Kashmiri poet, Amin Kamil, started an Urdu weekly, *Wadi*, from Srinagar. The promo of the newspaper introduced it as representing teachers, students, youth, writers, artistes and intellectuals. It highlighted its objective as dismantling ignorant, conscienceless and self-centered politicians as well as sycophant and corrupt officers and anti-social and narrow minded people. No wonder, the newspaper did not last long.

The decades of 1960 and 1970, otherwise a flourishing period for vernacular journalism in Kashmir, were a hard time for newspapers. G.M. Sadiq's Government (1964-71) was especially tough. As many as 11 newspapers including *Hamdard*, *Roshni*, *Zamindar*, *Hurriyat,* and *Mahaz* were banned in 1965. Two years later, during the Pandit Agitation over conversion and marriage of a Hindu girl with her Muslim colleague, the *Martand*, *Roshni* and *Nawa-i-Kashmir* were temporarily banned. In 1970, the *Srinagar Times* was banned for two months for critical writings against the government. In 1977, the newspaper faced a privilege motion in the State Assembly for publishing a cartoon which the members found derogatory to legislators.

Punitive actions against newspapers, or their editors, that the incumbent governments felt crossed the red line, were taken in many cases during the post-1989 years. Editors Ghulam Nabi Shaida (*Wadi Ki Awaz*), Mohammad Shaban Vakil (A*l-Safa*) and Ghulam Jeelani Qadri (*Afaq*) faced criminal cases in 1990 for, what the government felt, publishing seditious material. Twenty-nine years after the case was filed, Qadri was arrested on 24 June 2019 but released on bail next day. The case is still pending with the court of Chief Judicial Magistrate, Srinagar for want of the record which the prosecution has failed to produce till date. The *Kashmir Reader* was banned for about three months in the wake of a massive public upsurge following the killing of a militant commander, Burhan Wani, in 2016. Asif Sultan, a reporter with the newspaper, was arrested in 2018 for allegedly writing a seditious piece and is still in jail. Earlier, freelance photojournalist, Kamran Yusuf, was arrested in 2017 for, what his colleagues say, 'doing his professional duty'. In 2020, Gowhar Geelani, Peerzada Ashiq and Masrat Zahra were booked on charges of 'unlawful activities'.

The weekly *Chattan* launched in 1985 was seen as a serious effort to fill the void created by the demise of Shamim on 1 May 1980. Edited by Tahir Mohiuddin, the newspaper published analytical and well researched pieces on current issues which set a precedent for doing incisive write-ups in Urdu. Since 2011, the newspaper is published as a daily. In 1986, Urdu weekly, *Ishaet*, was published from Srinagar with this author and Javed Azar as ghost editors. Published through the litho printing process, the newspaper caught the eye of readers for its quality material and in-depth analysis. However, the weekly could not pull on beyond seven months due to transfer of one of its ghost editors to Leh, Ladakh after his identity was disclosed to the government by a journalist friend.

The year 1985 proved very propitious for the development of journalism in Kashmir, for that year the University of Kashmir established the Media Education Research Centre (MERC). About 1200 students have passed out from the department so far, a large number of whom is now ably holding important news beats within and outside Kashmir.[780] Besides MERC, the Media Departments of the Islamic University of Science and Technology and Central University Kashmir have started producing trained journalists. With an odd exception, all of the MERC pass-outs took English language journalism as their profession even as there was no strong tradition for this stream in Kashmir. However, there were professional journalists around who worked for different English news organizations outside Kashmir. They were source of encouragement for the youngsters. Many of these senior journalists were frequent guest speakers at the MERC.[781] They included Jagan Nath Sathu, Radha Krishen Kak, Pran Nath Jalali, Shyam Koul, Ghulam Nabi Khayal, Mohammad Sayeed Malik, Makhan Lal Kak, Yusuf Jameel, Zafar Meraj and Altaf Hussain.[782]

In 1984, English fortnightly, *Submission*, was issued from Srinagar. Its owner and editor, Mohammad Saleem Pandit, first converted the newspaper into a weekly in 1988 and then a daily in 1990. The newspaper stopped publication in 1991. Pandit joined the *Times of India* in 2000 and continues to work for the newspaper. In 1988, another English newspaper, *Samachar Post*, was launched by Pushkar Nath Koul Vakil. The post-1990 years proved to be very productive for journalism in general and the English newspapers in particular. With online editions, their efficacy in highlighting ground realities, as against the dominant official narrative on Kashmir, was recognized. The change came with the *Greater Kashmir*, launched by Fayaz Ahmad Kaloo as a weekly in 1987. The newspaper was converted into a daily in 1993 and soon became the largest circulated newspaper of Kashmir. It provided a platform for the young crop of journalists, many of whom honed their skills here and later joined national and international media outlets. In 1992, Imtiaz Bazaz launched an English news and views magazine, *Mountain Valley Kashmir*. Other English language newspapers like *Kashmir Images* (1996), *Kashmir Monitor* (1997), *Kashmir Observer* (1997) and *Kashmir Reader* (2012) broadened the landscape.

With the launch of the *Rising Kashmir*, the horizon of English language journalism in Kashmir brightened up further. Shujaat Bukhari with a young team of professionals started the daily from Srinagar on 10 March 2008. The newspaper provides analytical pieces on current topics. At least four journalists associated with the newspaper have won international (Ford and Fulbright) fellowships in a short span. Bukhari also published an Urdu daily *Buland Kashmir*, a weekly *Kashmir Parcham* and a Kashmiri daily *Sangarmaal*.

Masood Hussain's weekly *Kashmir Life*, launched in 2009, introduced exhaustive, in-depth and narrative form of journalism on issues concerning various facets of life in Kashmir. Long reportage on subjects, besides politics, such as history, culture, economy and environment earned the newspaper a distinct identity. Eight of its former staffers have won international fellowships and quite a few are now holding important media beats outside the Valley. In 2008, Ved Bhasin started the Srinagar edition of his Jammu based *Kashmir Times*. A year later, English monthly, *Conveyor*, was launched by Mohammad Hayat Bhat. The magazine stopped publication in 2012. Showkat Motta, a MERC pass-out launched a monthly English news magazine, *Narrator*, in 2016. The periodical is a serious attempt at producing quality journalism.

Compared to the English press, the vernacular press in Kashmir had already established a firm footing. Individuals such as Prem Nath Bazaz (*Vitasta* and *Hamdard*), Mohammad Sayeed Masoodi (*Khidmat*), Abdul Aziz Shora (*Roshni*), Sanaullah Bhat (*Aftab*), Ghulam Mohammad Arif (*Hamdard*), Nand Lal Wattal (*Khidmat*) and, later, Sofi Ghulam Mohammad (*Srinagar Times*) had laid a sound foundation for Urdu journalism in Kashmir. Over the years, more Urdu newspapers were added. These include *Uqab* (1972 as fortnightly, 1974 as weekly and 1994 as daily), *Srinagar News* (1977), *Afaq* (1985) and *Nida-i-Mashriq* (1992), to name only a few. The *Al-Safa* started as a weekly was soon converted into a daily in 1989 and instantly became popular. The weekly *Kashmir Uzma* launched in 2003 as a sister publication of the *Greater Kashmir*, further lifted the standard of Urdu journalism in Kashmir. The newspaper was converted into a daily in 2006. Through in-depth reporting and incisive write-ups, its editor, Javed Azar, was able to soon make it a leading Urdu newspaper of Kashmir. The *Greater Kashmir* also brings out weeklies, *Kashmir Ink* and *Nawa-i-Jhelum,* in English and Urdu, respectively.

In late 2007, a local business house run by politician Iftikhar Hussain Ansari started daily newspaper, *Etala'at*, in Urdu language and, later in 2008, issued its English edition with Wajeeh Ahmad Andrabi and Zahiruddin as editors of the two dailies, respectively. The owners of the newspapers hired journalists on handsome salaries forcing competitors to fatten pay packets of their staff. The newspapers did not last long. The English edition ceased publication in 2009 while Urdu edition lasted till 2012.

In 2015, another Urdu weekly, *Belaag Sahafat*, was started by a young duo, Mohammad Haroon Reshi and Tariq Ali Mir, which made quite an impression on readers with its standard and range of subjects.

Post-1990, many journalists, not all with formal degree in journalism, successfully took up the challenge of filling the vacuum created by the migration of Kashmiri Pandit journalists who till then held monopoly over the media in Kashmir, especially when it came to representing the news organizations outside Kashmir. They joined both print and electronic media.[783] Almost all Indian electronic news channels are today represented in Kashmir by local journalists.[784]

The otherwise productive period (post-1990) for quality journalism in Kashmir has seen mushrooming of newspapers in both English and Urdu languages. Serious journalists consider it all but a healthy trend. As of today, the total number of newspapers published from the two provinces of Kashmir and Jammu is about 660. Of these, Kashmir accounts for 295. These include all categories—daily, weekly, fortnightly and monthly. In 1999, the number was 249 (Kashmir 84 and Jammu 165). The figures suggest that the number of newspapers published from Jammu & Kashmir has registered a 265 per cent increase, Kashmir province alone adding 211 newspapers. As against 1946, when newspapers receiving government advertisement support were 38 in number, including 19 from Kashmir, the count has now gone up to 422 (Kashmir 177 and Jammu

245),[785] thereby registering a huge 1110% increase. Of the 38 newspapers, *Hamdard, Roshni, Rehbar* and *Khidmat* from Kashmir and *Amar* from Jammu are still in circulation.

On the dark side, since the beginning of turmoil in 1989, journalists in Kashmir have come under crossfire of two sides of the conflict. Apart from suffering punitive actions like banning of newspapers, seizure of printing presses and cases filed against editors, they have been target of arson and fatal assaults. Several journalists including Mohammad Shaban Vakil, Mushtaq Ali, Parvaz Mohammad Sultan, Ghulam Rasool, Asifa Jeelani and Shujaat Bukhari were killed while many others including Yusuf Jameel and Zafar Meraj narrowly escaped murder attempts but suffered grievous injuries.

Photojournalism as a profession in Kashmir was started by Sanaullah Bhat when his daily *Aftab* shifted from litho to offset printing process in 1970s. Earlier, blocks of photographs, mostly supplied by the State Information Department or the Press Information Bureau of Government of India, were printed through litho printing. The first photojournalist of Kashmir was Mohammad Amin, a staffer of the daily *Aftab*. He was followed by Merajuddin who initially worked for the *Srinagar Times*. Today, we have a large crew of photojournalists and camera persons working for different print and electronic media organizations within and outside Kashmir.[786]

In recent years, Kashmiri journalists have received global recognition and many of them have won international awards for their work. In 1996, Yusuf Jameel won the International Press Award of the Committee to Protect Journalists (CPJ), first and so far the only given to any journalist in India. He also won the Best Journalist/Writer award instituted by the South Asian Free Media Association (SAFMA) in 2006 and the second PEN Gauri Lankesh Award for Democratic Idealism in 2020. Ajaz Rahi is the first Kashmiri photojournalist to have won, in 2000, an award from the Netherlands based the World Press Photo in the Spot News Category for his coverage of the Kargil War. Other photojournalists who have won international awards for their work in Kashmir in recent years include Altaf Qadri, Rafiq

Maqbool, Javed Dar, Showkat Nanda, Mukhtar Khan and Dar Yasin. Photojournalists Dar Yasin and Mukhtar Khan received the prestigious Pulitzer Prize in feature photography for the year 2020. The third winner was Chhani Anand from Jammu. Again, in 2020, freelance photojournalist Masrat Zahra won the Anja Niedringhaus Courage in Photojournalism Award instituted in the memory of a German photojournalist, Anja Niedringhaus, who was killed in Afghanistan.

At times, some newspaper editors in Kashmir, to the amusement of readers, have engaged themselves in war of words against each other as a result of professional rivalry. In 1968, noted poet of Urdu and Kashmiri languages, Mir Ghulam Rasool Nazki, launched an Urdu weekly, *Algufran*, which lasted for a year. For its standard, the newspaper caught the eye of famous Urdu writer and exegete of Holy *Qura'n*, Abdul Majid Daryabadi. At one point in time, the weekly got involved in a running feud with the daily *Aftab* when both produced literature in prose and verse caricaturing each other to the enjoyment of their respective readers. A similar feud was witnessed between Shamim Ahmad Shamim and Sofi Ghulam Mohammad through the columns of their respective newspapers, *Aayeena* and *Srinagar Times*.

Compared to 1930s when the number of newspapers could be counted on finger tips, the press corps in Kashmir is a large fraternity today, divided into different categories of print journalists, TV journalists, photographers and videographers, each having their own association, and some more than one. As of today, there are 11 associations of journalists in Kashmir. These include Kashmir Editors Guild, JK Press Association, JK Editors Forum, Journalist Federation of Kashmir, *Anjuman-e-Urdu Sahafat*, Kashmir Working Journalist Association, Kashmir Union of Working Journalists, Kashmir Working Journalist Association [second with this name], Kashmir Press Photographers Association and Kashmir Videographer Press Association.

Kashmir abounds in funny titles of newspapers. Few years back there was a newspaper named *Gausul Azam*. Another carried the name *Barg-i-Sabz*. Yet another was named *Gul-i-Khandaan*. Today also, we have many newspapers with unusual and funny names like *The Fish Eye*, *Vigorous News*, *Precious Kashmir*, *Aaj ki Jung*, *Cheshma-i-Faiz*, *Safinat-ul-Najat*, *Bekhof Awaz*, *Mashaal Times* and *Sarw-i-Gulistan*. Among Kashmiri journalists, at least two, Khizar Maghribi and Makhan Lal Mahav, were established humourists whose poetry enthralled people. The former edited the *Gul-i-Khandaan* and the later was a *Khidmat* staffer.

First Embedded Journalist

The term 'embedded journalism' was first used during the Gulf War in 2003 when the United States invaded Iraq and it came to light that media-persons in the theatre of war were attached to different military units and working under the oversight of the Pentagon. Over the years, however, the phrase has come to include 'independent media' offering or willingly subjecting itself to the control or influence of the Establishment—civil or military—both during war and peace time.

Media in Jammu & Kashmir has traveled a long way through a strict control and procedure of an autocratic government to harsh and intimidating censorship during the so-called democratic rule. In the course of this journey, as happens everywhere, governments have also liberally used money power to keep a section of the media on their right side. A study of the birth and development of the Press in the State would make an interesting read on governments coercing journalists in toeing a certain line while instances of scribes offering themselves for the job would also not be scarce to find, shining instances of independent and honest journalists notwithstanding.

The earliest case of embedded journalism in Kashmir relates to the Thirties of the last century when a premier news gathering agency of pre-Partition India offered itself to be represented in Kashmir by a high ranking in-service government official. Lo and behold! The official took up the assignment and, while being in government service, worked for the news agency on a monthly retainer. Here was a characteristic case of a government receiving, instead of paying, money for getting its propaganda material widely circulated.

During early 1930s when Kashmir had erupted against the rule of Maharaja Hari Singh, his government was drawing flak throughout the United India for its repressive measures. A section of the Indian Press was very critical of these measures. To counter a bad press, an arrangement was reached between the Associated Press of India (API), and the Kashmir Government according to which the latter paid a monthly subsidy of ₹ 100 to the former in lieu of circulation of its official viewpoint.

It so happened in October 1932 that Colonel Jhonson, correspondent of the API in Jammu & Kashmir, was to proceed on leave and go to London. On 22 October, he visited Prime Minister E.J.D. Colvin at Srinagar with a suggestion that during his absence Captain Hira Singh, Political Secretary in the Prime Minister's Office, be entrusted with "sending out news to the Associated Press [of India]" at the "monthly allowance of ₹ 50 that Colonel Jhonson gets".[787]

Prime Minister Colvin saw "no objection in this arrangement". On the same day, he submitted a note to the Maharaja, seeking his approval. "It will be very confidential that the P.S. [Political Secretary] should be correspondent of API and it will enable us to send out our communiqués direct as press telegrams",[788] Colvin wrote to Hari Singh. As a word of precaution, he added, "Captain Hira Singh being a Government servant would not like to take any remuneration without Government sanction. The Prime Minister is of the opinion that this amount may be accepted but credited to the State Treasury."[789] Hari Singh approved the proposal.

On 25 October, the Associated Press of India informed Captain Hira Singh about his engagement as "our correspondent" on a monthly remuneration of ₹ 50. A telegram was also sent by API to the Telegraph Master, Jammu asking him "to accept bearing press telegrams" from Singh on their behalf. Singh was conveyed that "we require reports of all important events in Jammu and in the State written from the standpoint of an impartial onlooker." However, it is not difficult to imagine how impartial he would have been as a reporter when his Prime Minister had asked his position as a correspondent to be kept "very confidential" and used for sending out "our communiqués direct as press telegrams".

Hira Singh worked as correspondent of the API till 31 December 1932 when his assignment with the news agency expired. However, Jhonson had not returned by then. So, on 6 January 1933, Singh asked the API to issue necessary instructions to the Telegraph Master Jammu "if you still wish me to carry on". The Telegraph Office in Jammu had stopped entertaining his press telegrams after 31 December. The arrangement was extended but till April Singh's press telegrams were not accepted. By June 1933, Jhonson returned to his beat.

In the meanwhile, there arose a dispute between the API and the Government of Jammu & Kashmir over how much the news agency owed to the Political Secretary as remuneration for working for them during Jhonson's absence. The API took the stand that since no press telegrams were received by them for the months of January, February and March 1933, the agency did not owe anything to Captain Hira Singh for this period. The government argued that non-acceptance of press telegrams by the Telegraph Office was not any fault of Singh and that he must be paid for the period. It threatened to deduct the amount from the subsidy payable to the API. The issue was finally resolved and an amount of ₹ 150 remitted by the API to Singh in December 1933.[790] To be fair with Captain Hira Singh, the amount of his remuneration was credited to the State Treasury.

Maharaja Hari Singh's Government used journalists to create a favourable public opinion and there were journalists who willingly offered their services to do the government's bidding. Baldev Prasad Sharma arranged to bring out a special supplement of the *Chand* and published a letter in his name in *The Tribune* in support of the government stand on a major controversy hitting Kashmir in early 1940s when Prime Minister Gopalaswami Ayyangar ordered introduction of Devnagri script in educational institutions. To prove that he was furthering the agenda of the government, Sharma forwarded to the State's Publicity Department a free translation of "the talk on the script issue" with Sheikh Mohammad Abdullah besides some clippings of *The Tribune* and the *Karachi Daily*. On 21 January 1942, he wrote a letter to the Publicity Officer of the government, in which the 'independent journalist' minces no words to suggest that he had worked for the government. Sharma writes:

> "I thank you very much for lending me the book entitled "NATIONAL LANGUAGE FOR INDIA". You will be glad to know that I have made full use of the chapter containing Pandit Jawahar Lal Nehru's views on the subject. I have in today's mail received a copy of the "HINDUSTAN TIMES" containing a letter on the subject, which I am submitting herewith. In addition to this I got an excellent opportunity the other day, when the President of the National Conference invited a press conference at Jammu. Mr. Abdullah, as you will see, could not answer my questions satisfactorily. A summary of the talk on the subject has appeared in todays "TRIBUNE" of which a cutting is enclosed. In addition, I arranged to bring out a Special Supplement of the "CHAND" containing fuller account. A free translation of the talk on the script issue is being submitted herewith."[791]

Appendixes

I

Telegram dated 31 July 1951 from Syed Abdul Qasim Kashani, Chairman of the Parliament of Iran to Sheikh Mohammad Abdullah, Prime Minister of Jammu & Kashmir

As you are perhaps aware my life-long ambition has been to achieve solid unity among Muslim countries thereby putting an end forever both to internal dissensions and to foreign exploitation. At the present delicate juncture in world affairs it is all the more essential that we should rise above petty selfish ambitions and resolve our differences for the greater cause of uniting all Muslim and Asiatic Countries together in a powerful unit. Any loss of time in realizing and acting on this most crying need of the day will be helping Western Imperialist Powers to strengthen their strangle-hold on Asia. It goes without saying that the unity cannot be possibly achieved with India and Pakistan quarrelling with each other in the heart of subcontinent. It is absolutely essential, therefore, that these countries should satisfactorily and speedily resolve their differences. I am assured that the people, the leaders and the governments of both countries are anxious to develop and maintain friendly relations with each other. These differences would have been resolved long ago to the immediate relief of over 100 million of Muslims inhabiting the Indo-Pakistan subcontinent and to the great joy and satisfaction of the 400 million Muslims of the world and Asia if the Kashmir problem had been solved. I appeal to you at this critical juncture to make a bold and determined contribution by voluntarily withdrawing your proposal to proceed with the Constituent Assembly. This step, I am sure, will help considerably in creating a congenial atmosphere so necessary for initiating negotiations for a peaceful and satisfactory solution of this most important problem. I am eagerly waiting for your reply to this communication and I have full confidence that you will act effectively in accordance with the best interests of the Muslim World and therefore of Asia. I have no doubt that you are fully aware of the extent to which a solution of this problem will help to ease the situation in Asia.

II

Letter dated 15 August 1951 from Sheikh Mohammad Abdullah to Syed Abdul Qasim Kashani, Chairman of the Parliament of Iran

I am thankful for your cablegram of 31st July. I was away on tour in the interior of the State and the cablegram awaited my return in Srinagar. I could not, therefore, send you a reply earlier. I am very sorry for this delay.

I greatly appreciate your concern for a peaceful settlement of the Kashmir dispute. As a matter of fact, no one should be more anxious that the present state of tension and uncertainty should be ended, than the people of the State who have had to undergo untold sufferings during the past four years as a result of the complications in which the State has been involved. Unfortunately, Pakistani leaders, who were primarily responsible for bringing about this state of affairs, refuse to fulfill their obligations in restoring peaceful conditions in the State, thereby preventing a speedy and amicable settlement of the dispute.

The present situation would not have arisen if Pakistan had not chosen to attack the State in 1947 as a consequence of which she continues to occupy a large area by force. This act of direct aggression was preceded by open hostility to the national aspirations of the people of Kashmir, an overwhelming majority of whom are Muslims, and later on by economic strangulation by means of withholding essential supplies to them. In order to avoid further animosity and bloodshed, we sought the assistance of the Security Council to bring about a satisfactory solution of the dispute. But, unfortunately, the U.N.O. had come to be engrossed with international intrigues and power-politics and consideration of every issue is based upon individual interests of big powers regardless of the fundamental principles that the issues may involve.

The people of the State have waited for four long years in the hope that justice would be done to their case. But, it is a tragic reflection on the work of the U.N.O. to see that in spite of patent facts, a clear decision has been avoided all along. Consequently, the people here have come to believe that some of the interested members of the Security Council wish to settle the Kashmir problem on their own terms irrespective of what the State's people desire. These quarters have found Pakistan a willing partner in this game. How else are we to understand the unhesitating and unreserved acceptance by Pakistan of such incredible proposals as that of stationing Commonwealth troops in Kashmir, which would surely endanger the security of not only India and Pakistan but of the whole of Asia? Such a fantastic suggestion should be repugnant to any self-respecting country which cherishes independence. This lays Pakistan's bona fides in regard to freedom and unity of Asiatic countries open to suspicion. On the contrary, no one can accuse us for lack of zeal to contribute towards Asian people's liberation.

In face of such a treatment, the people of Kashmir cannot remain indefinitely in a state of drift and uncertainty. Having been convinced that a fair and just solution was not likely to be effected soon through the Security Council, they have decided to take the initiative into their own hands. They have anxiously watched the prolonged deliberations about their State but they nowhere find a genuine desire to take into account the legitimate aspirations of the people. It is, therefore, understandable, that they should be gravely concerned in regard to their future.

In view of these facts, our decision of convening a Constituent Assembly is the only way out of the present impasse. Since everyone, including India and Pakistan, are agreed that the future of the State should be determined by the will of its people, this decision should have been welcomed and respected by all those who are eager to bring about a settlement. The Constituent Assembly representatives will be elected on the basis of adult franchise and will naturally reflect the wishes of the people on all vital issues concerning the future shape of their country.

This step embodies the fulfillment of the national aspirations of the people of the State who have succeeded after 18 years of bitter struggle in liberating themselves from imperialist domination and autocratic exploitation. As such the Constituent Assembly represents their sovereign right of national autonomy. It alone would assure them a constitutional government charged with the progress and economic stabilisation of the State as well as with the maintenance of its security.

So far we have been accused of not being the popular party in the State and our views have been challenged even though our party led the people through the struggle against autocratic repression for eighteen years. Now that we ask the people to choose their representatives afresh, this universally accepted procedure of democracy is being objected to. This clearly must lead us to the conclusion that Pakistan wants to secure the territory of the State by force.

In this connection her contention that Kashmir belongs to Pakistan because majority of its population are Muslims, is as interesting as it is presumptuous. Where is the need for a plebiscite and all the legal quibbling after she has pronounced this verdict? According to this logic, not only Kashmir, but Afghanistan, Iran and rest of the Muslim countries should dissolve their national identities and merge themselves with Pakistan which claims to be the biggest Muslim State in the World.

In the present state of the world, we have seen that many small nationalities have come to suffer due to the greed and hypocricy of their more powerful neighbours. Under false pretences, rights of these people are being sought to be trampled over. In order to justify her own creation, Pakistan ignored the existence of 40 million Muslims living in India. Now she seeks to grab Kashmir irrespective of what the people of this place feel about it. You are not unaware of the national movements of the Arab countries, the Iranians and other Asiatic peoples against imperialism. The people of Kashmir, suppressed for centuries, are similarly emerging into nation-hood and they wish to shape their own destiny. Any encroachment on their right to do so constitutes unwarranted intervention. Our State has been the victim of aggression in which Muslims suffered as much as others. Our case should therefore deserve sympathy and support of all those who genuinely feel that national self-determination should be the inherent right of all Asiatic countries.

I have written in some detail in order to clarify the issue and I hope that you will be able to understand our position more clearly. The decision of convening a Constituent Assembly is judicious and timely, and I have no doubt that you will use your good offices to secure recognition of our viewpoint and support for our just cause.

III

Letter of Maharaja Hari Singh to President of India, Dr. Rajendra Prasad, complaining about the shabby treatment meted out to him by the Government of India.

Poona, 16/17th August, 1952

Dr. Rajendra Prasad,
President of India,
New Delhi

Sir,

I am making a direct approach to you in the matter of the affairs of the State of Jammu and Kashmir and its Ruler as the situation has become acute owing to the rapid developments that are taking place and the further steps which are being taken in the next few days as these will vitally affect me personally apart from the repercussions they will have on the subjects of the State.

It is necessary to set out very briefly the events that have happened so far as the State of Jammu and Kashmir is concerned since my accession to the Gaddi.

I became the Ruler of the State in 1925. I then found that the British had strengthened their hold on the State by taking advantage of certain circumstances because, it being a border State of great strategic and political importance, they wanted it to be completely in their grip. The British created in the myth of paramountcy without any historical or political sanctions and exploited the State as a set off against the fast approaching political awakening and urge for freedom in what was then known as British India.

Realizing what was coming. I took it upon myself to shake off the British yoke by insisting that the relations of the State with the British should be governed by the Treaty and all other strings which had been attached to such relationship with a view to gain domination over the State should be removed.

I succeeded in my efforts to a large extent but incurred the wrath of the British who thenceforth became openly hostile to me. Simultaneously with this, I started taking measures to ameliorate the condition of my people and to organize my government on progressively democratic lines.

I enacted laws to relieve rural indebtedness and to improve generally the lot of the agriculturist and the economic and social condition of my people. Some of these enactments were resented by my Hindu subjects who thought that their interests were being sacrificed in the cause of Muslim uplift. I established industries and made provisions for education and medical relief far in advance of any other State. Special provision was made for the educational advancement of Muslims who were then considered backward.

I was even more enthusiastic as regards the better organization of my government. In this, I had the assistance of men of unquestionable integrity and ability from British India as my Prime Ministers and other Ministers and heads of Departments. It will not be out of place to name a few of them, such as, Raja Hari Kishen Kaul, Mirza Sir Zaffar Ali, Mr. V.N. Mehta, Mr. Vijahat Husein, Sir Burjor Dalai, Sir Abdus Samad Khan, Sir K.N. Haksar, Sir N. Gopalaswami Ayyangar, Sir B.N. Rau.

As a result, the administration of the State in the matter of efficiency and organization was better than even in some of the Provinces of British India. One further fact to which I wish to draw your attention in this connection is that I invariably acted on the advice of such Ministers and did not interfere or overrule their directions. It, therefore, follows that if any fault is now to be found with the administration of the State and/or the policies then pursued, the blame cannot be laid at my door alone.

It is significant that for six years (1938-43) Shri N. Gopalaswami Ayyangar was the Prime Minister of the State and he will bear me out that I never interfered with his policies and decisions adopted and taken from time to time. Consequently, with my desire to give to the people of the State complete self-government, I discussed in 1945 with my Prime Minister, Sir B.N. Rau, in the presence of Sir Tej Bahadur Sapru and Sir Kailash N. Haksar, the inauguration in the State of

Full Responsible Government with Provincial Autonomy and a Central Government comprised of Representatives of the Provinces and a Board of Judicial Advisers with myself as the Constitutional Head. I was prepared to do this even with the knowledge that it would not be relished by the British. Sir B.N. Rau wanted this to be put into execution within the next fortnight.

I was of opinion that it should be done in about six months so as to enable us to complete the scheme. The news leaked out, there were intrigues, position became very difficult and Sir B.N. Rau left shortly thereafter.

The finances of the State were governed on modern principles. My expenditure was strictly limited and kept separate and distinct from the State finances and proper and well defined limits were laid down as between my personal and private matters and matters of the State. Thus, I had a well organized and efficient executive, a democratically elected Legislature, an independent judiciary, definite policies for expansion of education, medical relief and all other essential features of a progressive state. The eminent administrators and judges who worked for the State from time to time will bear testimony to this. All that I did aggravated the hostility of the British towards me as they were not sincerely inclined towards ameliorating the conditions of the people or for the freedom of the country.

In those days, the Rulers of the Indian States were judged by the condition and feelings of their subjects and I can say, without fear of contradiction, that the people of my State were content and had no cause for grievances against me or the administration of the State.

It is not unknown that trouble started in the State in 1931 and what has on occasions been described by so-called 'national leaders' of the State as 'the Freedom Movement' was engineered by elements outside the State under the instigation of the British. The movement in the beginning was a religious movement with slogans like 'Down with Hindu Raj' and 'Islam in danger'. The leaders of the movement were men who now figure as Ministers and Administrators in Azad Kashmir under Pakistan such as Chaudhary Ghulam Abbas and Maulvi Yusuf Shah and some others, to gain sympathy and cooperation from those fighting for freedom from the British yoke in British India, the Muslims who were running this movement gave it the name of 'National Conference'. The name was adopted also to fall into line with the movement carried on in other States in the name of the 'States Peoples Conference' and to take advantage of the declining prestige of the British. The movement thus gained the sympathy of the Indian National Congress. It became known in British India as the National Movement in the Jammu and Kashmir State.

These facts clearly showed that my people had no grievance against me, that the movement was started by disgruntled people with the British behind them and that those in charge of the movement gained the confidence and sympathy of the Indian National Congress by adopting the name of the 'National Conference'.

I have been accused by the Prime Minister of not listening to the advice of the Congress leaders during the fateful period 1946-47.

I deny that charge. In 1946, when the leaders of the Indian National Congress formed the Viceroy's Cabinet for the Interim Government, I had occasion to meet Mahatma Gandhi and Shri J.B. Kripalani, the then President of the Indian National Congress, when they both visited the State. Mahatma Gandhi suggested that I should have the backing of the people in whatever I did, Shri J.B. Kripalani suggested the immediate release of Sheikh Abdullah because the nominees of the National Conference who were in the government had resigned. I pointed to them that I had already set up a Constitutional Government which included two nominees of the National Conference and that it was not then possible to entrust the government entirely in the hands of one group, viz., the National Conference. I said to them that I was willing to make such further changes as might be suggested towards making it a completely popular government in consonance with the safety of the State and to keep the balance between the divergent views of different parts of the State. The matter rested there for the time being.

Then came the development of 1947 and the question of accession. The position of my State was very different, situated as it was in contiguity to India and Pakistan as also to Afghanistan, Tibet and Russia. The situation therefore required to be dealt with more tact and foresight than in the case of other states.

Mahatma Gandhi and the Prime Minister were anxious that I should not make a declaration of Independence and the Prime Minister was anxious to secure the release from prison of Sheikh Abdullah. Having regard to what my government had done when the Prime Minister visited the State in 1946, Lord Mountbatten chose to visit the State in June 1947 and we had several talks. Lord Mountbatten then urged me and my Prime Minister, Kak, not to make any declaration of Independence but to find out in one way or another, the will of the people of Kashmir as soon as possible and to announce our intention by the 14th August to send representatives accordingly to one Constituent Assembly or the other.

Lord Mountbatten further told us that the newly created States Department was prepared to give an assurance that if Kashmir went to Pakistan, it would not be regarded as an unfriendly act by the Government of India. Lord Mountbatten stressed the dangerous situation in which Kashmir would find itself if it lacked the support of one of the two Dominions by the date of the transfer of power.

The impression which I gathered from my talks with Lord Mountbatten who explained the situation with plans and maps was that, in his opinion, it was advisable for me to accede to Pakistan. I thought that in the circumstances it was advisable to have Standstill Agreements with India and Pakistan and get breathing time to decide which accession would be in the interests of the State.

Pakistan very quickly and willingly agreed to a Standstill arrangement, perhaps with mental reservations, as appears from their subsequent conduct. On the other hand, the Government of India did not make up their mind and, if I may be permitted to say so, dealt with the situation in a half-hearted and desultory manner; thus giving an opportunity to Pakistan to do mischief, as they did. This gave rise to misunderstandings on both sides resulting in dissatisfaction and delay in coming to an understanding. The results have been detrimental to both the State and India. Pakistan became impatient and, having failed to force accession, started with blockading the supplies to the State and ended by invading the State. Lord Mountbatten realizing the uncertain and dangerously unstable position of the State, asked Lord Ismay to approach me and get me to decide on accession without further delay to whichever Dominion I and my people desired. This was at the end of August, 1947.

My difficulties were as follows:

The People of the State were divided in several groups, each group having its own ideas about accession;

The Border Feudatory Territories such as Hunza, Nagar and Chitral and the District of Gilgit, where British influence was supreme were definitely for accession to Pakistan and were pressing me to accede to Pakistan without delay and threatening me with dire consequences if I did not act according to their suggestion;

The Muslim population of the State was also divided into groups with divergent views. Muslims from parts of Jammu such as, Mirpur, Poonch, Muzaffarabad, were for accession to Pakistan because of Pakistan propaganda inside the State;

Muslims of Kashmir and some Muslims of Jammu who were led by Sheikh Abdullah and the leaders of the National Conference did not want the question of accession to be decided at that stage but wanted me to part with power in their favour so that they could decide the question independently of me. They made no secret of their views and obstructed me in deciding the question of accession instead of helping me to accede to India;

Hindus of Jammu and all the people of Ladakh were for affiliation with or Accession of India; A portion of the population of Kashmir was also for accession to Pakistan.

Thus, there was a sharp division of opinion. The partition aggravated the situation and unhinged and unbalanced the minds of the people with the result that the people of the State were not in a position to give any considered opinion if I chose to consult them.

In September 1947, it was suggested to me that it would be a wise move on my part to appoint Shri Mehr Chand Mahajan as my Prime Minister as he would be able to handle the affairs of the State in the then critical period firmly and in a statesmanlike manner. Before Shri Mehr Chand Mahajan took up his appointment he discussed with Sardar Patel about immediate requirements of the State and Sardar Patel promised him full support and cooperation on behalf of the Government of India.

Sardar Patel also wrote to me stating this and adding that the Government of India fully realized how difficult the situation in the State was and assured me that the Government of India would do their best to help the State in the critical period. I then wrote to Sardar Patel that a little further elucidation of the points of view regarding the essential requirements of the movement would result in a satisfactory solution. Sardar Patel replied on October 2, 1947 that he had a further talk with Shri Mahajan and understood that Shri Mahajan was joining my service very shortly. As by that time I had proclaimed a general amnesty, Sardar Patel expressed his pleasure at the step I had taken and stated that this would rally round me the men who might otherwise have been a thorn in my side. He also stated that he was expediting as much as possible the linking up of the State with the Indian Dominion. Shri Mahajan then received Sardar Patel's letter of the 21st October, 1947 in which he said that he had further discussion with Sheikh Abdullah, that Sheikh Abdullah seemed to him genuinely anxious to cooperate and sincerely desirous of assisting the State in dealing with the external dangers and the internal troubles with which the State was threatened.

He further said that at the same time Sheikh Abdullah, as was natural, felt that unless something was done and done immediately, to strengthen his hands, both in popular eyes and in dealing with the dangers, it would be impossible for him to do anything substantial. He said he felt that the position which Sheikh Abdullah took up was understandable and reasonable, that in the mounting demands for the introduction of a Responsible Government in the State, such as was witnessed in Travancore and Mysore, it was impossible for me to isolate myself, that the upsurge was bound to affect me sooner or later, that the Government of India on their part had pledged to give me the maximum support and would do so, but without some measure of popular backing, particularly from amongst the community which represented such an overwhelming majority in Kashmir, it would be difficult to make such support go to the farthest limit that was necessary if the disruptive forces which were being raised and organized, were to be crushed. He advised me in the circumstances to make a substantial gesture to win Sheikh Abdullah's support. He said he had no desire to suggest that I should do so in a manner which would be completely revolutionary in character, that such a step might undermine the loyal and willing support which the State had commanded from strong elements of the body politic.

Shri Mahajan also received the Prime Minister's letter dated October 20, 1947 in which he referred to the friendliest feelings the Government of India had towards Kashmir and its people and their desire to help to the best of their ability in providing Kashmir with the commodities it needed. He said the Government of India would like to do so for humanitarian reasons as well because of their deep interest in the future of the people of Jammu and Kashmir State. That the self-interest of India also demanded that and that Government of India were strongly of the opinion that no coercion should be exercised on Kashmir and its people and that they should be allowed to function in their own way and to make such decision as they thought fit and proper and that in the furtherance of this policy the Government of India would direct their efforts.

The Prime Minister in his letter dated October 21, 1947 to Shri Mahajan said that the future of Kashmir was of the most urgent importance to the Government of India and for him, it was both a personal and a public matter that it would be a tragedy so far as he was concerned, if Kashmir went to Pakistan. The Prime Minister referred to the urgent need of Pakistan to get

Kashmir's accession to Pakistan and that they were threatening every now and then to that end and that everything else that they did was an accessory to the same, that the top ranking leaders of Pakistan were continually approaching the Kashmir National Conference leaders, that they assured to them for their best behaviour and promised them something approaching Independence if only they would agree to Kashmir acceding to Pakistan. They were even prepared to give the right of secession. The Prime Minister then suggested the urgency of taking some step like the formation of a Provincial Government and that Sheikh Abdullah, who was obviously the most popular person in Kashmir, might be asked to form such a government. The Prime Minister further added that in view of all the circumstances he felt that it would probably be undesirable to make any declaration of adhesion to the Indian Union at that stage that this should come later when a popular Interim Government was functioning.

After the amnesty proclaimed by me, Sheikh Abdullah wrote to me on September 26, 1947, in which, after referring to his incarceration for about a year and a half, he said as follows:

> In spite of what has happened in the past I assure Your Highness that myself and my Party have never harboured any sentiment of disloyalty towards Your Highness's person, throne or dynasty. The development of this beautiful country and the betterment of its people is our common aim and interest and I assure Your Highness the fullest and loyal support of myself and my organization.

He added:

> In order to achieve the common aim set forth above, mutual trust and confidence must be the main step. Without this it would not be possible to face successfully the great difficulties that upset our State, on all sides at present.

He concluded:

> Before I close this letter, I beg to assure Your Highness once again of my steadfast loyalty and pray that God may grant me opportunity enough to make this country

> attain under Your Highness' aegis such an era of peace, prosperity and good Government that it may be second to none and be an ideal for others to copy.

I wrote to Lord Mountbatten on October 26, 1947 informing him of the situation in the State. I received his letter dated October 27, 1947 stating as follows:

> In the special circumstances mentioned by Your Highness my Government have decided to accept the accession of Kashmir State to the Dominion of India.
>
> It is my Government's wish that as soon as law and order has been restored in Kashmir and her soil cleared of the invaders the question of the State's Accession should be settled by a reference to the people. My Government and I note with satisfaction that Your Highness has decided to invite Sheikh Abdullah to form an interim Government to work as your Prime Minister.

The Prime Minister also wrote to me on October 26, 1947 stating as follows:

> Shri V.P. Menon returned from Jammu this morning and informed me of his talks there. He gave me the Instrument of Accession and the Standstill Agreement which you had signed and I saw also your letter to the Governor General of India. Allow me to congratulate you on the wise decision that you have taken. I earnestly hope that they will lead not only to the effective protection of Kashmir State in the present but also to the freedom and well-being of Kashmir and India as a whole.

I then acceded to India.

The Prime Minister in his letter dated November 13, 1947 pointed out to me that the only person who could deliver the goods in Kashmir was Sheikh Abdullah, that he was obviously the leading and popular personality in Kashmir, that the way he had risen to grapple with the crisis had shown the nature of the man, that the Prime Minister had a high opinion of his integrity and his general balance of mind and that he was likely to be right in regard to major decisions.

Shri Gopalaswami, who was then a Minister without Portfolio, wrote to me on December 9, 1947 indicating for my consideration his views on the changes which in the critical situation of the State were immediately called for in the then existing constitutional and administrative set up in the State.

A draft of the Proclamation which I was intended to issue, was sent to me by the Government of India.

It was seen by Sheikh Abdullah. Sheikh Abdullah also saw the correspondence which had passed between Sardar Patel and myself. Shri Gopalaswami wrote to me on March 1, 1948 as follows:

March 1, 1948

My dear Maharaja Sahib,

> Messrs. V.P. Menon and Mahajan are going to Jammu this afternoon to discuss and finalize with you the draft of the Proclamation which Your Highness has to issue for appointing Abdullah as Prime Minister and others on his advice. The draft has been very carefully considered by myself, Pandit ji and Sardar ji, and we are of the opinion that the whole of it should be accepted by you. Anything less would not satisfy the requirements of the present situation.
>
> As a friend of yours, I consider it most important that Your Highness must make a very big gesture in order to rally the maximum percentage of the population of the State behind you with the help of Abdullah. Things are moving very fast and we have yet to fight a great battle at Lake Success. I have already stated during the discussion at Lake Success that Your Highness had only been waiting for Sheikh Abdullah to return from America to convert the Emergency Administration into an Interim Council of Ministers with Abdullah as Prime Minister. I am leaving Delhi for Lake Success the day after tomorrow, and it would be a great strength to the cause I have to plead there on behalf of Kashmir if this Proclamation is issued before I leave. I have not the slightest doubt that the issue of this Proclamation at

> this juncture is, in the circumstances that confront us at present, in the best interests of yourself and your people.
>
> It is further very important that everything that has happened in the past should be forgotten and forgiven and that Your Highness should take Sheikh Abdullah into your fullest confidence. In fact, I was almost going to suggest that you should give up your usual reserve, come out in the open and put yourself at the head of your people, both Muslims and non-Muslims, for the purpose of consolidating and strengthening the large volume of support for preserving the integrity of the State and maintaining its accession to India, which thanks to Sheikh Abdullah and the Indian Army, you have already behind you.
>
> With kind regards,
> Yours sincerely,
> Gopalaswami

Sheikh Abdullah in his letter dated March 24, 1948 stated as follows:

> The situation in Jammu and Kashmir State is, as you are well aware, a difficult one and requires the utmost careful handling. The emergency continues and has to be dealt with as such till normal conditions are restored. The burden of a Prime Minister in these circumstances will be a heavy one. He cannot function effectively without the fullest cooperation of his colleagues and the people as well as, of course, Your Highness.
>
> I have consulted some of my colleagues, who were available, and have come to the conclusion that it is my duty in these circumstances to undertake this burden. I trust that in the heavy work ahead I shall have Your Highness's full help and cooperation. I appreciate the spirit in which you have made the offer of the Prime Minister to me and on my part I assure Your Highness that I shall fully reciprocate it.

Then came the Proclamation dated 5th March, 1948 which was drafted by Shri Gopalaswami and approved by the Government of India and Sheikh Abdullah. It has been referred to in Article 370 of the Constitution of India that the State of Jammu and Kashmir has so far been governed under the constitutional set up for that Proclamation.

It is necessary to set out briefly what happened in the State and between the Government of India and Sheikh Abdullah in relation to the State after the Proclamation of March 5, 1948 and my leaving the State at the end of April 1949. Sheikh Abdullah and the men of his party took all power to themselves, ignored my existence and where they felt necessary, they got the consent of the Government of India to do what they liked in the State disregarding me and my wishes. This gradually led to deterioration and to the outside world, the State and Sheikh Abdullah became convertible terms. The people of Kashmir were utterly ignored and everything that Sheikh Abdullah desired to do was done in the name of the State with the express or tacit consent of the Government of India. At this juncture on a suggestion from Sardar Patel, I and my wife began a tour of the State. This did not suit the books of Sheikh Abdullah. He approached the Government of India with the result that I was asked to stay out of the State for a few months. I accepted the advice of Sardar Patel and agreed to stay out. The Yuvraj was appointed Regent. It need hardly be pointed out that the Yuvraj became a figurehead and had to take orders from Sheikh Abdullah. In this connection it may also be pointed out that although my Proclamation of March 5, 1948 was based on the Mysore Constitution, which stipulated the appointment of a Dewan and reserved subjects, yet gradually Sheikh Abdullah succeeded in getting the approval of the Government of India to making changes in the Constitution of the State, so as to make it very different from what was expressly intended to be. The mischief began with Sheikh Abdullah going direct to the Government of India on certain points over my head and the Government of India countenancing him and giving the desired directions and then informing me of what they had done at the instance of Sheikh Abdullah. The correspondence on the subject and the events following on each change bear testimony to what Sheikh Abdullah was trying to achieve in breach of the solemn promises and assurances given by him and also by the Government of India on his behalf. After my leaving the State things went from bad to worse.

Sheikh Abdullah was not satisfied with what he had achieved and aspired to absolute control of the State. He became openly inimical and hostile to me. He even interfered with my private properties and personal belongings, issued order to humiliate me and even interfered with the administration of the Dharmarth Trust, a Trust created by my forefathers of which I am the Trustee and which is being administered from day to day by the President of the Dharmarth Council appointed by me. The charities and institutions maintained from the revenues of Trust are starved. Even the routine expenses of the Trust, such as, for Puja in temples and Devasthans cannot be met because it pleases Sheikh Abdullah to prevent the income of the Trust coming to my hands or to the hands of President of the Dharmarth Council. The Jammu branch of the Imperial Bank of India refused to pay even to me the amounts of the fixed deposits of the Trust and also the State and to my Proclamation of March 5, 1948 wherein the setting up of such an Assembly was foreshadowed and stated that it appeared to the States Ministry that the time had come to reduce the uncertainty in Kashmir by going ahead with this proposal. He sent a draft Proclamation to set up the Constituent Assembly, for my comments.

I took exception to the proposed manner and method of setting up the Constituent Assembly. I summarized my objection to it as follows:

(i) That the Proclamation with the object and spirit of which I wholeheartedly agree be issued by me as Ruler who is the properly constituted authority in law to promulgate it and not by my Regent.

(ii) The powers and functions of the body intended to be constituted should be express, well-defined and accurately worded and should exclude from the purview of their enquiry and consideration matters not expressly entrusted to them.

(iii) They should report to the authority that constitutes it, i.e. the Ruler who shall seek the advice of the Parliament of India in the matter.

I refer to the correspondence that took place, the interview which Mr. Menon had with me in Bombay in February 1951 under the instructions of the Prime Minister and the subsequent negotiations which ended with my giving consent to the Yuvraj for setting up the Constituent Assembly. I also refer to the assurance given to me by the Minister of States (Shri N. Gopalaswami Ayyangar) in the course of the negotiations as to the position of myself and my dynasty and other important matters. I am constrained to refer to the relevant portions of his letter which, I quote below:

5th April, 1951:

> Developments have, however, since taken place both in the State and at Lake Success which make it imperative that the issue of this proclamation is not delayed any longer. The Government of India are committed to the convening of a Constituent Assembly, the preparations for which are in active progress in the State. That Assembly will be held whether the formal Proclamation issues or not. In the view of the Government of India it must be convened, if both their commitments to the people of Kashmir and their stand at Lake Success are to be implemented in spirit and in the letter. From the beginning they have held that this Constituent Assembly should be called under the provisions of the Constitution of India and that this should be done from both a tactical and constitutional point of view, on the authority of Proclamation issued by the Head of the State. The draft of the Proclamation has been agreed between the Government of India and the Government of Jammu and Kashmir. No purpose will, therefore, be served by any act of Your Highness which holds up the signing and issue of this Proclamation by Shri Yuvraj.
>
> On neither of the two matters about which I can understand your entertaining apprehensions, namely, the

> continuance of the accession of the Jammu and Kashmir State or of part thereof to India and the connection of the Headship of the State with your dynasty, no final decision could be taken by the Constituent Assembly to be convened. They are essentially matters which could be decided only as a matter of agreement between the Government of India and Parliament on the one side and the Government of Jammu and Kashmir and the State Constituent Assembly or Legislature on the other. The Government of India will, no doubt, at the proper time take the decision on these matters, which, I need hardly assure you, will be essentially just from the standpoint both of your dynasty and the people of the State.
>
> You have obviously to put your trust in the people of the State and the Government of India in respect of this matter. I hope, therefore, you will immediately lift the ban which you have placed on Shri Yuvraj affixing his signature to the agreed Proclamation and which naturally has placed him in great embarrassment.

Apprehending what was coming and in order not to embarrass the Government of India and the Yuvraj, I have been prepared to abdicate provided that a satisfactory arrangement was to come with me by the States Ministry and provided also that the Yuvraj's position as the Head of the State was assured. The negotiations in this behalf which were carried on with Shri Gopalaswami as the States Minister were left in an indecisive state because of Shri Gopalaswami having been succeeded as the States Minister by Dr. K.N. Katju. Having regard to the trend of events I wrote to Dr. Katju on June 29, 1952. I waited for Dr. Katju's reply as foreshadowed in the Prime Minister's letter. I then received Dr. Katju's reply dated July 30, 1952.

I replied to Dr. Katju by my letter dated August 8, 1952.

I enclose copies of these letters as they have an important bearing on the situation.

These letters speak for themselves Dr. Katju's reply is not a reply at all. The legal position, it appears to me, has not been considered and it further appears that it is being taken for granted by the Prime Minister and Dr. Katju that the relevant Articles, particularly Article 370, of the Constitution of India can be altered and/or amended to suit the present attitude of Sheikh Abdullah.

It would not be out of place to point out that Article 370 refers specifically to my Proclamation of March 5, 1948. That is the law which governs the State of Jammu and Kashmir until a new Constitution is framed, approved and adopted not only by the Constituent Assembly of the State but also approved by me and then by you and yet, I learn that the Prime Minister has asked the Yuvraj (who is acting only as my Regent and represents me) to agree to be the elected Head of the State forthwith, that is to say, even before the Constitution of the State is framed much less approved and adopted thus throwing over not only me but also the dynasty. I do not know what reply Dr. Katju proposes to make to me but it appears that the Prime Minister is dealing with the matter (vide his letter dated July 5, 1952). I have, therefore to specifically deal with the charges made in the Prime Minister's letter.

The Prime Minister in para 4 of his letter refers to the Constitution of India as having been based on and derived from the people of India and says with regard to the Jammu and Kashmir State that the Government of India felt that the people would prefer accession to India but the matter was delicate and not beyond dispute and, therefore, the Government of India did not press for the Accession of Jammu and Kashmir State but suggested that the matter should be considered at a later stage when the people's wishes could be ascertained in some form or the other and the suggestion was that some kind of a Constituent Assembly might be set up in the State to decide the question of accession as well as other questions.

I grant all this but how can the Government of India take all these steps over my head on whose authority they entered the State and are continuing there and who was the Chief Author of the Proclamation on which is based the future construction of political set up in the country?

In para 5, the Prime Minister says that on the invasion of the State by tribal raiders and others in late October 1947 the crisis arose and at that time I left Srinagar at the dead of night for Jammu and many of my officers followed me and the State was left without leadership or means of defence in so far as official authority was concerned. This is in fact untrue, as pointed out above. I left Srinagar for Jammu on the advice of the Government of India conveyed to me through Mr. Menon. The Prime Minister says further that in the basic picture of the crisis of Kashmir I do not come in at all. That statement amounts to suppression very and suggestion false.

I have acted all throughout from September 1947 under the advice of the Government of India, Lord Mountbatten, the Prime Minister, Sardar Vallabhbhai Patel and Shri Gopalaswami and, as pointed out herein above, Sheikh Abdullah himself made promises and gave assurances, which he is now backing out of. Even in the book called New Kashmir published by the Kashmir Information Bureau, New Delhi, in 1950 and which is the political Bible of Sheikh Abdullah, Sheikh Abdullah has based his case for a Responsible Government in the State under the aegis of the Maharaja and even gone to the length of setting out what functions the Maharaja was to perform. The Prime Minister in his letter says that the people of Kashmir must decide their own future. I may well ask whether Sheikh Abdullah is a synonymous term with the people of Kashmir. The people of Kashmir have not been consulted.

According to Sheikh Abdullah, the people of Kashmir have changed their mind to such an extent that they are determined to get rid of the idea of a hereditary ruler of the State. The Constituent Assembly has been packed with Sheikh Abdullah's men and even that Assembly has not yet come to a decision nor has it framed any constitution providing for the functions of the Head of the State either hereditary or elected and what one would like to know is where is the reason for this frightful hurry to elect the Head of the State thus doing away with me and my dynasty before the Constitution is framed and before the fate of the State is determined in the fight that is raging before the UNO between India and Pakistan.

Are myself and my dynasty to be pawns in the game which Sheikh Abdullah is playing with the Government of India on the representation that he is actively helping India in the case before the UN Security Council?

The Prime Minister says that he has seen no evidence of any sympathy on my part for the people of Kashmir who have gone through fire and suffering during the past four and a half years. May I ask who is responsible for this state of affairs? Have the Government of India given any choice of action to me during the last four and a half years? Have they at any time pulled up Sheikh Abdullah knowing as they did, on what promises and assurances Sheikh Abdullah became the Prime Minister? May I again point out that even before I left the State under the advice of Sardar Vallabhbhai Patel, I and my wife had started on a tour of the State as Sardar Patel had told me that I should see more of my people and they should see more of me. Sheikh Abdullah did not like this tour and approached the Government of India with the result that I was called at Delhi and asked to desist from returning to the State and finally to leave it.

The Prime Minister says at the end of this letter that the only assurance he can give to me is that the first place will be given always to the rights of the people and to the wishes of the people and that if I fall in with those rights and wishes, the government will endeavour to help me to the best of their ability.

I am prepared to take up the challenge. Let the people of Jammu and Kashmir freely decide between me and Sheikh Abdullah without interference from the Government of India. Let me point out what has been happening. The world has been given to understand that the march of events, the changed political values have brought about rapid and inevitable changes and we must accept them no matter what the obligation of the Government of India, Government of Jammu and Kashmir, the assurance of both the governments to me and their duties under certain legal and constitutional arrangements may be. With all due deference to this opinion, I must say that I emphatically challenge the contention that whatever has happened is in accordance with the will of the people and that the sovereignty has effectively and really passed to the people as it should and that they are consciously exercising their will and ask for changes which are being brought about by an oligarchy backed by Government of India. I cannot conscientiously recognize the changes in the Proclamation of March 5, 1948 which governs the relations of the State with India. But if the Government of India and you, Sir, feel that in the present stage of negotiations with Dr. Graham it would be inconvenient for the Government of India to allow this matter to be raked up, then at least, the Government of India should not succumb entirely to the wishes of Sheikh Abdullah but hold the balance equally between him and me and at least preserve the status quo as regards the headship of the State until the field is clear for the necessary steps to be taken to determine the will of the people of Kashmir.

Copies of the following documents are attached for your ready reference:

Note given to Prime Minister of Kashmir by Prime Minister of India on October 26, 1947;

Letter dated October 26, 1947 from the Prime Minister of India to the Prime Minister of Kashmir;

Letter dated October 27, 1947 from Prime Minister of India to the Prime Minister of Kashmir;

Letter dated October 27, 1947 from Prime Minister of India to me; Letter dated October 26, 1947 from me to Lord Mountbatten;

Letter dated October 27, 1947 from Lord Mountbatten to me;

Letter dated December 24, 1947 from Shri N. Gopalaswami to me.

Secure in the knowledge that I was out of the picture and could not reply, I was, by a series of false statements and speeches intended to humiliate and malign me, painted black and unpatriotic. The Government of India who had assured me that I would be protected against such onslaughts remained an unconcerned spectator. Not only that, it is most distressing to know and feel that whenever Sheikh Abdullah and his party talked of me in disparaging and spiteful terms, the highest authority in the Government of India immediately endorsed it. If Sheikh Abdullah said I could not return to the State, the Prime Minister with all the authority, prestige and might at his back, endorsed it. If Sheikh Abdullah said I had lost the confidence of the people, the Prime Minister referred to my alleged wrong-headed and mistaken policies, without saying exactly what they were and said the people had suffered on account of these. This no doubt had the effect of suppressing what is said to be the will of the people. Being placed as I was, I was absolutely unable to answer any of these accusations. I feel grievously wronged in that the Government of India whom I looked up to as the ultimate authority I could go to for redress, instead of stopping such malicious and false propaganda, not only went on countenancing it but endorsing it disregarding their solemn assurances.

Having eliminated me in a manner which had neither the sanction of law nor political morality, it was the duty of the Government of India to protect me. But that was not done and the matter did not end there. My properties and privileges etc., were attempted to be interfered with. I protested and asked for redress but never got it.

As I have said above, I was eliminated by a process which was neither fair nor honourable. It was not and it has never been due to the will of the people. It was due entirely to the machinations of Sheikh Abdullah and his party. They got themselves appointed on the definite assurance and later, with the connivance of the Government of India, systematically ignored all their legal and moral obligations and ultimately without rhyme or reason but to suit the books of Sheikh Abdullah successfully got me out of the State. Taking advantage of my absence and helplessness, started a campaign of vilification and harassment and thus created conditions wherein they could tell an unknowing world that they were doing what the people desired. I have taken the responsibility of making these statements and I earnestly request you, Sir, to ascertain the views of your government about them and then come to an independent opinion as to whether I have not been seriously wronged and to redress the wrong.

I may be permitted to summarize the position:

The Government of the State of Jammu and Kashmir was more advanced and enlightened than that of any other Indian State in the pre-partition days;

I employed men of undoubted ability and standing to be my Ministers from time to time;

In August 1947, Lord Mountbatten gave me the impression that I should accede to Pakistan, Government of India was undecided about the matter, wanted every step by me endorsed by Sheikh Abdullah, the people of Jammu and Kashmir were divided in their opinion and I decided to enter into Standstill Agreements with both India and Pakistan in order to have time for things to settle down;

Pakistan did not act up to the Standstill Agreements, blocked supplies to the State and aided and abetted the raiders;

I released Sheikh Abdullah as advised by Sardar Patel and relied on the assurance given by Sheikh Abdullah backed up by assurances given by the Government of India; I took Sheikh Abdullah in my Government; I issued the Proclamation of March 5, 1948; Sheikh Abdullah with the connivance of the Government of India started tinkering with the Constitution of 5th March, 1948; Sheikh Abdullah persuaded the Government of India to drive me out of the State; I left the State and appointed the Yuvraj, my Regent; My rights of personal property and the affairs of Dharmarth Trust were interfered with by Sheikh Abdullah; Sheikh Abdullah by maligning me created an impression that the people of Kashmir were against me; The Constituent Assembly was set up; The will of the people of Jammu and Kashmir is now judged by the whims and caprices of Sheikh Abdullah; Sheikh Abdullah having made up his mind to get rid of the Ruler and his dynasty, persuaded the Government of India to see eye to eye with him and to lay down that this could be done even before the new Constitution was framed much less approved by you on behalf of India;

I get no redress and am told that I am in the wrong, the will of the people is all that counts and I must abide by such will;

The Press carries reports from day to day creating feelings against me. False reports are not contradicted; The Prime Minister got angry as evidenced by his letter dated 5 July 1952 because I stated facts; The States Minister avoids giving a proper reply to me and yet the Press says I have been asked and have not replied;

The Yuvraj is being coerced by the Prime Minister and Sheikh Abdullah to accede to their suggestions.

Finally, I have to say that I had my range of controversy with Sheikh Abdullah and the Prime Minister and I am bitter about the fact that the Government of India have been unable to afford me protection and safeguard my rights in spite of the fact that throughout these four and a half years, I have given full cooperation and the fact that my pre-1947 conduct did not compare unfavourably with that of the other Rulers who at present enjoy Government of India's protection and favour. During the last three years of my enforced absence from the State I have given them no cause for grievance and at the most, I have been charged with delay in permitting the Yuvraj to take action which having regard to the consideration involved and my bitter experience, was natural and understandable. Even in this matter ultimately I did fall in line with the Government of India. If the result of all this in the final stage has again to be a betrayal by the Government of India of their assurances and promises etc. and is to result not only in my final removal from the State but also of the sacrifice of the Yuvraj whom I had entrusted to the Government of India's protection, I can only say that it would be an ill return for the faith which I and the Yuvraj placed in the government and the help and cooperation to the extent of self-effacement that we rendered to it. Only history and posterity will be able to do justice to our respective points of view.

In these circumstances, I appeal to you to consider the matter impartially in all its aspects with your sagacity and wisdom and guide me as to what would be in the best interests of the State.

I remain,

Yours faithfully,

Hari Singh

Glossary

aatash	fire
adda	station
adhan	the call for Muslim prayer
aelve bab	potato patron
ahram	unstitched cloth a pilgrim wears during the five days of Haj
ahrar	activists of the Majlis-e- Ahrar-e-Islam, Muslim religo-political party founded during the British Raj in 1929; also means 'the free ones'
ajaib ghar	museum
Allahu Akbar	God is Great
Allama	an honorary title carried by scholars, especially of Islamic jurisprudence and philosophy
Anjuman Darsul Islam	Association of Islamic Teaching
anjuman	association
anna	one-sixteenth of a rupee
aya	governess
badyan	fennel seed
Bakarwals	a tribe of nomadic goatherds and shepherds
basmati	a type of rice with long grains
Bharat	India
bidi	cheap cigarette made of unprocessed tobacco wrapped in leaves

Bikrimi	Hindu calendar using lunar months and solar sidereal years
Brahman zaadah	scion of Brahmans
chadar	blanket
chakdar	holder of large, uncultivated land
chapati	flat, round South Asian bread made without yeast
charpoy	a traditional cot used in the Indian subcontinent
chaudhri	transport agent
chela	disciple
chhakra	cart
chhari	mace
chhatank	equivalent to 1/8 of a *seer*
chillum	an earthen straight conical pipe with end-to-end channel used by mendicants to smoke
chinar	huge ornamental and shade tree indigenous to Kashmir; *Platanus orientalis*
chowki	police post
chowkidar	a watchman or a gatekeeper
coolie	an unskilled labourer especially in South Asian countries whose job is to carry things, especially traveller's bags at railway stations, airports, etc.
dandi	a seat carried on the back of a person to transport a traveller
darshan	view, exhibition
deechiwaer	small copper cooking vessel used in Kashmiri kitchen
Dewan	special congregational prayers held by Sikh community; also a designated high government official or a minister

	especially found in erstwhile princely states of India
dharmshala	religious hospice
dhobee	washerman
doonga	a living boat
Doordarshan Kendra	television center
dumdaar sitarah	meteorite
Eid or *Id*	Muslim festival observed twice a year, one, on the conclusion of the fasting month of *Ramadan* and, second, on the 10th day of *Dulhajah,* the last month of Islamic calendar, in commemoration of Prophet Abraham's offering his son Ismail for sacrifice on Allah's command.
Eidi	gift money given to children on the festival of *Eid*
farash khana	a room where carpets and tents are kept
farash	a bedmaker; chamberlain; a servant whose job is to spread carpets and prepare lamps, etc.; a tent pitcher
gaddi	seat
galladar	one who deals in stock and sale of rice
gaz	equivalent to 0.91 meter
ghat	a flight of steps leading down to a river
ghee	clarified butter used in South Asian cuisine
Giriftaar Committee	Arrest Committee
Goonda or *gunda*	goon
gotra	clan, descendants in an unbroken male line from a common male ancestor
Gujjar	an ethnic agricultural and pastoral community; also a member of the community

guli myooth or *vartaav*	gift money
guru	spiritual guide
haji	Muslim who has performed *haj*
hamam	an exclusive room with stone slab flooring underneath of which exists a hollow space for burning timber to keep the room warm
hangul	Kashmiri stag
Har Har Mahadev	a Hindu religious slogan meaning 'Mahadev or god Shiva lives in every human being'
hawalat	police lock-up
hijri	Islamic calendar year
hookah	hubble-bubble
huzoor minister	minister-in-waiting
ikka or ekka	a one-horse carriage
Imam of Eidain	one who leads the two congregational *Eid* prayers
Imam	leader or one who leads Muslim congregational prayers
Inqilab Zindabad	Long Live the Revolution
inqilab	revolution
intikhab-i-jamabandi	extract of quadrennial land record
jagar	a woolen cap
jagirdar	large land estate owner
Jaith	third month of the Bikrimi calendar
jama bandi	four-yearly record of ownership of land
jamawar	an exquisite shawl made in Kashmir
jatha	body of armed or unarmed people
Ka'ba	the cube-shaped building inside the Grand Mosque in Makkah in which direction Muslims all over the world pray five times a day

kacha	a mud house, dirt road
kahar	carrier of palanquin
kahcharai	grazing land
kalima shahadah	Testimony of Faith
kamkhwab	brocade woven of silk and gold or silver thread
kashmakash	conflict
Kashmir Darbar	Kashmir Government
khaat	a traditional cot used in the subcontinent
khaddar ka kurta pyjama	long shirt and trouser made of hand woven cotton fabric
Khan Bahadur	title conferred by the British Raj on pro-Government influential subjects
kharwar	ass-load, equivalent to 80 *seer*
khillat	grant
kishti	boat
kokar sahab	Mr. Rooster
kul devta	clan god
lakh	a hundred thousand
maalia	land revenue
Madarulmiaham	a high ranking administrator
Mahant	priest at a temple
maharaja	king, ruler
mahatmya	a guide book of a Hindu shrine
Mahaz-i-Azadi	The Freedom Front
majzoob or *moat*	ascetic
manjdhaar	whirlpool
maqboozai ahl-i-Islam	under the occupation of Muslims
marg	meadow
marla	a unit of area equivalent to 272.25 sq. ft.

masala dosa	popular south-Indian food
maund	equivalent to 37.32 kg.
Mazar-i-Sho'ra	Cemetery of Poets
Mirwaiz	chief cleric
Mirzaiyat	belief system propagated by Mirza Ghulam Ahmad (1835-1908) which Muslims consider as against the fundamental Islamic belief that Prophet Muhammad (pubh) is the last and final Messenger of Allah. People practicing *Mirzaiyat*, also known as *Qadianis* and *Ahmadis*, were declared non-Muslims in Pakistan in 1970s
Mirzayi	one who professes *Mirzaiyat*
misel-i-haqqiyat	record of rights
Mohtamim Dharmarth	Administrator of Dharmarth or Hindu Endowment
mohtamim	administrator
molvi	an honorific Islamic religious title given to Muslim religious scholars
muallim	teacher
mufti	an Islamic jurist qualified to issue a non-binding opinion on a point of Islamic law
mukarari	grant
murshid	spiritual guide
Naar-e-Takbeer	an Islamic slogan in response to which the crowd shouts *Allahu Akbar* (Allah is Great)
naat	versified eulogy of Prophet Muhammad, peace be upon him
naer	water jug
nambardar	village headman
namda	a woolen rug

nawab	an honorific title bestowed by the Mughal kings to semi-autonomous Muslim rulers of princely states in South Asia, Muslim ruler of a princely state
niaz	offering in cash and/or kind made at a shrine as an act of thanksgiving
Padre Sahib	Christian priest
paigham	message
paisa	one-fourth of an *anna*
pao	equivalent to ¼ of a *seer*
paranda	an open long Kashmiri boat used by a dignitary to participate in a river procession taken out in his/her honour
pir or peer	Muslim spiritual person, also a surname common between Muslims and Hindus of Kashmir
pheran	a traditional, loose, almost ankle-length outfit worn by Kashmiris, especially during winter to resist severe cold
Praja Sabha	people's assembly
puja	prayer
pujari	priest
qayamat	Doomsday
qayamat-i-sugra	little Doomsday
Quad-e-Azam	The Great Leader
Raghu	Hindu god Rama
Raghupati Raghav Raja Ram	popular Hindu devotional song in praise of Hindu god Rama
rai-shumari	plebiscite
raja	ruler
Rajab	seventh month of Islamic calendar
rajguru	spiritual guide of a ruler
riyakaar	a hypocrite

roti	bread
Rumi	of Rome
sad	member
sadhu	ascetic
Sadr-e-Riyasat	Head of the State
samadhi	memorial built upon a cremation site
sang baaran	rain of stones
sankalp	resolution
sarai	inn
satyagrah	non-violent civil resistance
Satyagrahi Aashram	hermitage of resistance
Sawan	the fifth month of Hindu calendar
seer	equivalent to 0.93 kg
sehar khan	one who awakens by drum beating Muslims for pre-dawn meal during the fasting month of *Ramadan*
Shab-i-Baraat	The Night of Fortune; the night between 14 and 15 Shaban, the eighth month of Islamic calendar, when Muslims believe Allah writes the destiny of people for the coming year and when He may forgive sinners.
shaivite	follower of Hindu god Shiva
shali	paddy
shaneel	velvet
shanti puja	peace prayers
shastra	a treatise, book or instrument of teaching, a manual or compendium on any subject in any field of knowledge, including religious
shawlbaf	a shawl weaver
Sheikh-ul-Hadith	honorific title given to an outstanding scholar of *Hadith* or sayings of prophet of Islam (pubh)

shikar	game
shikara	a ferry boat
shivala	Shiva's abode, a Hindu religious structure
singhara-nuts	water caltrop
Sipar-i-*Saltanat-i-Inglishia*	royal title adopted by Dogra rulers of Kashmir taking pride in calling themselves 'A Sword of the English Empire'
sonth	dry ginger powder
suji	semolina
surya devta	Sun god
suryavanshi	Sun dynasty
swami	a Hindu ascetic initiated into a religious monastic order
Tareekh-i-Kashmir	history of Kashmir
tarr	fabricated news
Tawarikh-i-Kashmir	histories of Kashmir
tehvildar	curator
thale baan	a spherical copper rice eating plate with an elevated base
thana	police station
tola	equivalent to 10 gm
tonga	horse-driven carriage
tooer	a round copper rice eating bowl
toofaan	tempest
toshkhana	a royal treasure house
trae'm	large plate in which food is served to 4 people
trak	equivalent to 5 seer
urs-i-shareef	auspicious festival
vihar	Buddhist monastery
Vitasta	ritualistic or mythological name of the Jhelum River

wajd	spiritual ecstasy
waza	Kashmiri chef who specializes in *wazwan*
wazir	political advisor or minister
wazir-i-wazarat	deputy commissioner
wazwan	famous Kashmiri multi-cuisine feast
yag	sacrifice
zaildar	feudal title of revenue collector of an administrative unit called *zail* extending between two and forty villages
zamzam	miraculously generated water from a well inside the Grand Mosque of Makkah
zanana	ladies
zari kulah	a turban worked with gold thread
zindabad	long live
zulm	cruelty

Bibliography

Abdullah, Sheikh Mohammad. *Aatash-e-Chinar*. Gulshan Books: Srinagar, 2008.

Ahmad, Ghulam. *My Years with Sheikh Abdullah: Kashmir 1971–1987*. Gulshan Books: Srinagar, 2008.

Ahmad, Khalid Bashir. *Kashmir: A Walk Through History*. Gulshan Books: Srinagar, 2018.

——. *Kashmir: Exposing the Myth Behind the Narrative*. SAGE, 2017.

Bakshi, Shiri Ram. *Kashmir: Valley and its Culture*. Sarup & Sons: New Delhi, 1997.

Bamzai, P.N.K. *A History of Kashmir*. Gulshan Books: Srinagar, 2008.

Bates, Charles Ellison. *A Gazetteer of Kashmir*, Gulshan Books: Srinagar, 2005.

Bazaz, Prem Nath. *Daughters of the Vitasta*. Pamposh Publications: New Delhi, 1959.

——. *The History of Struggle for Freedom in Kashmir*. Srinagar: Gulshan Books, 2009.

Biscoe, C.E. Tyndale. *Kashmir in Sunlight and Shade*. Mittal Publications: New Delhi, 1995.

Bruce, C.G. *Peeps at Many Lands—Kashmir*. Adam & Charles Black: London, 1911.

Charak, Sukhdev Singh. *Life and Times of Maharaja Ranbir Singh*. Jay and Kay Book House: Jammu, 1985.

Chaudhri, Ghulam Abbas. *Kashmakash*. Kashmir Book Foundation: Srinagar, 2017.

Collett, John. *A Guide to Kashmir*. W. Newman Publication: Calcutta, 1889.

Cultural Resource Mapping of Srinagar—*Shehar-i-Kashmir* (2 Vol). Indian National Trust for Art and Cultural Heritage: J&K Chapter.

Dass, Diwan Jarmani. *Maharaja*. Hind Pocket Books Pvt. Ltd: New Delhi, 1972.

Doughty, Marion. *Afoot Through the Kashmir Valleys*. Sagar Publications: New Delhi, 1971.

Fauq, Mohammad Din. *A Complete History of Kashmir*. Gulshan Books: Srinagar, 2009.

Ganai, Showkat Ahmad. *Kashmir: Accession and its Manipulation*. Gulshan Books: Srinagar, 2009.

Gockhami, Dr. Abdul Jabbar. *Kashmir: Politics and Plebiscite*. Gulshan Books: Srinagar, 2011.

Gundevia, Y.D. *The Testament of Sheikh Abdullah*. Abhinav Publications: New Delhi, 1974.

Hassnain, Fida Mohammad. *British Policy Towards Kashmir (1846–1946)*. Gulshan Books: Srinagar, 2009.

Hussain, Syed Tafaazull. *Sheikh Abdullah—A Biography: The Crucial Period 1905-1939*. Bloomington: Wordclay, 2009.

Hussain, Syed Tassaduque. *India Kashmir Twining of Night & Day*. Gulshan Books: Srinagar, 2012.

Iqbal, Javed. *Zindah Rood: Allama Iqbal Ki Mukammal Sawaneh Hayat* (Complete Biography of Allama Iqbal). Ilmi Academy: New Delhi, 2014.

Ishaq, Munshi Mohammad. *Nida-e-Haq*. Markaz-i-Ishaet: Srinagar, 2014.

Jagmohan. *My Frozen Turbulence in Kashmir*. Allied Publishers: New Delhi, 1991.

Kalhana. *Rajatarangini* (Trns. Stein). Gulshan Books: Srinagar, 2007.

Kashmiri, Fazil. *Tasveer-i-Haj*. Self published: Srinagar, 1958.

Kashmiri, Mulla Ahmad Bin Abdus Saboor. *Khawariqus Salikeen*. Department of Libraries & Research: J&K, 2011.

Kaw, M.K. *Kashmir and Its People-Studies in the Evolution of Kashmir Society*. A.P.H. Publishing Corporation: New Delhi, 2004.

Khan, Ghulam Hassan. *Freedom Movement in Kashmir (1931–1940)*. Light & Life Publishers: New Delhi, 1980.

Khan, Khurshid Alam. *Aftab aur Srinagar Times: Urdu Sahafat ke Sang-e-Meel*. Qasmi Qutub Khana: Jammu, 2013.

Khan, Mohammad Ishaq. *History of Srinagar (1846–947): A Study in Socio-Cultural Change,* Aamir Publication: Srinagar, 1978.

Khayal, Ghulam Nabi. *Iqbal Aur Tehreek-e-Azadi-e-Kashmir*. Kashmiri Writers' Conference: Srinagar, 1997.

Khoihami, Hassan. *Tareekh-e-Hassan* (Persian). Research and Publication Department. J & K Government: Srinagar, 1954.

——. *Tareekh-i-Hassan,* (Kashmiri Trans. Ahmad, 3 volumes). J&K Academy of Art, Culture & Languages: Srinagar, 1998, 1999, 2002.

Koul, Mohan Lal. *Kashmir: Wail of a Valley*. Gyan Sagar Publications: Delhi, 1999.

Kour, Ravinder Jit. *Political Awakening in Kashmir.* Ashish Publications: New Delhi, 1996.

Kwarteng, Kwasi. *Ghosts of Empire—Britain's Legacies in the Modern World*. Bloomsbury: London, 2011.

Lawrence, Walter R. *The Valley of Kashmir*. Oxford University Press Warehouse: London, 1895.

Madhok, Balraj. *Kashmir—The Storm Center of the World.* Houstan Texas, 1992.

Makhdoomi, Pir Mohammad Afzal. *Kashmir ki Tehrik-i-Azadi: Khwaab, Azaab, Saraab*. Meezan Publishers: Srinagar, 2017.

Mehta, Ved. *Mamaji*. Oxford University Press, 1979.

Mohi-ud-Din, Akhtar. *A Fresh Approach to the History of Kashmir*. Book Bank: Srinagar, 1998.

Mohi-ud-Din, Sofi. *Jammu Wa Kashmir Mai Urdu Sahafat*. Times Publications: Srinagar, 1973.

Mullik, B.N. *My Years with Nehru*. Bombay: Allied Publishers, 1971.

Neve, Arthur. *Thirty Years in Kashmir*. Gulshan Books: Srinagar, 2008.

Neve, F. Ernest. *A Crusader in Kashmir*. Gulshan Books: Srinagar, 2007.

——. *Beyond the Pir Panjal—Life and Missionary Enterprise in Kashmir*. Church Missionary Society: London, 1915.

Neve, Major Arthur. *The Tourist's Guide to Kashmir, Ladakh, Skardo & C*: Lahore, 1923.

Qayoom, Shabnam. *Kashmir ka Siyasi Inquilab*. Waqar Publications: Srinagar, 2007.

Raghavan, G.S. *The Warning of Kashmir*. The Pioneer Press: Allahabad, 1931.

Sa'dat, Molvi Mohammad Shah. *Tareekh-i-Kashmir ki Rozana Dairy*. Ghulam Mohammad Noor Mohammad: Srinagar, [Year of publication not printed].

Saraf, Muhammad Yusuf. *Kashmiris Fight for Freedom (1819–1946)*. Feroz Sons: Lahore, 2005.

Schofield, Victoria. *Kashmir in Conflict—India, Pakistan and the Unending War*: London, 2003.

Sethi, Krishen Dev. *Yaad-e-Rafta*. Jid-o-Jahad Publications: Jammu, 1986.

Singh, Harbans. *Maharaja Hari Singh: The Troubled Years*, Brahaspati Publications: New Delhi, 2011.

Singh, Karan. *Autobiography*. Oxford University Press: New Delhi, 1994.

Singh, Neerja. *Nehru-Patel: Agreement within Differences*, Select Documents and Correspondences 1933-1950. National Book Trust India: New Delhi, 2010.

Swinburne, Major T.R. *Kashmir—A Holiday in the Happy Valley With Pen and Pencil*. Tredition Classics, 2017.

Taing, Mohammad Yusuf. *Kashmir Qalam*. Meezan Publishers: Srinagar, 2009.

Taseer, Rashid. *Tehrik-i-Hurriyat-i-Kashmir*. Muhafiz Publications: Srinagar, 1984.

Younghusband, Francis. *Kashmir: Described by Sir Francis Younghusband*. Adam and Charles Black: London, 1911.

Journals, Reports, Files

Administration Reports of the Jammu & Kashmir State for the years 1913-14, 1940-41, 1941-42, 1942, 1943-44, 1959-60.

Detailed Report of a Tour in Search of Sanskrit MSS Made in Kashmir, Rajputana and Central India. Georg Buhler. *Journal of the Bombay Branch of the Royal Asiatic Society*. Bombay: 1969.

Encyclopaedia of Hindi Cinema. (Ed.) Gulzar, Govind Nihalani, Saibal Chatterjee. Encyclopaedia Britannica (India) Pvt. Ltd. and Popular Prakashan Pvt. Ltd: Bombay, 2003.

Hamara Adab. *Mashaheer Number*. J&K Academy of Art Culture & Languages, 1978.

Journal of the Bombay Branch of Royal Asiatic Society, 1877.

Kashmir—Appeal to World Conscience. Sheikh Mohammad Abdullah. Principal Public Relations Officer: Government of Jammu & Kashmir, [Year of publication not printed].

Kashmir Question in the Security Council—Miscellaneous correspondence between Sheikh Mohammad Abdullah. Government of India, Paris Delegation and others: Archives Repository Kashmir, 1949-53.

Koshur Encyclopedia. Vol 1, second edition: Jammu & Kashmir Academy of Art, Culture & Languages, 2006.

Mainstream Weekly. Vol LI, No. 35: New Delhi, August 17, 2013.

Monthly *Qaumi Digest* (Urdu): Lahore, 1997.

Randhawa Committee Report on the Reorganization of Libraries, Research & Museums for the Government of Jammu & Kashmir, 1976.

Report of the Commission of Inquiry constituted under SRO 39 dated 30th January 1965 issued by the Home Department, J&K Government to inquire into certain charges of misconduct against Shri Bakhshi Ghulam Mohammad, Srinagar: June 30, 1967. Accession No. 597/Report. Archives Repository Library: Srinagar.

Shabistan, Sheikh Abdullah: Dost ya Dushman (Special Publication). Shama Distributers Pvt. Ltd: New Delhi, January 1968.

Sheeraza (Urdu). Mohammad Yusuf Taing Number (Vol. 49, No. 4-7): J&K Academy of Art, Culture & Languages: Srinagar, 2011.

The Alpine Journal: London, 1997.

Travel Guide to Kashmir. [ed. G.R. Sarup]. Department of Tourism. J&K Government: Srinagar, 1955.

References and Endnotes

1. MUSLIM CONFERENCE TO NATIONAL CONFERENCE

1. Sa'dat, Molvi Mohammad Shah, *Tareekh-i-Kashmir ki Rozana Dairy*, pp. 694-95.
2. *Ibid.*, p. 695.
3. On 12 November 1931, Maharaja Hari Singh appointed a commission headed by B.J. Glancy, a European officer of the Government of India, which came to be known after his name as the Glancy Commission. Glancy was asked to "enquire into and report on the various complaints of a religious or a general nature already submitted to His Highness' Government and also such complaints as might be directly laid before the Commission." Besides Glancy as its Chairman, the Commission comprised four non-official members including one Hindu and one Muslim each from the two provinces of Kashmir and Jammu nominated by their respective communities.
4. Makhdoomi, Pir Mohammad Afzal, *Kashmir ki Tehrik-i-Azadi: Khwaab, Azaab Aur Saraab*, p. 186.
5. Hussain, Syed Taffazul, *Sheikh Abdullah: A Biography* (Second edition), p. 218.
6. Abdullah, Sheikh Mohammad, *Aatash-e-Chinar*, (Gulshan Books, 2008), p. 113.
7. *Ibid.* Mohammad Sayeed Masoodi credits Abdullah and himself with the decision taken in the Central Jail Srinagar where the two were lodged, "to form a party and name it [the] Muslim Conference." [Saraf, Muhammad Yusuf, *Kashmiris Fight for Freedom*, Vol. 1, p. 482.]
8. Abbas, Chaudhri Ghulam, *Kashmakash*, p. 118.
9. Saraf, Muhammad Yusuf, *Kashmiris Fight for Freedom*, Vol. 1, p. 481.
10. *Ibid.*
11. *Ibid.*, p. 482.
12. Abbas, Chaudhri Ghulam, *Kashmakash*, p. 121.

13. Fateh Kadal and Zaina Kadal are among several bridges spanning the Jhelum River within its course through the old Srinagar city. The Fateh Kadal was originally built in 1499 AD by Fateh Shah who ruled Kashmir in three stints between 1489 and 1516 AD. The Zaina Kadal was first built in 1427 AD by Zainul Aabideen, ruler of Kashmir between 1420 and 1470 AD.
14. Makhdoomi, Pir Mohammad Afzal, *Kashmir ki Tehrik-i-Azadi: Khwaab, Azaab Aur Saraab*, p. 229.
15. Saraf, Muhammad Yusuf, *Kashmiris Fight for Freedom*, Vol. 1, p. 483.
16. Speech made by Waliullah Zainul Aabideen on 15 October 1932 at the convention of Muslim representatives at Srinagar.
17. The Committee comprised leaders like Khawaja Saad-ud-Din Shawl, Chaudhri Ghulam Abbas, Khawaja Ghulam Ahmad Ashai, Aga Syed Hussain Shah Jalali, Maulvi Mohammad Abdullah Advocate, Pir Hisssam-ud-Din Gilani, Khawaja Ghulam Ahmad Bhat, Mian Ahmad Yar, Maulvi Mohammad Hussain, Munshi Abdul Aziz and Abdul Majid Qarshi.
18. Sa'dat, Molvi Mohammad Shah, *Tareekh-i-Kashmir ki Rozana Dairy*, p. 732.
19. Saraf, Muhammad Yusuf, *Kashmiris Fight for Freedom*, Vol. 1, p. 488.
20. *Ibid.*
21. Makhdoomi, Pir Mohammad Afzal, *Kashmir ki Tehrik-i-Azadi: Khwaab, Azaab Aur Saraab*, p. 112.
22. Abbas, Chaudhri Ghulam, *Kashmakash*, p. 128.
23. Makhdoomi, Pir Mohammad Afzal, *Kashmir ki Tehrik-i-Azadi: Khwaab, Azaab Aur Saraab*, p. 254.
24. Sa'dat, Molvi Mohammad Shah, *Tareekh-i-Kashmir ki Rozana Dairy*, p. 750.
25. *Ibid.*, p. 741.
26. Saraf, Muhammad Yusuf, *Kashmiris Fight for Freedom*, Vol. 1, p. 493.
27. Sa'dat, Molvi Mohammad Shah, *Tareekh-i-Kashmir ki Rozana Dairy*, p. 758. [Other members of the party included Gohar Rehman, Abdur Rahim Banday, Munshi Asadullah Vakeel, Khizar Mohammed Zaroo, Abdus Salam Parimoo, Allah Rakha Saghar and Sheikh Ghulam Qadir.]
28. *Ibid.*
29. *Ibid.*
30. *Ibid.*, p. 775.

31. *Ibid.*, p. 782.
32. *Ibid.*
33. Ishaq, Munshi Mohammad, *Nida-e-Haq*, p. 117.
34. *Ibid.*
35. Sa'dat, Molvi Mohammad Shah, *Tareekh-i-Kashmir ki Rozana Dairy*, p. 780.
36. *Ibid.*, p. 784.
37. The *Kashmir Times*, 10 December 1935.
38. Abbas, Chaudhri Ghulam, *Kashmakash*, p. 159.
39. Abdullah, Sheikh Mohammad, *Aatash-i-Chinar*, [Gulshan, 2008], p. 569.
40. *Ibid.*, pp. 159-60.
41. Taseer, Rashid, *Tarrikh-i-Hurriyat-i-Kashmir*, Vol. I, pp. 227-28.
42. Abdullah, Sheikh Mohammad, *Aatash-i-Chinar* (Second edition, 2008), p. 164.
43. Makhdoomi, Pir Mohammad Afzal, *Kashmir ki Tehrik-i-Azadi: Khwaab, Azaab Aur Saraab*, p. 258.
44. *Ibid.*
45. In his memoirs published in 1986, four years after his death, Abdullah claims that his was a middle class family engaged in manufacture and trade of Kashmiri shawls. [*Aatash-i-Chinar*, Gulshan (Reprint 2008), p. 3.]
46. Sa'dat, Molvi Mohammad Shah, *Tareekh-i-Kashmir ki Rozana Dairy*, p. 774.
47. *Ibid.*, p. 777.
48. *Ibid.*
49. *Ibid.*
50. *Ibid.*, p. 778.
51. *Ibid.*, p. 784.
52. *Ibid.*, p. 791.
53. Ishaq, Munshi Mohammad, *Nida-e-Haq*, p. 128.
54. The *Kashmir Times*, 18 August 1936.
55. *Ibid.*
56. Hussain, Syed Taffazul, *Sheikh Abdullag: A Biography* (Second edition), p. 276.
57. Ishaq, Munshi Mohammad, *Nida-e-Haq*, p. 118.
58. *The Albarq*, Srinagar, 14 July 1938.
59. Abbas, Chaudhri Ghulam, *Kashmakash*, p. 169.

60. *Ibid.*
61. Ahmad, Khalid Bashir, *A Walk Through History*, p. 210.
62. *Ibid.*, pp. 210-11.
63. Sa'dat, Molvi Mohammad Shah, *Tareekh-i-Kashmir ki Rozana Dairy*, p. 806.
64. Taseer, Rashid, *Tehrik-i-Hurriyat-i-Kashmir*, Vol. 2, pp. 56-57.
65. Sa'dat, Molvi, Mohammad Shah, *Tareekh-i-Kashmir ki Rozana Dairy*, p. 806.
66. *Ibid.*
67. *Ibid.*
68. *Ibid.*, p. 813.
69. Hussain, Syed Taffazul, *Sheikh Abdullag: A Biography* (Second edition), p. 290.
70. *Ibid.*
71. Abbas, Chaudhri Ghulam, *Kashmakash*, p. 169.
72. *Ibid.*, p. 170.
73. *Kalam-i-Niaz Kamraji*, Part-I, *Aansoon ka Haar*, Munshi Manzoor Ahmad Khan Niaz, Printer: Ghulam Mohiuddin Fazili, Associate Editor, *Haqeeqat*,Srinagar, published at the Kashmir Printing Press, Srinagar.
74. Bazaz, Prem Nath, *The History of Struggle for Freedom of Kashmir*, Third Edition, Gulshan, 2009, p. 145.
75. Abdullah, Sheikh Mohammad, *Aatash-i-Chinar*, Second Edition, Gulshan Books, 2008, p. 163.
76. Sethi, Krishen Dev, *Yaad-i-Rafta*, 1986, Jid-o-Jahad Publications, p. 16.
77. Ishaq, Munshi Mohammad, *Nida-e-Haq*, p. 124. On 21 June 1931, at a massive rally at *Khanqah-i-Moalla* the Muslim leaders resolved to fight for the rights of the oppressed Muslim community. That day, a young man named Abdul Qadeer Khan, appeared on the stage from nowhere and made a fiery speech against the Dogra rule asking people to rise and put an end to it. He was arrested and a case of sedition filed against him. On 13 July, when people in large number had gathered outside the Central Jail Srinagar where hearing of the case was scheduled, the police fired bullets killing 22 people. The incident ignited an organised movement against the autocratic rule of Hari Singh.
78. *Ibid.*, p. 817.
79. Abbas, Chaudhri Ghulam, *Kashmakash*, pp. 177-78.
80. *Ibid.*, p. 178.

81. Abdullah, Sheikh Mohammad, *Aatash-i-Chinar* (Second edition, 2008), p. 164.

82. Abbas, Chaudhri Ghulam, *Kashmakash*, p. 179.

83. *Ibid.*

84. Ahmad, Khalid Bashir, *Kashmir: A Walk Through History*, p. 158.

85. Khan, Ghulam Hassan, *Freedom Movement in Kashmir 1931-1940*, Gulshan Books, 2009, p. 272.

86. *The Statesman* dated 6 April 1939, *the Civil and Military Gazette*, Lahore dated 7 April 1939, and the *Weekly Aina*, Srinagar dated 21 December 1975, [Khan, *Freedom Movement in Kashmir*, p. 396].

87. Abbas, Chaudhri Ghulam, *Kashmakash*, p. 181.

88. *Ibid.*

89. Annual Administration Report of the Jammu & Kashmir State for the Samwat 1997-98 (16th Oct. 1940-15th Oct. 1941), Jammu, 1942, p. 65.

90. Sa'dat, Molvi Mohammad Shah, *Tareekh-i-Kashmir ki Rozana Dairy*, p. 817.

91. *Ibid.*, p. 819.

92. Makhdoomi, Javed, Facebook post dated July 7 at 12:05 AM.

93. Abdullah, Sheikh Mohammad, *Aatash-e-Chinar* (Gulshan Books, 2008) p. 174.

94. *Ibid.*, p. 650.

95. Ahmad, Khalid Bashir, *Kashmir: Exposing the Myth Behind the Narrative*, p. 154.

96. File No. 88, Subject: The Desh Sewak case, Chief Secretariat, Publicity Branch, His Highness' Government, Jammu & Kashmir, Archives Repository Jammu.

97. *Shabistan*, *Sheikh Abdullah: Dost ya Dushman*, Special publication, January 1968.

98. Sa'dat, Molvi Mohammad Shah, *Tareekh-i-Kashmir ki Rozana Dairy*, pp. 820-21.

99. *Ibid.*, p. 823.

100. Dar, Mohammad Yusuf, *Jawaharlal Nehru and Kashmir*, Mainstream Weekly, Vol. LI, No. 35, August 17, 2013.

101. Others who attended the meeting and issued a signed statement with regard to the revival of the Muslim Conference include Sardar Fateh Mohammad Khan, Mirza Attaullah Khan, Qazi Abdul Gani Delinah, Pir Zia-ud-Din, Babu Mohammad Abdullah, Chaudhri

Abdul Karim, M.I. Saghar, Ghulam Haider Gauri and Syed Mirak Shah [Saraf, p. 554].

102. Qayoom, Shabnam, *Kashmir ka Siyasi Inquilab*, Vol. 2, p. 39.

103. Saraf, Muhammad Yusuf, *Kashmiris Fight for Freedom*, Vol. 1, pp. 553-54.

104. *Ibid.*, p. 553.

105. Ayyangar was a civil servant from the Madras Civil Service who served as Prime Minister of Kashmir from 1937 to 1943. Later, he became a minister in the first cabinet of Jawahar Lal Nehru and held different portfolios including defence.

106. Weekly *Chand*, Jammu, 20 January 1942.

107. Abbas, Chaudhri Ghulam, *Kashmakash*, p. 83.

108. *Ibid.*

109. Abdullah, Sheikh Mohammad, *Aatash-e-Chinar* (Gulshan Books, 2008), p. 234.

110. Sa'dat, Molvi Mohammad Shah, *Tareekh-i-Kashmir ki Rozana Dairy*, pp. 825-26.

111. Ishaq, Munshi Mohammad, *Nida-e-Haq*, p. 133.

112. *Ibid.* [The Muslim Conference leader, Mohammad Yusuf Qureshi, privy to this development, had shared the information with Munshi Mohammad Ishaq who has transferred it to his book, *Nida-e-Haq*.]

113. *Ibid.*

114. Shabistan, *Sheikh Abdullah: Dost ya Dushman*, Special publication, January 1968, p. 138.

115. *Aatash-i-Chinar*, (Gulshan Books, 2008), p. 220.

116. *Ibid.*

117. Sethi, Krishen Dev, *Yaad-i-Rafta*, p. 16.

118. Qayoom, Shabnam, *Kashmir ka Siyasi Inquilab*, Vol. II, p. 114.

119. *Ibid.*, p. 115.

120. Sa'dat, Molvi Mohammad Shah, *Tareekh-i-Kashmir ki Rozana Dairy*, pp. 778-79.

121. Saraf, Muhammad Yusuf, *Kashmiris Fight for Freedom*, Vol. 1, p. 491.

122. Taseer, Rashid, *Tehreek-i-Hurriyat-i-Kashmir*, Vol. 3, p. 213.

123. Qayoom, Shabnam, *Kashmir ka Siyasi Inquilab*, Vol. II, p. 53.

124. *Ibid.*, pp. 54-55.

125. Written complaint No. 1321 dated 6-4-1943 addressed to the Governor, Kashmir Province by Mohammad Yusuf Khan, General Secretary, Muslim Conference, Srinagar, File No. 7, Year 2000

[Samwat], Subject: Complaints made by the Muslim Conference against the National Conference, Office of the District Magistrate Kashmir, Archives Repository Kashmir.

126. Written complaint No. 1742 dated 6-4-1943 addressed to the Governor, Kashmir Province by Anjuman Darsul Islam, Reshi Mohalla, Srinagar, File No. 7, Year 2000 [Samwat], Subject: Complaints made by the Muslim Conference against the National Conference, Office of the District Magistrate Kashmir, Archives Repository Kashmir. [The attackers were identified as Aziz Kumsuru, Nabir Gada and Nunda Gada.]

127. Letter of Mohammad Yusuf Khan, Secretary Anjuman Darsul Islam, addressed to the Governor, Kashmir Province dated 17 April 1943. File No. 7, Year 2000 [Samwat], Subject: Complaints made by the Muslim Conference against the National Conference, Office of the District Magistrate Kashmir, Archives Repository Kashmir.

128. Application of Jabbar Khan son of Sidiq Khan, resident of Khoja Yarbal, Srinagar, dated 9-4-1943. The alleged attackers included Ahmad Shah Tramboo of Anzmar, Khanyar accompanied by a police constable, Shamsuddin, File No. 7, Year 2000 [Samwat], Subject: Complaints made by the Muslim Conference against the National Conference, Office of the District Magistrate Kashmir, Archives Repository Kashmir. The owner of the house alleged that one Kashmiri Pandit, an employee of the Srinagar Municipality, accompanied by Ghulam Ahmad Baqal, President National Conference Halqa Committee, Rainawari, policeman Shamsuddin, Jabbar Bhat, Kabir Zargar, Sona Bhat and Mohammad Shaban Darzi intimidated and threatened him and demanded from him to pull down the Muslim Conference flag assuring that the National Conference will make good the loss suffered by the building. The owner of the building was accused of having constructed the house without permission from the Municipality which allegation he denied. The police vide Assistant Superintendent of Police City's letter No. 405/C dated 6-5-1943 also confirmed that the building was an existing one which had only been repaired.

129. Letter No. 1354 dated 16-4-1943 addressed to the Governor Kashmir Province by General Secretary, All J&K Muslim Conference, Srinagar, File No. 7, Year 2000 [Samwat], Subject: Complaints made by the Muslim Conference against the National Conference, Office of the District Magistrate Kashmir, Archives Repository Kashmir.

130. Other assaulters identified in a written complaint made by Ali Mohammad, President Muslim Conference, Halqa Committee Maharaj Bazar include Ghulam Mohammad Darzi son of Mam Joo Darzi of Goni Khann, Ghulam Mohammad Control of Goni

Khann, Amma alias Dala of Tankipora, Ghulam Mohammad Khan alias Tunda of Goni Khann, Ghulam Mohammad Wani son of Qadir Wani of Goni Khann and Ghulam Mohammad Driver son of Noor Mohammad of Goni Khann. A case was filed against the seven persons under Section 107 Cr.P.C. and challaned to the court of First Additional Munsiff; File No. 7, Year 2000 [Samwat], Subject: Complaints made by the Muslim Conference against the National Conference, Office of the District Magistrate Kashmir, Archives Repository Kashmir.

131. In its report vide letter No. 406/C dated 6 May 1943, the police downplayed the incident describing it as a fracas between the two parties in which "4 Muslim Conferencites received some injuries which were opined by the Medical Officer to be simple and to have been caused by a blunt weapon". File No. 7, Year 2000 [Samwat], Subject: Complaints made by the Muslim Conference against the National Conference, Office of the District Magistrate Kashmir, Archives Repository Kashmir.

132. File No. 7, Year 2000 [Samwat], Subject: Complaints made by the Muslim Conference against the National Conference, Office of the District Magistrate Kashmir, Archives Repository Kashmir.

133. *Ibid.*

134. Ahmad, Khalid Bashir, *Kashmir: Exposing the Myth Behind the Narrative*, pp. 166-67.

135. Qayoom, Shabnam, *Kashmir ka Siyasi Inquilab*, Vol. II, p. 55. Earlier, on 8 September 1933, Bakhshi Ghulam Mohammad had been beaten to pulp at Genz Khod and, as a result, lost his consciousness. To avoid embarrassment, he later came up with an explanation that he had fainted due to getting caught up in a swell of people at a narrow place and that nobody had beaten him up. [Sa'dat, Molvi Mohammad Shah, *Tareekh-i-Kashmir ki Rozana Dairy*, p. 753.]

136. Qayoom, Shabnam, *Kashmir ka Siyasi Inquilab*, Vol. II, p. 57.

137. *Ibid.*, p. 59.

138. Ishaq, Munshi Mohammad Ishaq, *Nida-e-Haq*, p. 135.

139. *Ibid.*, p. 97.

140. *Ibid.*, pp. 97-98.

141. *Ibid.*, p. 99.

142. *Ibid.*

143. Abstract of newspapers in vernacular, 10 June 1947, File No. PR-NK/6, Year 1946-48, Subject: Noor from the jail, State Archives Repository, Jammu.

144. Ishaq, Munshi Mohammad, *Nida-e-Haq*, p. 251.

145. Abstract of newspapers in vernacular, 10 June 1947, File No. PR-NK/6, Year 1946-48, Subject: Noor from the jail, State Archives Repository, Jammu.

146. Taseer, Rashid, *Tehreek-i-Hurriyat-i-Kashmir*, Vol. 3, p. 192.

147. Rashid Taseer quotes a local politician and later Abdullah's cabinet colleague, Sham Lal Saraf, as disclosing that Dr. Khan Sahib, the Red Shirt nationalist leader and brother of Abdul Gaffar Khan, came to Kashmir for a secret meeting with Hari Singh to know his views on Jammu & Kashmir's accession to India as the Khan Brothers and other nationalist leaders from the Frontier Province thought that in case the Maharaja acceded to India it will also provide them access through Abbottabad and Muzaffarabad to follow the suit. Dr. Khan had quite a few times earlier also met Hari Singh at Bombay with the same purpose. [*Tehreek-i-Hurriyat-i-Kashmir*, Vol. 3, p. 222].

148. Taseer, Rashid, *Tehreek-i-Hurriyat-i-Kashmir*, Vol. 3, p. 212.

149. The protest was organized by Muhammad Yusuf Saraf, a student leader who later rose to the position of Chief Justice of the High Court of Pakistan Administered Jammu & Kashmir.

150. Taseer, Rashid, *Tehreek-i-Hurriyat-i-Kashmir*, Vol. 3, p. 217. Ishaq (*Nida-e-Haq*, p. 154) writes that at Chhatabal when some Muslim Conference supporters raised pro Pakistan and pro Quad-i-Azam slogans, Gandhi responded by repeating these slogans.

151. *Ibid.*, p. 218. Taseer quotes journalist Mir Abdul Aziz who was present in the meeting and wrote about it in his weekly *Insaf* on 24 November 1981.

152. *Ibid.*, 221.

153. Mahajan was later appointed Chief Justice of the Supreme Court of India.

154. *Nehru-Patel: Agreement within Differences*, Select Documents and Correspondences 1933-1950, ed. Neerja Singh, p. 135.

155. *Ibid.*, p. 140.

156. Taseer, Rashid, *Tehreek-i-Hurriyat-i-Kashmir*, Vol. 3, p. 228.

157. *Ibid.*, p. 395.

158. *Ibid.*, pp. 245-46.

A LOYAL REBEL

159. Hari Singh's letter to President Rajendra Prasad written from Poona (now Pune) on 16/17 August 1952; *Maharaja Hari Singh: The Troubled Years*, Harbans Singh, p. 300. The letter can be also accessed @ https://cbkwgl.wordpress.com//?s=acted+all+throughout+from+September+1947+under+the+advice+of+the+Government+of+India&search=Go

160. Abdullah, Sheikh Mohammad, *Aatash-i-Chinar*, [Second Edition 2008, Gulshan Books], p. 307.
161. Maharaja Hari Singh's Order No. 176-11/47 dated 30 October 1947.
162. The document of oath signed by Abdullah and submitted to and countersigned by Ghose, is now part of archive on Kashmir's turbulent history.
163. Hari Singh's letter to President Rajendra Prasad written on 16/17 August 1952; *Maharaja Hari Singh: The Troubled Years*, Harbans Singh, p. 303.
164. Abdullah, Sheikh Mohammad, *Aatash-i-Chinar*, [Second Edition 2008, Gulshan Books], p. 307.
165. Hari Singh's letter to President Rajendra Prasad written on 16/17 August 1952; *Maharaja Hari Singh: The Troubled Years*, Harbans Singh, p. 305.
166. Temporary headquarter of the United Nations from 1946 to 1951.
167. Hari Singh's letter to President Rajendra Prasad written on 16/17 August 1952; *Maharaja Hari Singh: The Troubled Years*, Harbans Singh, p. 306.
168. *Ibid.*
169. Press Communiqué, 17th March 1948, The Jammu & Kashmir Government Gazette, 13th Chet 2004, p. 232.
170. *Ibid.*
171. Hari Singh's letter to President Rajendra Prasad written on 16/17 August 1952; *Maharaja Hari Singh: The Troubled Years*, Harbans Singh, p. 318.
172. *Ibid.*, pp. 318-19.

THE PLEBISCITE RUSE

173. Resolution adopted at the meeting of the United Nations Commission for India and Pakistan on 5 January, 1949. (Document No. 5/1196 para. 15, dated the 10th January 1949).
174. Hari Singh's letter to President Rajendra Prasad written on 16/17 August 1952; *Maharaja Hari Singh: The Troubled Years*, Harbans Singh, p. 299.
175. *Ibid.*
176. *Ibid.*
177. *Ibid.* According to the Census of 1941, the population of Hindus and Sikhs of Jammu Province was 4,22,299. Compared to this, Muslims of the Province numbered 5,85,358. The total population of Ladakh district (Leh, Kargil and Skardu) was 98,007 which included 77,925 Muslims. As regards Kashmir Province (including

Muzaffarabad), the population of Hindus and Sikhs accounted for 62,919. The population of Muslims of the Province was 8,71,499. So, if we go by Hari Singh's account, out of a total population of 40,21,616 of Jammu & Kashmir, 520,306 (12.93%) were "for affiliation with or Accession to India" while the rest were either for accession to Pakistan or wanted to decide the question independently.

178. File No. P.179, Subject: Kashmir Question in the Security Council-Miscellaneous correspondence between Sheikh Mohammad Abdullah, Government of India, Paris Delegation and others, Year 1949-53, Archives Repository Kashmir.
179. Mullik, B.N. *My Years with Nehru: Kashmir*, p. 185.
180. *Ibid.*, pp. 185-86.
181. *Ibid.*, p. 186.
182. File No. 58/CU/DK/64, *Fortnightly Diary, District Magistrate Anantnag,* Office of the Divisional Commissioner, Kashmir, Year 1964, Archives Repository Kashmir.
183. *Ibid.*
184. Puri, Balraj, How the Indira-Abdullah Accord was Signed in 1974, *Mainstream Weekly*, Vol. L, No. 17, April 14, 2012.
185. Abdullah, Sheikh Mohammad, *Aatash-i-Chinar*, [Second Edition 2008, Gulshan Books], p. 349.
186. M.C. Chagla's address to the Security Council on 5 February 1964, Foreign Affairs Record, *Pakistan*, Volume X, No. 1, January 1964. Abdullah's observation had invited an uncharitable comment against him by Pakistan Prime Minister, Liaquat Ali Khan, who dubbed the Kashmir leader as a "quisling" and "an agent of the Congress for many years."
187. Letter of D.P. Dhar to Sheikh Mohammad Abdullah dated New Delhi, August 18, 1952, File No. P.179, Subject: Kashmir Question in the Security Council—Miscellaneous correspondence between Sheikh Mohammad Abdullah, Government of India, Paris Delegation and others, Year 1949-53, Archives Repository Kashmir.
188. *Ibid.*
189. Munshi, Mohammad Ishaq, *Nida-e-Haq*, p. 229.
190. *Ibid.*
191. Telegram of Abul Qasim Kashani, Chairman of the Parliament of Iran, to Prime Minister of India, Jawaharlal Nehru dated 31 July 1951, File No. P.179, Subject: Kashmir Question in the Security Council—Miscellaneous correspondence between Sheikh Mohammad Abdullah, Government of India, Paris Delegation and others, Year 1949-53, Archives Repository Kashmir.

192. Telegram of Abul Qasim Kashani, Chairman of the Parliament of Iran, to Sheikh Mohammad Abdullah dated 31 July 1951, File No. P.179, Subject: Kashmir Question in the Security Council—Miscellaneous correspondence between Sheikh Mohammad Abdullah, Government of India, Paris Delegation and others, Year 1949-53, Archives Repository Kashmir.
193. *Ibid.*
194. Letter of Sheikh Mohammad Abdullah, Prime Minister of Jammu & Kashmir to Abul Qasim Kashani, Chairman of the Parliament of Iran vide No. 35/51/PRS dated 15 August 1951, File No. P.179, Subject: Kashmir Question in the Security Council—Miscellaneous correspondence between Sheikh Mohammad Abdullah, Government of India, Paris Delegation and others, Year 1949-53, Archives Repository Kashmir.
195. Letter of Sheikh Mohammad Abdullah to G.S. Bajpai, Secretary General, Ministry of External Affairs, New Delhi dated 30 October 1951, File No. P.179, Subject: Kashmir Question in the Security Council—Miscellaneous correspondence between Sheikh Mohammad Abdullah, Government of India, Paris Delegation and others, Year 1949-53, Archives Repository Kashmir.
196. *Ibid.*
197. *Ibid.*
198. Abdullah, Sheikh Mohammad, *Aatash-i-Chinar*, [Second Edition 2008, Gulshan Books], p. 390.
199. *Ibid.*
200. Letter of R.C. Raina to D.P. Dhar written from Jammu Tawi on 19 January 1952, File No. P.179, Subject: Kashmir Question in the Security Council—Miscellaneous correspondence between Sheikh Mohammad Abdullah, Government of India, Paris Delegation and others, Year 1949-53, Archives Repository Kashmir.
201. Abdullah, Sheikh Mohammad, *Aatash-i-Chinar*, [Second Edition 2008, Gulshan Books], p. 468.
202. *Ibid.*, pp. 467-68.
203. Hassan, Munshi Ghulam Hassan in his foreword for his father's memoir, *Nida-e-Haq*, p. 20.
204. Ishaq, Munshi Mohammad, *Nida-e-Haq*, pp. 349-50.
205. *Ibid.*, p. 350.
206. *Ibid.*, p. 361.
207. Abdullah, Sheikh Mohammad, *Aatash-i-Chinar*, [Second Edition 2008, Gulshan Books], p. 692.

208. In 1939, Abdullah had converted the Jammu & Kashmir Muslim Conference, the representative political party of the majority Muslim population, into the Jammu & Kashmir National Conference and opened its doors for other minorities of the State.
209. Abdullah, Sheikh Mohammad, *Aatash-i-Chinar*, [Second Edition 2008, Gulshan Books], pp. 360-61.
210. Ishaq, Munshi Mohammad, *Nida-e-Haq*, p. 361.
211. *Ibid.*
212. *Ibid.*
213. *Ibid.*
214. *Ibid.*
215. *Ibid.*, p. 362.
216. *Ibid.*, pp. 362-63.
217. Hassan, Munshi Ghulam, Foreword to *Nida-e-Haq*, p. 16. The resolution was opposed by Sheikh Mohammad Ibrahim Bhaderwahi, Maulana Ghulam Rasool and Malik Mohiuddin. Munshi Mohammad Ishaq did not attend the meeting. Those who spoke in favour of the resolution included Ghulam Nabi Kochak, Attaullah Suharwardy and Ghulam Mohiuddin Hamdani.
218. *Ibid.*
219. Shah, G.M., Ban on Jammu & Kashmir Plebiscite Front: Proceedings of the Unlawful Activities (Prevention) Tribunal, p. 31.
220. *Ibid.*, p. 163.
221. Ishaq, Munshi Mohammad, *Nida-e-Haq*, p. 388.
222. *Ibid.*
223. *Ibid.*, p. 389.
224. *Greater Kashmir*, 9 August 2010.
225. As told by Mandloo to the author.

A LETTER TO NEW YORK

226. Abdullah, Sheikh Mohammad, *Kashmir: Appeal to World Conscience*, p. 6. Text of the speech printed and published by the Principal Public Relations Officer, Government of Jammu & Kashmir.
227. The *Khidmat*, 2 October 1948.
228. Abdullah, Sheikh Mohammad, *Aatash-i-Chinar*, [Second Edition 2008, Gulshan Books], p. 451.
229. Letter of Sheikh Mohammad Abdullah addressed to D.P. Dhar dated 31 January 1950, File No. P.179, Subject: Kashmir Question in the Security Council—Miscellaneous correspondence between Sheikh

Mohammad Abdullah, Government of India, Paris Delegation and others, Year 1949-53, Archives Repository Kashmir.

230. *Ibid.*

231. *Ibid.*

232. *Ibid.*

233. *Ibid.*

234. *Ibid.*

235. *Ibid.*

236. *Ibid.*

237. *Ibid.* Begum Abdullah is not mentioned in the gift list.

238. *Ibid.*

239. *Ibid.*

240. Abdullah, Sheikh Mohammad, *Aatash-i-Chinar*, [Second Edition 2008, Gulshan Books], p. 343.

241. Letter of R.C. Raina, Private Secretary to Prime Minister of Jammu & Kashmir to D.P. Dhar, then in Paris, dated 19 January 1952, File No. P.179, Subject: Kashmir Question in the Security Council—Miscellaneous correspondence between Sheikh Mohammad Abdullah, Government of India, Paris Delegation and others, Year 1949-53, Archives Repository Kashmir.

242. *Ibid.*

243. Letter of the Deputy Secretary to the Government of India, Ministry of External Affairs, New Delhi to the Accountant General, Central Revenues, New Delhi vide No. F-14 (43)-EII/51 dated 24 January 1952, File No. P.179, Subject: Kashmir Question in the Security Council—Miscellaneous correspondence between Sheikh Mohammad Abdullah, Government of India, Paris Delegation and others, Year 1949-53, Archives Repository Kashmir.

TALE OF A MAMMOTH LOSS

244. *Himalayan Mail*, 4 April 2007.

245. Greater Kashmir, 10 June 2011.

246. Letter of the Public Information Officer, Jammu University No. PIO-II/JU/17/2807 dated 04/12/2017.

247. Government Order No. 1369-GAD of 2018 dated 11-9-2018. The Order reads: "Sanction is hereby accorded to the constitution of a committee, comprising the following, to suggest necessary measures for safety and preservation of Elephas nomadicus fossil discovered on 30th August 2000 at Galandar, Pampore and presently lying at Jammu University:

1. Director Archives, Archaeology & Museums, J&K, Chairman; 2. Professor G.M. Bhat, Department of Geology, Jammu University, Member; 3. Dr. Mohammad Ajmal Shah, Assistant Professor-cum-Curator, Center of Central Asian Studies, University of Kashmir, Member; 4. Abdul Majid Bhat, Retired Geologist/Civil Servant (Head Center for Himalayan Geology/Environment Protection Group, Kashmir, Member.

Mr. Mushtaq Ahmad Beigh, I/C Assistant Director, Archives, Archaeology and Museums, J&K shall assist the committee.

The terms of reference of the committee shall be as under: (a) Safety and preservation of the discovered fossil (Elphas nomadicus) (b) To ascertain the age of the fossil based on paleontological and archaeological studies (c) Outcome/response of the international labs/bodies on the samples of pre-historic stone tools, found with the fossil, sent by Jammu University (d) since Kashmir Triassic Park (Permian Triassic Era) at Guryul Ravine, Khonmoh, is coming up, relevance of the discovered fossil and stone tools as regards exhibition and preservation.

The committee shall be serviced by the Directorate of Archives, Archaeology & Museums and shall submit its recommendations by 15-10-2018.

By order of the Government of Jammu & Kahsmir."

248. This author took up the matter with the government through an open letter to the Advisor to Governor, Department of Culture, pointing out the folly in the impugned order and the urgent need to recover the stolen fossil but, sadly, it did not ruffle any feathers. The letter was not even acknowledged. The letter e-mailed to Advisor (G), Department of Culture at advisorjkganai@gmail.com on 17 September 2018 and shared on Facebook on 19 September 2018 is reproduced here:

An Open Letter to Advisor (G), Department of Culture

Mr. Khurshid Ahmad Ganai
The Advisor (G),
Department of Culture,
Government of Jammu & Kashmir,
Civil Secretariat, Srinagar.
Dear Mr. Ganai

I am writing this mail in the backdrop of the Government Order No. 1369-GAD of 2018 dated 11-9-2018 (copy attached) with regard to the fossil elephant discovered at Pampore in the year 2000, to express shock and anguish over the insensitivity and thoughtlessness that this order reflects. There cannot be any other instance as brazen as this where a government has literally handed over the custody of a stolen treasure to the thief himself.

It is an old adage that when governments want to obfuscate an issue they hand it over to a committee. Indeed that is precisely what the current J&K Government appears to have done about the theft of the fossil elephant from its discovery site in Kashmir. It has constituted a committee, apparently after public and media uproar for the return of the fossil. However, completely ignoring the basic demand of return of the fossil and rather than mandating the Committee to identify the people involved in the brazen heist and recommend action against them, the Committee has been asked to suggest measures for the safety of the fossil and identify its age. This is a clear sign that the government does not intend to attend to the basic issue—return of the fossil and punishment to the culprits.

The composition of the Committee is beyond belief; it is in fact very offensive to both public sentiment and demands of legal morality. The 5-member Committee includes the alleged mastermind and implementer of the fossil heist. Rather than hauling him to face criminal charges the government has bizarrely honored him with the membership of the Committee. How could he be asked to decide about the property he is alleged to have stolen? Moreover, it is common sense that his presence on the Committee would hamper efforts of bringing back the fossil to Kashmir. Over the years, he is on record to have tried every manner to justify the criminal act of stealing the fossil from Kashmir, depositing it with the Jammu University and, against all internationally accepted norms, retaining it there, illegally.

Ordinarily what was expected of the government was to, on priority basis, first order return of the fossil, and other discovered archaeological items, to its place of discovery (Kashmir) in accordance with law and international norms, and simultaneously, though belatedly, file an FIR with the concerned police station about the theft for initiating due process against the culprit(s) and partners in the crime. The preservation, determination of the age of the fossil, outcome/response of the international labs/bodies on the samples, etc. as included in the terms of reference for the Committee, could follow.

With due respects to their persons and professional experience, there is a serious doubt about the ability and expertise of the members of the Committee to determine the age of the fossil. None of them, I fear, is a vertebrate paleontologist. It is no less than a joke to ask them to determine the age of the fossil which involves highly technical and sophisticated science, when the University of Jammu with one of the oldest PG Departments of Geology in India and one of the Members of the above referred to committee on its staff, has not been able to do it for the last 11 years. What would be the worth of the finding of this committee whose supposed 'only expert' among its members [Dr. G.M. Bhat], in a bizarre and unprofessional manner and without conducting any investigation, declared at the excavation site itself the find as "a 50,000 year old mammoth fossil" [The Asian Age, 29 November 2000] and 'the largest ever found in the world" [The Reuters, 6 September 2000]. He reportedly also made unsubstantiated claim of striking oil, gas and coal from the site if enough money was made available to him, apart from 'misbehaving with media persons at the excavation site' [The Asian Age, 29 November 2001]. What good does the government expect from such an unprofessional 'expert'?

I do not know if you have gone through the elaborate write-ups published by newspapers here on the discovery of the fossil, its theft and the alleged criminal connivance by the Jammu University in its illegal removal from the site of discovery, and equally criminal negligence and lack of will displayed by the Kashmir University to bring back the stolen property. I hope and urge that you find time to go through the write ups (here, here, here) to appreciate the seriousness of the issue and how badly the government has addressed it.

In the meanwhile, I find it worthwhile to broadly rewind here the sequence of events leading from the discovery of the fossil to its theft to help you recognize the folly of the government's action.

Two teachers of the Department of Geology, Degree College Sopore initially located the outline of the fossil at an earth excavation spot at Galander. One of them, Dr. Abdul Majid Dar, happened to be the former research student of Prof. G.M. Bhat at Jammu University. At the time Dr. Bhat was on lien from Jammu University and had joined as Reader only a few months earlier the new Department of Geology & Geophysics (since re-christened Department of Earth Sciences) at the University of Kashmir. Dr. Dar contacted Dr. Bhat to seek help which in due course of time led to the excavation and extraction of the fossil as well as some stone implements of archaeological significance. The whole excavation process as well as securing the fossil from any damage from elements (through creating a tin housing until it was shifted to a well-designed and designate place in the University campus) was funded by the University of Kashmir. For whatever reasons, the fossil was not shifted from the site of discovery to the University of Kashmir or the State Museum and one day in 2007 the news broke out that it had been stolen from the site and taken to the University of Jammu.

While the theft of the fossil and other stone implements caused uproar in Kashmir, Dr. G.M. Bhat who is now the member of the just constituted Government Committee, was reported by the media bragging about illegally taking away the fossil from Galandar and installing it in the University of Jammu. He was even quoted challenging a reporter to go to the court, if he must, against him. The shameful manner in which the University of Jammu financed and assisted stealing of the fossil also was highlighted by the media. The matter was agitated in the State Legislature also and reportedly the former Governor had taken a serious note of and called for a report on the matter. The matter rests there. The University of Jammu has not returned the fossil despite assurances by its Vice Chancellor to this effect and the University of Kashmir has failed to get it back irrespective of its commitment on record. As you would appreciate from the history of the case, the foremost important thing for the government to do is to restore the stolen fossil to where it belongs (Kashmir), place the responsibility of the theft and proceed under law against the culprit(s). The preservation and identification of the fossil and other archaeological items would follow. Handing the matter over to the accused amounts to granting infinity to the illegal holding back of the fossil by the University of Jammu, besides mocking at law and justice.

As regards relevance of the fossil and other finds from Galandar with the Triassic Fossil Park 'coming up' at Guryul Ravine, Khonmoh, it is premature. The proposed Park is only at the conceptual stage, save a chain-link fencing of an identified piece of land.

Having said that, I hope you would take a fresh look at the matter and take immediate, urgent and appropriate steps to, first, recover the fossil from the University of Jammu and, later, ensure its identification through a team of experts, and installation at a relevant and secured place in Kashmir.

In the end, I am tempted to recall an incident of similar nature and how differently the government of the time reacted. In 1931, an elephant tusk and bones were excavated from the same area at Pampore by Dr. de Terra, then research associate at the Carnegie Institution of Washington. On his return, he took the mammoth with him and installed it in New Haven. When Maharaja Hari Singh came to know about it, he ordered its immediate return and, believe you me, Dr. de Terra had no option but to bring it back.

With regards,
Khalid Bashir Ahmad

249. *The New Yorker*, 10 May 1947, p. 22.

250. *Ibid.*

251. *Times of India*, 10 December 1935.

252. File No. N-127/15, Year 1917, Chief Secretariat, Political Department, Archives Repository, Jammu.
253. The Afghans, the Sikhs and the Dogras ruled Kashmir from AD 1747 to 1819, 1819 to 1846 and 1846 to 1947, respectively.
254. File No. N-127/15, Year 1917, Chief Secretariat, Political Department, Archives Repository, Jammu.
255. *Ibid.*
256. *Ibid.*
257. Report submitted by Chief Secretary, Jammu & Kashmir before the J&K High Court in compliance to its order dated 5 June 2013.
258. Deputy Superintending Archaeological Engineer (CPIO), ASI, Srinagar Circle's letter No. 8/196/2017-M-3141 dated 20 December 2017 in response to an RTI application by KB Ahmad.
259. As told to the author on phone on 30 November 2017.
260. Order No. ALM-184-ADL-1/80 dated 25-8-1980.
261. *Greater Kashmir*, 6 June 2007.
262. As told to the author in a telephonic interview on 27 November 2017.
263. Report submitted by Chief Secretary, Jammu & Kashmir before the J&K High Court in compliance to its order dated 5 June 2013.
264. *Ibid.*
265. *The Tribune*, 22 June 2016 http://www.tribuneindia.com/news/jammu-kashmir/community/govt-has-no-record-of-artefacts-stolen-during-militancy-years/255050 [accessed on 4 August 2020.]
266. *Indian Express*, 7 October 2015 http://indianexpress.com/article/india/india-news-india/angela-merkel-returns-indias-stolen-10th-century-durga-idol-to-narendra-modi/ [accessed on 4 August 2020.]
267. Banday, Dr. Ajaz Ahmad in a telephonic interview on 26 November 2017.
268. Deputy Superintending Archaeological Engineer (CPIO), ASI, Srinagar Circle's letter No. 8/196/2017-M-3141 dated 20 December 2017 in response to an RTI application by this author.
269. *Greater Kashmir*, 19 April 2007.
270. Deputy Superintending Archaeological Engineer (CPIO), ASI, Srinagar Circle's letter No. 8/196/2017-M-3141 dated 20 December 2017 in response to an RTI application by KB Ahmad.
271. In an interview over phone on 18 December 2017.
272. Taing, Mohammad Yusuf, *Heun Tsang*, Soan Adab, Tawareekh Naveesi Number-4, (1087), J&K Academy of Art, Culture & Languages, pp. 56-80.

273. Kennedy, Dane Keith, *Reinterpreting Exploration: The West in the World,* p. 202.

274. Kaw, M.K., *Kashmir and Its People: Studies in the Evolution of Kashmir Society*, p. 268. Sharda script is an ancient abugida writing system of the Brahmic family which was widespread between the 8th and 12th centuries in Kashmir.

275. Author and scholar, Prof. Shafi Shouq, however, believes that European scholars have preserved this intellectual wealth by using these to write thousands of systematically analyzed books published from London and other parts of the world.

276. *Kashmir Times*, Jammu, 3 May 1999.

277. Taing, Mohammad Yusuf, *Kashmir Qalam*, p. 302.

278. *Ibid.*, p. 303.

279. The South Asian Life & Times (SALT), Summer 2015 (April-June) [http://www.the-south-asian.com/aug2004/Gilgit_manuscript.htm]

280. Dayak, Manzoor Ahmad, *Gilgit Musawwadaat- Kitni Haqeeqat Kitana Afsana*, Sheeraza (Urdu), Vol. 45, No. 8-11, J&K Academy of Art, Culture & Languages, pp. 124-25.

281. *Ibid.*, p. 123.

282. *Ibid.*, p. 124.

283. Sheeraza (Urdu), Mohammad Yusuf Taing Number, Vol. 49, No. 4-7, J&K Academy of Art, Culture & Languages, p. 162.

284. Press Note dated 2 March 1948 issued by the Kashmir Bureau of Information, Government of Jammu & Kashmir.

285. Randhawa Committee Report on the Reorganization of Libraries, Research & Museums for the Government of Jammu & Kashmir (1976), p. 17.

286. In a telephonic interview on 15 December 2017.

287. Ganjoo, T.N., *Bilhana, Mashaheer Number*, Hamara Adab (Academy), p. 263.

288. *Biography of Hazrat Shaikh Yaqub Sarfi*, [www.mohrasharif.com/index.php/al-qasim-library/biography/sufis/613-biography-of-hazrat-shaikh-yaqub-sarfi]

289. Buhler, Georg, *Detailed Report of a Tour in Search of Sanskrit MSS Made in Kashmir, Rajputana and Central India*, Journal of the Bombay Branch of Royal Asiatic Society, (1877), p. 27.

290. *Ibid.*, pp. 27-28.

291. Koul, Mohan Lal, *Kashmir: Wail of a Valley*. [http://ikashmir.net/wailvalley/b2chap11.html]

292. Report on Conservation of Collection affected by Flood of Jammu & Kashmir Academy of Art, Culture and Languages, Srinagar,

National Research Laboratory for Conservation of Cultural Property, Lucknow.

293. *Ibid.*

294. *Ibid.*

295. *Ibid.*

296. *Ibid.*

297. Jain, R.C. and Savita, R.P., *Report of visit to SPS Museum, Srinagar*, (From 8th October, 2014 to 10th October, 2014).

298. *Ibid.*

299. In an interview with the author over phone on 7 December 2017.

THE CELLULOID YEARS

300. In a telephonic conversation with the author on 15 December 2017.

301. Letter No. PR. 881/B dated 21 September 1940, Chief Secretariat (Publicity Department), Archives Repository Jammu.

302. File No. 674, Governor of Kashmir, *Grant of land to S.L. Nanda for cinema purposes*, Year 1926, Archives Repository Kashmir.

303. Programme of films screened in the Kashmir Talkies Srinagar, File No. PR/5/A, Year 1947, Publicity Department, Archives Repository Jammu.

304. *Ibid.*

305. *Greater Kashmir*, 19 April 1917.

306. Annual Administration Report of the Jammu & Kashmir State for the Samvat 1997-98 (16th Oct. 1940-15th Oct. 1941) [Published 1942], p. 5.

307. Note dated 3 July 1936 signed by Hira Singh, Prime Minister's Office, Publicity Branch, Archives Repository Jammu.

308. Telegram sent by Man Singh, Dina Nath, Gulam Mohammad, Ahmadullah, Ghulam Qadir, Govind Ram, Mahisher Nath, Sri Kant, Gopi Nath, Habibullah etc., Prime Minister's Office, Publicity Branch, Archives Repository Jammu.

309. Letter sent by the Minister-in-Waiting to the Chairman Board of Censors, Srinagar vide No. 6006 dated 25 August 1936, Prime Minister's Office, Publicity Branch, Archives Repository Jammu.

310. *The Kashmir Times*, 13 August 1935.

311. The Annual Administration A Report of the Jammu & Kashmir State for 16th Oct. 1941 to 12th April 1943 talks about another cinema hall having come up during the period under report, p. 64.

312. Report of the Commission of Inquiry constituted under SRO 39 dated 30th January 1965 issued by the Home Department, J&K

Government to inquire into certain charges of misconduct against Shri Bakhshi Ghulam Mohammad, Srinagar, June 30, 1967, p. 71; Accession No. 597/Report, Archives Repository Library, Srinagar.

313. Gate Collections in Cinemas, Information Department, File No. ID/54/56, Year 1957-58, Archives Repository Jammu.
314. *Ibid.*
315. File No. 55/CU/DK/64, *Fortnightly Diary, District Magistrate Srinagar,* Office of the Divisional Commissioner, Kashmir, Year 1964, Archives Repository Kashmir.
316. Report of the Commission of Inquiry constituted under SRO 39 dated 30th January 1965 issued by the Home Department, J&K Government to inquire into certain charges of misconduct against Shri Bakhshi Ghulam Mohammad, Srinagar, June 30, 1967, p. 183; Accession No. 597/Report, Archives Repository Library, Srinagar.
317. *Ibid.*, p. 184.
318. *Ibid.*, p. 185.
319. *Ibid.*
320. *Ibid.*, p. 189.
321. File No. 2892/PR/11 /A/ 46151, Year 1946, Archives Repository Jammu.
322. Kashmir's Palladium Cinema, BBC Radio 4, 17 July 2017, https://www.bbc.co.uk/programmes/p058gh24 [accessed on 4 August 2020].
323. *Ibid.*
324. Letter dated 5 March 1942 sent by Universal Pictures Ltd. to the Secretary Board of Censors, Jammu, Programme of films screened in Regal cinema, File No. PR/CN-23, Year 1943, Archives Repository Jammu.
325. Encyclopaedia of Hindi Cinema, ed. Gulzar, Govind Nihalani, Saibal Chatterjee, Encyclopaedia Britannica (India) Pvt. Ltd. and Popular Prakashan Pvt. Ltd., Bombay, pp. 254-55.
326. Bazaz, Prem Nath, *Daughters of the Vitasta*, p. 232.
327. Weekly *Amar*, Lahore, 31 August 1931.
328. As told to this author in an interview on 12 May 2019.
329. *The Kashmir Times*, 5 May 1936.
330. Letter of Manager, Kashmir Talkies Limited No. 4029 dated 26 November 1940 addressed to The Secretary Board of Censors, His Highness' Government, J&K, Jammu.
331. *The Kashmir Times*, 19 May 1936.

332. Monthly *Jauhar*, December 1944, Chief Secretariat, Publicity Department, File No. 386/A/54, Year 1944, Archives Repository Jammu.
333. *Ibid.*
334. *Ibid.*
335. File No. 2892/PR/11 /A/ 46151, Year 1946, Archives Repository Jammu.
336. Annual Administration Report of the Jammu & Kashmir State for the Samvat 1997-98 (16th Oct. 1940-15th Oct. 1941) [Published 1942], p. 57.
337. Order No. 1156 C of 1939 dated 17-10-1939, Chief Secretariat (General), File No. No. PR/1148/B/CN-50, Chief Secretariat, Board of Censors, Archives Repository Jammu.
338. Committee Resolution No. 135 dated 1 *Phagun* 1996 Bikrimi, Chief Secretariat (General), File No. No. PR/1148/B/CN-50, Chief Secretariat, Board of Censors, Archives Repository Jammu.
339. Annual Administration Report of the Jammu & Kashmir State for the year 1943-44, p. 6, Archives Repository Jammu.
340. Prohibition against the screening of certain cinema films, File No. CN-12, Year 1937, Chief Secretariat, Publicity Department, Archives Repository Jammu.
341. *Ibid.*
342. *Ibid.*, *Sudarshan*, Jammu, 15 August 1940.
343. Display of Film Shorts in the Cinema Halls, File No. 7/A/45/CN, Chief Secretariat, Publicity Department, Archives Repository Jammu.
344. Nazir Bakhshi in an interview with Rajesh Prohit, http://www.thecherrytree.in/2013/10/04/nazir-bakshi-part-one/ [accessed on 4 September 2019]
345. *Ibid.*
346. Manmohan Singh Gauri, in a telephonic conversation with the author on 15 December 2017.
347. Jammu and Kashmir Legislative Debates (Official Report), 6th Session, February-March 1964, Vol. VI, No. 18, Monday The 23rd March 1964, p. 75.
348. *Kashmir*, 13 March 1947.
349. *Ibid.*
350. Non-official Members of the Board, File No. PR/1148/B/CN-50, Chief Secretariat, Board of Censors, Archives Repository Jammu.

KASHMIR TO KA'BA

351. Rehman's story was narrated to the author by Jalaluddin Shah on 17 July 2018.
352. Shaifta, Nawab Mustafa Khan, *Shaifta ka Safarnama Haj*, Monthly *Qaumi Digest,* Lahore, 1997, p. 72. From Delhi, Shaifta travelled through Jaipur, Ajmer, Chitore, Baroda and Surat to arrive in Bombay and it took him two years to return to Delhi on 23 Dilqadah 1256 Hijra corresponding to 14 February 1841. The sail-ship in which he was travelling hit an underwater rock and broke up. The passengers of the ill fated ship had to take shelter in a desolated island for one month and five days before being rescued by a search boat.
353. Kashmiri, Fazil, *Tasveer-i-Haj*, 1958, p. 55.
354. File No. 418/P. N.- 24, The Prime Minister, Publicity Branch, 1936, Archives Repository, Jammu.
355. *Ibid.*
356. *Ibid.*
357. In 1975, The Mughal Line introduced another ship named Noor Jehan to ferry Haj pilgrims from Bombay to Jeddah and back. The ship remained employed till 1985 after which it went for scrap. In the meanwhile, the company also employed another ship, MV Akbar, which was latter the only ship ferrying Haj pilgrims from Bombay when in 1995 it was withdrawn due to its bad condition and sea route pilgrimage was stopped. Recently, the Government of India announced a plan to revive the sea route. A modern ship can carry about 5000 pilgrims at a time and cover the distance between Mumbai and Jeddah in two-three days only.
358. Kashmiri, Fazil, *Tasveer-i-Haj*, 1958, p. 50.
359. This author accessed the correspondence between the Governor's office and Amir Gul Khan resting in Archives Repository, Jammu.
360. Central Haj Committee, Mumbai, www.hajcommittee.gov.in/previous_records.aspx
361. Dost Mohammad's one-time neighbour in Uri, Mir Abdur Rashid has vivid recollection of this incident.
362. Official press release No. 170 dated 11 September 1956 issued by the Department of Information, Jammu & Kashmir Government.
363. The notification was issued by the Chief Secretariat, Political Department, Jammu & Kashmir Government on 13 May 1958.
364. *Ibid.*
365. Kashmiri, Fazil, *Tasveer-i-Haj*, 1958, p. 56.
366. *Ibid.*, p. 66.

367. *Ibid.*
368. *Ibid.*, p. 53.
369. *Ibid.*, p. 89.
370. *Ibid.*, p. 40.
371. *Ibid.*, p. 43.

CHANGING PLACE NAMES

372. Proposal sent vide letter No. DL/Admn-Constt/39-719 dated 10-8-2011.
373. Khayal, Ghulam Nabi, *Iqbal aur Tehrik-i-Azadi-e-Kashmir,* pp. 26-27.
374. *Sheerazah (Urdu),* 1984, Vol. 23, No. 3-4.
375. *Ibid.*
376. Kalhana's Rajatarangini (Trns. Stein), Book I, verse 341.
377. Kalhana's Rajatarangini (Urdu trns. Thakur Chand Shahpuria), Vol. I, pp. 106-07.
378. Koshur Encyclopaedia, Vol. I, p. 304.
379. Kalhana's Rajatarangini (Trns. Stein), pp. 464-67.
380. *Kashmir: A Walk Through History*, p. 218.
381. File No. 12, *Subject: Private correspondence with various European friends in India from 1905 to 1906*, His Highness English Office, Year 1905-06, Archives Repository Jammu.
382. *Kaeshir Dictionary*, Vol. 2, p. 75, Jammu & Kashmir Academy of Art, Culture & Languages, Second edition, 2011.
383. *Ibid.*, p. 177.
384. File No. Q-a/12, Governor of Kashmir, Petition of Rasul Wani of village Dodharhama for contract to supply baggage to visit Ganderbal-Sonmarg Road. On 18 January 1917, the Revenue Minister, through his letter No. A/2336, informed the Governor of Kashmir that the issue of plantation was "Not yet referred to Darbar.", Archives Repository Kashmir.
385. *A Fresh Approach to the History of Kashmir* (Akhtar Mohiuddin), p. 45.
386. Qayoom, Shabnam, *Kashmir ka Siyasi Inquilab*, Vol. 4, p. 337.

STORY OF AN UPTOWN QUARTER

387. Kalhana, Rajatarangini, Book I, Verse 341.
388. Kalhana's Rajatarangini, Vol. II, p. 290.
389. File No. 468PR/ M-180, European Residents in Kashmir, Prime Minister's Office, Year 1937, Archives Repository Jammu.

390. Farooq Khan's elder brother, Afsar Khan, also performed such stunts in other parts of Kashmir.

391. Some other known inhabitants of Sonawar include Abdul Ahad Malik, Khalil Muhammad, Major Mohammad Akbar, L.N. Dhar, Mohammad Ramzan Guroo, Jan Mir, artist S.A. Rehman, mountaineer and tourism promoter Mohammad Yusuf Chapri, footballer Mohammad Ismail Chapri, Doctors Ali Mohammad Rather, Manzoor Ahmd, Nisar Ahmad Wani, Mohammad Yususf Bhat, Mohammad Shafi Bhat and Bashir Ahmad; Engineer Ali Mohammad Mir, Professors G.M. Parray, Ghulam Ali Wani, Abdul Hamid Bhat, Bashir Ahmad Wani (Mathematics) and Bashir Ahmad Wani (Zoology); writers Umar Majid, S.M. Qamar, M.M. Sidiq and Nazir Nazar, teachers Master Ghulam Qadir, Abdul Aziz Bhat, Adil Bashir, Ghulam Mohammad Mir, Ghulam Mohammad Wani, Ghulam Mohammad Rather and Ghulam Nabi; former General Secretary, Kashmir Motor Drivers' Association, Ghulam Mohammad Bhat, geo-scientist M.I. Bhat, and civil servants Abdur Rashid Bhat, Ali Mohammad Bhat, Zafar Ahmad, Mohammad Rafi and Khalid Bashir Ahmad, the present author.

392. Kashmiri, Mulla Ahmad Bin Abdus Saboor, *Khawariqus Salikeen*, p. 529.

393. File No. A/12, Part 5/4, Applications of certain persons praying for permission to build their houses in restricted area, Year 1911-14, Ex-Governor, Archives Repository Kashmir.

394. Report of the Wine Manufactory for the year 1892-93, p. 123.

395. Annual Administration Report for the year 1913-14.

396. File No. 58/B-80, Year 1904, Chief Secretariat, Political Department, Archives Repository Jammu.

397. *Ibid.*

398. For instance, 2 acres of land were allotted on lease to R. Mukerji son of Deb Nath Mukerji at Bonamsar in 1905 through an order of the Chief Minister issued vide No. 4325 dated 2 October 1905. Likewise, in 1907, Ali Mohammad and Mohammad Bux (merchants) were allotted 51 kanals and 15 *marlas* of land, again, at Bonamsar for setting up a dairy. The order of allotment was issued on 18 March 1907. Other beneficiaries of the Government munificence between 1906 and 1908 include Aziz Din Kausa son of Khawaja Samad Shah (1 acre 7 kanals and 10 marlas), Aziz Contractor son of Mohammad Yakub (2 acres), Mohammad Sultan son of Assad Ullah Shah, merchant (2 acres), S. Ganda Singh son of Dhian Singh (2 acres 4 kanals 1 marla), M. Suraj Bal son of Dewan P. Manphul (3 kanals 13 marlas), Khan Bahadur Allah Baksh (12 kanals 6 marlas), Dr. A. Mitra son of S. Mitra (2 acres), Byramji Ratanji (2 acres), Messrs N.D. Harri Ram and

Bros. (7 kanals), Pandit Ikbal Nath Kaul (34 kanals 15 marlas) Ram Nath Chopra and Bros. (4 acres), R. Mukerji (9 kanals 12 marlas), L. Radha Kishen Seth son of Narain Das Sethi (2 acres), D. Fateh Chand (26 kanals 15 marlas), L. Har Narain (2 acres), Bhai Dayal Singh (26 kanals 12 marlas), Pandit Bhagat Ram Vaid (16 kanals), L.N. Sharma (16 kanals) and P. Amar Nath Purbi (2 acres). [Report of the Committee on Grant of Land for Building Purposes, 1915, Accession No. 1981, Archives Repository Kashmir.]

399. Acquisition of land for Parsee cemetery, File No. 151, Office of the Governor Kashmir, (also marked as Nazool Office File No. 137/N/1993-94).
400. *Greater Kashmir*, 27 August 2013.
401. File No. 187, Acquisition of land for Parsee cemetery, Ex-Governor, Archives Repository Kashmir.
402. *Ibid.*

OF PRICES AND FARES

403. Lawrence, Walter, *The Valley of Kashmir*, p. 243.
404. *Ibid.*
405. *Ibid.*
406. *Ibid.*, p. 244.
407. Bates, Charles Ellison, *The Gazetteer of Kashmir*, (Gulshan 2005), p. 88.
408. Lawrence, Walter, *The Valley of Kashmir*, p. 245.
409. Swinburne, Major T.R., *Kashmir: A Holiday in the Happy Valley*, [Reprint Gulshan 200], p. 250.
410. Report of the Administration of the Jammu & Kashmir State for the Sambat Year 1968 (1911-12), Appendix XXXVII, Archives Repository Kashmir.
411. *Ibid.*, Sambat Year 1969 (1912-13), Appendix XVIII.
412. File No. C-a/12/75, Supply of rice for Hospital use, ex-Governor, Archives Repository Kashmir.
413. Neve, Major Arthur, *The Tourist's Guide to Kashmir, Ladakh, Skardo&C*, Lahore, 1923, p. 12.
414. *Ibid.*
415. *Ibid.*
416. *Ibid.*, pp. 12-13.
417. *Ibid.*, p. 11.
418. *Ibid.*, p. 13.
419. Administration Report of Jammu & Kashmir for the year 1959-60, Archives Repository Kashmir.

420. *Travel Guide to Kashmir*, ed. G.R. Sarup, 1955, p. 104.
421. *Ibid.*, pp. 104-05.
422. *Ibid.*, p. 105.
423. A resident of Sonawar, Bhat was the father of this author. He died on 7 July 1969.
424. Till late 1960s, the Jhelum River was the main mode of transport of goods and cargo in Kashmir.
425. Al-Biruni, *India*, (ed. Qeyamuddin Ahmad), National Book Trust, India, [Reprint 2008], p. 99.
426. Stein, M.A., Kalhana's Rajatarangini, Vol. I, p. 34.
427. Drew, Frederic, The Jummoo and Kashmir Territories, p. 164.
428. Collett, John, *A Guide to Kashmir*, Calcutta, 1889, p. 185.
429. *Ibid.*
430. *Ibid.*, pp. 190-91.
431. File No. 250/BK-8, Miscellaneous Publications of the Publicity Department since 1935, Year 1936, Publicity Department, Archives Repository Jammu.
432. Kant, Shams-ud-Din, *Wounded Memories of the Tribal Attack on Kashmir* (Asad, Muhammad Saeed), [PDF, p. 28].
433. *Ibid.*
434. *Travel Guide to Kashmir*, ed. G.R. Sarup, 1955, p. 106.
435. *Ibid.*, p. 107.
436. *The Jammu & Kashmir Government Gazette*, Vol. 93, Jammu, Sat., the 17th Jan., 81/27th Pausa, 1902, No. 42-d.
437. We live in times when the government has willfully abdicated its responsibility of controlling prices except for occasionally issuing price lists of essential commodities which carry no more than archival value. Any consumer item of same quality is sold at different prices in different pockets of the city or, worse, at different shops in the same market. For an item of same quality, a departmental store will charge you much higher than a nearby grocer. To give an idea of how food items mentioned in the preceding cost today, one may quote per kilogram prices obtained from a south Srinagar city grocer. Honey sells at ₹ 750, rice (China) ₹ 30, potato ₹ 25, onion ₹ 30, mutton ₹ 440, Dalda *ghee* ₹ 120, walnut ₹ 300, poultry ₹ 120, ginger powder ₹ 600, fennel seeds ₹ 100, red chili powder ₹ 280, semolina ₹ 80, sugar ₹ 50, pepper ₹ 20 (12 gm), ginger ₹ 140, turmeric powder ₹ 230 and moong ₹ 120. A bundle of *nadru* sells at ₹ 400 and a dozen of eggs at ₹ 60. A liter of milk costs ₹ 40, curd ₹ 120, mustard oil ₹ 140 and petrol ₹ 77.96 (as on 24 November 2018). A Pashmina *dussa*

costs anything between ₹ 15,000 and ₹ 20,000. A *tola* of saffron is sold at ₹ 2,000 and gold at ₹ 31,000. A cup of coffee sells at ₹ 120 and a *masala dosa* at ₹ 150. A cubic feet of *deodar, pine and fir* is sold at ₹ 2800, ₹ 1800 and ₹ 800, respectively. A truckload of A-grade bricks (2000 pieces) costs ₹ 14,000. A quintal of walnut wood sells at ₹ 900.

While more swift, and costlier, modes of transport are available today, the per passenger bus fare for Baramulla, Sopore, Bandipore, Kupwara, Handwara, Budgam, Pulwama and Annatnag is ₹ 52, ₹ 48, ₹ 55, ₹ 87, ₹ 74, ₹ 11, ₹ 37 and ₹ 60, respectively. The per passenger to and fro bus fare between Srinagar and Muzaffarabad is about ₹ 3377 INR which includes ₹ 1560 INR between Srinagar and Kaman Post (zero point on LoC) and ₹ 1000 PKR between Kaman Post and Muzaffarabad.

ROMANCE WITH RUMOURS

438. Ashiq Hussain, *The Hindustan Times*, https://www.hindustantimes.com/india/panic-grips-kashmir-over-child-death-rumour-from-polio-drops/story-n4BYY01l0TeqthqB7EUyyJ.html [accessed on 4 August 2020].
439. Stein, M.A., *Kalhana's Rajatarangini*, Vol. II, f.n. 706-10, p. 56.
440. Lawrence, Walter, *The Valley of Kashmir*, p. 314.
441. Biscoe, Tyndale. *Kashmir in Sunlight and Shade*, p. 167.
442. *Ibid.*
443. Makhdoomi, Pir Mohammad Afzal, *Kashmir ki Tehrik-i-Azadi: Khwab, Saran aur Azab*, pp. 320-21.

SIR MOHAMMAD IQBAL: THE UNTOLD STORY

444. Kour, Ravinderjit, *Political Awakening in Kashmir*, p. 152.
445. A copy of the letter was shared with this author by Peerzada Mohammad Ashraf from his private collection.
446. Weekly *Guru Ghantal, Kashmir Number*, Lahore, 30 August 1931.
447. Ahmad, Khalid Bashir, *Kashmir: Exposing the Myh Behind the Narrative*, p. 124.
448. Daily *Siasat*, Lahore, 16 August 1931.
449. Iqbal, Javed, *Zindah Rood: Allama Iqbal ki Mukkamal Sawaneh Hayat*, p. 500.
450. *Ibid.*, pp. 500-01.
451. Letter of Advocate Amar Nath Chona to Mirza Zafar Ali Khan
452. *Ibid.*
453. Mehta, Ved, *Mamaji*, Oxford University Press, p. 238.
454. *Ibid.*, p. 240.

455. Iqbal, Javed, *Zindah Rood: Allama Iqbal ki Mukkamal Sawaneh Hayat*, p. 350.
456. *Ibid.*, p. 329.
457. *Ibid.*, p. 209.
458. File No. 12, *Subject: Private correspondence with various European friends in India from 1905 to 1906*, His Highness English Office, Year 1905-06, Archives Repository Jammu.
459. Khan, Ghulam Hassan, *Freedom Movement in Kashmir (1931-1940)*, p. 1136.
460. Daily *Inqilab*, Lahore, 13 August 1931.
461. Iqbal, Javed, *Zindah Rood*, pp. 35-36.
462. *Ibid.*, p. 36.
463. Iqbal, Waleed (grandson of Iqbal), at the inaugural ceremony of *Jeshan-e-Iqbal* at Kolkata on May 30, 2015. [*Times of India*].
464. Nehru, Jawaharlal, *Discovery of India*, p. 350.
465. *Ibid.*, p. 351.
466. *Ibid.*, p. 352.
467. *Ibid.*
468. Iqbal, Javed, *Zindah Rood*, p. 483.
469. *Ibid.*, p. 612.
470. *Ibid.*
471. Raghavan, G.S., *The Warning of Kashmir*, p. 59.
472. *Guru Ghantal*, Lahore, 30 August 1931.
473. *Daily Siasat*, Lahore, 16 August 1931.
474. *Weekly Amar*, Lahore, August 31, 1931.
475. File No. 509 PR-21/N, Year 1939, Archives Repository, Jammu.
476. Singh, Khushwant, *Iqbal's Hindu Relations*, The Telegraph, Calcutta, June 30, 2007.
477. Khoihamai, Hassan, *Tarikh-i-Hassan,* vol. II, p. 730.
478. *Ibid.*, p. 738.

THE TEMPLE AGITATION

479. *Kashmir: Exposing the Myth Behind the Narrative*, Ahmad, Khalid Bashir, p. 146.
480. *Ibid.*
481. Cultural Resource Mapping of Srinagar, Shehar-i-Kashmir, Vol. II, p. 600, Indian National Trust for Art and Cultural Heritage, (INTACH), J&K Chapter.
482. In a telephonic interview with the author on 15 January 2019.

483. *Koshur Encyclopedia*, Vol. 1, [Second edition, 2006], pp. 342-44, Jammu & Kashmir Academy of Art, Culture & Languages.

484. *Kashmir: A Walk Through History*, Ahmad, Khalid Bashir, p. 212.

485. Bande Matram, Lahore dated 12 March 1936.

486. File No. 297/PR/M-144, The Prime Minister (Publicity Branch), 1936, Archives Repository Jammu.

487. In an interview with the author on 21 December 2018.

488. Sa'dat, Molvi Mohammad Shah, *Tareekh-i-Kashmir ki Rozana Dairy*, p. 818. A contemporary of Ratangir, Sa'dat, wrote a 2-part history of Kashmir published by the then leading publishing house of Kashmir, Ghulam Mohammad Noor Mohammad Tajraan-i-Kutub, Maharajganj, Srinagar. The first part, *Tareekh-i-Kashmir Urdu* covers the 40 years of Maharaja Pratap Singh's rule, while the second part, *Tareekh-i-Kashmir Ki Rozana Dairy* gives a day-to-day account of events from 1925—when Maharaja Hari Singh ascended the throne—to 1947, a period to which the author himself was a witness. Sa'dat was admitted by Maharaja Hari Singh to his Darbar as a historian of Kashmir [Rafiqi, Mohammad Amin, *Hamara Adab, Shakhsiyat Number-I*, 1984-85, J&K Academy of Art, Culture & Languages, p. 284]. He also helped G.M.D. Sufi and Munshi Mohammad Din Fauq a great deal in their works of history titled *Kashir* and *Tawarikh-i-Kashmir*, respectively. On 1 August 1939, Sa'dat records the death "yesterday of Mahant of Durga Nag Shiv Ratangir who had occupied the Muslim cemetery during the reign of Maharaja Pratap Singh and built a temple and a house over it." Former Inspector General of Police, Javid Makhdoomi, who has edited and published his father, Pir Mohammad Afzal Makhdoomi's political diary titled *Kashmir Ki Tehreek-i-Azadi: Khwab, Azab Aur Sarab*, also alludes to the "forcible" occupation of the graveyard at Durga Nag by the government and making Mahant Shiv Ratangir as "its custodian and caretaker. Makhdoomi writes, "During the summer of 1939 heightened activities of various religious, political [and] social groups were clearly noticed. It may be interesting to note that Kashmiri Pandits suddenly became hyper active. The reason being that during Maharaja Pratap Singh's rule a graveyard located at Durga Nag, Srinagar was forcibly occupied by the govt. [government] and made one 'Mahant' namely Shiv Rattan Gori as its custodian and caretaker. The Mahant, over a period of time, raised a structure on the occupied land." [Makdoomi's Facebook post dated 19 November 2018, accessed on 30 March 2020]

489. In a telephonic interview with the author on 16 January 2019.

490. Letter of Wazir Tej Ram, President Dharmarth Council to District Magistrate, Kashmir vide No. 1669 dated 1st August 1939, File

No. 141, Subject: Regarding Durga Nag Affair, Archives Repository, Srinagar.

491. Letter of District Magistrate, Kashmir to Senior Superintendent of Police, Srinagar No. C.P./42/D.O. dated 1st August 1939, File No. 141, Subject: Regarding Durga Nag Affair, Archives Repository, Srinagar.

492. Letter of District Magistrate, Kashmir to President Dharmarth Council, Srinagar No. P.C./43/D.O. dated 1st August 1939, File No. 141, Subject: Regarding Durga Nag Affair, Archives Repository, Srinagar.

493. Letter of District Magistrate, Kashmir to Senior Superintendent of Police, Srinagar No. C.P./45/ dated 1st August 1939, File No. 141, Subject: Regarding Durga Nag Affair, Archives Repository, Srinagar.

494. Official Press Note No. 122 of 2 August 1939, File No. P.N. 29 of 1939, Subject: Durga Nag Agitation Press Notes, Archives Repository, Srinagar.

495. *Ibid.*

496. *Ibid.*

497. Sa'dat, Molvi Mohammad Shah, *Tareekh-i-Kashmir ki Rozana Dairy,* p. 818.

498. Official Press Note No. 123 of 4 August 1939, File No. P.N. 29 of 1939, Subject: Durga Nag Agitation Press Notes, Archives Repository, Srinagar.

499. File No. 141, Subject: Regarding Durga Nag Affair, Archives Repository, Srinagar.

500. *Ibid.*

501. *Ibid.*

502. Taseer, Rashid, *Tehrik-i-Hurriyat-i-Kashmir,* Vol. II, p. 64.

503. Letter of District Magistrate of Kashmir addressed to the Chief Secretary, Political Department, No. CP/72 dated 8 August 1939.

504. Letter of Chief Secretary to District Magistrate Kashmir vide No. B-263/39-PB dated 12 August 1939, File No. 141, Subject: Regarding Durga Nag Affair, Archives Repository, Srinagar.

505. Letter of Senior Superintendent of Police, Kashmir to District Magistrate Kashmir vide No. 3024 dated 1 September 1939, File No. 141, Subject: Regarding Durga Nag Affair, Archives Repository, Srinagar.

506. Letter of District Magistrate Kashmir to Chief Secretary, Political Department vide No. C.P. 84 dated 9 August 1939, File No. 141, Subject: Regarding Durga Nag Affair, Archives Repository, Srinagar.

507. City Situation Report No. 3850 dated 7 August 1939, File No. 141, Subject: Regarding Durga Nag Affair, Archives Repository, Srinagar.
508. Letter of District Magistrate Kashmir to Wazir Wazarat Baramulla No. CP/89 dated 9 August 1939, File No. 141, Subject: Regarding Durga Nag Affair, Archives Repository, Srinagar.
509. Taseer, Rashid, *Tehrik-i-Hurriyat-i-Kashmir,* Vol. II, p. 65.
510. City Situation Report of 9 August 1939 signed by Balwant Singh, Inspector of Police City, File No. 141, Subject: Regarding Durga Nag Affair, Archives Repository, Srinagar.
511. City Situation Report of 15 August 1939 signed by Balwant Singh, Inspector of Police City, File No. 141, Subject: Regarding Durga Nag Affair, Archives Repository, Srinagar.
512. City Situation Report of 10 August 1939 signed by Balwant Singh, Inspector of Police City, File No. 141, Subject: Regarding Durga Nag Affair, Archives Repository, Srinagar.
513. City Situation Report of 14 August 1939 signed by Balwant Singh, Inspector of Police City, File No. 141, Subject: Regarding Durga Nag Affair, Archives Repository, Srinagar.
514. City Situation Report of 16 August 1939 signed by Balwant Singh, Inspector of Police City, File No. 141, Subject: Regarding Durga Nag Affair, Archives Repository, Srinagar.
515. *The Hindu,* Madras, 19 August 1939, File No. 141, Subject: Regarding Durga Nag Affair, Archives Repository, Srinagar.
516. *The Hindu,* Madras, 19 August 1939.
517. Statement signed by SSP, Kashmir Province, File No. 42 of Samvat 1995-96, Archives Repository, Srinagar.
518. *Ibid.*
519. *The Martand*, 11 August 1939.
520. Letter of Governor and District magistrate Kashmir to Wazir Tej Ram, President Dharmarth Council vide No. C.P./101/D.O. dated 11 August 1939, File No. 141, Subject: Regarding Durga Nag Affair, Archives Repository, Srinagar.
521. Taseer, Rashid, *Tehrik-i-Hurriyat-i-Kashmir,* Vol. II, p. 66.
522. http://www.earlytimes.in/newsdet.aspx?q=148581 [accessed on 15 March 2020].
523. https://swarajyamag.com/insta/jammu-and-kashmir-pandits-want-shrines-bill-to-protect-temples-temple-properties [accessed on 15 March 2020].

THROUGH THE DOGRA RULE

524. File No. 229/P-21, Year 1912, Archives Repository Jammu.
525. *Ibid.*

526. *Ibid.*
527. *Ibid.*
528. *Ibid.*
529. Letter No. 1595 dated June 10, 1912 from the Assistant Secretary to Chief Minister to the Superintendent of Police, Kashmir. [File No. 229/P-21, Archives Repository Jammu.]
530. According to the Accession Register of the S.P.S. Museum, Srinagar, the meteorite was received in the Museum on 25 May 1912. The object is accessioned as item number 1810 and the description details show that four pieces of meteorite were found at Shopian in some villages and the object was received from the Superintendent of Police. One piece was sent to Resident Mr. Frasin and the other to the Principal Jammu College. The Prince of Wales College happened to be the only college in Jammu then.
531. Author and expert in Kashmir Studies, Mohammad Yusuf Taing who hails from a village in Shopian, told the author in an interview.
532. *Ibid.*
533. File No. 229/P-21, Year 1912, Archives Repository Jammu.
534. Meteorite Fall Statistics, [http://en.wikipedia.org/wiki/Meteorite_fall] accessed on October 21, 2016.
535. TWA Flight 800 [http://en.wikipedia.org/wiki/TWA_Flight_800]. There were other possible causes also put forward to explain the accident including a terrorist attack and mechanical failure. The accident resulted in the death of all 230 on-board passengers.
536. American Folklore Society, The Worship and Folklore of Meteorites, *The Journal of Folklore*, p. 199.
537. File No. 80/M-331, Year 1914, Archives Repository Jammu.
538. Kalhana's *Rajatarangini* (Trns. Thakur Achhar Singh Shahpuria), Vol. I, pp. 54-55.
539. *Ibid.*
540. Neve, Ernest F., *Beyond the Pir Panjal: Life and Missionary Enterprise in Kashmir*, p. 68.
541. Gulab Singh was the ruler of Jammu. After the British defeated the Sikhs who then also ruled Kashmir, they sold him the Valley along with its inhabitants and resources for a sum of 7.5 million *Nanakshahi* rupees in lieu of the indemnity Ranjit Singh had to pay to them.
542. Biscoe, C.E. Tyndale, *Kashmir in Sunlight and Shade*, p. 165.
543. Neve, Ernest, F., *A Crusader in Kashmir*, Gulshan Books [Reprint], pp. 11-12.
544. *Ibid.*, p. 80.

545. *Ibid.*
546. Greater Kashmir, 14 March 2015, https://www.greaterkashmir.com/news/kashmir/mirwaiz-concerned-at-christian-missionaries-mysterious-activities/ [accessed on 17 October 2016].
547. Greater Kashmir, *Apostasy Unveiled!*, January 20, 2011.
548. File No. 204/L-197, Year 1915, State Archives Repository, Jammu.
549. *Ibid.*
550. *Ibid.*
551. *Ibid.*
552. *Ibid.*
553. *Ibid.*
554. *Ibid.*
555. In 1924, there was a major labour agitation in Srinagar against poor wages and ill treatment of workers at the Sericulture Factory which resulted in a mass agitation and severe government reprisal.
556. KashmirForm.org, http://kashmirforumorg.blogspot.com/2009/09/not-bad-even-beggar-can-make-rs-10000.html accessed on 17 October 2016.
557. Abdul Qayoom Shah, Social Activist, http://kashmirforumorg.blogspot.com/2009/09/not-bad-even-beggar-can-make-rs-10000.html [accessed on 4 August 2020.]
558. Archives Repository, Jammu (File No. 173).
559. *Ibid.*
560. Lawrence, Walter R., *The Valley of Kashmir*, p. 233.
561. *Ibid.*, 223.
562. Archives Repository, Jammu (File No. 173).
563. *Ibid.*
564. *Ibid.*
565. *Ibid.*
566. Krishan Dev Sethi in a telephonic interview with the author on November 9, 2014.
567. *Ibid.*
568. Karan Singh, *Heir Apparent: An Autobiography*, Oxford, 1989, p. 37.
569. Kwasi Kwarteng, *Ghosts of Empire: Britain's Legacies in the Modern World*, p. 121.
570. *Ibid.*
571. Shiri Ram Bakshi, *Kashmir—Valley and its Culture*, p. 251; Sheikh Mohammad Abdullah, *Aatash-e-Chinar* [Gulshan], p. 311.

572. Jagmohan, *My Frozen Turbulence in Kashmir*, p. 84.
573. Sheikh Mohammad Abdullah, *Aatash-e-Chinar* [Gulshan], p. 311.
574. *Ibid.*
575. File No. 283/V-7 of 1925, Archives Repository, Jammu.
576. *Ibid.*
577. File No. 163/130G/1926, Archives Repository, Jammu.
578. Karan Singh, *Heir Apparent: An Autobiography*, Oxford, 1989, p. 37.
579. Kwasi Kwarteng, *Ghosts of Empire: Britain's Legacies in the Modern World*, p. 121.
580. Karan Singh, *Heir Apparent: An Autobiography*, Oxford, 1989, p. 5.
581. Sati Sahni, A Conversation, http://ikashmir.net/pakraid1947/sahni2.html [accessed on 10 January 2019].
582. Karan Singh, *Heir Apparent: An Autobiography*, Oxford, 1989, p. 37.
583. Tapan Bose, Kashmir Times, 1 September 2014.
584. Karan Singh, *Heir Apparent: An Autobiography*, Oxford, 1989, p. 55.
585. Bakshi, Shiri Ram, *Kashmir—Valley and its Culture*, p. 251.
586. Shimla or Simla, the capital of Himachal Pradesh, was then part of the province of Punjab.
587. Khan, G.H., *Freedom Movement in Kashmir* (1931-1940), p. 140.
588. *Ibid.*
589. *Ibid.*, pp. 146-47.
590. IGP's Report submitted to Prime Minister of Kashmir on August 29, 1931.
591. *Ibid.*
592. *Ibid.*
593. Karbala, a city in Iraq, is the venue of the Battle of Karbala fought in 680 AD between the army of Umayyad Caliph Yazid and a handful of men of Imam Hussain, grandson of Prophet Muhammad (peace be upon him) in which Imam Hussain (Allah be pleased with him), along with his 72 family members and companions, was martyred.
594. Khan, G.H., *Freedom Movement in Kashmir* (1931-1940), p. 146.
595. The Simla Agreement was signed by India and Pakistan on 2 July 1972 following the December 1971 war between the two countries that resulted in the birth of an independent country, Bangladesh, out of the erstwhile East Pakistan. The Agreement bound the two

countries "to settle their differences by peaceful means through bilateral negotiations." The Accord converted the Cease-fire Line into the Line of Control (LOC) along the divided State of Jammu & Kashmir.

596. File No. P-Ch-51, Archives Repository Jammu.
597. *Ibid.*
598. *Ibid.*
599. *Ibid.*
600. *Ibid.*
601. *Ibid.*
602. Abdullah, Sheikh Mohammad, *Aatash-i-Chinar*, Second Edition, Gulshan Books, 2008, p. 166.
603. Sethi, Krishen Dev in a telephonic interview with the author on 25 March 2018.
604. Sethi, Krishen Dev, *Yaad-i-Rafta*, 1986, Jid-o-Jahad Publications, p. 15.
605. *Ibid.*
606. Official Press Release, File No. P. N. 11/B, Publicity Branch, Chief Secretariat, Year 1938, Archives Repository Jammu.
607. *Ibid.*
608. Press Communique No. 71 dated 2 September 1938, File No. P. N. 11/B, Publicity Branch, Chief Secretariat, Year 1938, Archives Repository Jammu.
609. Abdullah, Sheikh Mohammad, *Aatash-i-Chinar*, Second Edition, Gulshan Books, 2008, p. 166.
610. Identified by Krishen Dev Sethi as Ali Mohammad Tariq.
611. Abdullah, Sheikh Mohammad, *Aatash-i-Chinar*, Second Edition, Gulshan Books, 2008, p. 166.
612. Press Communique No. 71 dated 2 September 1938, File No. P. N. 11/B, Publicity Branch, Chief Secretariat, Year 1938, Archives Repository Jammu.
613. *Ibid.*
614. *Ibid.*
615. Official Press Release, File No. P. N. 11/B, Publicity Branch, Chief Secretariat, Year 1938, Archives Repository Jammu.
616. Press Note No. 69 dated 31 August 1938, File No. P. N. 11/B, Publicity Branch, Chief Secretariat, Year 1938, Archives Repository Jammu.
617. *Ibid.*

618. Note No. 70 dated 1 September 1938, File No. P. N. 11/B, Publicity Branch, Chief Secretariat, Year 1938, Archives Repository Jammu.
619. *Ibid.*
620. Press Note No. 69 dated 31 August 1938, File No. P. N. 11/B, Publicity Branch, Chief Secretariat, Year 1938, Archives Repository Jammu.
621. Press Note No. 70 dated 1 September 1938, File No. P. N. 11/B, Publicity Branch, Chief Secretariat, Year 1938, Archives Repository Jammu.
622. Press Communique No. 71 dated 2 September 1938, File No. P. N. 11/B, Publicity Branch, Chief Secretariat, Year 1938, Archives Repository Jammu.
623. Bazaz, Prem Nath, *The History of Struggle for Freedom of Kashmir*, Third Edition, Gulshan, 2009, p. 144.
624. *Ibid.*
625. *Ibid.*
626. Press Communique No. 71 dated 2 September 1938, File No. P. N. 11/B, Publicity Branch, Chief Secretariat, Year 1938, Archives Repository Jammu.
627. Press Note No. 72 dated 2 September 1938, File No. P. N. 11/B, Publicity Branch, Chief Secretariat, Year 1938, Archives Repository Jammu.
628. *Ibid.*
629. Press Note No. 76 dated 5 September 1938, File No. P. N. 11/B, Publicity Branch, Chief Secretariat, Year 1938, Archives Repository Jammu.
630. *The Statesman*, 1 September 1938.
631. Press Note No. 92 dated 16 September 1938, File No. P. N. 11/B, Publicity Branch, Chief Secretariat, Year 1938, Archives Repository Jammu.
632. Sethi, Krishen Dev in a telephonic interview with the author on 25 March 2018.
633. Secret D.O. No. D. 827-C/38 dated 18th October 1938 from Residency to Chief Secretary, Jammu & Kashmir, Political Department, Pandit Ram Chandra Kak, State Archives Repository, Jammu File No. 148/Pl-12, Year 1938.
634. The information withheld from the Maharaja was about the visit of Muhammad Ali Jinnah in 1927, the news about which was broken by daily *Pratap* published from Lahore.
635. Letter of the Resident to Prime Minister Raja Hari Krishan Koul dated 10th August 1931.

636. Tikoo, P.N., *Story of Kashmir*, p. 94.
637. Yasin, Madhavi, *British Paramountcy in Kashmir*, p. 22.
638. *Ibid.*, p. 25.
639. *Ibid.*, p. 26.
640. Tikoo, P.N., *Story of Kashmir*, p. 98.
641. *Ibid.*, pp. 98-99.
642. File No. 12, *Subject: Private correspondence with various European friends in India from 1905 to 1906*, His Highness English Office, Year 1905-06, Archives Repository Jammu.
643. *Ibid.*
644. *Civil and Military Gazette*, Foreign and Political Department, File No. 7(5)-R of 1929, Government of India, 'R' Branch Nos. 1-2, NAI; Bazaz, *The History of Struggle for Freedom in Kashmir*, [Gulshan, 2009], p. 119.
645. Archives Repository, Jammu, Publicity, File No. I/8 B, Year 1944.
646. *Ibid.*
647. *Ibid.*
648. *Ibid.*
649. *Ibid.*
650. Bazaz, Prem Nath, *The History of Struggle for Freedom in Kashmir*, [Gulshan, 2009], p. 170.
651. *Ibid.*, p. 172.
652. *Ibid.*

A BOWL OF HISTORY

653. Bates, Charles Ellison, *A Gazetteer of Kashmir*, p. 196.
654. *Ibid.*
655. Younghusband, Francis, *Kashmir*, London, Reprint 1911, p. 98.
656. *Ibid.*, p. 102.
657. Bruce, C.G., *Peeps at Many Lands: Kashmir*, Adam & Charles Black, London, 1911.
658. Younghusband, Francis, *Kashmir*, London, Reprint 1911, p. 98.
659. Neve, Ernest F., *Beyond the Pir Panjal: Life and Missionary Enterprise in Kashmir*, p. 6.
660. Today, there are over fifty hotels and commercial structures, about a hundred other buildings including offices and assets of the Gulmarg Development Authority and various government departments. Add to this alarming scenario, a township in concrete including double-storied buildings erected by the defence forces within the

bowl itself. Indiscriminate constructions, vehicular movement deep into the bowl and unregulated rush of people have badly told upon the health of the Queen of Hills. On a given day during peak season, four to five thousand people descend on the bowl to have the Gandola ride.

661. Younghusband, Francis, *Kashmir*, London, Reprint 1911, p. 98.
662. *Ibid.*
663. *Ibid.*, p. 99.
664. Sahni's observations were sourced from his interveiew available @ikashmir.net/memoirs/sahni2.htmlhttp://ikashmir.net/memoirs/sahni2.html [accessed on 1 April 2019]
665. File No. 28/C.E.7, Year 1940, Archives Repository Jammu.
666. *Ibid.*
667. *Ibid.*
668. *Ibid.*
669. http://nedoushotels.com/home/ [accessed on 3 April 209]
670. Andrew Whitehead's Blog, https://www.andrewwhitehead.net/blog/srinagar-nedous-reborn [accessed on 3 April 2019]
671. File No. 8, Chief Secretariat, General & Political Department, Subject: Lease of Nedous Hotel Gulmarg, Yaer 1890, Archives Repository Jammu.
672. In his response, Nedou explained that he did not seek loan of ₹ 10,000 to merely repair the Bloc-B of the hotel but proposed to increase accommodation from 6 to 20 or 25 rooms and carry out other costly improvements.
673. File No. 8, Chief Secretariat, General & Political Department, Subject: Lease of Nedous Hotel Gulmarg, Year 1890, Archives Repository Jammu.
674. File No. 3 of 1906, Private Secretary to H.H. The Maharaja, Subject: Execution of repairs to the palaces at Gulmarg through Mr. Nedou, Archives Repository Jammu.
675. File No. 53/P-28, Chief Secretariat, Political Department, Year 1900, Archives Repository Jammu.
676. *Ibid.*
677. *Ibid.*
678. *Ibid.*
679. File No. 19/K/99, Chief Secretariat, Political Department, Year 1902, Subject: Visit of HE Lady Curzon to Gulmarg, Archives Repository Jammu.
680. *Ibid.*

681. *The Tribune*, Lahore dated 21 October 1936.

682. Dass, Diwan Jarmani, *Maharaja,* Hind Pocket Books Pvt. Ltd., New Delhi, pp. 43-44.

683. *Ibid.*

684. File No. 12, *Subject: Private correspondence with various European friends in India from 1905 to 1906*, His Highness' English Office, Year 1905-06, Archives Repository Jammu. C.E. Tyndale Biscoe was a promoter of sports including cricket in Kahsmir. His C.M.S. School, as he informed Maharaja Pratap Singh in a letter dated 10 July 1906, annually spent about ₹ 1,000 on cricket and other sports "to train the boys under our charge that they make become true men, strong in body, mind and soul."

685. *Ibid.*

686. *Ibid.*

687. *Ibid.*

688. *Ibid.*

689. *Ibid.*

690. Sir Francis Younghusband, the British Resident in Kashmir in 1906 and author of *Kashmir.*

691. File No. 12, *Subject: Private correspondence with various European friends in India from 1905 to 1906*, His Highness English Office, Year 1905-06, Archives Repository Jammu.

692. *Ibid.*

693. *Ibid.*

694. A famous hill station in South Kashmir, about 100 kms from capital Srinagar.

695. File No. H-P-18, Year 1926, Archives Repository Jammu.

696. *Ibid.*

697. *Ibid.*

698. *Ibid.*

699. *Ibid.*

700. *Civil & Military Gazette*, 30 July 1935.

701. *Ibid.*

702. File PLS-5, Year 1925, Archives Repository, Jammu.

703. *Ibid.*

704. *Ibid.*

705. File No. 145/V.B.30, Year 1927, Archives Repository, Jammu.

706. File No. 59, Year 1928, Archives Repository, Jammu.

707. File No. PU-16, Year 1926, Archives Repository, Jammu.

708. State Council Resolution No. X dated August 3, 1923.
709. *Ibid.*
710. *Ibid.*
711. *Ibid.*
712. File No. 136, Year 1934, Archives Repository, Jammu.
713. *Ibid.*
714. *Ibid.*
715. *Ibid.*
716. File No. 53/P-3, Year 1928, Archives Repository, Jammu.
717. *Ibid.*
718. *Ibid.*
719. *Ibid.*
720. *Ibid.*
721. *Bikrimi* calendar year, corresponding to 1929-30 AD.
722. File No. 53/P-3, Year 1928, Archives Repository Jammu.
723. File No. 83, Year 1928, Archives Repository Jammu.
724. File No. 249/CUB.200, Year 1938, Archives Repository Jammu.
725. *Ibid.*
726. *Ibid.*
727. *Ibid.*
728. *Ibid.*
729. File No. 232-T.18, Archives Repository Jammu.
730. *Ibid.*
731. File No. 184/30, Year 1930, Archives Repository Jammu.
732. *Ibid.*
733. *Ibid.*
734. *Ibid.*
735. *Ibid.*
736. Biscoe, C.E. Tyndale, *Kashmir in Sunlight and Shade*, p. 40.
737. *Ibid.*
738. Younghusband, Francis, *Kashmir*, London, Reprint 1911, p. 99.
739. *Ibid.*, p. 100.
740. File No. 339, Year 1931, Archives Repository Jammu.
741. *Ibid.*
742. *Ibid.*
743. *Ibid.*

744. *Ibid.*
745. *Ibid.*
746. *The New Yorker*, May 27, 1939, pp. 89-90.
747. File No. 521, Year 1932, Archives Repository Jammu.
748. *Ibid.*
749. *Ibid.*
750. *Ibid.*
751. Hunt, John, *Beyond Gulmarg: Exploring the Pir Panjal in the Thirties*, Alpine Journal, 1997, p. 191.
752. Ashraf, M., *Winter Tourism in Kashmir*, Greater Kashmir, 22 November 2018.
753. *The Civil & Military Gazette* and *The Tribune*, 6 March 1936.
754. *The Statesman*, 7 March 1936.
755. *The Civil & Military Gazette* and *The Tribune*, 7 March 1936.
756. *The Statesman*, 8 March 1936.
757. *The Civil & Military Gazette* and *The Tribune*, 8 March 1936.
758. File No. P.N.- 9/D, Subject: *Office copies of press notes and communiques and connected correspondence from 24 October 1935 to 24 April 1936*, year 1936, Archives Repository Jammu.
759. Hunt, John, *Beyond Gulmarg: Exploring the Pir Panjal in the Thirties*, Alpine Journal, 1997, p. 194.
760. *Ibid.*
761. The worst hit areas included Gurez, Karnah, Uri, Bunji and Hajibal where hundreds of persons were overwhelmed by avalanches and killed. The affected areas being cut off and communication disrupted, it took weeks for information of the massive devastation to reach Srinagar. In Gurez alone, 110 persons perished. Reports from Bunji (Gilgit-Baltistan) spoke of "great damage" to life and property with a large number of residential houses overrun by avalanches and taking a large toll of humans and cattle. From Karnah tehsil, 86 deaths were reported till 12 March. In Geetra village of Teetwal, 24 people in five houses died under a heavy snow avalanche, destroying houses and cattle as well. Eleven persons were buried alive under an avalanche in Dodran, Uri tehsil, of whom six victims were rescued. A small village, Kail in the Neelam Valley suffered 24 deaths. Given the magnitude of the disaster, officially designated as "dreadful", the government started Avalanches Relief Fund to help the affected families. Maharaja Hari Singh and his wife contributed ₹ 1500 to the Fund. The officiating Prime Minister, Barjor Dalal, and his wife donated ₹ 150 and ₹ 100, respectively.

762. File No. 224/VB-243), Archives Repository Jammu.
763. *Ibid.*
764. *Ibid.*
765. File No. PR/CN-28, Chief Secretariat, Publicity, Year 1943, Archives Repository Jammu.
766. Letter of General Manager, Universal Pictures Ltd., No. AR/7153 dated 22 June 1944, File No. PR/CN-27, Chief Secretariat, Publicity, Year 1943, Archives Repository Jammu.
767. Singh, Karan, *Autobiography*, p. 161.
768. Taseer, Rashid, *Tehrik-i-Hurriyat-i-Kashmir* (1949-1953), Vol. 4, p. 374.

DATELINE KASHMIR

769. Khan, Khurshid Alam, *Aftab aur Srinagar Times: Urdu Sahafat ke Sang-e-Meel*, p. 32. Professor Abdul Qadir Sarwari gives the year of its first publication as 1866. Some others have mentioned the year as 1882.
770. *Ibid.*, p. 33.
771. Nazki, Ayaz Rasool, *Ar-Rafiq: Abdul Salam Rafiqi*, Urdu Sahafat ke Do Sau Saal, National Council for Promotion of Urdu Language, New Delhi, p. 813.
772. Mohiuddin, Sofi, *Jammu Kashmir Mai Urdu Sahafat*, p. 21.
773. *Ibid.*, p. 55.
774. *Ibid.*, p. 60.
775. Modern Jammu & Kashmir State-1925-42, Accession No. 2059, Archives Repository Kashmir.
776. *The Daily Herald*, Lahore, 28 May 1937.
777. *The Kashmir Times*, 8 June 1937.
778. *Weekly Khalid*, 21 March 1941.
779. *Weekly Chand*, Jammu, 20 January 1942.
780. Some of the names that quickly come to mind include Muzamil Jaleel (*The Indian Express*), Parvez Bukhari (*AFP*), Ajaz Hussain (*Associated Press*), Showkat Nanda (*Washington Post*), Zahoor Malik (*Kashmir Times*), Naseer A. Ganai (*Outlook*), Taufiq Rashid (*Hindustan Times*) Basit Umar (*Barcroft*) Gowhar Geelani (*Catch News*), Tariq Bhat (*The Week*), Ishfaq ul Hassan (*DNA*), Murtaza Shibli (*Freelancer*), Muzaffar Raina (*The Telegraph*), Majid Jahangir (*The Tribune*), Athar Pervez (*Freelancer*), Hakim Irfan (*Economic Times*), Peerzada Arshid Hamid (*Xinhua*), Aliya Bashir (*Global Press Institute*), Bilal Handoo (*Free Press Kashmir*), Aarish Bilal (*News X*), Shafat Kira (*Kashmir Vision*) and Rakib Altaf (*Hindustan*

Times). Among such prominent MERC pass-outs as are successfully running the show of local print media are Hilal Mir, Zahiruddin, Riyaz Wani, Majid Maqbool, Haroon Mirani, Haroon Rashid Shah and Tahir Bhat. The MERC pass-outs also have a prominent presence in the electronic media—Shahana Bhat (*Press TV*), Mufti Islah (*CNN News 18*), Asif Quraishi (*ABP News*), and Baba Umar, Mohsin Mughal and Mehboob Jeelani (*TRT World*). Some MERC pass-outs including Athar Zia, Sabeha Mufti, Nasir Mirza, Syeda Afshana, Shahnaz Bashir, Shahid Rasool, Munir ul Islam, Mussarat ul Islam and Tariq Ahmad Rather have opted for careers in teaching, administration or official media. Tariq A Bhat and Arshad Mushtaq have established their own film and documentary making units.

781. Jagan Nath Sathu, Radha Krishen Kak, Pran Nath Jalali, Shyam Koul, Ghulam Nabi Khayal, Mohammad Sayeed Malik, Makhan Lal Kak, Yusuf Jameel, Zafar Meraj, Altaf Hussain, *et al.* were among such seniors whom the young journalists looked upon as their inspiration.

782. Srinagar based Kashmiri journalists who have ably represented Indian and foreign English language media include Jagan Nath Sathu, Radha Krishen Kak, Mohammad Sayeed Malik, Ghulam Nabi Khayal, M.L. Kak, Yusuf Jameel, Altaf Hussain, C.B. Koul and B.L. Kak. In early 1940s, Khurshid Hassan Khurshid represented the *Orient Press*, then the only Muslim news agency in India. He was picked by Mohammad Ali Jinnah in 1944 as his private secretary, a position which he held till the latter's death in 1948. Prominent among those who have distinguished themselves while serving with different media outlets based outside Kashmir is M.L. Kotru who was editor of India's reputed newspaper, *The Statesman*, for several years. Others who have earned a name in the field include M.K. Dhar, Sheikh Manzoor Ahmad, Iftikhat Gilani, Muzamil Jaleel, Nidhi Razdan, Arun Dhar, Harpal Singh Bedi, Basharat Peer, Waheed Mirza, Sumir Koul, (Late) Jay Raina, Ashutosh Handoo, Aurangzeb Naqshbandi, Rajesh Koul, Ramesh Bhan, Niti Raina, Ajay Koul and Arti Dhar.

783. Among those who established themselves as journalists are Rashid Ahmad, Mukhtar Ahmad, Ahmad Ali Fayaz, Ali Mohammad Sofi, Bashir Ahmad Sofi, Riyaz Masroor, Riyaz Wani, Zulfikar Majid, Athar Parvaiz, Khurshid Wani, Ehsan Fazili, Peerzada Ashiq, Mohammad Salim Pandit, Fayaz Bukhari, Inayat Jahangir, *et al.* Those who joined subsequently and made a mark include Riyaz Masroor, Shuja ul Haq and Basharat Masood.

784. They include Nazir Masoodi (*NDTV*), Idrees Lone (*News Nation*), Khalid Hussain (*Zee News*), Mir Fareed (*Times Now*), Ashraf Wani (*Aaj Tak*), Manoj Koul (*News 18 Urdu*), Afzal Bhat (*ANI*), Sibti Mohammad Hassan (*IRIB*), Asif Suhaf (*News 24*), Manzoor Mir

(*India TV*), Rifat Abdullah (*IBN 7*) and Zeenat Zeeshan Fazili (*Republic TV*).

785. The figures pertain to the year 2018.

786. They include Merajuddin, Habib Ullah Naqash, Sheikh Tariq, Farooq Javed, Nisar Bhat, Tauseef Mustafa, Fayaz Kabli, Bilal Bahadur, Mukhtar Ahmad, Amin War, S. Fayaz, Javaid Dar, Mohammad Aslam, S, Irfan, Danish Ismail, Tariq Mir, Hilal Bhat, Tariq Lone, Qazi Irshad, Arshad Hussain, Shabir Shah, Bashir Lone, Shakeel ur Rehman, Dar Yasin, Aman Farooq, Syed Waseem Andrabi, Yawar Nazir Kabli, Arshad Hussain Shah, Aamir Amin Bhat, Irfan Manzoor Shah and Shuaib Masoodi.

787. File No. PP-59, His Highness' Government, Publicity Department, Subject: *Representation of API by the Political Secretary*, Year 1933, Archives Repository Jammu.

788. *Ibid.*

789. *Ibid.*

790. *Ibid.*

791. Ahmad, Khalid Bashir, *Kashmir: A Walk Through History*, pp. 192-93.

Index

E

F

G

T